General Lesley J. McNair

General Lesley J. McNair

Unsung Architect of the US Army

Mark T. Calhoun

University Press of Kansas

© 2015 by the University Press of Kansas
All rights reserved

Published by the University Press of Kansas (Lawrence, Kansas 66045),
which was organized by the Kansas Board of Regents and is operated and
funded by Emporia State University, Fort Hays State University, Kansas
State University, Pittsburg State University, the University of Kansas, and
Wichita State University

Library of Congress Cataloging-in-Publication Data

Calhoun, Mark T.
General Lesley J. McNair : unsung architect of the US Army /
Mark T. Calhoun.
pages cm. — (Modern war studies)
Includes bibliographical references and index.
ISBN 978-0-7006-2069-2 (cloth : alk. paper)
ISBN 978-0-7006-2070-8 (ebook)
1. McNair, Lesley James, 1883–1944. 2. Generals—United States—
Biography. 3. United States. Army—Officers—Biography. 4. Military
education—United States—History—20th century. 5. United States.
Army—Officers—Training of—History—20th century. 6. Soldiers—
Training of—United States—History—20th century. 7. World War,
1939–1945 United States. 8. World War, 1914–1918—Biography. 9. World
War, 1939–1945—Biography. I. Title.
E745.M42C45 2015
355.0092—dc23
[B]

2015002822

British Library Cataloguing-in-Publication Data is available.

Printed in the United States of America

10 9 8 7 6 5 4 3 2 1

The paper used in this publication is recycled and contains 30 percent
postconsumer waste. It is acid free and meets the minimum requirements
of the American National Standard for Permanence of Paper for Printed
Library Materials z39.48-1992.

For Mark Taylor Calhoun Jr.

Contents

Illustrations

Preface

Many historians advised me not to pursue this topic for my first book, mostly because of their concern that insufficient archival records existed to support a detailed analysis of Lesley McNair's career. I did receive encouragement from a few individuals, but most reminded me that no single source of "McNair Papers" exists, and they warned me that I would have to visit many different archives in hopes of finding adequate sources, risking much on the conviction that such records existed. Despite this well-intentioned advice, I stubbornly continued my potentially fruitless quest—and through a combination of luck, persistence, and the help of many talented archivists and supportive colleagues, I managed to amass a much larger collection of papers than I ever imagined I would.

When I first began to discuss with colleagues and friends my desire to work on this topic, I heard an often-repeated story, which soon took on the form of folk wisdom. It always centered on an unnamed graduate student who had supposedly begun work on a dissertation on McNair but could not complete it because he could not find adequate sources. After much searching for this mysterious graduate student, I finally found one historian who thought he knew who it might be. This historian had a student some years hence that did intend to write his dissertation about Lesley McNair, but he dropped out of his PhD program for personal reasons in his first year, before he even began to conduct dissertation research.

I also often heard the rumor that Clare McNair, Lesley's wife of nearly forty years, burned his papers out of grief in 1944, after her husband died in Normandy, and only twelve days later, their only son, Doug, died in Guam. I soon found evidence that she did not burn her husband's papers. In 2010, I discovered a set of McNair papers at the Library of Congress. The first of the nine boxes included a short letter that Clare McNair wrote when she donated the papers. This collection consisted of various personal items including letters, poster-sized promotion orders ("sheepskins"), and several scrapbooks of photos and newspaper clippings that Clare collected throughout her husband's career. Interestingly, the letters in the collection of personal papers include none between Lesley and Clare (or between McNair and any family members or colleagues); they consist entirely of Clare's communications with friends of the family and Lesley's professional acquaintances. However, no evidence exists that Clare selectively destroyed any of Lesley's personal records or letters. The collection appears complete, with no chronological gaps or signs of Clare removing any documents from the scrapbooks or other collections.

Army personnel who worked with McNair soon learned of his habit of working long hours and doing little else. One can see this aspect of his personality in the documents he left behind, as they consist almost exclusively of professional correspondence. He rarely wrote personal letters (and those few located in various archives usually address both business and personal matters). He also did not maintain a journal or diary, although he did accumulate a small collection of articles and board reports related to projects that he worked on throughout his career. These files now reside in Record Group 337 at the National Archives in College Park, Maryland (NARA 2). An exhaustive search turned up no more personal files or correspondence at other archives than those located at NARA 2.

Another fact helps explain the lack of personal correspondence in archival collections of McNair papers. He spent most of his career, and nearly all of World War II, in stateside assignments. Although he worked long hours, he lived at home and saw Clare regularly, and therefore he did not need to maintain a lengthy written correspondence with her. If he exchanged letters with her during any of his early career deployments (the Vera Cruz Expedition, the Punitive Expedition, and World War I), they apparently did not find their way to an archive. One aspect of this lack of personal correspondence seems rather odd: the absence of letters to Doug McNair, his only child and fellow artilleryman who served during World War II, both stateside and overseas. McNair appears to have kept track of his son's career indirectly, through correspondence with colleagues who had regular contact with him. No evidence exists that he corresponded with Doug directly—at least not regularly. This probably merely serves as an example of McNair's formal demeanor, which might have led him to see Doug first as a junior army officer and then as a son. (This formality comes across, at least, in the few letters located in various archives that he wrote to Doug, or in which he mentioned him.[1]) The reliance on his wife to handle their social correspondence fits with McNair's businesslike demeanor, as well as with the culture of the era, but his limited interaction with his son seems indicative of an unusually formal, even distant, attitude toward personal relationships.

McNair also generally avoided the public eye. He disliked engaging the media, and he did not do so regularly until his duties during World War II required it. He exhibited no interest in fame or notoriety. One can only speculate whether he might have produced a memoir had he survived the war, like so many of his peers did, but no evidence exists that he began work on one during his career. While the various archives cited in the bibliography collectively contain a great deal of material on McNair's career—most of which does not appear to have been used in any previous secondary work—they consist almost exclusively of official documents.

This book therefore serves as an analysis of one army officer's career and the impact that he had on the army's effectiveness in the caldron of battle during World War II. It contains minimal biographical information, instead focusing on Mc-Nair's military life. It provides the first comprehensive analysis of McNair's duties, professional experience and performance, and development as a military leader and thinker over the full forty years of his career. Most importantly, this study identifies the connections between McNair's key formative experiences during his early career and the thinking that guided his actions during his last five years of service, when he rose to the highest levels of rank and responsibility of his career and made a significant impact on America's war effort from 1939 to 1944.

Some colleagues discouraged me from devoting my time to this project because McNair only served as a staff officer during World War II. In my view, Mc-Nair's service as a senior staff officer actually underscores the significance of this study. It highlights the critical role that staff officers played during World War II in developing the organizations, training programs, and combined arms doctrine that US army unit commanders relied on for success in combat. Staff officers have long fulfilled critical functions at various unit echelons, often overlooked in commander-centric histories of the US army in combat. The army has a long history of relying heavily on its staff officers in the performance of its day-to-day operations, but historians rarely produce studies of officers who spent the majority of their wartime duty in staff positions. In contrast, commanders attract a great deal of attention from historians, given their unique authority and responsibility. Nevertheless, even the best commanders in US army history would have found themselves severely hindered by the absence of the many skilled staff officers who served throughout their organizations (and often transitioned to command positions after gaining invaluable experience as general staff officers).

Lesley McNair served in two high-level staff positions in the War Department during World War II, including his final role as commander, Army Ground Forces—a functional command subordinate to the War Department responsible for preparing the Army Ground Forces for war rather than leading those troops in combat. However, McNair possessed a broad range of previous experience serving in command and staff positions, in peacetime and combat, throughout his career, which ran from 1904 to 1944. The numerous biographies of commanders like General George Patton, Field Marshall Erwin Rommel, and Field Marshall Sir Bernard Law Montgomery illustrate the popularity of the "great captains" approach to military history, but the field would benefit from more studies of the hardworking yet underappreciated staff officers who helped translate their commanders' intent into executable orders. Although America's World War II commanders and campaigns deserve further study, historians should devote more time to the many staff officers on whom the War Department and field command depended. Perhaps the following work will encourage more historians to explore this relatively barren terrain.

Disclaimer: Opinions, conclusions, and recommendations expressed or implied within are solely those of the author, and do not represent the views of the US Army School of Advanced Military Studies, the US Army Command and General Staff College, the United States Army, the Department of Defense, or any other US government agency. Cleared for public release: distribution unlimited.

Acknowledgments

I owe a great many people my deepest gratitude for helping me complete this project. I began my academic journey as a military historian while pursuing a master of military arts and sciences degree with a specialty in history. My thesis adviser and first mentor as a budding historian, Dr. Christopher Gabel, helped me narrow down my dilettante's broad but shallow understanding of military history by introducing me to the fascinating and still controversial early twentieth century of the US army, particularly the interwar period (1919–1939). Dr. Gabel and other historians, including Dr. Robert Baumann and Dr. Michael Pearlman, taught me to read history critically and from varying perspectives. I carried the focus these professors helped me develop into my second graduate program at the US Army School of Advanced Military Studies, where professors including Dr. James Schneider and Dr. Michael Epstein exposed me to the juxtaposition of military theory and history, emphasizing the importance of historical, cultural, and intellectual context in military thought and action.

The pivotal moment in my development as a historian took place when I began the PhD program in American history and US military history at the University of Kansas. There I was fortunate enough to study under many talented professors, in particular my dissertation director, Dr. Theodore Wilson, a brilliant historian, gifted teacher and scholar, and dear friend. I learned a great deal from many other talented historians during my studies at KU, including Dr. Roger Spiller, Dr. Jeff Moran, and Dr. Kim Warren. These and many other professors guided, encouraged, and prodded me to this point in my career. They taught me a great deal, and I continue to learn as I reflect on my time studying history under their guidance. They also helped me to see how much I did not know, encouraging my conviction to never stop learning, to think critically, and to always base my historical interpretations on a foundation of sound, scholarly research. I would not have had the courage to pursue this topic without their support and guidance.

Many other historians and archivists provided essential assistance, without which this project could not have come to fruition. I began my research concerned that I might not find enough material to enable me to complete this project, and I ended up with far more than I could use. Rusty Rafferty, Elizabeth Dubuisson, and the dedicated staff at the Combined Arms Research Library (CARL) at Fort Leavenworth went to heroic lengths to find archive documents, electronic files of out-of-print doctrine and technical manuals, and books through interlibrary loan. Timothy Nenninger and the many other talented archivists at the National Archives and Research Administration provided me invaluable assistance, as did archivists at the Library of Congress, US Army Heritage and Education Center (USAHEC) at Carlisle Barracks, and the Center of Military History at Fort McNair. Special mention also goes to Mr. Eric Voelz who was as surprised as I was to find General McNair's entire personnel file intact in a fire safe vault at NARA, St. Louis, and happily sent me a copy of the entire file. Similarly, Dr. Boyd Dastrup, US Army Field Artillery Branch historian, filled in many gaps in my knowledge of McNair's service at the Field Artillery School, and the archivists at the Morris Swett Technical Library and Fort Sill, Oklahoma, provided me with various documents and photographs that proved essential to my research. Finally, Mary Sego, Neal Harmeyer, and Stephanie Schmitz scoured the collection at the Purdue University archives, locating and sending me many documents and photographs from McNair's service at Purdue as professor of military science and tactics.

I am also extremely fortunate to work at the US Army School of Advanced Military Studies, an institution that shaped my intellectual development as a field-grade officer and prepared me for four years of the hardest assignments in which I served during my active-duty army career. As a member of the faculty, I am fortunate to have the opportunity to work with a new class of incredibly talented students each year, surrounded by military and civilian faculty members with a diverse and impressive range of educational backgrounds, who share a dedication to the SAMS mission while maintaining an environment that encourages intellectual curiosity and creative thinking. My daily interaction with these students and peers, along with the school's dedicated and professional leadership and staff, has enabled me to continue pursuing my goal of lifelong learning.

A few of my colleagues at SAMS and Fort Leavenworth's Combined Arms Command (CAC) Headquarters deserve special mention. Judith Price, a fellow army retiree, SAMS graduate, and dear friend who works at CAC, read every word of this document, providing editorial advice and, more importantly, encouragement at a time when I desperately needed it. I came to know Judi because of her husband, a wonderful friend, and a colleague on the SAMS faculty whom I greatly admire, Eric Price, also a retired army officer and currently a PhD candidate at the KU history department. Eric also read the manuscript, offering substantive advice and another shoulder to lean on. Finally, both Bruce Stanley, a fellow army retiree and SAMS professor, and Rich Dixon, a former supervisor and now retired and serving as the SAMS deputy director for operations, provided me friendship, advice, and an encouraging nudge when they knew I needed one. The past year and a half have taught me the value of friendship, and these individuals stand out among the many wonderful colleagues I am proud to work with and consider friends.

The staff at the University of Kansas Press is an incredibly hard-working, dedicated, and friendly group of professionals. Working with them was an absolute pleasure, and they made a very daunting process as painless as possible for me. I am particularly grateful for the patience with which the press granted me extensions on submission deadlines when life put obstacles in my way during a difficult year. No matter what distraction came next, Mike Briggs and the editorial board gave me the time I needed to sort things out so that I could once again devote my attention to this project. For that, I will be forever grateful. Naturally, while each of these people and institutions played a key role in my development as a historian and my completion of this project, any errors or misinterpretations in this book are mine alone.

I would also like to acknowledge General McNair's two living direct descendants: his great-granddaughter, Lisa Juliet (McNair) Katnic, and her daughter (his great-great-granddaughter), Hallie Miranne (McNair) Katnic. These two wonderful women come from a long line of McNairs (with several spelling variations) from several countries and a long lineage of military professionals tracing back to the fourteenth century, when the king of England approved the McNair family crest. They have waited far too long for a comprehensive military life of their most famous American ancestor to appear. I hope they are pleased with the result.

Finally, I owe my greatest debt of gratitude to my son, Mark Taylor Calhoun Jr., for his patience during far too many nights and weekends when I was stuck in my home office, surrounded by books and tapping away at a keyboard rather than spending time with him. He has been patient, supportive, and helpful, doing more than any father could expect to help keep our household together while I completed this project, demonstrating maturity rare in a young man of his age. This book is as much a reflection of his hard work and dedication as it is of mine.

General Lesley J. McNair

Brigadier General Lesley J. McNair, AEF GHQ Staff G-5 Training Division, Chief of Artillery Training and Tactical Procedures, Chaumont, France, 1919. Courtesy of US National Archives II, College Park, Maryland

Introduction

General George C. Marshall once called General Lesley J. McNair "the brains of the Army" in recognition of the exceptional intellectual capacity that he demonstrated throughout his career, particularly during the process of organizing and training the hastily mobilized US army that fought during World War II.[1] The influence that McNair exerted throughout his career on mechanized combined arms doctrine and training, equipment development, and unit organization placed him among the handful of generals most responsible for both the effectiveness and the flaws of the army that the United States sent to war in 1942. Through his broad experience, tireless work ethic, and effective leadership, McNair played a key role in guiding the army's modernization efforts during the two decades between the world wars, known as the interwar period. Various studies have addressed his participation in that process, particularly his efforts during the few years preceding America's direct involvement in the war. The army's official histories of World War II also describe McNair's role in the procurement, mobilization, organization, and training of personnel to enable the growth of the army from its prewar strength of just over 100,000 to more than eight million by the end of the war.

Despite the key role he played in the early twentieth-century's army, few works of history exist that focus directly on Lesley McNair, and none provides a detailed description of his long and influential career. Perhaps historians have not attempted a comprehensive analysis because he left behind no collection of personal letters, memoirs, or diaries when he died of wounds inflicted by errant American bombs in Normandy in 1944. A larger body of literature exists that consists of various analyses of US army effectiveness during World War II and studies of the army's preparations for the war during the interwar period. This body of work, taken as a whole, depicts a somewhat negative image of the US army's effectiveness during World War II, although some notable exceptions do exist. Many of these histories mention McNair, but their authors focus on the last few years of his career, particularly his role in preparing the army for combat during World War II. Working with the limited information available at the time, these authors tended either to attribute the perceived ineffectiveness of the US army in World War II—at least in part—to McNair's influence, or to disregard his influence as insignificant, creating an enduring but incomplete image of his capability as an army officer. The resulting idea that McNair's skills and experience did not prepare him for his duty requirements during World War II had a long-lasting effect on the history of both the war and McNair's role in it.

This book offers the first detailed study of McNair's entire career from his graduation at West Point in 1904 to his death in 1944, including the wide variety of positions he held, the experience he gained in these positions, and his lifelong pursuit of innovation, all of which prepared him for high-level service during World War II. The previously limited access to this information does not necessarily mean that historians who have written about McNair in the past erred in their interpretations of his duty performance, but one wonders how the information contained in the previously unused primary sources might have altered their findings.[2] This book assesses McNair's strengths and weaknesses, how they influenced his efforts to prepare the rapidly mobilizing US army for combat during the pivotal events of World War II, and the role they enabled him to play in shaping American senior leaders' thinking about modern warfare.

Assessments of McNair have often described him as a career staff officer and field artilleryman, and many of these argue that he possessed unrealistic ideas about combat organization, training, and doctrine, the result of limited practical experience outside his basic branch. Such assessments beg the question how McNair rose to such a high level of responsibility during the final years of his career (1939–1944), working in positions that required a broad understanding of mechanized combined arms operations, procurement, organization, war economy, and many other issues related to mobilization for war—and for which generals Malin Craig and George C. Marshall selected him by name.[3]

An intensive scouring of the archives turned up many official documents and reports but few personal papers. The primary sources most often seen in works that mention McNair come from one small collection of boxes held at the National Archives and Records Administration in College Park, Maryland. This collection (a subset of Record Group 337) contains records dating from throughout McNair's career, but the majority focus on his service after 1939. Historians who have referenced this collection in their work tended to focus on the papers related to the World War II years. During these five years McNair served as commandant, Command and General Staff College from 1939 to 1940; chief of staff, General Headquarters from 1940 to 1942; and commander, Army Ground Forces (AGF) from 1942 to 1944. Some much older papers reside in this small collection, but with few exceptions, historians appear to have paid these documents little attention.[4] Although access to the newly revealed primary source material cited here does not reveal a spotless record, it does shed new light on many aspects of the current historical understanding of McNair's career and indicates that a reassessment might be warranted.

Analyses of US army effectiveness during World War II often serve as case studies in books containing arguments pertinent to the modern-day army. For example, during the army transformation era of the early 2000s, many books appeared that used the army's interwar (1919–1939) modernization and reorganization efforts as source material for comparative analysis with the ongoing Department of Defense transformation process. Such analyses often compared the testing and procurement of weapons systems or organizational changes in the interwar years versus modern eras, like the army transformation years. These studies offered either support for or criticism of new weapons systems or doctrinal concepts that senior leaders in the Department of Defense considered fundamental to the army transformation process. McNair often appeared as a key figure in such works because of his involvement in the mobilization and training of the US army for World War II. He played an important role, for example, in the development of the World War II army's antitank doctrine, and he oversaw a variety of efficiency-based initiatives like streamlining, pooling, and task organization. He also significantly influenced prewar doctrine development, and he led the effort to train mobilized personnel and newly formed units on approved and emerging doctrinal concepts.[5]

This book engages many previously unused sources to analyze both General McNair's ideas about modern warfare in the 1930s and 1940s, and how those ideas developed during a career marked by participation in many equipment tests, boards, experiments, and other innovation-focused activities. Similarly, it provides an examination of the other factors that affected his thinking and prepared him for the duties he performed as America mobilized for and took part in the war. For example, McNair enjoyed less decision-making authority and autonomy during World War II than some accounts assert. The War Department imposed many limitations on McNair's authority, giving him little control over decisions regarding issues that purportedly fell under his purview. Even at the height of his responsibilities as commander of AGF, he remained subordinate to the War Department General Staff, which did not always operate at peak efficiency.

Once America entered the war, the War Department's Operations Division assumed key roles, including that of key adviser to General Marshall, and the division often deferred to commanders in the field when their advice conflicted with that of McNair or other senior staff officers in the Zone of Interior (the Home Front). McNair supported the policy of deferring to field commanders without question in the final years of the war, but he believed that this made less sense in the early years, when most divisions had not yet deployed, mobilization and training remained the army's primary effort, and the bulk of expertise resided in McNair's General Headquarters, and later AGF. When considering the full cast of characters involved, one finds that many of the army's most significant shortcomings during the war stemmed from inefficiencies or infighting within the War Department. McNair lacked the ability to exert any control outside of his own organization, so instead he spent much of his time trying to anticipate the effects of various War Department inefficiencies and find ways to overcome them before they grew out of control. His recommendations often had a limited effect on War Department decision making.[6]

The experience that McNair gained during his forty-year career—and the manner in which he influenced the US army's effectiveness at planning and conducting modern mechanized combined arms warfare during World War II— serves as the central topic of this narrative. Few day-by-day accounts of fighting or detailed campaign analyses appear, although in some cases such accounts provide evidence to illustrate key points. The pressures of military service during this difficult period revealed weaknesses in McNair's personality and flaws in his thinking—just as they did in all of the senior leaders who served during the first half of the twentieth century. His vision of modern warfare largely reflects prevailing views among the regular army's more influential personnel, and his efforts to prepare the US army for another mass mobilization and large-scale war appear quite reasonable, particularly when one considers other key factors outside of McNair's control that influenced his ability to perform his duties during World War II. He, like many of his fellow general officers, developed a logical and largely accurate view of the changing nature of modern warfare, even if optimizing the US army's organization and doctrine to account for its unique nature made army operations and the generals who led them seem rather dull and workmanlike.[7] Studies have created a well-established view of America's army in World War II as poorly led, marginally effective, and reliant on material superiority for success. Analysis of McNair's career and the experiences he gained—in some cases individually, but in others via events or opportunities available to most officers who served in the interwar years—casts doubt on this interpretation.

With a tiny regular army, no army reserve, and an unevenly trained National Guard, America's generals faced the challenge of preparing to fight complex, mechanized combined arms warfare while leading an army made up almost entirely of raw recruits, using far more advanced equipment than anything used in the previous war. McNair played a key role in this effort and stands among many great leaders who contributed to the army's success in combat. The evidence provided here also contributes to the growing body of literature that has reevaluated over the past twenty years the combat effectiveness of the US AGF during World War II.

The current accepted wisdom regarding America's war effort, which a small but growing subgroup of military historians has worked for about the last two decades to change, holds that the US army never matched the Wehrmacht in combined arms war-fighting capability. Instead, the historical record supports the idea that America's mere entry into the war guaranteed an Allied victory—not because of American combat effectiveness but because of overwhelming American superiority in matériel and personnel. FDR's admonition to the American people in a Fireside Chat on December 29, 1940, that America must serve as the Allies' arsenal of democracy has only served to reinforce this interpretation.[8] This deeply entrenched narrative includes many components, but it relies largely on the idea that America made up for the poor fighting ability of its mediocre generals and inept ground forces with almost limitless material resources, personnel reserves, and firepower. Many historians, particularly during the past twenty years, have demonstrated through various means that American soldiers fought effectively during World War II, while the arsenal of democracy on which they supposedly relied began to falter in 1942, and national-level prioritization decisions left them with a disproportionately low share of available resources. Despite these historians' efforts, the image of inept and poorly led US army combat troops compensated only by America's vast industrial strength remains central to the remarkably resilient accepted wisdom regarding American soldiers' combat effectiveness.

Some historians have emphasized the fact that the Soviets bore the brunt of the fighting in Europe from Germany's invasion of Russia in 1941 until June 1944, when the Allies finally opened the long-promised second front. This has led many to conclude that the Red Army had bled the Wehrmacht white by the time the Americans entered the war. The Red Army did stand largely alone against Hitler's forces in the land war in Europe for nearly three years, making extraordinary sacrifices to keep Hitler at bay until its coalition partners could open a second front in Western Europe. Yet ample evidence exists to show that the Germans committed many high-quality combat forces to the Western Front after the Allied invasion on June 6, 1944 (D-Day), and the Wehrmacht remained a dangerous and resilient enemy until its collapse during the final weeks of the war. The Anglo-American alliance achieved a remarkable series of victories over Hitler's forces in both the Mediterranean and the Western European theaters while the Americans simultaneously fought a costly campaign against the Japanese in the Pacific theater. These victories had geopolitical repercussions that still ripple through the fabric of American society and today's world order.

The insights gained from the study of McNair's professional development and contributions to the army between the world wars help explain how the US army fought effectively during World War II. Throughout his career, McNair led innovative efforts that contributed to the modernization of the army, and he played a key role in reorganizing the army and updating its doctrine. These activities contributed to the solid foundation on which the small but professional regular army began mobilization in 1940, after which McNair designed and led the most thorough and intensive individual and collective training effort the army had ever undertaken before a war. Without knowledge of these activities, undertaken between the wars by Lesley McNair and many other military professionals, one can see how the historical interpretation of America's success during the war developed into a story of material superiority and adaptation to the challenges of modern warfare.

In fact, it took far more than industrial might or personnel strength to enable America to contribute as effectively as it did to the Allied war effort. In particular, mobilizing a massive conscript army on a foundation of coherent doctrine and thorough training enabled American infantrymen, or GIs, upon deployment to the front, to learn through experience and adapt when necessary. A subtle but important difference exists between the meanings of these two terms. Often the need to fight in a particular environment or set of conditions when prepared to deal with an entirely different situation requires soldiers and their leaders to adapt to that new set of conditions. This often involves developing new fighting techniques in the heat of battle to replace inappropriate doctrine or making other ad hoc modifications to correct flaws in organization or mobilization training.

Many studies of the US army during World War II attribute GIs' success in combat primarily to their ability to achieve these rapid adaptations, necessary— as the argument goes—to enable them to overcome their poor preparation for war. In many accounts, this adaptation to fill gaps in mobilization training and equipping explains how, despite initial setbacks, the army ultimately prevailed in combat. Instead, a careful reading of the historical record indicates that the US army went to war with suitable doctrine and a mix of adequate to excellent equipment that, combined with thorough training and battle hardening, enabled GIs to fight effectively. The AGF had completed the most thorough mobilization training program in America's history, accomplishing not only individual but also large unit training in mechanized combined arms warfare. Nevertheless, despite the benefit of this foundation, GIs had to learn to apply in the harsh reality of combat those skills that they had studied in peacetime. Although many historians' accounts of the war describe this process as one primarily of adaptation, emphasizing lack of preparedness overcome by determination and ingenuity, some historians emphasize thorough preparation followed by learning. For example, historians Williamson Murray and Allan R. Millett described how "American combined-arms tactics, emphasizing firepower with maneuver, *steadily improved in the harsh classroom of war.*"[9]

Studying McNair's career reinforces the idea that a well-prepared army learned how to fight on the deadly battlefield of World War II rather than relying on individual or unit methods of adapting to it. However well prepared they might have been, typical American soldiers entered service as untrained volunteers or draftees—new recruits, not professional soldiers. This meant that the preparation soldiers received before engaging in combat remained merely a set of skills and procedures practiced in simulated combat conditions. Lacking experience in the reality of war, GIs had to learn on the battlefield how to use the skills and equipment effectively that they had studied and practiced during mobilization training. Thus, even soldiers in the few divisions that received years of training before their eventual use during World War II required battle hardening to develop combat proficiency. Battle hardening proved to be a particularly important process during the mobilization for World War II, given the degree to which the US government had downsized the army after the World War I, which resulted in a severe lack of personnel, modern equipment, or opportunities to train before protective mobilization began in 1940. Combat is the only truly effective test for anything military, from the soldier to any piece of equipment that soldier might use when facing a determined foe. Training exercises could only narrow the gap between the GI's image of war and the reality of war once he engaged in it. The rest happened on the battlefield, for which McNair saw one solution: "Drill them into such a state of discipline that the men, in the excitement of battle, will instinctively do the things which they have been taught to do in the classroom, on the drill field and on maneuvers."[10]

The US army's senior leaders undertook a massive effort to overcome these challenges by updating doctrine, building new combat systems, and conducting training on an unprecedented scale before deploying troops to war. Although imperfect, this process did prepare the US army's combat divisions for the challenges they faced on the World War II battlefield. As soldiers deployed and adjusted to the realities of combat, they had to learn how to fight the way they had trained, but against a skilled and ruthless enemy, leading to challenges in units' initial confrontations with the enemy. Although individual units did adapt to specific, unanticipated conditions, prewar doctrine and training served as the foundation for these soldiers' learning and adaptation, providing a relatively uniform approach to modern warfare that proved effective because it was optimized for the US army's strengths and weaknesses. As time passed, units at the front received new equipment and learned from their own experiences and those of others, disseminated in the form of combat lessons. This accelerated the learning process and improved GIs' ability to conduct mechanized combined arms maneuver as described in army doctrine and to defeat a determined enemy.

By synthesizing topics often addressed separately in works on World War II and the interwar period, this book seeks to demonstrate that despite the US army's shortage of funds, troops, and equipment between 1919 and 1940, its regulars did not sit on their hands between the world wars.[11] Rather, led by many dedicated professionals like Lesley J. McNair, a small but motivated core of American Expeditionary Force veterans maintained a lively discourse and an innovative spirit throughout the interwar years. They sustained this discourse in professional journals, diverse career opportunities, equipment tests, experiments in unit organization, and a first-class professional military education system.[12]

Michael Matheny, in *Carrying the War to the Enemy*, helped explain why the US army's officer corps, contrary to Blumenson's assertions, possessed the intellectual foundation necessary to enable them to lead an effective army in the 1940s. During this period, war moved at a much faster pace and inflicted unprecedented levels of destruction on the enemy, along with anything else in a mechanized army's path. Despite America's lack of experience in this sort of war, its officer corps engaged in an educational process and ongoing discourse throughout the preceding decades that instilled in their minds all of the key elements of the modern concept of operational art. As Matheny argued, "The key elements of American operational art as developed in the interwar school system centered on theater structure, jointness [combined arms], phasing, and establishing a firm connection to both tactical and strategic objectives." Grounded in this educational system, "in application, American operational art took the form of continuous concentric pressure to overwhelm the enemy." [13]

Matheny rejected Russell Weigley's claim that American military thought before World War II focused on strategy and tactics while neglecting operational art. He countered, "Clearly, the Army War College studied strategy and the Staff School taught tactics, but both studied and exercised large-unit operations. Precisely because the military school system dealt with large-unit operations as well as strategy and tactics, the curriculum bridged the gap with operational art. The national military planning system adopted during the interwar years started with strategic objectives and then detailed the military resources necessary to achieve them." This method instilled in American officers "the Clausewitzian notion that war must serve a political purpose." By combining this awareness with a foundation in "the geometry of global warfare" structured as "theaters of war and theaters of operations," American officers understood the importance of logistics planning, the usefulness of operational phasing, and combination of tactical actions to achieve strategic aims. They might have lacked the dash and daring of officers like George Patton and Erwin Rommel, but they understood operational art—in theory initially, but soon validated by experience—making the workmanlike methods of most American officers also the most appropriate to the US army's ends, ways, and means.[14]

Returned to their permanent rank after World War I, the army's midgrade officers found themselves frozen at the rank of captain or major, held up by the so-called hump: senior officers allowed to remain on active duty long after age and ossification should have led to their retirement. Facing the prospect of retiring in the midst of an economy trembling under the weight of the approaching Depression, the army's senior officers remained entrenched in their positions, while many captains and majors stalled in their postwar rank for a decade or more, waiting for the logjam to break. These dedicated regulars continued to study the changes in the nature of warfare and the challenges they would face if they had to mobilize America for another large-scale war. They remembered the army's poor state of readiness before World War I, and they had no desire to experience such conditions again. If they could not be ready with a large army or modern equipment, they could at least prepare mentally for what the future might hold.

In seeking solutions, these midgrade officers (the future senior leaders of the army) envisioned the emerging changes in the nature of warfare, including the significance of mechanization and air power. As they thought through these challenges, the regulars developed doctrine for combined arms mechanized warfare. Although they lacked the personnel and equipment required to practice the concepts they developed and the doctrine they wrote, the regulars did their best to simulate them in peacetime maneuvers (not conducted on a large scale until after mobilization began in 1940). Given America's isolationist foreign policy and the economic conditions wrought by the Depression, only another unavoidable world war would lead the government to rebuild a powerful combat force like the American Expeditionary Force and provide it the resources it needed to put these new ideas into practice against a determined enemy. Nevertheless, when the time came, the regulars intended to be ready.

Once the nation began to mobilize in 1940, War Department chief of staff George C. Marshall imposed age and fitness standards that forced out many older officers and disqualified others for unit command, creating opportunities for more energetic and often better-educated junior officers to fill key command and staff positions across the army. Simultaneously, President Franklin Delano Roosevelt flooded the American military and the civilian industrialists who would build its combat equipment with resources and money that facilitated both the production of equipment and the completion of a comprehensive training program. Although this shift from a determined isolationist stance to a decision to prepare for war resulted in a rapid expansion, American Expeditionary Force veterans in the War Department remembered well the challenges with the mobilization for World War I and worked hard to avoid making the same mistakes. Still, given the realities of civilian control of the army, the War Department lacked the ability to reverse the profit motivation, personal ambition, and bureaucratic inefficiency that took hold during protective mobilization in 1940. These issues led to many of the same mobilization setbacks experienced during World War I, and many new ones as well.

As the American soldiers and their leaders deployed and entered combat, the AGF also had to contend with War Department inefficiency and infighting. This manifested in many ways, from interbranch disputes to disruption of predeployment unit training, but the AGF conducted effective mobilization training and deployed with a solid foundation in US army doctrine. This provided the army's senior leaders with a force that could learn how to conduct combined arms modern warfare with all of the skill and tenacity of its enemies. Nevertheless, few histories of the US army in World War II take this view, many of which emphasize German tactical prowess and American industrial might while offering a negative assessment of McNair's contributions or overlooking him entirely.

In his comparison of German and US army performance during the war, *Fighting Power*, Martin van Creveld argued, "The American officer corps of World War II was less than mediocre." Creveld qualified this assessment by pointing out the challenge presented by time pressure during the hasty mobilization of US army divisions, but his assertion that "between them and their German opposite numbers there simply is no comparison possible" seems unjustifiably oversimplified. Creveld's comparative analysis exhibits a common bias held by admirers of German tactical prowess and an uninformed acceptance of the American material superiority myth that, in Creveld's view, explains the US army's eventual success in combat.[15] *Fighting Power* serves as a perfect example of the result of what historian William J. Astore referred to as "*A Case of* Wehrmacht *Penis Envy.*"[16] Astore focused on a primarily American post–World War II phenomenon, but the excessive admiration of German fighting prowess he described has also long existed among non-American historians, as demonstrated by works like Creveld's *Fighting Power.*[17] Finally, Creveld's book and others like it oversimplify the issues that most affected the outcome of World War II, emphasizing tactical fighting ability while overlooking the combatant armies' ability to conduct operational art by arraying those tactical actions for complementary effect and setting the conditions for their success.

Such historical criticisms of American officers usually focus on their supposed lack of boldness and daring, and Blumenson ranks among many historians who hold Patton up as the exception among an otherwise mediocre American officer corps. Part of the reason for this view probably lies in the historical focus on the better-known commanders of armies and army groups, and to a lesser extent the most famous senior aviators and navy admirals. Such histories often laud the boldness of these great captains. For example, Patton repeatedly requested more resources and freedom of action when commanding the 3rd US Army in Western Europe, promising that he could end the war quickly if only Eisenhower would grant his requests. Various historians have supported Patton's assertion, but few histories present the alternative view: that Patton did not understand the operational approach that was central to Eisenhower's broad-front strategy, the criticality of that strategy, or the disruption that giving him priority of supply to support a narrow thrust would cause to the Allied campaign. Eisenhower emphasized keeping pressure up along the entire western front and avoiding any action that might overextend part of the line and form a salient for German counterattacks to exploit. Often interpreted as a lack of boldness, too few historians have acknowledged that the success of this strategy may indicate its appropriateness to the operational environment on the western front of the European Theater of Operations. A full chapter of Eisenhower's papers addresses this issue, explaining clearly the reasons why Eisenhower insisted on a broad front strategy and viewed a deep thrust by either Montgomery or Patton as too risky and logistically unsupportable.[18] Nevertheless, histories still repeat Patton's claims. For example, the back cover of Dennis Showalter's *Patton and Rommel: Men of War in the Twentieth Century* contains this sentence: "Had his superiors given [Patton] free rein, the US army could have claimed victory in Berlin as early as November of 1944."[19]

Historians continue to criticize Eisenhower for his adherence to this strategy, supporting the image of the unimaginative American general capable only of grinding down the Germans in a laborious and bloody attrition-based strategy. In *Decision at Strasbourg: Ike's Strategic Mistake to Halt the Sixth Army Group at the Rhine in 1944,* historian David P. Colley quoted historian Stephen Ambrose, who claimed that "attrition is always a cautious and unimaginative strategy." Building on this broad oversimplification, Colley argued, "With Ike in command, there would be no grand envelopments, no surprise or bold maneuvers by the 6th Army Group to outwit or outflank the Germans," and he asserted that General Eisenhower "lacked the boldness of a Patton or a Rommel; and he did not have Montgomery's detailed understanding of tactics and strategy."[20] Colley made these claims to support his criticism of Eisenhower's decision to refuse Lieutenant General Devers's request to attack across the Rhine into Germany in November 1944. Colley blamed this "mistake" on Eisenhower's supposed lack of boldness and imagination while discounting the many reasons Eisenhower found Devers's plan flawed. Primarily, Eisenhower concluded the attack would create unacceptable risk by creating weak points in the Allied line while offering little promise for the decisive results Devers imagined, thanks to the rough terrain that Allied forces would encounter once across the river. Eisenhower had learned from the disastrous results of giving Montgomery free rein to launch the bold and complex Operation Market-Garden two months earlier.[21]

Even in those areas where terrain might have favored more bold maneuvers, limited logistics capacity meant that supplying a bold localized offensive would require limiting fuel, ammunition, and other supplies along the rest of the front—a significant risk Eisenhower wisely chose not to take. Harold R. Winton's

Corps Commanders of the Bulge highlighted the fallacy of equating officer quality with boldness and daring by focusing on six corps commanders who provided crucial leadership during the two-month-long operation. Winton revealed the key contributions of six American general officers—Gerow, Middleton, Ridgway, Millikin, Eddy, and Collins—many of whom remained in relative obscurity in the historical record as a result of historians' tendency to focus on large unit commanders. (Even Ridgway remains better known for his service in the Korean War than during World War II.) Historians should produce more studies like Winton's because they help shatter the myth of the workmanlike American general.[22]

David E. Johnson stands out among historians of World War II as a particularly strident critic of both the US military in the interwar period and McNair's role in the events of that era. Emphasizing what he viewed as the imagination-inhibiting influence of McNair's field artillery background, Johnson mistakenly identified McNair as the individual solely responsible both for the army's adoption of antitank guns as the primary weapon to defend against enemy tank attacks, as well as for the army's adoption of the tank destroyer and the creation of the tank destroyer command.[23] He also criticized McNair's role in the McNair Board, which assessed the potential of air power, coast artillery, and antiaircraft artillery to defend a coastline against attack from the sea, and he asserted that McNair "accomplished little" during his one-year assignment as commandant at Fort Leavenworth from 1939 to 1940.[24]

William O. Odom also found fault with McNair's performance in his historical analysis of the development of doctrine during the interwar years. Focusing on McNair's involvement in the long-overdue update of the army's *Field Service Regulations 1923* (*FSR 1923*), Odom described McNair's keen interest in the development of the 1939 update, which took place while McNair served as commandant of the Command and General Staff School (CGSS) at Fort Leavenworth. He noted that the bulk of the changes in the new manual came from the CGSS faculty, many written by McNair himself. McNair pushed Chief of Staff George C. Marshall for quick approval of the updated manual and requested authorization to begin incorporating the new doctrine into the CGSS curriculum while awaiting a decision, which he received. Marshall tentatively approved the new manual within a month of its completion, but a subsequent armywide review of the tentative manual drew a great deal of criticism, prompting McNair and his faculty to begin a more thorough review, which eventually led to the publication of the much improved *FSR 1941*. While Odom only singled out McNair for criticism in one particular area—his involvement in the inclusion of the pooled antitank unit concept in the doctrine—he spent far more time enumerating the many flaws of the 1939 manual than describing the improvements in the *FSR 1941*, which would guide army operations for most of the war. McNair contributed significantly to the content of both of these manuals.[25]

Other authors who have written about World War II included criticisms of McNair in their work, in some cases unsupported by anything other than anecdotal evidence. For example, in *Nothing Less than Full Victory,* Edward G. Miller oversimplified the media reaction to McNair's 1942 Armistice Day address to the troops, titled "The Struggle is for Survival: The Importance of Training and Personnel." After hearing many reports of American combat troops confronting the enemy for the first time, apparently unprepared for the deadly seriousness of the situation, McNair recognized the inexperienced soldier's typical reaction upon experiencing combat for the first time. He intended his speech to remind GIs that they now faced an experienced, tenacious enemy bent on killing them, and to help instill in them the determination to do what had to be done to survive. Miller asserted that McNair's remarks about the need for American troops' battle hardening in combat (in a speech later referred to as the "kill or be killed" speech) led "the media [to have] a field day."[26] Although McNair's broadcast over the Blue Network did attract a great deal of attention from the media and the American people, Miller's wording implies that the speech was poorly received, and his vague assessment of its impact leaves the reader unaware that a large majority of listeners appreciated the appropriateness of McNair's remarks. Miller also demonstrated the problem with assessing McNair's performance without knowledge of his assignment history and experience when he placed much of the blame for what he called the US armor problem on McNair's shoulders. Like many historians, Miller saw McNair as just "an artilleryman" that lacked the imagination to handle his varied responsibilities during World War II, including matters related to armored warfare.[27] McNair's assignment history demonstrates the flaw in this assessment.

In other works in which one would expect McNair to play a key role, the authors barely mention him, if they mention him at all. For instance, McNair rarely makes an appearance in the historians Allan Millett and Williamson Murray's three-volume *Military Effectiveness* on interwar military innovation or military effectiveness in the early twentieth century. Similarly, McNair's name does not even appear in the index of Martin Blumenson's *Kasserine Pass,* despite the many topics that the author addressed that McNair worked on not only during the mobilization period but also in some cases for many years before World War II began. In fact, assessments of the US army's preparation for World War II and resulting American combat effectiveness that do not mention McNair, or do so only briefly, far outnumber those that do.

Many possible reasons exist for the lack of a detailed assessment of McNair's role in the pivotal events of World War II and the interwar period. Many historians apparently believed the rumor that no primary sources on McNair existed in the archives, leading them to the conclusion that a lack of reference material made a detailed analysis of McNair impossible. If this is true, these historians probably arrived at the logical conclusion that it was better to leave him out of their narrative than make unsupported assertions about him. Others might have believed that his role in their particular topic did not warrant the time and effort it would take to ferret the necessary details out of the limited sources available. Finally, several historians did analyze his role in those events for which they believed they had found adequate supporting evidence, and several of these historians did so with admirable success. Others, however, derived a more negative description of him than the full record of his career supports, or more often simply underestimated McNair's influence on the US army throughout his career, including his influence on the ground forces' preparation for combat during World War II. Many histories, for example, did not account for McNair's vast experience in field tests of various organizations and equipment throughout his career, including his central role in the design of the new infantry division organization that the army adopted before the war. Similarly, much of the literature on US army performance in World War II emphasized its missteps while often overlooking its accomplishments and the significant efforts made by men like Lesley McNair during the interwar period to prepare the army for war.

By contrast, several historians have worked in recent years to illustrate the US army's combat effectiveness during World War II while simultaneously dismantling the material preponderance argument. These authors have demonstrated the fact that the US army could and did stand toe to toe against the German army and win, in battle after battle and campaign after campaign. These works show that American success during World War II resulted largely from the army's logical organization and sound doctrine, as well as the arduous training that helped American citizen-soldiers learn this doctrine and overcome their lack of combat experience to develop into highly skilled and professional warriors. McNair played a key role in all of these activities related to the US army's preparation for war. The historians working to modify perceptions of American military effectiveness face a challenge similar to Brian Linn's, when he so convincingly overturned Weigley's grand theory of American military operations in his 2002 critique of Weigley's *The American Way of War*.[28] Such long-standing views contained in many histories and supported by noted historians' views resist change, but careful research and compelling arguments can eventually change even the most well-entrenched narratives.

One of the earliest of these so-called revisionist histories, Keith E. Bonn's *When the Odds Were Even*, provided a comparative analysis of the training and doctrine of the US and German armies that met in the Vosges Mountains in the winter of 1944–1945. Bonn argued that "the published American tactical and operational doctrine was so similar to the German army's that it shared its Clausewitzian validity almost point for point." Further, Bonn described the differences in American and German organization as an American advantage. Often criticized for his strict adherence to the principle of generalized training, McNair argued for the creation of specialized units during mobilization only when necessary (for example, airborne divisions and ranger units) because he believed specialized training should take place upon the soldiers' arrival in their units. Bonn pointed out that the American adherence to three basic division types throughout the war, as opposed to the Germans' reliance on many specialized divisions, not only simplified American logistics but also, "most importantly, diminished the friction in command and tactics so prevalent on the German side." Finally, Bonn argued that US army unit organization was particularly well suited to work in concert with its doctrine, particularly the triangular division, which could easily break down into combat commands and regimental combat teams task organized for the needs of the specific missions that they would perform. This meant, "unlike the Germans . . . whose organization for combat sometimes failed to accurately reflect the needs of tactical and operational doctrine, the Americans' organization was admirably suited to the task."[29]

Writing the same year as Bonn, Michael D. Doubler significantly added to historical understanding of the GI's application of peacetime training to fight effectively on the modern battlefield. Doubler focused in his book, *Closing with the Enemy: How GIs Fought the War in Europe, 1944–1945*, on how the US army prepared for and fought the campaign on the Western Front of the European Theater of Operations. Doubler described how the GI not only benefited from the doctrine he learned in the predeployment training that he conducted, but also from the detailed study of the army's lessons learned in past campaigns. Doubler explained that this process enabled the GI to expand on the foundation of army doctrine by molding those core concepts to fit the specific context in which he would apply them against the Germans in the final campaign to secure Germany's unconditional surrender. Despite his frequent use of the term "adaptation," the processes Doubler described seem like learning, combining the general concepts learned in predeployment training with the specific methods learned by studying the keys to past successes and finding solutions to past failures.[30]

These combat lessons continued to inform the GI's doctrinal foundation as he added to them by overcoming new challenges like the complex *bocage* terrain of Normandy. Meanwhile, personnel from various arms and echelons began to resolve longstanding challenges like the initially poor air-ground cooperation that had its roots in the Army Air Corps' quest for independence and the conviction of

Roosevelt and several of his senior military advisers that the Allies would win World War II from the air. This led to limited joint training and tardiness developing tactical procedures to facilitate close air support, scarcity of aircraft well suited to the fighter-bomber role, and challenges establishing communications between aircraft, tactical air controllers, and ground forces supported by air power. Despite these problems, ground and air personnel soon learned to overcome their differences and develop new procedures, conduct joint air-ground training, and use (with mixed success) heavy bombers in a close air support role. While some obstacles to effective air-ground coordination were too deeply entrenched to overcome them completely, the Allies proved that they could set aside parochial differences and even develop sincere pride in learning new methods to assist their fellow members of the combined arms team. The "doctrinal vacuum" that Doubler described simply prevented the integration of air power into the combined arms team until the final year of the war, when it finally achieved its true potential effectiveness—already excellent when made up of infantry, artillery, and armor—and all the more powerful with the air forces finally integrated. Certainly the strategic bombing and theater strategic interdiction missions the aviators executed before post-summer 1944 benefited the war effort, but as Doubler illustrated, addition of a powerful and well-coordinated close air support capability significantly added to the capability of the combined arms team.[31]

In *Victory at Mortain,* historian Mark J. Reardon added another counterpoint to the material preponderance school by focusing on Germany's first major counteroffensive against an American unit on the European continent. On August 7, 1944, five Panzer divisions attacked a single American infantry division defending in the small French town of Mortain. Reardon argued, "For the first time since D-Day, American small-unit commanders were remaining alive long enough to learn their trade [how to apply their doctrine in combat conditions]. By examining the fighting that took place, one can discern how the US army was beginning to evolve into the proven and professional military machine that went on to win the war in Europe." Among the many interesting insights in Reardon's work, he revealed the usefulness of the towed antitank gun in the hedgerows of Normandy, where the rough terrain made this weapon far more effective than tanks in frontline antiarmor defense. Although Reardon acknowledged the risk of a thin frontline antitank defense, lacking depth or the means to reinforce the line at a point of penetration, the effectiveness of the guns deterred the Germans from risking the heavy losses necessary to achieve a penetration. Reardon also emphasized the effectiveness of the infantry–artillery team, whose doctrine the army had firmly established before the war. Reardon argued, "Combined training was carried on until infantry and artillery became thoroughly indoctrinated in the operational procedures necessary to coordinate their actions on the battlefield."[32]

Reardon acknowledged the fact that the infantry–tank component of the doctrinal infantry–artillery–tank combined arms team lacked the efficacy of the infantry–artillery relationship, but he made the important point that this gap proved just as common among infantry and armor units from the same division as it did between infantry units and reinforcing General Headquarters tank battalions. In other words, the hedgerows of Normandy presented the primary challenge facing the infantry–armor team, not the lack of habitual relationships, because this terrain made the motorized or mechanized infantry particularly vulnerable to concealed German defenders and deterred the infantry from accompanying the better-armored tanks on the attack. Over time, however, training and combat experience enabled the infantry and armor to mature into the effective combined arms element envisioned in doctrine, and combined with the power of massed, observed artillery fires, it enabled US combat forces to maintain a steady advance in extremely difficult terrain against well-trained and well-equipped German units enjoying the advantage of the defense. This maturation process did not rely on adaptation—or the creation of new doctrine on the spot, as some histories imply. It simply involved the learning and battle-hardening process necessary to enable American combat units to execute their doctrine effectively in demanding combat conditions. Within a month of establishing the beachhead, combat units in Normandy had learned to operate effectively as combined infantry–artillery–armor–engineer teams, supplemented with close air support when available. This enabled them to fight their way methodically through some of the toughest terrain imaginable against the vaunted German army and maintain steady progress despite the lack of reserve divisions and their reliance on inexperienced individual replacements to replenish the ranks of units as they suffered combat losses.[33] Reardon's work stands out as a superior narrative that tells this story clearly and convincingly.

Historian Peter Mansoor, in *The GI Offensive in Europe*, sought to rejuvenate the image of the American infantry soldier by arguing, "The Army of the United States accomplished its mission in western Europe because it evolved over time into a more combat-effective force than Germany could sustain on the battlefield." *The GI Offensive in Europe* made a significant contribution to the rejuvenation of the GI's image by using detailed case studies from America's campaigns in Western Europe to demonstrate that American infantrymen performed much more effectively in combat than some historians have asserted. Mansoor identified many of the challenges McNair had to deal with during the war, focusing on how GIs dealt with the results of these challenges, whereas this book focuses more on how McNair sought to resolve the cause. Mansoor emphasized adaptation over learning, and adaptation did play a key role in the World War II GIs' battle hardening into effective combat troops when the doctrine they learned did not fit a particular situation, just as adaptation serves the same purpose today. Mansoor's book provides a deeply researched, detailed, and influential addition to the revisionist American school of World War II history. The present study arrives at many of the same conclusions as Mansoor did in *The GI Offensive in Europe,* although the emphasis here remains on McNair and his efforts to create an effective combat force from his staff positions on the home front. Analysis of the army's development into an effective organization from McNair's perspective logically emphasizes the learning process combat soldiers underwent in battle, while the GIs' perspective could naturally lead one to focus on adaptation's role in GIs' transformation from green recruits to effective, battle-hardened soldiers. I argue that the doctrine that US army divisions practiced in training and learned to use in combat worked quite well, and army units required no more adaptation in battle during World War II than American soldiers have in the nation's other wars.[34]

Robert Sterling Rush, in *Hell in Hürtgen Forest,* sought to present a "different perspective of US Combat effectiveness against German units in the European Theater" than that found in most works on the US army in World War II. Rush sought to contribute to the new interpretations of American combat performance in World War II provided by authors like Bonn and Mansoor—authors that he applauded for having "slowly stripped away the aura of German ground superiority in the face of overwhelming odds," leading to a significant change in the accepted wisdom. This has created a situation in which, as Rush argued, "some quarters now accept that, on par, American divisions were superior to those German ones they faced."[35] Writing in 2001, Rush did not have access to several more works that have added to this line of reasoning. Mark J. Reardon's *Victory at Mortain: Stopping Hitler's Panzer Counteroffensive* fits within the earlier works Rush mentioned and used a similar argumentative approach. Additionally, books have since appeared that make similar arguments but from a different angle. For example, Peter J. Schifferle's *America's School for War* and Michael R. Matheny's *Carrying the War to the Enemy: American Operational Art to 1945* emphasized education and discourse among officers on duty during the interwar period as the key to the US army's ability to conduct effective operational art during World War II.

In *America's School for War,* Schifferle highlighted the significant contributions made by the faculty of the Leavenworth schools and the benefit of the education that US army officers received there in maintaining a lively discourse regarding the evolving nature of modern warfare. Schifferle pointed out key gaps in the education that officers received at Leavenworth in the 1920s and 1930s, particularly the lack of focus on logistics and Army Air Forces. However, he argued that the school's contributions far outweighed its shortcomings, concluding that officers received an excellent and appropriate education at the Leavenworth schools that prepared them for the task of leading and training a hastily mobilized and rapidly expanding US army on the eve of America's involvement in World War II.[36]

Critics of America's World War II officers have expressed admiration for the bold, charismatic leadership styles of officers like Patton and Rommel, describing them as far superior to officers with less panache. Maverick behavior certainly drew public attention and helped such officers establish their reputations as superior battlefield commanders, but it also lessened their effectiveness and made them poor followers. In contrast, workmanlike competence served the American officer corps well, establishing a reasonable performance standard while producing many truly excellent general officers. Schifferle provided an explanation for this phenomenon:

> Perhaps the greatest irony of the interwar General Staff School education was that the failure to resolve a very controversial issue—whether to focus on teaching future commanders or teaching future staff officers—was itself of great benefit to the fielded force in World War II. The conflation of commandership and staff officer skills, exemplified in the name change in the early 1920s to the Command and General Staff School, actually assisted the leaders of combat divisions in World War II. They were educated like the dragoons of old who, when on foot, were told they could defeat any mounted force and, when on horseback, were told that they could defeat any dismounted unit. Leavenworth students were continually informed that as general staff officers they needed to know everything the generals had to know so they could assist them with proper staff work. As potential generals, they were told they would need to know everything that their staff knew to better teach less qualified subordinates and to better appreciate the estimates they would receive from a staff during combat.

This dual focus on generalship and staff skills enabled the relatively small pool of Leavenworth-trained officers to not only bring their own individual skills to either job but also train and assist those officers around them who found themselves in a command or staff role having had no Leavenworth education or only the abbreviated course offered during mobilization. Combined with the War College education received by most of the army's senior leaders, the American officer corps' broad and challenging educational experience during the interwar period resulted in a level of competence that enabled them to fight effectively despite the reliance on untrained recruits at all ranks and in the most demanding combat positions in the AGF.[37]

In *Carrying the War to the Enemy*, Matheny took issue with works such as David E. Johnson's *Fast Tanks and Heavy Bombers* and William O. Odom's *After the Trenches* for their overemphasis of tactical doctrine and adoption of (or failure to adopt) new technologies. Matheny argued that this approach caused these historians and many like them to miss the interwar "evolution of US military thinking at the operational level of war. It was at this level, particularly in dealing with logistically supportable joint and combined-phased operations, that senior American commanders did particularly well and laid a foundation for the Allied victory in World War II." Matheny emphasized the army's interwar education system rather than the "published doctrine or scholarly works of American officers" as the source of "the rudimentary understanding of joint and combined operational art developed [at Command and General Staff College and the American War College] and . . . imparted to a generation of senior American officers."[38]

These works illustrate the growing awareness of the importance of sound doctrine and effective education in that doctrine to the success of American combat units during World War II. The authors understood the fundamental skills and educational experiences that made the regular army officers of the interwar period both effective leaders and skilled trainers of the American soldier or junior officer—usually raw recruits who needed someone to teach them the basics rather than giving them an example of brilliant combat leadership. These American combat personnel defeated the vaunted German army despite its long tradition of militarism, extensive combat experience, advantage of fighting on the defensive in extremely rough terrain, and moral determination that came from knowing that with each step back, it came closer to defending its homeland and its soldiers' families from unconditional surrender.

Although presented in a very different manner than the various books referenced above, Robert Goldich wrote a review of the final book in Rick Atkinson's Liberation trilogy, *The Guns at Last Light,* that offered a unique and thought-provoking argument to show that Atkinson's book deserves a place among the revisionist works described above. In this book review, Goldich pointed out five reasons why Atkinson's book is "even better than you think." Goldich's first reason merits a long direct quotation:

> *The Guns at Last Light* is an American book, written by an American author . . . in which the narrative and interpretation of the American components of the Northwest Europe campaign are stressed. It's about time. For far too long, general histories of the campaign, and particularly of the Battle of Normandy, have been dominated by supercilious British historians. These men almost never fail to grasp an opportunity to criticize American military performance from privates to generals, up to the highest-ranking American leader of all, Dwight D. Eisenhower. From Chester Wilmot in the early 1950s, to Max Hastings in the early 1980s, to Antony Beevor over the past couple of decades, the

British have monopolized the popular historiography of the Northwest Europe campaign (largely, I suspect, because Britain has done nothing beyond the tactical level of war since 1945, and American military historians have had four major wars involving forces of field army size to write about). This narrative of alleged American military bungling would simply make an American uncomfortable if there was any substantive truth in it. But there isn't. By being scrupulously fair in his evaluation of American, British, and Canadian commanders, Atkinson shows that the latter two were not one iota better, and arguably slightly worse, than American leadership at the division, corps, army, army group, and theater level.

Goldich next emphasized a point that Atkinson made clear but is too often forgotten: "When armies of roughly equal military competence and weaponry clash, tactical and operational deadlock are almost inevitable, and usually the only way to break it is through attrition. This was particularly true in Normandy."[39]

Goldich illustrated the quality of Atkinson's analysis by describing his emphasis on the often overlooked topic of logistics, which remained a significant constraint for months after D-Day. Lack of supplies made the deep, thin thrusts that Montgomery constantly agitated for simply infeasible, and Eisenhower's better grasp of the impact of logistics on Allied operations illustrates the wisdom of his broad front strategy, which struck the best balance between Allied capabilities and limitations. Goldich also praised Atkinson's identification of physical and moral stamina as key requirements for high-level command during the war. Finally, he emphasized Atkinson's identification of Eisenhower's main strength as supreme Allied commander—not simply his ability to hold the coalition together but also his recognition that to do so, he could not let any one nation seem to be winning the war on its own while the others played purely supporting roles. This too had a significant impact on Eisenhower's theater strategy and the operational art that emerged from it as Eisenhower took direct control of Allied ground operations in the fall of 1944.[40]

Goldich effectively summarized several key arguments that Atkinson made in *The Guns at Last Light* that make this book a significant contribution to the increasingly widespread view that the US army deployed to combat reasonably well-trained and well-equipped troops. Atkinson's work supports the idea that GIs went to war prepared to fight based on sound doctrine. Perhaps this indicates that the trajectory of the accepted wisdom on US army effectiveness during World War II has begun to change.

This book, while primarily intended to describe details of Lesley J. McNair's career that have previously been absent from the literature on World War II, also supports the reevaluation of US army effectiveness during World War II that one finds in the books described above. It does, however, vary somewhat in approach, not only because of its primary purpose—revealing the details of a military life—but also because it emphasizes learning rather than adaptation as the primary reason for the American army's successes. Many historians who have offered fresh perspectives on US army effectiveness during World War II have emphasized GIs' ability to adapt. This collective body of work might have led to an impression, intentional or not, that the US army faced a situation for which it lacked the appropriate training, equipment, and leadership—yet somehow it possessed a unique ability to find novel and innovative approaches to fight and thereby overcome its many limitations. Although cases of adaptation of doctrine, equipment, and organization to deal with particular circumstances took place during World War II, as in any war, the following study presents evidence that this process merely augmented the primary means of US army success: learning how to fight as it was trained, organized, and equipped against an experienced and determined enemy. One finds the intersection of McNair's story and that of the US army's effectiveness here; McNair spent the majority of the interwar period working to organize the World War II army and write its operational doctrine.

In the early American campaigns, both in the South Pacific and in the Mediterranean theater, the Americans usually sent unseasoned units into combat for the first time—a situation for which mobilization training can only partially prepare a unit, at best. One sees the true success of American combined arms doctrine in World War II when reading the accounts of units that, after their initial exposure to combat conditions, gained the experience that enabled them to apply the doctrine they learned in unit training and large-scale maneuvers in actual combat conditions. One typically finds the best examples of this process of learning and battle hardening in the post-D-Day campaigns in Normandy through the fall of Berlin. Such examples support the arguments found in most of the books referenced earlier. Further, the body of work on US army operations during World War II reveals a growing awareness of the fundamental importance of well-trained and competent staffs to success in modern warfare. Unsurprisingly, the US army focused a great deal of effort on the development of staff officer competence both during the interwar years and during the mobilization for war.

The following analysis demonstrates that McNair deserved the nickname that Marshall gave him: the brains of the army. In a military not known for producing famous and prolific military theorists, McNair stands out as a key figure in moving American thinking about modern warfare forward. Like most military thinkers, he worked within a military bureaucracy, which itself existed within a larger national and social system. He faced challenges navigating the complex terrain of these systems, as did all military intellectuals, and unsurprisingly, not all of his predictions regarding the nature of future warfare were completely accurate.

In other cases, he simply lacked the ability, being only one man (albeit an influential one) to resolve the flaws he recognized in those larger systems. Americans in the decades between the world wars still harbored a distrust of large standing armies, and, as Edward M. Coffman put it, "had little interest in and less respect for soldiers in peacetime. Many civilians may have lived through the 1920s and 1930s without ever seeing one, while a few might not even have known about their existence."[41] Their prevailing isolationist views led these civilians to support congressional actions to constrain military progress through stringent cuts in War Department budgets and personnel authorizations. McNair, like all regular army officers during the interwar period, struggled against these constraints, advising the best possible course given a limited range of options. In short, McNair got some things wrong, but given the challenges he faced, he still managed to get more right.

As James Wheeler pointed out in an *Army* article, McNair now ranks among Marshall's forgotten men. Wheeler described these men as the leaders Marshall observed to be particularly capable early in his career and called on for senior leadership when the need arose in 1939. Wheeler wrote his article in response to an earlier article by Cole Kingseed entitled "Marshall's Men," adding these "forgotten men" to Kingseed's list of Marshall's better-remembered subordinates. As Wheeler pointed out, McNair's service "and that of the other forgotten Marshall men, is unknown to most Americans." Nevertheless, even Wheeler, as he sought to remind his readers of McNair's contributions, painted him with a broad brush. For example, he emphasized Marshall's role in selecting general officers for the army's senior leadership positions, but he did not acknowledge McNair's perhaps equally significant responsibility of recommending who should command every division and corps the army activated to fight World War II—recommendations Marshall usually endorsed. Stephen R. Taaffe, however, corrected this oversight in *Marshall and His Generals*. As Taaffe pointed out, "Despite all his years in the small prewar army, it was impossible for Marshall to personally meet and evaluate every officer eligible for the highest ranks and positions." Therefore, "he had to depend increasingly upon the recommendations of others . . . especially General Lesley McNair of Army Ground Forces."[42]

The following analysis synthesizes historical perspectives from a variety of different subfields. These include the interwar officer education system; the military and industrial mobilization effort before both World War I and World War II; the challenges associated with coalition warfare; and the organization and internal relationships of the War Department General Staff, the functional commands, and the various army branch chiefs and schools before and during World War II. Drawing on topic areas that writers often address independently reveals the often overlooked interconnectedness of seemingly disparate factors and how this interconnectedness influenced the effectiveness of the US army. This synthesis often suggests new interpretations for McNair's views and actions and indicates that he understood the nature of modern warfare better than much of the existing literature suggests.

The narrative presented here serves the primary purpose of revealing the history of General Lesley J. McNair's full forty-year-long army career. It highlights the many contributions he made to the US army's doctrine, organization, and training—not just during the mobilization for World War II but throughout the preceding thirty-six years. Key themes recur that offer new perspectives on McNair's role in the modernization and mechanization of the US army between the World Wars. These themes include McNair's belief in the value of officer education, his strong convictions regarding the qualities required in a competent commander, his keen interest and involvement in military innovation, and his vast experience in field tests and experiments before mobilization for World War II began.

McNair also sought to overcome interwar resource constraints by gaining efficiencies in unit organization through various measures of streamlining and pooling of assets—a task the War Department assigned to him formally when the members of the General Staff began to acknowledge the scarcity of resources in 1942 that McNair and other key leaders had anticipated years earlier. He understood the value of arduous, realistic training, and perhaps more importantly, he grasped that innovative concepts and equipment required objective, detailed experimentation to test their practical value. He also recognized the criticality of the use of combined arms fighting methods, and he consistently sought to optimize army organization and doctrine to enable this in a resource-constrained, hastily mobilized army—something he experienced several times as a young officer and knew would characterize any future American war effort.

As he strove to inculcate these values in the army, McNair maintained an exhausting schedule, regularly working sixteen-hour days and rarely taking leave. As a senior officer, he traveled thousands of miles on the road and in the air to visit units in training. Even after assuming command of AGF, he did administrative work himself that other officers might have delegated to someone else, not only to ensure it met his exacting standards but also because completing it all required working late into the night—something he preferred to do himself rather than requiring such sacrifices from his subordinates.

Perhaps unsurprisingly, one can discern the roots of these ideas and traits in McNair's education and practical experience during the early years of his long career. McNair did not always predict the nature of future warfare perfectly, but he certainly did not struggle as intently to build the size and influence of his staff as his peers who commanded the Army Air Forces and Army Service Forces. He became increasingly detached as a result of his hearing loss as he aged, and he grew despondent over the inefficient War Department bureaucracy and policies that created unnecessary challenges for AGF while seemingly favoring the Army Air Forces and Army Service Forces. Perhaps most frustrating of all, he constantly found his freedom of action hamstrung by the limitations to his authority imposed by the War Department's staff procedures. Nevertheless, a full recounting of his military life reveals a career marked by far more successes than missteps. McNair's military record sets him apart as a general officer who contributed far more than currently recognized to the US army's successful participation in the Allied war effort during World War II.

Part I

Innovation in Peace and War

1

From Cadet to Commander: Birth of an Innovator

By analyzing in detail the early years of McNair's four-decade-long career in both staff and command positions, during peace and war, the first few chapters of this book reveal much about his varied experiences and the sources of his ideas about modern warfare, which, once developed as a young officer, he championed throughout the interwar period.

McNair as a Young Man and Cadet

Lesley James McNair lived a small-town existence for most of his youth. His father, James McNair, immigrated to America from Comphelltown, Scotland, at the age of eight in 1854. James lived in Ohio with his seven siblings and his parents, William and Mary McNair, until the 1870s, when he moved with his family to Neoga, Illinois. James met and married Clara Mantz McNair in Dayton, Ohio, in 1880 and moved to Verndale, Minnesota, the following year. Today Verndale boasts a population of just over 500, but in the 1880s, the town enjoyed a bustling economy, attracting merchants and farmers seeking an entry point to new agricultural areas in the northern Midwest. Verndale's economy centered on packaging wheat brought in from the northern prairies, then shipping it to Minneapolis and onward to satisfy demands from across the nation. James and Clara McNair operated a general store near the central part of town and lived in a small home a block and a half from the store. They raised four children: two sons and two daughters. They celebrated the birth of Lesley James, their second child and first-born son, on May 25, 1883.[1]

Lesley McNair attended school in Verndale through ninth grade—the highest grade available at the local school—consistently excelling academically. However, no opportunity existed near Verndale for a bright young man to complete high school, prompting the McNair family to leave Verndale after fourteen years there. The family genealogy, a multivolume project completed by James Birtley McNair between 1923 and 1960, covered the history of the extended McNair family, including those originating in Scotland and other parts of Great Britain, many of whom adopted variant spellings of the family surname. The genealogy described James and Clara as prominent members of the Verndale community. In addition to his general store, James dealt in timber products, and he spent a great deal of time in camps looking after his timber interests in Nimrod, Minnesota. According to one account, Verndale residents described Clara as a "model housewife, devoted mother, and steadfast friend," whom neighbors regarded as an accomplished musician. She also maintained a strong interest in local educational affairs. Perhaps this interest helped her convince James to sell his timber business and leave behind his beloved camps in the woods so that he could move his family to Minneapolis in 1894, thus enabling Lesley and his siblings to finish high school.[2]

Lesley took full advantage of this opportunity. Driven by the goal of serving as a US navy officer, he finished high school in 1897 with a strong record and competed successfully for a position to attend the US Naval Academy at Annapolis. However, he soon grew frustrated with the academy's long waiting list, and he enrolled the following year in the Minnesota School of Business in Minneapolis. There he pursued a degree in mechanical engineering, studying ordnance construction, woodworking, metalworking, ordnance design, bookkeeping, and statistical work. By spring 1900 he had completed this program, and, still on the waiting list to attend the Naval Academy, he sought admittance to the United States Military Academy (USMA) at West Point. The academy accepted him for immediate admittance into the next class, notifying him of his new status as a West Point cadet on August 1, 1900, requiring him to make due haste to report in time to begin the fall semester.[3]

McNair continued his record of outstanding academic performance at USMA. When he earned his commission in 1904, he ranked eleventh out of the 124 graduates in his class. He received an appointment as a second lieutenant in the field artillery, a branch that suited him well because of his skill in mathematics—consistently among his strongest subjects during his four years as a cadet. Besides his commission as a field artillery officer, McNair earned a nickname at West Point. As Larry and Dorothy Lehner recall in "McNair: Verndale to St. Lô," McNair's "West Point colleagues remembered him as a mathematical shark, and called him 'Whitey' [because of his strikingly white hair], a nickname that followed him the rest of his life."[4]

McNair's particular interests, most notably mathematics, stand out when one compares his class rank in each topic to his overall class rank during each of his four years at USMA. For example, McNair completed his first year ranked number 31 out of 154 fourth class (first year) cadets, but he ranked number 24 in mathematics—his highest standing among all subjects that year. In his second year, he earned his highest overall ranking of his West Point career, taking posi-

Lesley J. McNair, Cadet, United States Military Academy, circa 1901. Courtesy of the Military History Institute

tion number 6 among the 142 third class cadets, ranking number 4 in drawing and 10 in mathematics—his two best subjects that year. McNair struggled a bit in his third year, falling to number 30 out of 125 cadets; but he ranked number 5 in drawing, 20 in conduct, and 23 in mathematics. When McNair finished his senior year as number 11 out of 124 graduating cadets, he ranked number 8 in ordnance and gunnery, 12 in mathematics, and 18 in military efficiency.[5]

Always committed to strict discipline both for him and for others, McNair experienced only one lapse in conduct during his four years in the notoriously strict program of instruction at West Point. He returned late from leave on one occasion after visiting a young woman named Clare Huster in New York City. Because he married Clare soon after graduation and spent the rest of his life with her, the demerit probably seemed a small price to pay.[6] However, before the young cadet married Clare, he headed west to begin active service as a second lieutenant in the mountain artillery. In the early twentieth century, officers faced stiff competition to earn a commission in the field artillery. Second Lieutenant McNair overcame this competition to earn a slot in the branch; the artillery also proved a perfect fit for the talented young mathematician. (His desire to serve in the artillery probably resulted from the mentorship of West Point's mathematics department faculty, composed at the time primarily of field artillerymen.[7]) Although he enjoyed and performed well in his basic branch, McNair soon found a way to put his exceptional talent in drawing and ordnance design to use, resulting in a four-year detour from the standard field artillery officer's career path.

Branch Detail to Ordnance

The newly commissioned McNair arrived at Fort Douglas, Utah, in September 1904 to undertake his first tour of duty after three months of leave. He served as a platoon leader assigned to the 12th Battery, Mountain Artillery. While learning the duties of a young leader of field artillerymen, McNair requested in 1905 an examination for detail to the Ordnance Branch. He took the exam in February, and the board of examiners recommended approval of his request in May. On May 22, 1905, McNair received orders reassigning him to the Ordnance Branch, and he arrived at Sandy Hook Proving Ground in New Jersey on June 14. Although McNair possessed exceptional talent for drafting and ordnance design, the presence in New York of Miss Clare Huster might also have influenced his decision to request a branch detail to ordnance, with its promise of an assignment on the East Coast. He certainly did not waste any time; he married Clare on June 15, 1905, soon after his arrival in New Jersey.[8]

McNair spent the next four years serving in a wide variety of Ordnance Branch positions. Despite his academic proficiency and evident interest in the Ordnance Branch, McNair's efficiency reports from this period reflect mixed performance. This appears to have resulted from a shaky relationship with a particular supervisor, but he may also have found it difficult to achieve a reasonable balance between his personal and professional life after experiencing five years of military routine at West Point and the remote army outpost at Fort Douglas.

First Lieutenant G. R. Green, his battery commander at Fort Douglas, made only positive remarks in McNair's first efficiency report. Green described the young lieutenant as an officer who possessed excellent "attention to duty, profession zeal and general bearing and military appearance," and very good "intelligence and judgment shown in instructing, drilling, and handling enlisted men." Green identified McNair as a good equestrian, suited for service in the field artillery, or as an instructor at the US Military Academy, and—largely due to his "special ability in mechanical drawing and map making"—particularly fit for "detail in Ordnance Department." However, Green found McNair best suited, in the event of war, for service with the field artillery.[9]

By contrast, McNair's efficiency reports from his four-year detail with the Ordnance Department provide a mixed assessment of the young officer. His first two reports reflect performance on par with that of his assignment at Fort Douglas. Colonel G. S. Smith, his supervisor during the first year of his branch detail, when he served as a staff officer in the office of chief of ordnance, commended his basic skills and characteristics as an army lieutenant. Smith judged McNair "well fitted for detail on the General Staff," but wrote, "To a limited extent he appears to be qualified for command of troops." With no performance deficiencies noted, one can only speculate why Smith believed McNair possessed limited potential for command; however, this could have been merely a result of his youth and lack of experience. Regardless, Smith summarized his report by finding McNair "qualified for his position," stating that he "should be entrusted with important duties commensurate with his experience and rank." Smith recommended McNair for either artillery or ordnance duty in time of war.[10]

In 1906, McNair left the office of the chief of ordnance for Watertown Arsenal in Boston. His first supervisor, Lieutenant Colonel F. E. Hobbs, seemed impressed with McNair's performance, finding him excellent or very good in all the basic officer leadership qualities. He deemed McNair fit for detail as "an instructor in the Department of Ordnance and Gunnery" or in "command of troops." Further, Hobbs made note of a commendation that he wrote for McNair "in a special report made by me to the Chief of Ordnance as to character and service of detailed officers who had served under my command." McNair spent the final two years of his detail to the Ordnance Branch working for Major C. B. Wheeler, and given the fact that the two efficiency reports McNair received from Wheeler stand out as the only ones from his branch detail that contained any poor marks, it appears that the two officers did not work particularly well together.[11]

For example, Wheeler judged McNair in 1908 reasonably well qualified in the basic skills of an officer, but Wheeler found McNair possessed "no peculiar fitness for detail," and he wrote that McNair's "capacity for work is not large." Wheeler clearly did not think highly of McNair, writing, "I would not object to his being under my immediate command but I would prefer to have an officer of greater capacity." Wheeler also noted that he had mentioned McNair unfavorably in an Ordnance Office report earlier that year, and he believed McNair was "unwilling to devote more time to routine work than the daily office hours, no matter how much his work may be in arrears. He has at times worked over hours but there is a general spirit of unwillingness."[12]

McNair's problems with Wheeler continued the following year. His 1909 efficiency report, in which Wheeler seemed more pleased generally with McNair, provided positive assessments of his performance and potential, but it closed on a negative note that revealed the most likely explanation for Wheeler's poor assessment of McNair's performance. It read, "Captain McNair's otherwise good efficiency is impaired by his lack of power of appreciating the best methods of conducting his duties in accordance with the wishes of his commanding officer for whose judgment he has appeared at times to be willing to substitute his own." Even with two somewhat negative efficiency reports prepared by Wheeler, McNair's overall performance during his branch detail led to his promotion to captain in ordnance, although this promotion did not apply in his basic branch—field artillery—where he remained a first lieutenant.[13]

Despite his difficulties with Major Wheeler, McNair learned a great deal during his four years working for the Ordnance Branch. At Watertown Arsenal in particular, McNair undertook an intensive "course of practical profession" that included instruction in a diverse range of applied skills. In this yearlong course, McNair performed hands-on studies of laboratory test machines and methods. This included breaking test specimens, metallurgical analysis, foundry skills including the melting of bronze and cast iron, the manufacture of steel and pouring of castings, and the use of equipment including the forge, steam hammer, bolt machine and shears, lathes, planes, shapers, milling and boring machines, and test devices. McNair received practical experience during the day and completed academic work after hours, including the study of course notes, reference books, and technical drawings. The expertise he developed served him well in the coming years, when the army turned to him with increasing frequency to oversee various equipment tests and boards where he put this practical experience to use designing and conducting tests, and preparing detailed reports complete with graphs and detailed drawings.[14]

Return to Field Artillery

When McNair departed Watertown Arsenal in 1909, he possessed a uniquely broad range of skills compared to the average artilleryman. Building on his exceptional mathematical and technical drawing ability, McNair learned the value of methodological rigor and scientific objectivity in the conduct of equipment tests and experiments during his branch detail with ordnance. A traditional field artillery career path could not provide such a wealth of broadening opportunities. In five short years, Lieutenant McNair had developed a solid foundation of both technical and tactical proficiency.

With his new wife in tow, and restored to his previous rank in the field artillery, First Lieutenant McNair returned to the West for further service in his primary branch. He received orders reassigning him to the 4th Field Artillery at Fort D. A. Russell, Wyoming, on July 1, 1909, where he took command of Battery C two weeks later. McNair spent the next eight years with the field artillery at posts in Wyoming, Texas, and Oklahoma, or on combat duty in and around Mexico. In these assignments, McNair mastered the demands of service in remote and mountainous terrain, and he developed a reputation as an energetic, no-nonsense leader. Second Lieutenant Jacob L. Devers, a newly commissioned platoon leader assigned to McNair's battery after graduation from the 1909 West Point class, remembered McNair as an outstanding battery commander. In particular, Devers recalled that McNair set high standards, led by example, and possessed the ability to motivate his men to perform exceptionally well—skills critical for successful commanders, given the difficult conditions soldiers faced in austere Western outposts.[15]

In addition to the normal duties of a field artillery battery commander, the army soon began to give McNair responsibilities that would enable it to make use of the experience he gained during his detail to the Ordnance Department. In the decade after the turn of the century, much of the equipment in use by the mountain artillery served its purpose only marginally at best. Units of the mountain artillery still used the 2.95-inch Vickers-Maxim mountain gun, a weapon obsolete since 1905, when the Ordnance Department developed a three-inch howitzer for the light artillery. Although Ordnance had planned to develop an experimental battery to test a new mountain gun the same year, it had made no significant progress by 1909.[16] Therefore, the Ordnance Department tested various modifications to the obsolete 2.95-inch gun, seeking to improve its carriage and sight to make it more suitable for mountain duty. Furthermore, most mountain artillery units' packsaddles, other transport and pioneer equipment, and items including kitchen gear and the mobile forge ranged from unsuitable to nonexistent. McNair spent much of his four years in command of Battery C working to find solutions to these various equipment challenges, conducting tests and participating in boards while training his men in extremely arduous conditions.[17]

McNair's work to improve mountain artillery equipment and training contributed to a larger armywide effort to modernize the field artillery. This project dated to the turn of the century, when the poor performance of the field artillery during the Spanish-American War prompted American development of a new three-inch howitzer. Observers of the Russo-Japanese War of 1904–1905 reported dramatic improvements in field artillery procedures that increased the effectiveness of indirect fire. As historian Janice E. McKenney noted,

> That war involved the clash of large armies armed with modern weapons, resulting in the extensive use of trenches. The effectiveness of artillery fire drove both sides to cover, that is, in defilade. Laying guns indirectly while in defilade became standard, with centralized control provided through the use of telephone wire. Indirect fire control resulted in an increase in the number of potential firing locations, and the ability to shift the fire of a great number of pieces without physically moving them permitted the use of heavier, less mobile artillery in the field.
>
> However, field artillery leaders argued that their branch's organization and personnel management policies hindered its ability to take full advantage of the new 3-inch gun and employ the advanced firing methods observers had witnessed in the Russo-Japanese War.[18]

After much debate, Congress passed an act separating coast and field artillery into separate branches in 1907, based on the conclusion that the mission and function of the two subfields of artillery differed so much that having artillery officers rotate between assignments in the two types of units served no useful purpose. The same act, in McKenney's words, "authorized six additional field batteries and gave the heretofore provisional regiments legal standing. The regiments, numbered 1 through 6, each had two battalions of three four-gun batteries. The 1st, 3d, and 5th Field Artillery were authorized as light artillery to serve with infantry troops, the 2d and 4th as mountain or pack artillery, and the 6th as horse artillery to serve with the cavalry." The mountain artillery served the same infantry support role as the light artillery but relied on mules instead of horses to negotiate rough and mountainous terrain, and it used generally lighter, more mobile equipment. However, no mountain equivalent of the new three-inch gun yet existed by 1909, despite years of purported effort to develop one. One of McNair's first priorities therefore involved testing the existing gun to find ways to maximize the potential of a weapon most artillerymen considered obsolete.[19]

McNair's first step in this effort involved deploying with one section of his battery to Fort Riley, Kansas, in September 1909 to conduct firing tests for six weeks with the Ordnance Department's prototype 2.95-inch mountain howitzer. Upon his arrival at Fort Riley, McNair requested detailed drawings of the modified Vickers gun, which he used after his return to Fort D. A. Russell to prepare a detailed report on the Fort Riley firing tests. This report included his own engineering drawings for a customized mountain artillery piece designed to his specifications that he urged the Ordnance Department to build and test. He submitted this report on April 5, 1910, after which he began planning a battery training exercise. The Ordnance Department had not yet issued any of the new mountain guns to McNair's C Battery, so he took his unit to the Target and Maneuver Reservation, Pole Mountain, Wyoming, for a month of training with the equipment he had on hand in July 1910. This training gave McNair his first opportunity to test his battery in field conditions, identify needed equipment and training shortfalls, and prepare for more tests, which he planned for early the next year.[20]

Meanwhile, during the first few months of 1911, Major William Lassiter of the 5th Field Artillery conducted an inspection of the 4th Field Artillery for the inspector general, Maneuver Division, based in San Antonio, Texas. Major Lassiter issued his findings on May 6, 1911, having conducted his inspection in March and April of that year (he began the inspection on the same day the 4th Artillery's new commander, Colonel E. D. Hoyle, took command). Before describing his detailed findings, Lassiter introduced his report with several general observations concerning the challenges he observed in the mountain artillery. These supported his general finding that "the batteries are not thoroughly reliable agencies for the prompt delivery of effective fire. The officers are not, as a rule, well skilled in posting their guns and employing them to produce fire which is quickly effective. It is difficult to escape the conclusion that, so far as the officers are concerned, this condition is in a great measure due to an imperfect and incomplete system of training."[21] Lassiter qualified this assessment, however, noting the unique challenges facing the mountain artillery. These centered on the particularly onerous nature of their mission, combined with the austere conditions artillerymen endured at posts like Fort D. A. Russell.

Lassiter also made note of the poor material and organizational state of the mountain artillery, emphasizing that, "prompt attention should be given the matter of placing the mountain artillery on a better footing with respect to matters of equipment and of interior organization." He provided a list of equipment and methods that needed improvement, including the gun and packsaddle, mule loading procedures, and the training of enlisted men. In particular, he advised finding a way to simplify the pack mule loading procedures so that enlisted men could learn this skill in a reasonably short period. He stressed the importance of achieving the goal of replacing the civilian packers that the firing batteries currently required with military personnel—an important change that would reduce reliance on contractors during combat operations. Lassiter's observations provided a list of mountain artillery issues that McNair sought to resolve by leading his battery through even more tests and exercises over the next several years.[22]

Concurrent with Lassiter's inspection, McNair received orders effective March 13, 1911, to serve on a Mountain Artillery board with two other artillery officers from the 4th Artillery. The orders directed the board to observe McNair's battery as it tested various equipment under development for the mountain artillery, including the modified mountain artillery howitzer, potential replacements for the standard aparejo packsaddle, and miscellaneous other field equipment. The board's first test consisted of a long-range march from Fort D. A. Russell to San Antonio and back, completed between March 13 and July 14. After only a short break, McNair took his battery back to the field, conducting another round of firing tests and field exercises at Pole Mountain, Wyoming, between July 25 and August 13.[23] The War Department disbanded McNair's first Mountain Artillery board on February 26, 1912, the same day that it approved the board president's three-page report summarizing its findings. The board found that the tests McNair's battery conducted, both at the firing range and on the march from Fort D. A. Russell to San Antonio and back, confirmed, as written in the report, that "there is no arm of the service so deficiently equipped as the mountain artillery."[24]

The War Department soon turned to McNair for further tests of mountain artillery equipment. Less than a month after the Mountain Artillery board issued its final report, McNair received orders to conduct further analysis of the equipment identified as deficient in the initial series of tests, with a particular focus on the gun and packsaddle. To complete these tests, McNair began planning another, longer march that would take the battery through Colorado and then back to Fort D. A. Russell in the summer of 1912. Although most of the equipment tests would have to wait until this upcoming march through Colorado, McNair completed a detailed study of the packsaddle problem based on the findings of the previous years' tests, and he submitted this report on May 17, 1912.[25]

Most members of the field artillery considered the standard mountain artillery packsaddle—the aparejo—deficient as currently configured, primarily because of its excessive weight and the skill required for artillery personnel to load it correctly, requiring the service of civilian contractors. McNair set out on his own initiative to find a suitable replacement. The Ordnance Branch had already devised an alternative configuration for the 1911 field tests that used long canvas bags instead of wooden boxes to carry the ammunition. When McNair first saw this modified packsaddle, he knew that it would cause injury to the mules, and he made recommendations to the Ordnance Branch for improvements. However, the Ordnance Branch disregarded McNair's recommendations, issuing his battery a set of their modified packsaddles as originally designed. To overcome the Ordnance Branch's resistance to his recommendations, McNair designed a test that compared five packsaddle configurations, including three variants of the aparejo that the Ordnance Branch was already considering for adoption (or retention) as standard equipment. In addition to these three options, McNair's test also included the English packsaddle, currently in use in many European armies and considered by many mountain artillerymen a superior packsaddle to the aparejo. Finally, McNair's test included a fifth pack saddle of his own design, based on the standard aparejo saddle but equipped with a specially designed ammunition pack and other modifications to improve deficiencies he had observed in training and testing of all the other packsaddle variants.[26]

In his test, McNair found that the standard aparejo, in either of the two configurations currently in use by the Ordnance Department, performed the worst out of the five when tested against two evaluation criteria. The first of these, efficiency, equated to the percentage of the total weight of the packsaddle made up by the artillery ammunition it carried. The second, capacity, measured the percentage of a mule's 350-pound maximum load taken up by ammunition, as opposed to the weight of the pack itself (also taking into account carrying capacity left unused). When testing the other three saddles, McNair found that the variant of the aparejo developed by the Ordnance Department (equipped with canvas bags instead of wooden boxes) provided only slightly better efficiency and capacity than the two current configurations. The English packsaddle performed equally well in these two criteria and outperformed all three of the Ordnance Department's designs when taking into account other characteristics like durability, load distribution, and packing ease and efficiency.[27]

The packsaddle McNair designed performed quite well in comparison with the poor performance of any of the existing packsaddle variants, including the English version. In McNair's configuration, the aparejo supported a smaller, more durable, efficiently designed canvas ammunition carrier, which improved the packsaddle's load size, weight distribution, and center of gravity. This enabled pack mules to carry heavier loads with less risk of injury, and it made ammunition more readily accessible to the men unloading the packs when firing. McNair's men constructed the packsaddle to his specifications with materials on hand, and yet it withstood more than two weeks of near-constant use without breaking down. The Ordnance Branch's canvas ammo pouch, in contrast, demonstrated poor endurance as a result of the weak, lightweight canvas used to make it. McNair's packsaddle carried the most rounds in the smallest carrying configuration, in two-round packs that one man could easily remove from the pack and carry to the firing battery even in rough terrain. Finally, it exceeded all the other configurations in efficiency and capacity by 12 percent or more. On the basis of these results, McNair proposed his design for adoption by the mountain artillery, but given the short period McNair had available to test it, he recognized the need for more extensive tests and identified additional improvements from which he believed it would benefit. Therefore, he prepared a second report describing these additional modifications and recommending that the Ordnance Department construct eight sets of his proposed carriers for issue to his regiment for further testing.[28]

Shortly after submitting his initial packsaddle report, and while still working on his second, McNair began preparing his battery for the upcoming field test, scheduled for June 20 to August 17, 1912. Lieutenant Devers, still serving as a platoon leader in McNair's battery, participated in this particularly high-profile and arduous test, in which McNair led his battery—a unit consisting of three pack trains of fifty mules each—on a fifty-one-day, 844-mile march. The battery departed from Cheyenne, Wyoming, headed south through Denver, Colorado Springs, and Canyon City, and then returned to the Rockies to conduct a record-setting high-altitude firing mission at 14,000 feet before returning home to Wyoming. This field test provided a great deal of additional data supporting McNair's recommendation for further modifications and testing of his packsaddle design.[29]

Despite McNair's significant effort to develop a better packsaddle, as late as 1917 Captain Leroy P. Collins wrote a short article published in the *Field Artillery Journal* noting that the army had yet to accomplish the further tests McNair recommended. Therefore, the standard aparejo configuration remained in use:

> I believe that the further test recommended by Captain McNair has never been made. There has always existed in our service a strong prejudice in favor of the aparejo to the exclusion of other types of pack saddles, probably due to the feeling that what was good enough for the old Army in its severe frontier service, is good enough for us. This feeling has been strengthened undoubtedly by the influence exerted on the army by the old time civilian pack masters. While no one denies that the aparejo has played an important role in our past history, yet the great number of sore backs, ensuing after a long march make it a matter of great importance that a pack saddle which is easier on a mule's back be adopted, if such a one exists or can be developed. Many mules returned from the march mentioned with holes in their sides which could not be covered by two hands and these were months in healing with no work.[30]

Even at this early stage of his career, McNair demonstrated a strong interest in innovation by working to find the most effective equipment for the army's use and by demonstrating the skill and objectivity to conduct and prepare reports on detailed and methodologically sound tests of such equipment.

This conflict between McNair, an ordnance-trained unit commander, and Ordnance Department engineers regarding packsaddles for mountain artillery units illustrates the challenges caused by the bifurcation of responsibilities for military equipment procurement and use in the early twentieth century. This division of responsibilities caused significant problems for the US army as it attempted to incorporate new technologies when modernizing its organization and doctrine. Historian Daniel Beaver identified the root of the problem as the informal nature of the relationships that guided the functioning of the Board of Ordnance and Fortification, established in 1885 to conduct a Congress-mandated review of the army's planned coastal-defense system. Beaver pointed out,

> By 1888 it was clear that construction and location of the new fortifications required formal coordination of the technical and construction bureaus and the army combat arms as well as close cooperation with the navy. In an unprecedented piece of legislation passed on September 22, 1888, Congress mandated a permanent Board of Ordnance and Fortification chaired by the commanding general of the army and including representatives of the War Department staff as well as an independent civilian representative to integrate the coastal defenses of the United States. The first formal interbureau managerial experiment by the War Department, it brought together engineers, ordnance, signals, and artillery officers to discuss systematic weapons research and development, improve cooperation between themselves and with the navy, and cultivate technical connections with American industry.

Under its first commander, the competent general of the army John McAllister Schofield, the board performed quite well, but as Beaver pointed out, several inefficiencies in its inner workings meant its effectiveness relied largely on informal relationships and a spirit of cooperation between the commanding general, the secretary of war, and the bureau chiefs. In particular, the Ordnance Bureau and the engineers each had their own boards, and they controlled the contracting process. This meant "the successful operation of the Board of Ordnance and Fortification hinged on personal consultation and informal connections."[31]

As leadership changed among the various departments and agencies that worked with the board over the next ten years, the spirit of cooperation that existed under General Schofield's tenure eroded. By 1899, Secretary of War Elihu Root lost all confidence in the board, and he made no mention of it in his annual report that year. However, the War Department took no effective action to decisively disband or replace the board. Implementation of Root's general staff system at the turn of the century left the board overlooked, and its functions devolved to various agencies, with war planning falling under the purview of the War College Division of the General Staff, while the technical and supply bureaus or various special boards retained responsibility for weapons and equipment development and standardization.[32] Thus, McNair possessed the most experience with pack-saddles of any of the various individuals or agencies involved in their development, and he commanded the units that conducted the field tests, but ultimately the technicians in Ordnance Branch and industry decided what equipment they would procure and field to army units.

Meanwhile, McNair's experimentation with mountain artillery packsaddles and extensive field tests drew attention from senior leaders in the branch, including the commandant of the Field Artillery School at Fort Sill, Oklahoma. This led to the school's request for a one-year detail of McNair to Fort Sill, to put into tabulated and easy-to-understand form the statistical firing data instructors at the school had collected over the previous fifteen months, during which the school fired over 7,000 rounds of artillery during various tests and training events. Because of a shortage of instructors, the school had only collected the data, but they possessed no officer on the faculty capable of putting it into useful form. The commandant believed organizing the data into a useful format would fully occupy the time of an officer for one year. He requested McNair by name to complete the task, writing, "Lieut. McNair, as far as I have been able to observe is fitted by disposition and by temperament to accomplish this kind of work in an extremely efficient manner." The War Department approved this request on December 3, 1912, with a report date of February 1, 1913, also directing McNair to travel to France to observe French artillery fire about midway through this one-year detail.[33]

McNair earned permanent promotion to captain of field artillery during his detail at Fort Sill, on April 19, 1914. After ten years of peacetime training duty, he soon received the opportunity to apply his hard-earned skills in operational combat assignments. From 1914 to 1917 he served twice in combat, first as regimental commissary, 4th Artillery, during the Funston Expedition to Vera Cruz (April to September 1914), and later as a battery commander in the 4th Artillery in support of Major General John J. Pershing's Punitive Expedition to Mexico (July 1916 to February 1917). Between combat tours, McNair returned to the Field Artillery School at Fort Sill, where he continued to work on fire procedures and weapons development.[34]

Before McNair joined the Funston Expedition, Colonel Berry of the 4th Field Artillery requested that the War Department assign McNair to his regiment instead of the captain currently slated to fill the intended position. Today's generals still use this administrative action (known as a by-name request, or BNR) in their efforts to fill their organizations with officers of known competence or particular ability.[35] The War Department granted Berry's request, and McNair supported the 4th Artillery during the expedition. His efficiency report covering this period includes the following evaluation of his performance during the expedition: "Under

Captain Lesley J. McNair's First Command—C Battery, 4th Artillery, Mexico; Punitive Expedition, 1917. Courtesy of US National Archives II, College Park, Maryland

the semi-field conditions existing here: Excellent. He has attended to the supply of the regiment in a businesslike way."[36]

Upon his return from Vera Cruz, McNair remained at the School of Fire, where he conducted various tests and experiments intended to identify improved methods of fire direction and control. Evidently he had performed so well as statistical officer that senior leaders at the Field Artillery School managed to retain his services beyond the initial one-year detail. In his next annual efficiency report, after serving another year at the School of Fire, McNair's supervisor remarked on his particular expertise in ordnance construction and ballistics theory of field gunnery, and he ranked McNair "among the first 6 captains of field artillery in efficiency." In his final efficiency report at the School of Fire, completed in May 1916 as McNair prepared to deploy in support of the Punitive Expedition, his rater described McNair as "an officer of the highest type, thoroughly qualified and reliable" and rated him "excellent" in all categories.[37]

McNair returned to the 4th Field Artillery for the duration of the Punitive Expedition, serving as a battery commander and leading troops in combat for the first time. Although no records appear to exist that describe his experience of command in detail, his efficiency report for this period indicates that he served in an excellent manner while leading his battery 300 miles into Mexico and back. His rater and first endorser expressed great satisfaction with his performance, evaluating him excellent in all areas, including those related to leading combat troops in the field. Their observations included several comments regarding his general competence, including "an excellent officer in both theory and practice," and "this officer is in my opinion one of the best equipped, mentally, morally, and physically, in the service." Major General John J. Pershing signed the report under "First Indorsement," concurring with the evaluation written by McNair's rating officer, Colonel Allaire.[38] This demonstrates that they may not have served closely together during the Punitive Expedition, but at a minimum, Pershing read the high praise McNair received in his efficiency report and knew enough about his reputation to endorse the remarks.

These operational assignments further developed McNair's skill as a leader of artillerymen, but more significantly, they steeped the young captain in the principles of traditional American war-fighting doctrine. Building on its roots as a frontier constabulary, the turn-of-the-century American army remained confident of the primacy of the infantry and the power of moral superiority to win battles. Its experiences during the operations in Mexico under Funston and Pershing verified in many American officers' minds the effectiveness of their traditional fighting methods. Meanwhile, a radically new form of warfare took shape in Europe, where large armies adapted their doctrine to the superiority of the defensive enabled by machine guns, massed artillery, and elaborate systems of entrenchments. Nevertheless, the US army, paying little attention to a war they did not expect to fight, continued to emphasize morale over technology and expected the infantry to win battles with the rifle and bayonet. In the traditional American view, the infantry provided the main combat force, relying on artillery support only to the degree necessary to enable it to close within rifle range and finish the enemy with a bayonet charge.[39] In this respect, McNair proved unique in his particular expertise with the latest fire techniques and equipment, as well as in his efforts to increase the mobility of field artillery so it could provide effective support to the infantry.

The Punitive Expedition to Mexico in support of Brigadier General John J. Pershing's 8th Brigade proved to be particularly significant for McNair's career. Not only did the expedition offer practical lessons in the employment of mobile artillery but it also exposed McNair to a complex and difficult mobilization that revealed significant weaknesses in the army's ability to react to a threat to the US border. This experience surely made a significant impact on the young McNair. It also gave him another opportunity to serve under Pershing, one of the army's most capable leaders, soon selected to lead the American Expeditionary Forces during World War I. McNair's service with Pershing during this period began a lengthy association that played a key role in the young officer's career.[40]

McNair's participation in the American Expeditionary Forces' preparation for its involvement in the World War began immediately upon his redeployment from the Punitive Expedition. When he returned from Mexico, McNair reported in January 1917 to Camp Stewart in El Paso, Texas, where he joined the 1st Division and began predeployment organization and training. Working once again for T. E. Merrill and Major General William L. Sibert, his division commander, McNair continued to impress his superiors, as demonstrated by the efficiency report he received upon his arrival in France the following August. McNair was rated excellent in all areas. This efficiency report highlighted McNair's suitability for service on the General Staff. The report also reflected the excellent reputation McNair developed during his first thirteen years of service, expressed in Major Merrill's assessment of his particular skills: "This officer is especially competent in every class of duty that has devolved upon him while under my observation [ten months of combat service]. He has great ability as an organizer and executive which especially fit him for important staff duties in high command in war." Unsurprisingly, Merrill indicated he hoped the division would retain McNair's services, as indicated by his comment, "I earnestly recommend that he be given command of one of the regiments of field artillery in our temporary forces, preferably a regiment of new type material." For his part, Sibert summed up his evaluation of McNair with the recommendation to assign him to "General Staff or command with advanced rank." On the basis of his long and impressive service record and strong evaluation reports, McNair was sure to find himself entrusted with significant responsibility as America entered the World War.[41]

2
World War I

The United States observed the outbreak of World War 1 with both dismay and a sense of detachment. Although some citizens supported American involvement in the war, most Americans expressed the determination to remain neutral, a predisposition espoused by President Woodrow Wilson. However, as historian Ronald Schaffer argued, "After the outbreak of war in Europe, Wilson's administration proclaimed American neutrality but began taking actions that made it, before 1917, an undeclared participant." As a result, the government expended a great deal of effort shaping the perceptions of a divided public to gain their support for the war effort. Through propaganda efforts and decisive action to stamp out public dissent, enthusiasm for American participation slowly spread while dissidents learned to stay quiet, and Americans became mentally prepared to serve, whether at the front or supporting a war economy at home. America possessed perhaps the best-suited economy of the war's major belligerents to support the effort it entailed, but the nation's focus on internal development over the previous decades had done little to prepare it for the demands of rapid military mobilization.[1]

Preparing for a New Kind of War

Unlike its success preparing the public, the Wilson administration made little progress readying either the military or industry to fight a major conflict in Europe. By the time America entered the war on April 6, 1917, it had missed the opportunity to mobilize the nation's industrial capacity in support of the war effort. The military also prepared only marginally well. As historian Edward Coffman argued, "during the formative period, which continued into the early months of 1918, delays, mistakes, and confusion hampered the developing war effort: yet, progress was made."[2]

American transatlantic shipping capacity remained the same in 1917 as it had been in 1810, and shipbuilders completed only a few new ships during the prewar mobilization, the first of which they finally launched in 1918, just in time to support the war effort. In fact, the US navy lacked both operational and logistical capability at the start of the war because of congressional refusal to fund fleet construction requests submitted by the General Board through the secretary of the navy. This lack of funding meant those battleships that the navy did possess lacked both personnel and the various auxiliary vessels (cruisers, destroyers, transports, and supply ships) necessary to sail more than 10,000 miles.[3] Similarly, plans to produce airplanes, tanks, artillery, and machine guns all resulted in few if any weapon systems appearing in time to outfit the American Expeditionary Force (AEF), which had to rely mostly on French and British equipment in combat. Even the US-made Springfield rifle remained in short supply, requiring many American soldiers to use the inferior British Lee-Enfield instead.[4]

Throughout the mobilization period, the dysfunction in weapons and equipment design, procurement, and fielding continued as a result of the continued existence but unclear status of the Board of Ordnance and Fortification, which continued to perform tests and make recommendations that had little effect. In general, military equipment users provided desired performance specifications—which emphasized effectiveness in actual combat conditions—to the engineers in Ordnance Branch, who then worked with industrial leaders to create a system or weapon that achieved an acceptable fit with the field commanders' specifications, based more on the principles of efficiency and mass production than combat effectiveness. No key authority figure provided the centralized control or spirit of cooperation that had existed under Schofield's leadership, causing unresolved disputes to linger on for long periods while army units remained hamstrung in their efforts to modernize. Daniel Beaver argued that more effective use by the War Department of the Board of Ordnance and Fortification could have led to resolution of such disputes and improved the army's equipment development and acquisition process as it prepared for participation in the war.[5]

For example, two decades of controversy plagued the issue of fielding machine guns for the cavalry and infantry, beginning at the turn of the century when the weapons finally performed reliably enough for fielding to operational units. Ordnance standardized the Vickers-Maxim gun, and the Colt Fire Arms Company won the initial contracts to produce it. However, military personnel by that time realized the machine gun offered usefulness for all of the combat arms, but the Vickers-Maxim—a heavy, water-cooled weapon—offered only a defensive capability because it weighed over 100 pounds (including ammunition and tripod). The infantry managed to develop techniques to use the Vickers-Maxim, but the cavalry could not transport it effectively or deploy it quickly in action.[6]

The desire to find a single weapon suitable for both branches led to the examination in 1909 of the Benét-Mercié light machine gun by General William Crozier, the chief of ordnance. Weighing less than thirty pounds, the weapon was, in Beaver's words, "a technician's dream"—light, cheap, clip fed, air cooled, and equipped with a folding tripod and quick-change barrels. Ordnance placed the Vickers-Maxims in storage, replacing them with this apparently ideal weapon, soon nicknamed the Benny-Mercy. Once ordnance issued it to field units, this new machine gun performed consistently poorly. It lacked the defensive power of the heavy Vickers-Maxim, and it seemed more like an automatic assault rifle than a machine gun. Even after clamping it onto a forty-pound tripod, the infantry complained of the weapon's poor accuracy and its inability to provide sustained fire. The cavalry appreciated the Benny-Mercy's portability but otherwise found it unsuitable as a result of its instability (and resulting inaccuracy) caused by its low weight. Finally, the Benny-Mercy, machined to very fine tolerances, jammed far too easily even in slightly dusty conditions. Although some members of the infantry and cavalry saw potential in the light machine gun, ordnance had placed its bets on a single machine gun that served neither branch's needs rather than developing different weapons optimized for specific uses.[7]

Beaver highlighted a more fundamental issue than the eventual choice of a particular machine gun. The War Department finally solved the machine gun impasse as a result of the imminent threat of war, acknowledging that no single machine gun could satisfy the various capabilities that different branches and applications required of the weapon, and ultimately ordering in May 1917 the Browning water-cooled heavy machine gun and the Browning automatic rifle. Nevertheless, this and other last-minute expedients did nothing to resolve the root causes of the procurement problem: conflicting views between individual army officers from the combat arms and ordnance, the opportunism among private companies seeking to sell military equipment, congressional intervention based on political priorities, and most importantly the lack of a single individual or department leading the process. Beaver contended that had the individuals in power grasped the true scope and nature of the problem, they could have used the Board of Ordnance and Fortification to resolve the dysfunction that crippled the prewar procurement process.[8]

Army training proved similarly deficient, in large part as a result of the ineffectiveness of Secretary of War Baker and a succession of incompetent army chiefs of staff. The army benefited from the appointment in March 1917 of Peyton C. March as chief of staff, but he took office too late to significantly improve the AEF's readiness for combat. Therefore, soldiers received inadequate training resulting from outdated concepts of war, shortages of rifles and heavy weapons, and disruptions in unit cohesion resulting from the constant turnover caused when soldiers departed unit training early to deploy as replacements to the front. The army also suffered from an overemphasis on the moral element, demonstrated, as Mark Grotelueschen pointed out, by the "human-centered view of battle that dominated the Fort Leavenworth courses" leading to "the curriculum's blatant neglect of recent technological developments, including those in such crucial areas as artillery, machine guns, aircraft, and automobiles." Most American officers remained rigidly attached to the dogma of combat characterized by lightly armed infantrymen maneuvering rapidly by foot, unencumbered by heavy weapons, and intent on executing an offensive culminating in a heroic bayonet charge that would drive away a terrified enemy. No one seemed to notice that events on the battlefield in Europe proved this view increasingly outdated, or they argued that flaws in French and British doctrine limited their offensive effectiveness.[9]

The AEF sought to enable this unique doctrinal approach by creating massive units of infantrymen that far exceeded the size of comparable Allied formations at every echelon, most clearly embodied in the giant AEF square division of 28,000 men—double the size of Allied or German divisions. As Grotelueschen pointed out, historians have identified several reasons for this organizational decision beyond its supposed tactical superiority. These include a shortage of trained officers, Pershing's desire to place a limited number of qualified regular army officers in command of all AEF divisions, and—in support of national policy—the desire to maintain AEF uniqueness in organization and doctrine to deter the Allies from breaking up US units for piecemeal reinforcement of existing British and French units. However, the AEF's organizational decisions primarily supported the tactical approach envisioned in the open warfare doctrine, which Pershing and his adherents believed required these massive divisions to create and exploit penetrations in enemy lines on a stabilized battlefield, where poor mobility often prevented forward passage of lines by fresh divisions or support units with mobile heavy weapons systems. Battlefield experience since 1914 also led the AEF to expect extremely high casualty rates. Because they believed a division must possess the capability to attack an entrenched force, create a penetration, and conduct a pursuit after pushing the enemy onto open ground, AEF leaders believed it must possess enough men to absorb significant losses and keep fighting.[10]

These mobilization and training deficiencies and organizational decisions resulted in the AEF arriving in France sorely unprepared for combat. Although US forces and matériel provided invaluable support that contributed significantly to the eventual Allied victory, this resulted as much from the effect on German morale as any battlefield success. Further, while AEF combat performance generally improved with experience, the AEF suffered severe losses, particularly in the Meuse-Argonne, where twice as many American soldiers died than in the US army's second-deadliest battle (Okinawa, during World War II). One can only speculate how many losses a more effective prewar organization, training, and mobilization process might have prevented.[11]

Fighting the War

Secretary of War Newton D. Baker selected Pershing to serve as the overall commander of the US army in France in May 1917. Baker saw him as the obvious choice, given his recent command experience with the Punitive Expedition, his loyalty to the Wilson administration, and his robust health and soldierly appearance—factors that led Baker to choose him over his closest competitor, Major General Leonard Wood. Pershing also actively campaigned for the position. Pershing returned to America in February, recalled early from the yearlong Punitive Expedition that, by fortunate happenstance, provided a core of seasoned veterans around which to build the AEF from an otherwise poorly prepared army and National Guard. Upon his return, as S. L. A. Marshall recalled, Pershing

> called a conference of correspondents and said to them: "We have broken diplomatic relations with Germany. That means we will send an expedition abroad. I'd like to command it. Each of you must know some way in which you can help me. Now tell me how I can help you so that you can help me." Here was frank ambition, and nothing wrong with it. The history of America in World War I is written in Pershing's shadow because he wanted it that way.[12]

Marshall went on to describe the enigma that was "Black Jack" Pershing. He overshadowed the story of the war and the efforts of his various peers and rivals in a way unseen in any previous American war, yet he displayed no particularly "deep military wisdom." He inspired confidence in his political superiors, yet displayed an austere, introverted character to his subordinates and soldiers. Further, "he had fundamental qualities that went far in the shaping of an army—patience, sobriety, emotional balance, and an unshakable fortitude." He led soldiers to achieve their best not through ruthless discipline or charisma—he was never "popular with troops"—but through tough training, high standards, and an ethical code of fairness. Nevertheless, Pershing faced a daunting challenge, suffering shortages in every resource the AEF required, including trained soldiers, equipment, and time.[13]

In the years leading up to America's involvement in the war, divisions existed in both government and society with regard to issues such as whether the United States should send a military force to France and how it would form, equip, and prepare such an expedition. When Congress declared war against Germany in April 1917, the United States army consisted of only 5,971 officers and 121,797 enlisted men. Mobilization of the National Guard enabled the expansion of Pershing's AEF, but this added only another 174,008 marginally trained officers and enlisted soldiers—far short of the National Guard's authorized strength of

Brigadier General Lesley J. McNair, AEF GHQ Staff G-5 Training Division, Chief of Artillery Training and Tactical Procedures, Chaumont, France, 1919. Courtesy of US National Archives II, College Park, Maryland

450,000. The passage of the Selective Service Act in May 1917 established a wartime draft, leading to formation of the national army and enabling the AEF to grow in strength to more than two million men at war's end. Nevertheless, it took almost a year from the passage of the act before the first trained and equipped American forces finally arrived in France. In addition to an overall shortage of men, the prewar regular army's officer corps consisted mostly of men senior in age but junior in rank. A system of promotion based on seniority combined with a shortage of positions of higher rank, leading to slow promotions for promising young officers while senior officers often continued to serve long after they had passed their prime. This led to a situation in which most of the US army's senior leaders did not possess the fitness or drive necessary for combat service. This made it particularly difficult for Pershing to find qualified officers to fill command and staff positions in the AEF.[14]

The shortage of qualified senior officers in the prewar US army presented an opportunity for young and energetic leaders such as the thirty-four-year-old Captain McNair. When Pershing returned from Mexico on February 5, 1917, he began to move older army leaders aside in favor of more junior officers. McNair had to wait only three months before earning promotion to major and reassignment to the General Staff Corps.[15] Major McNair deployed to France as the 1st Division's assistant chief of staff for training. He first met Major George C. Marshall, the 1st Division's assistant chief of staff for operations, during this deployment; the two officers shared a stateroom during the voyage across the Atlantic Ocean.[16]

Soon after his arrival in France, McNair earned promotion to lieutenant colonel and found himself reassigned to the General Headquarters training division (G-5) of the AEF, as the chief of artillery training and tactical procedures. McNair impressed Pershing with his exceptional performance and military bearing, and Pershing rewarded this performance by promoting him to colonel in June 1918 and brigadier general in October 1918, making him, at the age of thirty-five, the AEF's youngest general officer. As the senior artillery officer of the General Headquarters training division, McNair worked closely with Pershing. He conducted frequent visits to the front on Pershing's behalf to report on unit training and performance, and he benefited greatly from his mentorship. This close working relationship resulted in Pershing's influence leaving its mark on McNair, who displayed similarities to Pershing in his views on doctrine, leadership style, and military bearing throughout the remainder of his career.[17]

In particular, McNair shared Pershing's views on open warfare doctrine—specifically the superiority of observed artillery fires to support infantry in the attack. As Boyd Dastrup noted,

> McNair, the senior field artillery officer on the AEF staff, reflected Pershing's thinking. In November 1918, he vehemently criticized European unobserved map firing techniques and advocated the superiority of the American doctrine of observed fire. He explained that the Europeans concentrated on unobserved indirect fire rather than focusing on observed fire and pushing field artillery forward to support the infantry advance. A strong sponsor of indirect fire, McNair wrote that unobserved map fire was causing too many infantry casualties because it seldom engaged obstacles to the infantry advance as observed fire could. Whereas observed indirect fire offered flexibility, unobserved fire was rigid and prohibited adjusting to meet changing tactical requirements like observed fire could, making American technique superior.[18]

Dastrup argued, however, that while Pershing and McNair agreed regarding the advantages of observed fire, even they did not grasp the true superiority of the method: its ability to paralyze the enemy in depth, an essential capability required to enable a war of maneuver. Nevertheless, McNair's support of open warfare concepts and observed fire set him apart not just from the European artillerymen that used unobserved map firing techniques, but also from those officers in his own branch who had a preference for European fire direction methods. This demonstrates that McNair, from an early stage in his career, grasped the potential of field artillery to break the deadlock of stabilized warfare.[19]

Pershing also held strong opinions regarding the desirable characteristics of army officers that he passed on to his close subordinates. He believed they should be physically fit, possess stamina, exhibit high standards of appearance, and exude confidence while also possessing the ability to grasp quickly and communicate with clarity the key points of a situation. This led Pershing to move many senior regular army officers aside because they did not meet his standards, even after the AEF's arrival in France, replacing them with younger and more capable junior officers. As a case in point, Pershing relieved Major General William L. Sibert, an engineer officer selected by Secretary of War Baker to command the 1st Infantry Division. Sibert possessed a high reputation in Washington, but Pershing disapproved of him on many counts: he was old, had no combat experience, demonstrated a poor grasp of training, and lacked confidence. Upon receiving reports that Sibert displayed a disturbing pessimism during a visit by a group of American dignitaries to his command post in France, Pershing finally ordered him to return to Washington on December 15, 1917. This step demonstrated both his lack of patience with substandard officers and his authority to appoint and relieve commanders in the AEF as he saw fit.[20]

Pershing relieved many other officers, including other division commanders. On the same day that he ordered Sibert back to Washington, Pershing relieved Major General William Mann, commander of the 42nd "Rainbow" Infantry Division. Mann was sixty-three, overweight, and not particularly energetic; however, he demonstrated a propensity to take advantage of his political connections back home to defy Pershing's wishes. Although Pershing possessed limited ability to influence congressional representatives, his authority in France was unquestioned, and Mann soon found he had picked a fight he could not win. Pershing had always lacked confidence in National Guard officers, and this episode only served to reinforce his already significant reservations, particularly concerning their appointment to command positions. Fortunately, Pershing selected a highly competent officer, Major General Charles D. Menoher, to relieve Mann, and the Rainbow Division went on to serve admirably in combat. Nevertheless, the implications were clear: a stagnating regular army officer corps and reliance on National Guard units to facilitate army expansion led to significant challenges for the AEF regarding officer competency, particularly at senior levels.[21] Further, hasty mobilization meant the army lacked sufficient time to resolve these challenges before unit deployment.

Service on the AEF staff exposed McNair to an influential mentor in General Pershing; it also provided a formative experience that significantly affected McNair's ideas regarding the army's organization and doctrine. Preparation of the AEF for war required a major transformation of the small American frontier army to a European-style conventional force, and the ensuing expansion meant raw recruits soon vastly outnumbered the core of regular army soldiers and officers. Nevertheless, the army's traditional view of war fighting lived on in the form of an infantry-centric doctrine championed by Pershing and his like-minded traditionalist cadres, known as open warfare. This term took on a particular meaning in the preparation for war, becoming a catalyst for debate both within the AEF and between the AEF and its French and British allies.

A US army manual for training platoons, published in 1917, described open warfare doctrine as consisting of two subcomponents: "The terms 'trench-to-trench attack' and 'attack in open warfare' . . . differentiate from an instructional point of view between the methodical attack of highly organized defenses and such attacks as may occur at a later period of an offensive after the main system of the enemy's defenses has been penetrated."[22] This description of open warfare conditions as distinct from those of trench warfare represents US army officers' efforts to resist adoption of European fighting methods developed in the early years of the war and tailored for the stabilized warfare that emerged on the Western front. This resistance emerged both from the army's desire to build on its own long-standing fighting traditions (which, ideally, would enable the AEF to break the deadlock on the Western front), and from the political imperative of retaining American forces' independence on the World War I battlefield.

President Wilson highlighted the latter imperative in guidance he issued on May 4, 1917, that made it clear that he did not intend to see AEF combat units piecemealed out to serve as reinforcements under British and French command. This explains in part why the AEF's open warfare doctrine and the British and French stabilized warfare fighting methods often resembled each other more than they differed. According to US army doctrine, ground forces would engage in trench-to-trench warfare when fighting from static positions at close range. In theory, this method always served as merely a temporary state pending the next opportunity to resume the offense. At this point, American forces would seek to dislodge the enemy from its defensive positions and then, following doctrine, transition to "attack in open warfare," with the goal of breaking through the enemy's remaining static defenses and pressing the attack to achieve penetration in depth.[23]

Many AEF senior leaders arrived in France convinced that their offensive-minded open warfare doctrine and their massive divisions would enable them to break the deadlock of the trenches—an illusion that did not fade until problems began to emerge on the battlefields of France. Once they actually engaged in combat, the effects of the rapid mobilization of AEF divisions began to show. The doctrine was always much more effective in theory than in reality, particularly given the lackluster effort AEF forces undertook in preparation to use it. Although open warfare dominated American military discourse before the war, the complexity of the mobile form of warfare exceeded the training capability of the AEF's rapidly mobilized and deployed units. Most troops received far more training in trench-to-trench warfare than open warfare methods during predeployment training, so naturally AEF forces experienced difficulty in their effort to return mobility to the battlefield. The rapid mobilization that prevented the AEF's divisions from preparing adequately for the combined arms fighting methods that open warfare required led to rigidly planned operations, poorly executed attacks, and ineffective use of supporting weapons. In addition, shortage of communications equipment and limited artillery mobility meant attacking infantry lacked sufficient fire support once it moved beyond the range of its supporting artillery. Many division commanders successfully adapted and found innovative solutions to the challenges they faced, but this breakdown between the peacetime discourse on warfare and the reality the AEF encountered in battle resulted in many casualties, highlighting the need to review army doctrine and unit organization after the war.[24]

Assessing the War's Lessons

Despite the AEF's difficulties conducting open warfare on the Western front, the army determined from a series of postwar evaluations that it possessed generally sound doctrine. Both the AEF and the War Department appointed formal boards to analyze the army's combat experience in detail. The AEF convened more than twenty boards between December 1918 and June 1919, chaired by the most senior, experienced officers serving with the AEF to study the lessons of the war and identify both the strengths and the shortcomings of army doctrine used during the World War. The findings of these boards would inform both the creation of updated postwar doctrine and the development of curricula by the faculty of army schools in preparation for their reopening after the war. Each board concentrated on a particular aspect of the war to develop a summary of combat lessons that would inform postwar reorganization, equipment acquisition, and doctrine development. Each board developed its own method of data collection, but most—particularly the branch-specific boards—sent questionnaires to units or personnel of the appropriate type from which to derive the data necessary to develop a board report of findings and recommendations.[25]

The members of the Lassiter (artillery) Board, formed on June 11, 1919, briefly included Brigadier General McNair.[26] The Lassiter Board tackled perhaps the single most significant challenge the AEF faced: the difficulty of providing adequate mobile fire support to infantry in the attack. The board made several key recommendations for postwar artillery development that its members believed would increase the artillery's mobility and firepower while enhancing its ability to provide timely and accurate fires in support of maneuvering infantry.[27] However, just one week after the formation of the Lassiter Board, McNair received orders reassigning him as one of the thirty-four members of the inaugural faculty of the Army School of the Line, reforming at Fort Leavenworth, Kansas. Thus, instead of assessing these critical lessons of the war on a board in France, McNair would teach them at the Leavenworth schools. He also helped incorporate them into postwar doctrine as the army sought to develop the means to conduct combined arms warfare—the essence of modern warfare, and the method that many saw as the means to break the defensive deadlock of the trenches of the World War.[28]

No clear consensus emerged from the postwar boards, including the findings of the most influential of the boards, the Superior Board, made up of the AEF's most powerful and respected leaders. As Mark Grotelueschen explained, articles published in professional journals after the war demonstrated the division of opinion about the lessons of the war into three camps: "Those arguing that the war confirmed the value of the Army's existing, prewar doctrine; those insisting that the Army needed to understand the inherent value of massive firepower; and a middle group that focused on incorporating as much firepower into the infantry as possible to keep it as the primary arm, while admitting that new weapons and technologies had increased the importance of heavy firepower in battle."[29] Significantly, Pershing added his particularly influential voice to the debate by including a "Wrapper Indorsement" with the individual board reports upon their submission to the secretary of war in June 1920. In addition to delaying the release of the boards' findings by several months, Pershing strongly criticized them in his endorsement. He wrote that proximity to the recent war's events and the influence of a stabilized front mentality influenced the boards' findings in a way that made them more applicable to the past war than the conditions the army would probably encounter in a future war. For example, Pershing strongly disagreed with retention of the massive AEF division, insisting that mobility should serve as the driving factor in determining army organization. Although the AEF division might have been appropriate for the war just fought (for various reasons), he doubted its efficacy in a future, and presumably more mobile, war. He advocated severe cuts in both overall size and in the attachment of specific capabilities and units like supporting artillery, and he also condemned the reliance on highly detailed plans of attack that included clearly defined unit sectors and both intermediate and final objectives that units should achieve on a predetermined timetable.[30]

Naturally, Pershing's Wrapper Indorsement only increased the stridency of the debate between the three camps while creating controversy among those officers who objected to his blanket criticism of their detailed findings based on objective surveys of combat units, many of which relied on the capabilities and techniques that Pershing suggested the army should abandon. This provided an early indication of the challenge the army would face over the coming years as it sought to anticipate the conditions it would encounter in a future war and to design organizations and equipment appropriate for those conditions, guided by suitable doctrine. Consensus on these issues seemed unlikely to emerge anytime soon.[31]

Reestablishing the Leavenworth Schools

As the army returned home from France in 1919 and closed the staff college at Langres, it reestablished the School of the Line and the General Service School— the first- and second-year programs of the prewar Leavenworth staff schools. Like its prewar predecessor, the General Service School concentrated on division-, corps-, and army-level operations while leaving matters at the regiment level and below to other army schools (mostly branch schools for company-grade officers). The Leavenworth schools relied on a small but hand-selected inaugural faculty chosen from among the AEF's best officers. McNair, having returned after the war to his permanent rank of major, served as a member of the General Service School's faculty of thirty-four officers, whose ideas about modern warfare influenced the army far out of proportion to their number. The members of this faculty established the foundation for an educational system that remained in place throughout the interwar period, building on the preexisting curriculum from Langres to develop an updated yearlong course for a new generation of general staff officers. Their role proved so important that the War Department sent a team from the inspector general's office in 1920 to evaluate the faculty's performance. The inspection team singled out McNair for particular praise.[32] Several members of this inaugural faculty, McNair included, eventually earned permanent promotion to general officer rank and returned to Fort Leavenworth later in their careers to serve as commandant of the Leavenworth schools.[33]

In addition to its influence on the army's education system, the postwar General Service School faculty carried on the tradition of Leavenworth's involvement in the writing of various doctrinal manuals. These included the *Field Service Regulations,* which the faculty updated by building on the foundation provided by the AEF board findings. This led to the creation of the 1923 *Field Service Regulations*. This updated manual incorporated the lessons of World War I while addressing changes in military technology since the preparation of the 1905 version, and it became the "authoritative basis for the instruction of the combined arms for war service."[34]

While the 1923 *Field Service Regulations* represented a comprehensive update to pre–World War I large-unit tactical doctrine, the key lesson the army drew from the AEF's experience during World War I attempting to conduct open warfare was the conviction that the fundamental characteristics of war had not changed. The innovative spirit represented by motorization, mechanization, and efforts to incorporate new military technologies remained focused on finding ways to fight more effectively according to traditional methods. The infantry, although increasingly viewed as a member of the combined arms team, remained the primary means to execute an offensive doctrine emphasizing maneuver, firepower, and the human element. It is illustrative that the 1923 *Field Service Regulations* was the first version to contain general principles of war—the "immutable" principles of the scientific, Jominian tradition of military theory.[35]

Although officers at Leavenworth and within the War Department embraced the concept of certain immutable general principles of war, they distinguished between war—a general term for the phenomenon as a whole—and the practice of specific forms of warfare. They discounted European methods of warfare as inadequate and developed a comprehensive doctrine based on American military tradition and experience. Military theory—often thought of as the sole province of European intellectuals—influenced the army's postwar revision of both its doctrine and its educational system. A small group of the army's most influential officers, including Major McNair, guided the army's interwar transformation process in keeping with the fundamental principles of war—principles they believed the AEF had validated on the battlefields of France while seeking to understand the evolution of warfare with the advent of new technology and fighting methods. Therefore, American military thinkers like McNair sought ways to use new military technology and doctrine or maximize organizational efficiency to develop new war fighting methods rather than merely update existing methods so that they could fight a future war in fundamentally the same manner they had fought the last one.[36]

Not all officers involved in the postwar discourse saw these matters the same way. Three schools of thought emerged after the war, each of which supported a different interpretation of its lessons. Traditionalists adhered to Pershing's view that highly mobile infantry relying on the rifle and bayonet would win America's future wars. Firepower advocates, led by Major General Summerall, argued that successful attacks depended on using overwhelming firepower to destroy enemy defenses before the infantry advanced. Finally, a small group advocated a combined arms approach in which infantry would enjoy the support of a great deal of mobile firepower, including automatic rifles, machine guns, grenades, mortars, 37mm guns, and mobile howitzers, all acting in concert as an integrated team. Some officers even foresaw the need to develop a capability to provide instantaneous support with heavier weapons. The combined arms approach emerged as the predominant view in the immediate postwar period, and the 1923 *Field Service Regulations* formally indoctrinated it. McNair, perhaps as a result of his general staff experience, emerged as one of its most vocal advocates. Thus, the appearance of principles of war in the 1923 *Field Service Regulations* does not indicate a stagnation of postwar US army doctrine. Instead, it serves as an early indication of the means by which innovative thinkers from all branches of the army sought to apply the lessons they learned during World War I. They all sought to develop the means—and gain the education—necessary to avoid another experience of the trench warfare that characterized the Western front in Europe during the World War.[37]

During the first seventeen years of McNair's career, he learned how to manage an artillery battery in rough terrain, how to lead men in arduous circumstances, and how to conduct sustained offensive operations on foreign soil. His World War I experience of the theory and reality of open warfare fixed these early military experiences and the American traditions they represented in McNair's mind. A 1921 article he wrote for the *Field Artillery Journal* reveals his early struggle to reconcile the realities of the modern battlefield with the traditional methods that remained at the core of army doctrine. In this article, entitled "Infantry Batteries and Accompanying Guns," McNair described the need for mobile artillery to accompany the infantry on the attack to enable them to overcome enemy strong points and support weapons that survived the initial bombardment. The article emphasized themes that recurred throughout McNair's interwar service, such as balancing the relative benefits of supporting versus attached artillery (that is, pooling assets at higher echelons versus assigning them directly to subordinate units), proper command structures and appropriate missions for supporting arms, and the need for combined arms training in common core tasks. McNair closed the article by reiterating this latter theme: "The full effectiveness of infantry batteries and accompanying guns cannot be developed merely through a high state of individual knowledge and training on the part of the infantry and artillery; a team-play is necessary which can be attained only by the two arms actually working together. This combined training should be acquired in the training area rather than on the battlefield."[38] For the remainder of his career, these ideas guided McNair's efforts to organize and train the army for its next great test in the caldron of battle.

General Pershing Awards Brigadier General McNair the Distinguished Service Medal at AEF GHQ, Chaumont, France, March 23, 1919. Courtesy of US National Archives II, College Park, Maryland

McNair remained committed to this concept even though the combined arms view remained unpopular among many officers, some of whom placed the perceived welfare of their branch over that of the army as a whole. With primacy came priority—for funding, new equipment, and specialized training.[39] Although an artilleryman at heart, McNair demonstrated early in his career that he would fight for the strength of the combined arms approach, even if this led him to strive for efficiencies through techniques like streamlining and pooling that

Marshal Petain Awards Brigadier General McNair the Legion D'Honneur at Metz, Lorraine, France, April 19, 1919. Courtesy of US National Archives II, College Park, Maryland

would affect—and therefore generate resistance from—traditionalists within his own branch. Many of his fellow artillerymen vehemently resisted such concepts, often protesting the loss of control this would mean over assets like division artillery or other tactical-level organic units. Nevertheless, McNair's extensive experience led to the conviction that modern warfare required combined arms fighting methods, and he doggedly fought to instill this mind-set throughout the army.

McNair served with distinction for almost three years before and during World War I under the close supervision of Pershing, one of America's most enigmatic and demanding generals. McNair learned a great deal from his mentor. He exhibited the traits General Pershing required of a successful army officer, and Pershing's leadership left its mark on McNair as well. Pershing demonstrated his approval by personally decorating McNair after the war with the Distinguished Service Medal, in recognition of his outstanding accomplishments as the AEF's chief of artillery training.[40] Shortly thereafter, with Pershing looking on, Marshal Henri Petain presented McNair with the award of Officer of the Legion of Honor.[41]

Upon his return from France, McNair reverted to his permanent rank of major—but unlike many who served with the AEF, he remained an up-and-comer among the army's officer corps, beginning his postwar service in the key position of instructor at the army School of the Line.[42] Here McNair served at the forefront of what modern commentators refer to as the interwar mechanization process. His experience in France convinced him of the benefit of close infantry–artillery coordination, leading McNair to view innovation as a means to improve combined arms fighting methods rather than a rationale for providing priority funding to a particular branch.

McNair's next assignment further broadened his already far-ranging base of experience. Building on several defining aspects of his career history to date, including his artillery expertise, combat experience, general staff service, and innovative spirit, McNair found himself serving once again on a general staff, but in a very different capacity than in the past. He also soon assumed duty as president of a board testing the capability of several types of military equipment, immersing him in an intense and growing debate that proved central to the army's modernization efforts. As this next assignment demonstrates, McNair had established by 1920 a reputation as an officer who could handle a wide variety of tasks and a high level of responsibility while maintaining remarkable objectivity—a set of capabilities that grew both increasingly essential and uncommon within the army over the coming years.

3

McNair: War Planner

Major McNair departed Fort Leavenworth in December 1920 and arrived in Hawaii after a brief period of leave on February 13, 1921.[1] Like all his peers who missed the opportunity to attend the Leavenworth schools as a result of the World War but who later served as instructors there, McNair also departed with credit for graduating, per General Orders No. 74, which ensured his inclusion on the Initial General Staff Eligible List.[2] When McNair reported for duty, Major General Charles P. Summerall, the Hawaiian Department commander, chose to use him in just this capacity, appointing him to serve as his assistant chief of staff for operations (G-3).[3]

After spending the previous twenty years as a company-grade leader, a staff officer responsible for training, or a faculty member at an army educational institution, McNair possessed no experience as an operations officer or war planner. Nevertheless, he applied the same dedication and energy to this new role as he had to his previous positions, and as always, he performed with distinction. Summerall soon entrusted him with a great deal of responsibility, directing him to lead the development of a joint defense plan to counter an attack on Oahu by the naval and air forces of Japan, the nation that currently represented the United States' chief strategic concern. This represented a significant change in perspective and an increase in responsibility for McNair, but as in the past, he welcomed the challenge and exceeded all of Summerall's expectations.[4]

McNair approached this daunting task with his usual determination and energy, despite the many challenges that stemmed from the army's long-standing and heated debates regarding the capabilities of coast artillery and aviation in defending against an attack from the sea. Summerall placed great trust in McNair by assigning him to lead this effort. Both the United States and Japan had signed the Five-Party Treaty in 1922, which prohibited fortification of military bases in the Pacific. America abided by the terms of the treaty, but US political and military leaders suspected Japan of secretly fortifying its Pacific military bases in violation of the treaty. Even when the treaty lapsed in 1930, Congress lacked the funds to invest in fortifications in the Pacific. Therefore, from 1922 until the late 1930s, US forces relied on the Coast Artillery Corps, along with army and navy aviation, to support naval and ground forces' efforts to defend Oahu against what many believed to be an imminent Japanese attack. Japan presented the major strategic threat to the United States in the Pacific, and navy leaders in particular remained convinced they "would sooner or later fight Japan," leading them to develop and continually update War Plan Orange throughout the interwar period.[5]

The McNair Board

Major McNair began the project of updating the Oahu defense plan by presiding over a board consisting of himself, two officers from the Coast Artillery Corps, and one officer from the Air Service. This board (aptly named the McNair Board) convened to "investigate, consider and report on the powers, limitations and combined training of the Coast Artillery Corps and Air Service in coast defense" as directed by the War Department in a letter dated April 21, 1923. The War Department directed the board to submit its findings by December 1923 to help resolve the growing debate both within the military and among national political leaders over the potential of coast artillery, antiaircraft artillery, and aerial bombers to defend coastal areas against attacks from the sea and air. The McNair Board began its investigation in May 1923 by collecting all available data on coast artillery and aviation capabilities, eventually citing nine references in Inclosure 1 of the final report. The board then developed and evaluated a detailed test methodology, enlisting the support of units based on Oahu to optimize the methodology and then conduct the actual tests. The board sought both to confirm existing data from the previous tests cited in the report and to collect additional data to support or deny the conclusions resulting from previous studies.[6]

The board, relying largely on the support of volunteer aircrews and coast artillery personnel, performed two types of tests. The Air Service conducted airplane-bombing tests "to determine the accuracy of airplane bombing as a function of altitude and to investigate the subject generally," while the Coast Artillery evaluated "anti-aircraft firing to determine the accuracy of anti-aircraft firing as a function of the altitude of the target."[7] Despite the seemingly distinct nature of the two types of tests overseen by the board, they did not suffer the ill effects of branch bias and lack of cooperation often associated with the postwar period, when the army found itself short on funds and therefore rarely in agreement about weapons development programs. On the contrary, the board made every effort to not only develop and describe in the report sound methods for conducting bombing and firing tests and calculating the accuracy of fire, but also to eliminate error and bias from the tests. As the board report attests, "In addition to the regular bombing crew, pilot, reserve pilot and bomber, each plane carried a Coast Artillery officer who observed and recorded the time of release of each bomb, the altitude by altimeter, the azimuth of the plane by ship's compass at the instant of the release and the approximate position of the point of impact of the bomb." Further, the onboard observer fired a Very pistol at the moment of release to notify ground observers, who observed the point of impact using standard Coast Artillery azimuth instruments manned by trained observers, both on the ground and on board the tug or bomber towing the target.[8]

Further, the board made every feasible effort to minimize error, using multiple trained observers and the latest observation equipment as well as conducting lengthy preparatory training to standardize bombing methods and improve the proficiency of the four bomber crews that flew the actual test missions. The board recorded the bombing results for each crew separately to enable identification of variations in test results resulting from differences in aircrew skill. This enabled the board to minimize erroneous interpretations in the test results. Further, the test participants met regularly to discuss ways to standardize and optimize testing methods, and they spent considerable time experimenting with various procedures before beginning the actual tests. This careful preparation resulted in thorough standardization of test equipment and parameters. Factors standardized by the test participants included altitude, airspeed, and procedures for bomb drops, the models of aircraft and bombing sights used, target towing cable lengths, and target types and colors. The board identified challenges associated with using dummy bombs and developed procedures to minimize error caused by their unique characteristics. Finally, participants developed improved maintenance procedures to optimize the performance of bombing mechanisms, and they considered the effect of meteorological data and other variables that could influence test results.[9]

Given the care and diligent effort the board committed to the tests, McNair demonstrated admirable objectivity in his final report, dated February 11, 1924. He closed the report with a tentative conclusion and a call for further analysis: "While it is by no means contended that the tests were exhaustive, they were nevertheless as thorough as possible with the time and means available, and it is believed that the results are a useful contribution in the solution of the problems involved." In fact, the board report stated the methods developed and preparations undertaken would "prove of continuing usefulness in carrying out similar investigations and more particularly in the training of bombardment aviation and anti-aircraft artillery." General Summerall agreed with this assessment, writing a letter of commendation that he sent to McNair and the other members of the board and included in their annual efficiency reports.[10]

The McNair Board report supported its findings with extremely detailed descriptions of the methods used, the preparations made, and the recorded results of the various tests. After describing the test procedures and data analysis methodology used, the board report summarized its overall conclusions, which it supported with twelve enclosures totaling ninety-two pages of detailed tables and charts. These enclosures contained the results of each individual bombing run or antiaircraft artillery target engagement, collective results depicted as scatter plots reflecting spherical probability analysis, and detailed descriptions of the equipment used and the mathematics performed to calculate the results. A particularly interesting chart depicted the relative anticipated distances of artillery and aircraft to the various types of ships based on their anticipated deployment in a possible enemy naval assault.[11]

Overall, the board came to positive conclusions, stating, "The major caliber coast gun is effective and essential against naval targets. Against large targets it is more accurate than the bomber, except beyond ranges of about 25,000 to 30,000 yards." Further, "the bomber is a powerful means of attacking naval targets at relatively great distances from the coast. Its methods are simple and direct." However, "its effectiveness may be impaired by weather conditions and visibility. It is vulnerable to hostile aviation and anti-aircraft agencies; hence it lacks the solidity and dependability of the seacoast gun." Finally, "the anti-aircraft artillery on land is a thoroughly effective means of defense against the bomber, provided it is available in adequate quantity and that searchlights and listening apparatus are capable of detecting and illuminating the target." Clearly, the board made every effort to include representatives from all the affected combat arms in the tests and sought to provide a fair and even-handed analysis of the results.[12]

The board also highlighted several observations secondary to the overall results but useful in considering future efforts to improve the effectiveness of the various means of defense tested. The report pointed out the relative survivability advantage of mobile over fixed coast artillery pieces, and it identified the need to develop antiaircraft guns capable of engaging bombers at their maximum bombing altitudes using timed fuse rounds with large burst radii. Significantly, some of the board's most useful insights came from the Air Service crews who flew the test missions. These included identification of imperfections in bomb release mechanisms and the accuracy of bombsights, supporting the finding that aerial bombing was "an art to a great extent; the perfection of instruments of precision which will render it less dependent on the personal element should be pushed."[13]

As mentioned above, General Summerall commended the board members for their diligent efforts and outstanding results. Furthermore, he endorsed the board report on March 12, 1924, highlighting some of the McNair Board's more original and significant findings. In particular, Summerall pointed out that the results demonstrated significantly better performance of aerial bombers in these tests compared to the findings reported by Lieutenant Commander Grow of the US navy in 1923. In Grow's report, which appeared in the *US Naval Institute Proceed-*

ings in December 1923, bombing attacks from 11,000 feet achieved only a 15 percent rate of hits, while bombing attacks from 3,000 feet achieved a slightly better 19 percent rate of hits. Using a target similar in size, aircrews flying McNair Board missions achieved significantly higher hit percentages, achieving an average hit rate against moving and stationary targets of 65.5 percent at 3,000 feet and 28 percent at 11,000 feet.[14]

It seems that no unbiased and comprehensive description of the methods and findings of the McNair Board has appeared in any previous source, other than the original board report (available only in the National Archives). In what appears to be the only other source that contains a description of the board, the author, David E. Johnson, provided an incomplete record of its findings. In his critical assessment of the US army's post–World War I modernization efforts, *Fast Tanks and Heavy Bombers,* Johnson distilled the lengthy and balanced conclusions provided in the McNair Board report into a few short phrases, which might lead some readers to misinterpret the board's work as the biased effort of a field artilleryman to demonstrate the coast artillery's superiority over aviation. Johnson wrote:

> In May 1923 the Hawaiian Department convened a board to examine "the powers and limitations of Coast Artillery and Air Service." Major Lesley J. McNair, himself an artilleryman, headed the board, which determined that the coast artillery provided a better defense against enemy naval forces than aviation, because air power is often "impaired by weather conditions and visibility" and "is vulnerable to hostile aviation and anti-aircraft agencies." McNair concluded that air power "lacks the solidity and dependability of the seacoast gun."[15]

In his short summary of the McNair Board's efforts, Johnson did not describe the board's composition or well-defined methodology. He also oversimplified the board's conclusions, focusing on portions of the report that mentioned the areas in which coast artillery demonstrated advantages over aviation while neglecting to mention those that described aviation's unique capabilities and advantages over the coast artillery. He also did not mention the fact that the McNair Board reported significantly better performance by aerial bombers than that described in Grow's analysis of previous tests.

Johnson also downplayed the impact of the McNair Board. He described the reaction of Major General Mason W. Patrick, chief of the Air Service, to the McNair Board's findings, claiming Patrick "was incensed at the assertion that bombers were highly vulnerable to anti-aircraft fire and that the coast artillery was a better naval defense agency than the Air Service." According to Johnson,

Patrick concluded that "the coast artillery, whose existence was jeopardized by the advent of the airplane, was trying to reassert its primacy in coast defense and perhaps even carve out a new niche as an anti-aircraft force." Johnson did not mention the inclusion of antiaircraft artillery in the test, which would have more accurately portrayed the McNair Board as an effort to determine the relative merits of all aircraft, coast artillery, and antiaircraft artillery. As written, Johnson's description could lead the reader to see the McNair Board as merely a competitive test of airpower versus coast artillery, with bias stemming from the appointment of an artilleryman as board president. Johnson also claimed that the McNair Board had little impact because in the ensuing debate the War Department sided with Patrick, who asserted, quoting Brigadier General H. A. Drum's statement at a 1925 aviation board of inquiry, "The development of aviation has rendered 'the continued maintenance of the majority of our Coast Artillery installations uneconomical.'" America's coastal defense fortification system did eventually prove economically infeasible, but this hardly made the McNair Board's findings irrelevant. On the contrary, the McNair Board had significant impact both within the Hawaiian Department—where it provided essential data that the G-3 section used when writing the updated plan of defense of Oahu—and at the highest levels of the government, where it prompted an executive-level investigation. Johnson mentioned neither of these outcomes in his account.[16]

The Oahu Defense Plan of 1924

The McNair Board's findings contributed directly to the other major project McNair completed as the G-3 of the Hawaiian Department in 1924. The War Department sent various documents to Summerall between January 1920 and September 1923 requiring input to their ongoing update of the overall War Department mobilization plan. These documents required a revision of the Hawaiian Department's defensive projects and plans and a reassessment of the army's role in the defense of Oahu. Summerall directed McNair to prepare the departmental response by writing an updated plan of defense for Hawaii, focusing on the port island of Oahu. McNair accomplished this through a detailed staff study titled "Basic Project for the Defense of Oahu," which he completed shortly after he submitted the McNair Board report, and which Summerall approved on February 9, 1924. Part 1 of the plan consisted of a detailed, forty-three-page "Estimate of the Situation," beginning with the following mission statement: "The mission of the Hawaiian Department in a Red–Orange situation is to protect the naval base at Pearl Harbor against naval and aerial bombardment, against enemy sympathizers, and against hostile expeditionary forces, supported or unsupported by a hostile fleet."[17]

The estimate rested on the assumption that Orange (Japan) might pursue one of two possible courses of action in a future war that would affect the Hawaiian Department: first, "naval action in the Pacific primarily, with only incidental military operations, referred to hereafter as the naval plan," and second, "military and naval action, referred to hereafter as the military plan." The enemy estimate also anticipated two possible strategic approaches by Orange. If Orange executed the naval plan, it would seek to "eject Blue [American forces] completely from the Pacific and to close the Pacific ports of Blue. The plan doubtless would contemplate the reduction of the Philippines, Guam, and Oahu. Oahu would be needed by Orange as a naval base." By contrast, the military plan would involve an attack directly against the continental United States, either through Canada or over the western US coast. In either of these military plan scenarios, the planners assumed Orange would "be inclined to ignore the Blue forces on Oahu, at least initially." The planners thought that the military plan would exert the greater pressure on Blue, but "Orange, however, for political, economic or other reasons, might be unwilling to assume so great a burden and decide to adopt the naval plan."[18]

Those familiar with contemporary colored plans like Plan Orange would probably not find anything atypical about the analysis contained in the 1924 Basic Project for the Defense of Oahu. The estimate of the situation thoroughly evaluated likely enemy and friendly courses of action to include the plans of action for the various Blue forces in response to the various possible actions of Orange. The estimate showed surprising prescience in its predictions, given the early date of its preparation, and its authors thought that Orange would benefit more from occupying than destroying the military facilities on Oahu—a debatable but insightful assessment, given the speed with which America restored its naval capability at Pearl Harbor in 1942. However, for the purposes of this analysis, the most striking characteristic is that Lesley McNair, usually known for his skill in mobilizing, organizing, and training ground troops, led this joint planning effort. Further, he thoroughly considered the wide range of possible enemy and friendly actions, as well as many other involved factors such as terrain, enemy sympathizers, and possible imposition of martial law. Finally, he based the plan on detailed staff work, exercises conducted between 1921 and 1923 that augmented and tested against reality the findings of the staff analysis, and the results of the McNair Board.

McNair's basic plan described a defense of Hawaii relying on 94,000 ground troops, reinforced by additional airplanes and coast artillery, and prepared to enforce martial law and use poison gas to repel Japanese invasion.[19] However, it also included branch plans and additional considerations, depending on possible variations such as whether the army would impose martial law, how many reinforcements would arrive in Hawaii and how quickly they could deploy, and the location of the majority of America's naval forces at the onset of Orange aggression. As stated in the G-3 appendix to the plan, signed by General Summerall in February 1924, "The plans of action governing the several basic war plans are set forth in the Basic Project in a more comprehensive and coordinated form than has existed heretofore."[20] Attesting to the high quality of the staff work and exercises supporting McNair's plan, Army Chief of Staff General John J. Pershing approved it with only slight modification in August 1924.[21]

While McNair overcame significant difficulties to develop a feasible and realistic plan of defense, this brief foray into war planning stands in stark contrast to the majority of postings he held over the course of his long career. It also serves to demonstrate the intense and divisive nature of branch and service rivalry that had emerged in the five years since the end of the World War. Soon after McNair left Hawaii for his new assignment to work with the Reserve Officer Training Corps (ROTC), the results of the McNair Board and the issues it studied came under scrutiny at the national level. The McNair Board report drew significant criticism, particularly from members of the Air Service. This criticism, exemplified by the findings of the 1925 President's Aircraft Board, did not bode well for future interservice cooperation when leaders such as McNair found their efforts to conduct objective analyses questioned by biased observers.

The President's Aircraft Board of 1925

The publication of the McNair Board report and the updated plan for the defense of Oahu marked the apogee of McNair's assignment in Hawaii. His tour of duty there ended officially on February 11, 1924, when he took several months of leave before reporting for duty on June 30, 1924, as professor of military science and tactics for Purdue University's reserve officer training course. However, this change of duty did not mark an end to McNair's involvement with the board he presided over in Hawaii or the reaction the McNair Board report prompted among various military and political leaders. Instead, his efforts as Summerall's G-3 soon gained national attention, particularly concerning the ongoing debates regarding the role and capabilities of aviation in the military service. Before shifting focus to McNair's service in the Purdue ROTC program, it seems appropriate to finish the current story by recounting the national-level events that took place in 1925, largely in reaction to McNair's war planning efforts in Hawaii, and which affected him directly in a high-profile event near the end of the year.[22]

The War Department convened a special naval board in early 1925 "to report to the president on the development of aviation." This board relied primarily on the McNair Board report of 1924 for documentary evidence because this report contained the results of the most recent and diligently conducted tests on the subject. The chief of the Air Service, Major General Mason W. Patrick, wrote to the adjutant general on February 12, 1925, commenting on the McNair Board's findings. General Patrick noted that the chief of coast artillery, Major General Frank W. Coe, made the following assertion in his annual report of September 8, 1924: "The bomber is outmatched by the anti-aircraft artillery at all altitudes which can now be reached by service bombers, provided that the target can be seen." Patrick pointed out that to support this assertion, Coe quoted the following passage from the McNair Board report: "The anti-aircraft artillery on land is a thoroughly effective means of defense against the bomber, provided it is available in adequate quantity and that searchlights and listening apparatus are capable of detecting and illuminating the target."[23]

Patrick wrote in his letter to the adjutant general that he and Coe attended a meeting called by the War Department assistant chief of staff for operations "for the purpose of coordinating the War Department testimony to be given before the Special Naval Board." Patrick claimed that at this meeting, he pointed out "certain obvious errors in the calculations of the McNair Board which, when corrected, practically nullified the value of the board's conclusions." According to Patrick, when he pointed out these unspecified errors, "General Coe admitted certain of the facts presented and I [Patrick] naturally assumed that no further reference would be made . . . to a document which presented conclusions based on calculations of such obvious inaccuracy. I therefore refrained from submitting the report to the War Department . . . believing that the necessity thereafter had ceased to exist."[24] Patrick went on to claim that despite his assumption to the contrary, it seemed "considerable credence is still given to the conclusions of the McNair Board."[25] This led him to provide technical criticisms of the McNair Board's methods and assumptions that he believed led to significant mathematical inaccuracies in the evaluation of the data collected by the board.

To support his criticisms, Patrick referred to the findings of Dr. Loring, an expert technician in the Ordnance Department, who conducted a purely mathematical assessment of the McNair Board data without considering the "fundamentally erroneous assumptions" that, according to Patrick, led the board to false conclusions. Patrick listed six "corrections" provided by Dr. Loring (listed as points b through g). In the first three corrections that Patrick quoted from Loring's report (points b through d), Loring found that the board "endeavored faithfully and impartially" in its conduct of an extended test to answer the War Department's questions; gave unanimous support to the findings reported; and revealed no indications of bias or unfairness against any arm of the service. In the next two (points e and f), Loring found that the results obtained by both the Air Service and the Antiaircraft Artillery "were not the best that could be expected with the latest equipment." In his final point (point g), Loring found that "the report of the McNair Board may not do full justice to the possibilities either of the Air Service or of the Antiaircraft Artillery," although he did not believe this resulted from any unfairness to one service in favor of the other.[26]

Upon receipt of this letter from Major General Patrick, the War Department forwarded it to the office of the chief of the coast artillery, Major General Coe, for comment. One interesting difference in Coe's response is that unlike Patrick's, it included point a from Dr. Loring's assessment of the McNair Board report: "That the board was made up of representatives of several branches of the Service and included an Air Service Officer." One cannot help but wonder why the chief of Air Service left this particular point out of his reference to Dr. Loring's assessment. In fact, because Loring only looked at the data and not the detailed description of the methodology and assumptions supporting the analysis of that data, his observations do not account for two key facts. He could not have known that in addition to the one Air Service officer who served as a member of the board, four aircrews volunteered many hours of their time training for and perfecting the methods of the tests before they actually measured any data. Further, he did not know that all the test participants met frequently to refine test methods and assess training progress before conducting the tests. Therefore, many members of the Air Service participated in the process, benefiting from the preparatory training both in individual flying and bombing skills and as a service in developing updated bombing techniques and maintenance procedures. Most significantly, these aircrews' long-term participation in this collaborative process gave them many opportunities to voice objections to the methods or assumptions guiding the tests, had they desired to do so.[27]

After quoting all seven of Loring's corrections to the McNair Board report, Coe argued, "The report of the McNair Board is entitled to weight as the impartial and dispassionate conclusions of a diligent and able board of officers and that quotations from this report when so described are entitled to weight as the best information now available." Finally, Coe concluded that although they represented the best findings currently available, the McNair Board's conclusions should not serve as "the approved conclusions of the War Department." Thus, the adjutant general made the following assessment, approved by the secretary of war, of the input provided by Patrick and Coe: "Matters of controversy have not yet been decided by the War Department."[28]

In September 1925, President Calvin Coolidge ordered Curtis D. Wilbur, secretary of the navy, and Dwight D. Davis, acting secretary of war, to appoint a group of retired military officers, judges, and congressional representatives to form the President's Aircraft Board. This came as a response to the ongoing and increasingly heated military debate regarding air power, combined with speculation in the popular media concerning the capabilities of the Air Service in defense of America against foreign attack. A handwritten note on the front cover of the final board report reveals the primary motivation behind formation of the board. The note reads, "Released for morning papers Dec 3."[29]

The President's Aircraft Board heard the testimony of ninety-nine witnesses. Aviators accounted for more than half of the witnesses because, in the board members' view, "there has been a widespread impression among flying men that their point of view and professional opinions have not been enough considered, that large matters of policy have been determined by men without flying experience." Further, the board made it clear to these "flying men" that they desired their testimony to reflect their own opinions, "whether or [not] those opinions coincided with the opinions of the departments." However, even this board faced great difficulty in finding clear answers to the matters in contention. On the third page of their report, the board members wrote that they encountered throughout their proceedings significant conflict in the testimony of the ninety-nine witnesses they questioned. Further, they expressed surprise that this conflict involved not only matters of opinion but also questions of fact. However, they found that in most cases "the apparent differences in fact are merely different conclusions resulting from partial statements of fact."[30]

After a brief description of the background to the controversy, the board members presented their findings by dividing the report into two parts. The first part addressed several of the primary questions regarding matters of controversy, while the second recommended actions the president should direct with respect to the army, the navy, and industry as the main supplier of aeronautical material. Several interesting conclusions, approved unanimously by the board, appeared in the report. The board recommended continuation of the separation between military and civilian aviation because any such union would only breed distrust of the intentions of commercial aviation as it sought to extend its domestic reach. However, the board also warned against the false notion that investment in a large air power would amount to a "peace movement." On the contrary, the board pointed out that despite the natural sea barriers America enjoyed, it must still invest adequately in its defense while sustaining its policy of avoiding becoming embroiled in a European-style arms race. Perhaps more importantly, the board cautioned against the belief that the appearance of a new style of weapon could "change the ultimate character of war. The next war may well start in the air but in all probability will wind up, as the last war did, in the mud."[31]

The board also made several recommendations for encouraging the growth of both civilian and military air strength and capability, including encouraging commercial uses of aviation; improving existing aviation law, insurance, and government oversight; encouraging investment; and basing decisions regarding military aviation strength on realistic assessments of potential enemy aviation capability. Although the board agreed that the nation currently faced no significant threat of aerial attack from another nation, they did not discount the possibility of such a threat in the future or the need to prepare to counter it. Finally, the board did not recommend formation either of a separate department of national defense encompassing the existing military services; nor did it recommend creation of a separate air force equivalent to the army and navy, as either action would run counter to the principle of the military services "acting as integral parts of a single command."[32]

In the second half of the report, focused on recommendations regarding the army, navy, and industry, the board recommended changing the name of the Air Service to the Air Corps and considering it equivalent to the other branches of the army, like artillery, infantry, and cavalry. However, it did not recommend supporting the Air Service's requests for removal from the control of the War Department, arguing that aviation officers' frustrations associated with serving under and competing for promotion against nonflying officers did not outweigh the need to maintain unity of command. Nor did it support the assertion that the military should make sufficient investments in aviation technology to replace all aircraft with the latest models. In short, the board found that "obsolete" did not equate to "unsafe," and that sufficient investment could be made to continue improving military aviation technology without constantly maintaining a fleet composed of only the most modern and capable aircraft available.[33]

Many other, relatively minor recommendations followed in the second section, but perhaps the most significant and prescient statement appeared in the closing paragraph of the report. After noting that initially they disagreed on the matters under deliberation, the members of the board described the mindset that enabled them to arrive at a consensus, ending their report with the following statement: "We have reached a unanimous conclusion because we have approached our task in a spirit of mutual accommodation and understanding. The same spirit may prove helpful both to those charged with the grave responsibility of developing the policies in regard to the use of aircraft in national defense and to those who encounter the hazards of actual operations in the air."[34]

This spirit of mutual accommodation among the various military branches or services remained elusive. Far from unique to questions of air power, similar disputes over funding, equipment capabilities, doctrinal roles, unit organization, and command hierarchies continued to hamstring the army, particularly in the realm of mechanization and the attempt to turn the ideal concept of combined arms into a reality. Neither the McNair Board nor the President's Aircraft Board did anything to forestall the increasingly volatile interbranch and political rivalries infecting both the War Department and national-level leaders in 1924–1925, which only grew worse as such debates and struggles for limited funds continued in the coming years.

Nevertheless, awareness of all the details regarding this little-known episode in McNair's early career provides a new perspective on the interwar army's challenges overcoming branch bias and competition for funds and independence. While these challenges certainly created problems as the army sought to modernize in the decades after the World War, a spirit of cooperation rather than competition guided the efforts of some personnel, such as the various members of the McNair Board. The inability to consider the board's findings objectively at higher levels should not lead to the assumption that this lack of objectivity existed throughout the army. With respect to McNair, his efforts as the Hawaiian Department operations officer and president of the McNair Board demonstrate that he possessed a broader range of experience than that of a typical field artilleryman, and they highlight his commitment to detailed, unbiased experimentation. McNair's peers and immediate superiors recognized him as a meticulous, hardworking, objective, innovative, and intellectually gifted officer. One can only imagine how frustrating he must have found this whole episode and how it must have affected his views as he faced similar challenges throughout the remainder of his career.

The Billy Mitchell Trial

One final event that transpired in 1925 deserves mention here because of Major McNair's little-known but direct involvement. On November 20, 1925, just ten days before the release of the results of the President's Aircraft Board, McNair received orders from the War Department's adjutant general directing him to travel to Washington on temporary duty to the trial judge advocate to testify at the court-martial of the famous advocate of air power, Billy Mitchell.[35] Mitchell found himself facing a court-martial for insubordination as a result of his ever-increasing stridency in claiming America lacked a competent air service, and would continue to lack one as long as it remained subordinate to the army. Although most historians of early twentieth-century American military history probably have some familiarity with the Mitchell court-martial, the historical record indicates most are probably unaware of McNair's involvement in the trial.[36]

As it prepared its case, the prosecution learned that Mitchell visited Hawaii during the same period that the McNair Board prepared for and conducted its tests of air service, coast artillery, and antiaircraft capabilities. After his visit, Mitchell based many of his assertions about the supposed ignorance of nonflying military men regarding the potential of airpower on what he claimed to have seen in Hawaii. His criticism and misrepresentations of the Hawaiian Department's attitude toward airpower infuriated Major General Summerall, who unsuccessfully sought appointment as president of Mitchell's court-martial. However, given the centrality of what he had supposedly witnessed in Hawaii to Mitchell's claims, the adjutant general ordered both Major McNair and Major General Summerall to testify at Mitchell's court-martial. Their testimony proved vital to the prosecution's case, enabling it to demonstrate the intentional misrepresentations and inaccuracies in many of Mitchell's statements.

For example, Summerall refuted Mitchell's claims that he observed a chronic lack of resources for the Air Service in Hawaii due to its nonflying superiors' lack of willingness to provide it adequate support. Instead, Summerall demonstrated that he had done just the opposite, redistributing resources from other branches of service within the Hawaiian department to augment the Air Service. Further, McNair's (and Summerall's) testimony refuted Mitchell's claims that during his visit to Hawaii in 1923, no plans for the defense of Oahu existed. As McNair pointed out, during this time, the Hawaiian department did in fact have a plan for the defense of Oahu, one that McNair and his operations staff had already begun to update, resulting in the revised plan they published in early 1924. McNair also refuted Mitchell's supposed prescience in predicting the possibility that Japan might initiate a war against America with some form of sneak attack against a vulnerable base like Pearl Harbor or the Panama Canal. He pointed out that these predictions held striking similarities to the planning assumptions in a 1920 document entitled *Joint Army and Navy Action in Coast Defense*—one of many references McNair and his staff used in developing their updated plan for the defense of Oahu.[37]

McNair also demonstrated that during his tour there, the Hawaiian department recognized Pearl Harbor, and particularly the oil storage tanks, as key vulnerabilities that defense plans must account for. Mitchell had long claimed a monopoly on this insight, but McNair exposed Mitchell's claims not only as unoriginal but also as a willful misrepresentation. His testimony demonstrated that simple ignorance could not explain Mitchell's false statements because Mitchell had made no effort to interact with the joint team involved in the McNair Board or Oahu defense planning when he was in Hawaii. Mitchell chose to remain secretive during his visit, and McNair made it clear that Mitchell could have known about current and ongoing defense planning if had he chosen to. Instead, he consistently refused to divulge why he was there. In doing so, Mitchell passed up the opportunity to talk to key people who could have divulged the true nature of the situation in Hawaii. Instead, he chose to spread rumor and falsehood upon his departure.[38]

The criticism that McNair's plan for the defense of Oahu attracted from men intent on furthering the interests of their branch or service illustrates the severity of the problem of branch bias, particularly in an era of increasing budget constraints. Always the selfless servant, McNair, along with his fellow board members, devoted six months of his career to an objective, detailed, and cooperative interservice study of the ability of existing weapons systems to contribute to the defense of Oahu from a naval assault. In stark contrast to this objective, diligent, and cooperative effort stands the example of Billy Mitchell, a man who explored military bases and key terrain around Hawaii, gathering intelligence like an enemy spy. Mitchell later claimed no defense plans existed when defense planning went on in earnest activity all around him. He also did not acknowledge (and may not have realized) that McNair included Air Service personnel in this planning effort—and recognized them by name for their contributions. Mitchell also asserted that the Hawaiian Department ignored and underresourced the Air Service when in fact Summerall reallocated resources from already underfunded ground units to support Air Service development.

This brief episode in Lesley McNair's career represents but one of the many fascinating periods in his four decades of service that remain unknown to most historians of the early twentieth-century army. Another development that could potentially put McNair's plans for a career in the army in jeopardy first emerged during his tour in Hawaii. In his 1922 annual physical examination, his hearing test revealed slight hearing loss in his left ear; however, the report indicated the doctor identified "no pathology" and recommended no further action. McNair's 1923 exam indicated the same reduced hearing, but in both his 1923 and 1924 exams, his doctors gave no treatment advice and ordered no additional tests. However, his doctor annotated the hearing section of the 1924 report, "drums slightly thickened," and he advised McNair to continue regular examinations at the ear, nose, and throat clinic that he had begun on his own initiative in 1923.[39]

The long, slow grind of the postwar years—they must have seemed interminable to McNair and his peers—tended to receive quick and broad-brush treatment from later historians. Some chose to ignore key events from this period, while others chose to reference these events without offering detailed or accurate representations of what actually took place. The McNair Board and its aftermath serve as an important example, given the objectivity, methodological rigor, and spirit of cooperation inherent in the McNair Board's efforts to study important and highly contentious issues, only for later interpretations to obscure the quality of the methods used in completing the detailed tests. Nevertheless, the peacetime regular army after World War I provided many diverse experiences to those officers who remained in the service. After four years of intensive experience as an operations officer and war planner, McNair received orders to report to Purdue University, where he served as professor of military science and tactics.[40] At Purdue, McNair gained his first experience in providing military training to civilians.

Part II

Interwar Education and Training

4
Professor of Military Science and Tactics at Purdue

While military officers such as Lesley McNair debated the meaning of the army's experience in the Great War and prepared for the likelihood of another such conflict, much of American society rejected out of hand the idea of American involvement in another European war. Simultaneously a pacifist movement spread from Europe across the globe. Pacifism arose in Europe as a reaction to the war's death toll, combined with the perception that the major powers' political and military leaders lacked the appropriate regard for the value of human life. Popular literature, poetry, and music recorded the misery and suffering caused by the war, as memorials appeared on battlefields and in cities around the world. Indicating the widespread power of the pacifist movement, sixty-one countries, including the United States, signed the Kellogg-Briand Pact of 1928, which outlawed war as a means to settle international disputes.[1]

Steven Trout highlighted the irony embedded in this agreement—an indication of the naively idealistic international postwar environment. As Trout argued, while the disarmament talks of 1921–1922 might have prevented a war in the 1920s, as time passed, it morphed into an opportunity for those governments that chose to ignore the limits set out by the treaty, thereby gaining advantage over those that did abide by its restrictions. This resulted, for example, in the growth in Japanese naval power that would contribute to the dangerous international imbalance of military power in the Northwest Pacific region a decade later. As Trout explained, "Thus, like the infamous Kellogg-Briand Pact of 1928, a renunciation of armed conflict signed (ironically enough) by all the major combatant nations of the Second World War, the [1921–1922 Naval Disarmament] conference ultimately demonstrated the irrelevance of diplomacy in the face of resurgent militarism and nationalistic fervor."[2]

ROTC in the Interwar Years

Well before this symbolic event, the US Congress acceded to the public's isolationist leanings and long-standing distrust of a large military by significantly reducing the army's size and budget. By passing the 1920 National Defense Act (NDA), Congress limited the size of the postwar army to 297,717 personnel (senior military leaders had recommended 500,000). Cuts in appropriated funds further reduced actual personnel strength to 175,000 in 1920. By 1923, the army reached a low of 118,750 personnel. In the event of a war America could not avoid, Congress envisioned mobilization of the National Guard and a pool of reserve officers to augment the small cadre of regulars.[3]

The regular army officers who remained on active duty after the war did not accept this optimistic vision of the future. They understood that war existed throughout history as one of the few constants of human culture, no matter the cost to the combatants who waged it. Further, they knew the risk involved in relying on mobilization of reservists in time of war. As McNair witnessed while on the American Expeditionary Force (AEF) staff, National Guard units often required as much training as units formed of inductees, and their officers rarely exhibited the necessary skill to command large units in combat. Fortunately, a small but talented pool of midlevel officers chose to remain in the regular army even though they soon encountered the hump—a stall in promotions caused by senior officers remaining on active duty for want of better career opportunities. This meant that midlevel officers typically spent more than a decade each at the grades of captain and major while they waited for senior officers to retire, eventually opening up new opportunities for promotion.[4] Nevertheless, many dedicated officers remained in the service, determined to ensure the army remained prepared for the possibility of another war.

The 1920 NDA cut the army to the bone and made provisions only for a navy reserve, relying on the National Guard as a substitute for a true army reserve, but it included several initiatives intended to improve the readiness of those forces that would defend the nation after the World War. In addition to serving as the nation's immediate defense force, the NDA called on the regular army to train the large civilian force that the nation would mobilize in the event of another large-scale war. The army would do this primarily through the Reserve Officers Training Corps (ROTC). Although its origins date to the nineteenth century, the ROTC program saw its first formal implementation in the 1916 NDA, passed as a measure to accelerate American preparedness for participation in the World War.[5]

In fact, after the Great War, many public figures, including Pershing, Theodore Roosevelt, and various politicians and special interest groups (like the Military Training Camps Association), advocated universal training at citizen military training camps. The opponents of universal military training defeated this initiative before it gained any real traction, successfully standing on the premise that the static, attrition-based nature of the Great War indicated that future combat, if necessary, would rely on machines, not men, to minimize bloodshed. Therefore, the states would shoulder the burden of training the National Guard, and the federal government would have no army reserve as well as the smallest possible army, devoting most of the limited funds available to equipment rather than personnel. The only federal training program to survive this debate was the ROTC, which comprised a group of men who received military training in college and would serve as a cadre to turn raw recruits into soldiers in the event of another war. The 1920 NDA renewed and updated the ROTC's charter after the war. By 1923, the program comprised 104,000 cadets, and 49 percent of army personnel had served in positions that involved training civilians, whether in the ROTC or a similar program.[6]

McNair reported for duty at Purdue University in Lafayette, Indiana, on May 1, 1924, after four months of leave. His service with the ROTC marked the beginning of a ten-year stretch of assignments as either an administrator or student at some form of military training institution. However, Purdue provided a new challenge for Major McNair, who found himself training civilians for the first time. His only similar experience to that point, working with recently mobilized national guardsmen during World War I, left him with a negative view of the potential of civilians inducted into military service. In contrast to that experience, McNair's assignment at Purdue gave him a chance to see the outcome of thorough peacetime military training provided to a large group of civilian officer cadets. This assignment not only gave him direct experience turning civilians into soldiers but also enabled him, because of the length of his assignment, to lead an organization to a much higher level of proficiency than an officer could expect to achieve while conducting such training in the midst of a large-scale mobilization.[7]

In addition to training cadets during his four years at Purdue, McNair also interacted with a variety of senior college officials, local and state politicians, and civilian activists. This was a broadening experience for a midgrade officer whose service over the previous twenty-one years consisted primarily of duty at isolated outposts and during combat deployments. McNair embraced the varied challenges of this new assignment and made great strides in developing Purdue's ROTC program into a first-class organization. This experience enhanced McNair's reputation as an officer who could handle the diverse responsibilities of senior leadership while making Purdue's ROTC department one of the best in the nation.[8] This period of his career also provides great insight into McNair's personal and professional views because of several articles that he published while at

Purdue—articles that expressed his strong opinions about pacifism, the need for national military preparedness, and the importance and nature of military training in colleges and universities.

When Major Lesley J. McNair reported for duty as the new professor of military science and tactics at Purdue University, he joined the ranks of officers responsible for leading one of the nation's many new ROTC programs. As designed by the 1920 NDA, ROTC departments offered both a two-year program for freshmen and sophomores—a compulsory program at many universities, including Purdue—and an advanced program for juniors and seniors who desired to continue military training and earn a commission upon graduation, whether in the army reserve, the National Guard, or possibly the regular army. Purdue conformed to this basic academic structure while operating since 1919 as a purely motorized field artillery unit. This made Purdue's ROTC program a perfect fit for Major McNair, a highly respected artilleryman with years of experience conducting experiments in new field artillery techniques—a practice he would continue at Purdue.[9]

This assignment also vastly increased McNair's exposure to civilian leaders and the public media. Other than his appearance at the Billy Mitchell trial, the young artilleryman had previously maintained a low public profile, even when serving as a general officer on the AEF staff. However, his assignment at Purdue placed McNair in a position involving interaction with both civilian trainees and community leaders, including leaders of the small but outspoken national pacifist movement. Perhaps surprisingly, considering his lack of experience in such situations, McNair proved quite effective in dealing with civilians. He also engaged in the pacifist debate with passion and eloquence, writing articles and delivering speeches at Purdue that recognized the virtue of pacifism as an ideal but that convincingly explained the necessity to maintain military readiness to confront the dangers presented by the real world.

Although Congress only halfheartedly implemented the 1920 NDA—primarily as a result of America's isolationist stance and budgetary concerns, along with other sociopolitical factors like pacifist sentiment—McNair found an ally in college president Dr. Edward C. Elliot, who believed that America required a strong national defense and who provided unwavering support to Purdue's ROTC program.[10] McNair wrote several articles while at Purdue that revealed his thoughts on the importance of military training in civilian institutions. As Edward Coffman described in *The Regulars,* "Americans traditionally had little interest in and less respect for soldiers in peacetime. Many civilians may have lived through the 1920s and 1930s without ever seeing one, while a few may not even have known of their existence."[11]

McNair recognized that this indifference or ignorance among much of the American public only added to the challenge that both the government's isolationist foreign policy and the pacifist vocal minority posed to the spirit of civic duty he believed necessary to prevent the interwar officer corps from falling into lethargy. He remained determined to do all that he could to prevent the army's physical and intellectual stagnation. While at Purdue, McNair took great strides both to serve as an example to his fellow midgrade regular army officers struggling to get over the hump and to instill in Purdue's student body a belief in the benefits and importance of military training.[12]

The first article McNair wrote while at Purdue, "Military Training at Educational Institutions," appeared in 1925 in the *Purdue Engineering Review*. McNair described the nature and value of military training at civilian institutions, responding to those critics of the ROTC who believed that students could use the time devoted to military training in colleges more effectively by studying academic subjects. He focused in particular on the "wondering freshmen and indignant sophomores" compelled to participate in ROTC. He pointed out that Purdue's president, Dr. Elliot, who had received military training while a student at the University of Nebraska, asked similar questions of his commandant, Lieutenant John J. Pershing. Although McNair admitted in his article that he remained unsure whether Elliot found Pershing's answers to his questions satisfactory, he pointed out that Elliot had emerged in the 1920s as one of the nation's most ardent supporters of military training for college students.[13]

In "Military Training at Educational Institutions," McNair explained the organization and history of the ROTC, identifying its roots in America's militia tradition and its evolution from the informal program of the nineteenth century to the NDA-formalized system established in 1920. Emphasizing the program's role in national military preparedness, McNair pointed out that despite its voluntary nature, the senior ROTC program existed in 1925 at 127 institutions across America, with 82,761 students enrolled in ROTC training. In fact, even more schools desired to form ROTC programs of their own but could not because the War Department lacked the required funds. However, with another 42,743 students enrolled in junior ROTC programs in high schools and other institutions across the country, the nationwide total of students receiving military training in 1925 exceeded 125,000.[14]

McNair described the various motives that led institutions to establish ROTC programs and the two main qualities students developed as a unique benefit of participation. He argued that colleges such as Purdue provided military training from both a sense of patriotism and a desire to produce good citizens. More importantly, however, military training prospered in institutions of higher education because it had proven its worth as a component of adult education. In other words, ROTC did not benefit students merely by preparing them for war, but also by providing general educational benefits that resulted primarily from two intangible forms of character development. McNair identified these two benefits as discipline, which he viewed as an essential trait in all successful adults, whether civilians or soldiers, and leadership, another important component of any adult's character.[15]

To illustrate his point, McNair pointed out that many of Purdue's students graduated college after an average or subpar academic performance, only to surpass their peers in their civilian careers. He attributed these cases largely to the benefits of leadership and discipline, and he pointed out that Dr. Elliot himself had stated that only the Military Department, among all those at Purdue, included leadership training in its curriculum. Thus, McNair sought to demonstrate that the benefit of military training extended not just to those students bound for active service but also to the large majority of ROTC students who planned to remain in civilian life after graduation. He argued their military training provided all ROTC participants discipline and leadership skills, contributing to the self-confidence necessary to put their "book learning" to maximum use.[16]

Also in 1925, McNair made an early foray into engaging the public media by writing a letter to the editor of the *Army and Navy Journal.* Perhaps emboldened by his participation in the Mitchell trial and the publicity over his Oahu defense tests and planning, McNair wrote this letter in response to a congressional bill, taking a position on the question of whether the War Department should adopt a selective promotion system for army officers. His letter exhibits the maturity and confidence of an officer willing to engage in debate on military matters with both fellow military officers and civilians. It also reveals his expertise in matters well outside the purview of the typical artillery officer and his deeply held convictions regarding the army's need for committed, high-quality officers. In his letter, he provided a detailed and well-reasoned argument in support of the principle of a selective promotion process, but he disagreed with the system proposed in the bill currently before Congress.[17]

McNair's argument for implementing the proposed selective promotion system included an additional consideration: the officer's rank. For example, he supported the system of selection for general officers and pointed out its broad acceptance throughout the army, noting, "We have far abler general officers by selection than we would have by seniority." He then made the case that, based on the vital importance of the positions they held, the army should also select its colonels—men it relied on to serve in key positions including brigade command and division chief of staff—using a selective promotion system. In particular, McNair argued that this would minimize the common experience among contemporary officers of observing regiments in training in which lieutenants colonel or even majors possessed greater potential for brigade command than that of the actual commander.[18]

However, McNair argued that the situation changed at grades below colonel. He admitted that "the grade of captain, the company commander, is, like that of colonel, of disproportionate importance," and he pointed out that in his own experience, many officers who made excellent company commanders could not meet the demands of higher rank. Many such men remained mired in the details that consumed the company commander's attention, "forever fussing with details and interfering with their subordinates." On the other hand, because often a captain "is only beginning to find himself as an officer," average company commanders often made effective colonels because their "real ability develops later." Thus, McNair concluded that merit-based selection of captains for promotion "should be undertaken with hesitation," and such a system should not govern promotion of lieutenants.[19]

Considering the question of promotion by selection (reward for individual merit) as a whole, McNair therefore supported the method in principle as a change that would serve the good of the army. However, he did not believe a merit-based promotion system would work equally well for all ranks of officers. He noted three main concerns with the proposed selection process. These included the possibility of improper outside influence, the tendency of officers serving on promotion boards to favor subordinates with whom they had served, and the imperfection of information that could lead to inaccuracies in an officer's personnel file.[20]

To avoid these pitfalls, McNair recommended safeguards, which he argued would prove effective only when formalized by law. Many of the safeguards he recommended still exist in today's officer promotion system. McNair's recommendations included providing promotion boards with clear and standardized criteria to govern their selection decisions. He believed boards should rely only on official (not personal) records and should base their promotion decisions on an officer's full history of performance under a variety of supervisors rather the completion of one exceptional assignment or the receipt of several glowing evaluations from the same supervisor. McNair also suggested that the army use a selective promotion system among officers who had served ten years or more and achieved the rank of captain, recommending a graduated use of promotion by selection depending on rank. Under McNair's proposed system, the army would promote all general officers based on merit, but only half of all colonels and only 10 to 20 percent of lieutenants colonel and majors. He also argued that such a system could only avoid branch bias by determining how many officers a board would promote from each branch before each selection board met. Finally, Mc-

Nair recognized that even with the most stringently applied control measures, governed by law, such a system might prove unpopular "with the majority of the Army, for the majority will be adversely affected individually. It is inevitable that the most carefully devised system will result in some injustice and some heart-burning, but it is nevertheless believed that the net result would be greatly increased efficiency."[21]

Pacifism at Purdue

The following year, 1926, McNair turned his attention to the problem of pacifism and its threat to the ROTC program at Purdue in an article he wrote for the *Purdue Alumnus* titled "Pacifism at Purdue University." Purdue had recently earned recognition by the War Department as a distinguished college for the sixth time (a distinction it earned during every year of McNair's tenure), standing out that year in comparison to other colleges' programs by a wider margin than ever. This demonstrated that Purdue possessed a high-performing and motivated body of ROTC cadets. Nevertheless, not everyone at Purdue supported the idea of compulsory military training in college. The first significant evidence of opposition to the ROTC program came to McNair's attention shortly after the college's November 11, 1925, Armistice Day observances. The guest speaker for the event, Colonel Paul V. McNutt, a member of the Officers Reserve Corps and dean of law at Indiana University, focused his remarks on pacifism, of which he had begun to see, in McNair's recollection of his speech, "unmistakable signs of activity."[22]

One Purdue ROTC cadet recalled McNutt in a 1926 *Field Artillery Journal* article as "a fine example of a leader of men, tall, of fine physique, piercing black eyes and a voice that commands attention and respect." Singling out McNutt's address as one of the best given that day, Cadet Major W. G. Hinckley highlighted the Dean's remarks regarding his concern with pacifism:

> I have been troubled of late by a serious matter. Certain groups of individuals, some of them honest and well-meaning, some of them not, are seeking to exact a pledge from persons of military age never again to serve this nation in time of war and to destroy their love for this nation as a nation. I have no abuse for those who are honest and well-meaning. I agree with them that the abolition of war is a consummation devoutly to be wished. I emphatically disagree with them as to the means of achieving that end.

Hinckley quoted McNutt on several points that supported his antipacifist position. McNutt reminded the more than 4,000 attendees of the Armistice Day events that America, as a rich nation in "a distracted, bankrupt, but armed world," must remain vigilant in its national defense. He recalled the futility of America's past efforts to lead nearby countries in disarmament, which only left the nation open to the threat posed by its more powerfully armed neighbors, including Mexico. McNutt particularly disagreed with the assertion that military preparedness made America a nation of militarists, arguing that neither he nor any other soldier who had seen war wanted to experience another one.[23]

However distasteful Americans might find the experience of war, McNutt rejected the concept "that the abolition of war can be brought about by the disarmament of America alone or by the taking of a slacker vow by the youth of this land." Disarmament would only lead to lawlessness within America and vulnerability to attacks from abroad. Reminding the audience of the sacrifice of America's fallen, McNutt stated, "I know what our soldier dead would say to the slacker vow, ... 'Be prepared. If the danger comes, fight on, fight on to victory.'"[24] In his *Alumnus* article, McNair described a debate that ensued in the student opinion column of the campus newspaper, *The Exponent,* over the several days following the Armistice Day observances. First, a student criticized both McNutt's remarks and military training at Purdue. Another student soon joined in with an editorial opposing military instruction in colleges, leading to growing debate among the student body and, in McNair's opinion, "definite indications of a desire to agitate the question of compulsory training."[25]

Two individuals added fuel to the fire over the coming months. First, leaders among the Purdue faculty and student body received in January 1926 copies of a thirty-one-page pamphlet written by Winthrop D. Lane and published by the Committee on Military Training, a group that included Jane Addams, Carrie Chapman Catt, John Dewey, W. E. B. DuBois, and James Weldon Johnson. As McNair pointed out, the pamphlet recited "in detail the progress of military training in educational institutions since the World War, asserting that the War Department is making great strides in militarizing the country." McNair quoted a particularly troubling passage from the pamphlet: "The deep danger of military training is not that it teaches a boy how to handle a rifle, but that it leads him to *think* in the *psychology of war.*"[26]

Close on the heels of the appearance of Lane's pamphlet, the executive secretary of the National Council for the Prevention of War, Frederick J. Libby, spoke three times in Lafayette, Indiana, on February 28, 1926. In his *Alumnus* article, McNair pointed out that Libby spoke "twice from pulpits and once at the YMCA." In these speeches, Libby voiced his advocacy of the United States' joining the League of Nations and abolishing compulsory military training in colleges and all military training in high school. He also, as McNair put it, "did not advocate disarmament, but opposed 'pyramiding of armament,' whatever that means." Anticipating the impact Libby might have on the Lafayette community and the student body at Purdue, McNair arranged for ROTC cadets to attend Libby's presentations. Overall, these attendees "were surprised at the weakness of his arguments, although impressed with their subtlety." To pin Libby down on some of these more subtle points, McNair had members of the ROTC Order of Military Merit (junior and senior honors students) prepare written questions. Libby sent written replies not long after he left Lafayette.[27]

Libby's responses demonstrated his standing as a pacifist based on Christian principles, his belief that "the Monroe Doctrine is being stretched too far nowadays," and his conviction that although America should not disarm, it also should not increase armaments because "it is the psychology accompanying increase of armaments that is endangering future peace." Libby advocated a return to armament reduction by international agreement—in short, making America's security subordinate to the international community's desire for peace. McNair followed this summary of Libby's responses to his students' questions with a description of the reaction among the student body at large. During the week after Libby's visit to Lafayette, the *Exponent* contained multiple attacks from students opposing his pacifist, internationally focused stance on national security. Only one person stepped forward in defense of Libby's position—a local preacher who criticized the *Exponent* as prejudiced for publishing only views that ran counter to those expressed by Libby. Eventually debate shifted away from Libby's remarks to the more general question of compulsory military training at Purdue. After Libby's visit, students found the Lane pamphlet—previously available only to select members of the faculty and student leadership—and distributed it to everyone on campus, both faculty and students.[28]

McNair next provided examples of similar events taking place at "practically every campus where there is military training," usually led by local ministers with the support of national organizations like Libby's, and generally opposing military training on the grounds that colleges should seek ways more in keeping with Christian ideals to avoid wars in the future. One leaflet that these organizations distributed to students before college enrollment, seeking to convince students to oppose military training, referred to "the Military Problem" on campuses and argued, "All groups might profitably take steps to abolish the requirement of compulsory military training in colleges as undemocratic and Prussian." This leaflet provided a list of pacifist references that included *War: Its Causes, Consequences and Cure,* by Kirby Page, author of the infamous "Pacifist Pledge":

> Let the churches of America say to their own government and to the peoples of the earth: We feel so certain that war is now un-Christian, futile and suicidal that we renounce the whole war system. We will never again sanction or par-

ticipate in any war. We will not allow our pulpits and classrooms to be used as recruiting stations. We will not again give our financial or moral support to any war. We will seek security and justice in other ways.

McNair referred to Kirby's "Pacifist Pledge" as "Treason under the guise of religion!"[29]

McNair next revealed links between the pacifist, antimilitary training movement and American communist and socialist organizations. He focused on one individual in particular: Paul Blanchard, publisher of the *Amalgamated,* the union newspaper of the Amalgamated Clothing and Textile Workers. As described in the Lusk Report of 1925, prepared by a committee of New York legislators, Blanchard fomented strikes among Amalgamated union workers and he spoke in February 1926 at Wyoming University against compulsory military training in colleges. McNair pointed out the similarity of Blanchard's argument to Libby's, both of which emphasized the supposed damaging psychological effect of military training on the young men who received it. However, McNair also brought into question the notion that Christian ideals motivated Blanchard, quoting from a recent issue of the *Amalgamated:* "It is up to the workers of this city to break up this criminal union (of the employers). They are digging graves for themselves and we will see that they are ducked into them. They try to do all in their power to crush and disorganize you, but we can stand and overpower the whole damned bunch." Apparently not all opponents of military training in colleges drew their motivation from Christian-inspired pacifist tendencies.[30]

McNair ended the article on a positive note, pointing out first that America emerged from the war with Spain having learned valuable lessons that strengthened the nation's defenses. Although this did not prepare America for the immensity of the task it would face during World War I, a war "the pacifists assured us would never occur," it left the country better prepared than it had been in 1898. Since the end of the World War, the nation had struggled with the tension between pacifist tendencies and the knowledge among senior political leaders that America must remain prepared for war. Despite the delay in passage of the 1920 NDA, as well as the relatively low funding and personnel strength with which it was provided, President Coolidge had firmly supported the act and ensured its continued funding even as he sought disarmament through international agreement.[31]

Focusing on Purdue itself, McNair highlighted the support provided to ROTC by Dr. Elliot. In a letter to McNair dated January 28, 1926, Elliot wrote,

Here, at Purdue University, the ROTC is regarded as an integral and valuable element in the plan of technical education, to which this institution is primarily devoted. However, entirely apart from the question of the specific training of men for reserve military commissions, and entirely apart from the relation of the military training to engineering instruction, I consider that the ROTC contributes largely and efficiently to the development of those essential qualities of which dynamic character is composed—the sense of personal responsibility, the inspiration of leadership, and a recognition of the eternal place of order and organization in human society. . . . I have always considered that this training had an equally important aim of giving to the young men, who are fortunate to receive it, something in sharp contrast to the present day tendencies toward personal irresponsibility and lawless individuality; making them realize that strength of character depended upon certain common realities of life rather than upon sentimental preachments.

Pointing out that Elliot wrote this letter before the pacifist stir caused by Libby and the Lane pamphlet, and not in response to them, McNair added his own assessment. He reminded his readers that America had pacifists before the World War, and despite their views falling victim to the facts of that war, pacifists remained active upon its conclusion. He assessed the situation at Purdue as "quiet after the recent exposure of the fallacy of Mr. Libby's views, but the fact must not be overlooked that the basic cause of the agitation, these national pacifistic and communistic organizations, are still very much alive. The pacifist strives to influence and exploit public opinion by propaganda. The best antidote is an enlightened and thoughtful public opinion." In this well-researched and well-written article, McNair made great strides in administering the antidote to Libby and the pacifist tendencies he sought to spread.[32]

Although the ROTC programs at Purdue and some other universities across America faced pacifist opposition, professional officers like McNair successfully defended their programs. McNair's *Alumnus* article serves as a reminder of the brief spike in pacifist activity at Purdue and the effort required to counter it, but this represented only a small minority of the difficulty regular army officers faced in their efforts to maintain military preparedness, particularly in securing government funding for army personnel, equipment, and training in the 1920s. Nevertheless, dedicated regular army officers and students across America continued ROTC training with War Department support, however minimal, based on the limited implementation of the 1920 NDA. However, one event in 1926 would demonstrate just how integral Dr. Elliot judged McNair's leadership to the success of Purdue's ROTC program.

Having arrived at Purdue in the fall of 1924, McNair had served less than two years when the chief of the Field Artillery branch, Major General William J. Snow, sent Dr. Elliot a letter on March 10, 1926, informing him that he would soon have

Purdue ROTC, May 31, 1926 (far left: President Elliot; third from left: Lieutenant Colonel Lesley J. McNair). Courtesy of Purdue University Archives

to relieve McNair for pressing duty at Fort Bragg. Snow wrote that he recognized the disruption this would cause to Purdue's ROTC program, but he assured Dr. Elliot that only McNair could suitably perform the work required by the Field Artillery board at Fort Bragg. He needed McNair to lead the board's effort to update the field artillery drill regulations, and he assured Elliot he would provide the best possible officer available as a replacement.[33]

The day after he received this letter, Dr. Elliot forwarded it to the acting secretary of war, J. R. Hines, voicing his strong objections to the planned relief of McNair. Elliot noted the dramatic improvements McNair had achieved in his short time at Purdue, having "completely demonstrated his distinctive fitness for the many and different tasks belonging to our corps, which numbers more than fourteen hundred men and is the largest light artillery organization in the country." Elliot explained that McNair arrived to find the detachment in disarray from the frequent changes of leadership preceding his assignment, but as a result of his "strong character, his personal force and his technical competency, Major McNair developed a morale and standards of performance which have the hearty approbation of the University and the State." Because of the recent challenges Purdue had faced with the rising specter of pacifism, as well as McNair's skillful handling of this challenge, Elliot feared McNair's early relief would result in far more than mere degradation in the program's quality. Rather, Elliot believed losing McNair at this critical juncture could make the provision of military training at Purdue unsustainable. In short, Elliot believed the early departure of McNair could lead to the end of Purdue's ROTC program, and he conveyed this concern in very clear terms to the acting secretary of war.[34]

Dr. Elliot's strident objections soon achieved the desired effect. On March 18, just one week after Elliot wrote his letter, the Acting Secretary of War Hines responded with a brief note granting Elliot his wishes. Hines assured Elliot, "The Department appreciates the valuable services being rendered by Major McNair at Purdue University, in view of which it is not contemplated relieving him until the completion of his normal tour of duty at his present station." Two days after Acting Secretary of War Hines wrote his letter to Dr. Elliot, Major General Snow also wrote a letter confirming he would not move McNair early. Snow wrote, "The situation as to personnel has changed somewhat so that an excellent officer, upon whom I did not count, has become available to me for the special work I contemplated using Major McNair for; and, accordingly, I shall leave him with you." This brief exchange demonstrates the outstanding reputation McNair had achieved by 1926, within his branch, at Purdue, and even at the level of the secretary of war.[35]

Before his departure from Purdue in 1928, McNair wrote two articles, one published in Purdue's 1928 *Debris* and the other in the February 1928 edition of the *Coast Artillery Journal*, summing up his experience of four years of training ROTC cadets. In his *Debris* article, McNair commended Purdue's program for its achievements during his tenure there, giving full credit to the student officers for earning recognition as a distinguished college in three consecutive annual War Department inspections. He also declared the program equally likely to earn distinction in the 1928 inspection, scheduled for the month after McNair's departure.[36]

McNair also addressed Purdue's struggles with the nationwide pacifist movement to eliminate military training in colleges, pointing out, "The University was by no means immune to these activities, but the authorities and the students were quick to reject the unsound propaganda." In fact, the struggle "served a useful purpose, however, in stimulating discussion of the principles and objects of military training." With the height of the debate well behind them, McNair found the students "increasingly thoughtful and responsive as to the educational possibilities of the training," recognizing the broad range of benefits it provided. Specifically, he found the sophomore class benefited in particular from this process of reflection. Once "more of a liability to The Corps than an asset," the sophomore class achieved a generally improved attitude toward compulsory military training.

McNair assessed the sophomore class, previously "indifferent" or even "trouble-some," in 1928, "by their proficiency, their budding leadership, their example and their numbers, are collectively the backbone of The Corps." As evidence, McNair pointed out that batteries with fewer sophomores than their peers tended to perform comparatively worse in training. Thus, McNair's ROTC program at Purdue emerged from the pacifism struggle a stronger unit that conducted more effective collective training, and that was composed of a cadre of cadets more dedicated to the ROTC mission and their own individual training than before the debates of 1926.[37]

McNair sought to achieve two basic goals by writing his article for the *Coast Artillery Journal,* titled simply, "The ROTC." First, he described the ROTC program and the nature and need for further training and development of its graduates. Second, he requested support for the program from members of the National Guard and the reserves, primarily to fight pacifist tendencies wherever they appeared, and he solicited their representatives to ensure that the ROTC continued to receive the funding it required. He described the quality of the ROTC officer, based largely on the more than 830 hours of military training received over four years in the program. Regarding this latter topic, McNair emphasized the breadth of ROTC training, beginning in the first two years with a focus on basic drill and soldier skills, then culminating in the final two years with an emphasis on practical experience in leadership development. In short, McNair argued, "Never before in our history have we produced officers so carefully schooled, except at the national academies."[38]

Regarding the latter points, McNair provided an assessment many citizens and perhaps many reservists likely found bold, if not truly surprising. He made his thoughts on pacifism particularly clear: "As to the spasmodic attacks against ROTC by pacifists, reds, pinks, chronic objectors, and publicity seeker, amateur, and professional, the line of action is simple and clear: *inform the people.* Once the cloud of misinformation, exaggeration, and false logic is dissipated, there need be no fears as to the verdict of the great mass of Americans."[39] To support this point, McNair provided several key points of fact. Military training at colleges, regardless whether required or elective, did not derive from any legal requirement or War Department coercion; it existed solely as a matter of institutional policy at each school. Further, the colleges decided the specifics of the training programs, conforming only to the general guidance that they should focus the first two years on individual discipline and the second two years on leadership. He argued that the success of the program stemmed mostly from the fact that both the colleges and the government derived significant benefit from ROTC; the former experienced dramatic educational benefits among program participants, while the government gained a pool of highly trained reserve officers for potential duty if the need arose for national defense. Finally, McNair debunked the common misperception that the government funded college ROTC programs. In fact, in Purdue's case, not only did the college receive no government funding for ROTC, but the program cost Purdue $8,000 per year—a cost the college gladly paid as a result of the evident benefit accrued to both the individual cadets and the institution.[40]

However, McNair expressed concern that—despite prior congressional support for the program—future developments could spell trouble for its continuation. Although colleges received no direct funds, they did depend on the large stocks of equipment remaining in the wake of the World War. Once depleted, these stocks would require replenishment for ROTC programs to continue providing realistic training, and this would require congressional funding "in spite of the very proper considerations of economy" and the ever-increasing "pinch of the budget." Thus, McNair sought both to educate readers of his article for the *Coast Artillery Journal* on the nature and successes of the ROTC program to date, and on the impending budget crisis that posed a significant threat to the program. He asserted that the army could only avert this threat with a concerted effort by the portion of the populace who understood and supported the need for national preparedness, which required trained officers—and much of the informed public served in the guard or reserves in some capacity.[41]

A physical challenge resurfaced near the end of McNair's tour that made his professional advancement problematic. While at Purdue, McNair's hearing loss worsened significantly, from a reading of 15/20 in his left ear—consistent throughout the previous several years—to a reading of 4/20 (he continued to test 20/20 in his right ear). This led the examining doctor to recommend that McNair report to Walter Reed General Hospital for further treatment, which the adjutant general, B. B. Parrott, approved on August 8, 1927. McNair proceeded to Walter Reed where, after a comprehensive examination conducted while an inpatient from August 11 to 27, the ward surgeon documented McNair's hearing loss, including the addition of tinnitus to his symptoms, and recommended his return to duty with no further action. McNair remained cooperative and frank (as described by one of his doctors) throughout the examination, admitting that his hearing loss began shortly after his graduation from West Point. With his condition fully documented, McNair returned to Purdue to finish his final year of duty there.[42]

McNair earned promotion to the permanent rank of lieutenant colonel on January 9, 1928, after serving only seven years as a major, or about half as much time in the hump as many others during the interwar period.[43] Furthermore, McNair had developed into far more than merely a field artillery officer with little or no experience outside his basic branch. His first twenty years of service included a diverse range of duty positions that made full use of his wide-ranging skills and

Being a soldier, the memories that must ever be uppermost in my mind are those of The Corps. I came with the Class of 1928, even as I leave with it, hoping that they may accept me as a sort of classmate. We found a great Corps when we came, new and green as we all were. We have watched it grow and succeed, and like to think that we have helped, at least we tried, and gave our best.

It may seem to those who remain to carry on at the Graduation Review that our departure leaves a void, but not so. The Corps is a living organization, dependent upon every individual in it, and yet not one of those individuals is indispensable or even necessary; otherwise it could not be great.

The traditions of The Corps are the deeds of those who have gone before; it is upon these deeds that those who come tomorrow can build higher and better. It is my studied opinion that The Corps of today only approximates the full development of which it is capable; the foundations have been laid, solidly I hope, but the full measure of realization is yet to come.

LIEUT. COL. L. J. McNAIR

Lieutenant Colonel Lesley J. McNair, PMS&T of Purdue ROTC, with Farewell to the Corps, The Debris (Purdue Yearbook), 1928. Courtesy of Purdue University Archives

interests. He served a four-year branch detail in ordnance soon after graduating from West Point, and the army put that experience to use in several field equipment tests before the World War. On the AEF staff, he oversaw artillery training among all the AEF's combat formations; as a general staff officer, he performed many tasks to improve overall AEF effectiveness, even leading an effort to resolve problems with current methods for the fitting of soldiers' boots at initial entry. His exceptional performance on the AEF staff earned him several promotions, leading to his distinction as the AEF's youngest brigadier general. After the war, he served as a member of the individually selected inaugural faculty of the General Service School at Fort Leavenworth, developing the field artillery curriculum and working with thirty-three peers from a variety of branches to reestablish a postwar system of field-grade officer education in the United States.

Upon his assignment in 1921 to the Hawaiian Department, McNair stepped well outside of his field artillery experience to serve as Brigadier General Summerall's operations officer. During this assignment, he gained extensive war plans experience, developing a comprehensive plan of defense for Oahu. He also put his innovative spirit to use, conducting detailed and objective tests of aviation's ability to defend the island from aerial and naval attack—tests that soon garnered attention at the highest levels of the American government. Upon departing Hawaii, he led one of the nation's largest and most highly regarded ROTC programs at Purdue University, demonstrating not only the ability to train field artillery cadets, but also to engage in high-level debate with civilian and government leaders on a wide range of topics. These included analyses of creating a potential officer promotion system based on merit, assessing the merits of military training in civilian universities, and confronting the dangers pacifism posed both to national defense and to military training programs across America. McNair proved so effective in his duties at Purdue that the university's president, Dr. Edward Elliot, believed at the height of the pacifist movement in 1926 that Purdue's ROTC program might not survive the campaign against military training at Purdue without his leadership. In short, by 1928 McNair no longer fit the mold of the typical officer of field artillery. After twenty-four years of service, he had developed a degree of maturity and experience that made him stand out among his peers as a multitalented and highly respected officer. His next assignment as a student at the US Army War College provided him a chance to expand the range of capabilities he had developed.

5

The Army War College Class of 1928–1929

McNair received the opportunity to build on the war planning experience he gained in Hawaii as a student at the US Army War College (AWC), class of 1928–1929.[1] Like all AWC attendees after the World War, McNair received an education emphasizing practical work that included participation in many student committees that analyzed and recommended updates to actual American war plans. As historian Michael Matheny has explained, after its reestablishment in 1919, the AWC "began as an adjunct to the War Department's General Staff to assist in the preparation of war plans. Unlike the General Staff School [at Fort Leavenworth], the War College worked with real war plan scenarios." The college emphasized joint training, including not only the various military services but also the political and economic considerations involved in national military mobilization.[2]

Before McNair's attendance, the AWC curriculum underwent significant changes, including an even greater emphasis on learning by doing and other improvements that led to the high-quality education the college's graduates received after 1928. Although various studies describe the simultaneous evolution of the curriculum at the Leavenworth schools, fewer analyses of this kind exist focusing on the AWC, and none describes the specific role that the AWC played in preparing Lesley McNair for his service as a senior officer after he graduated in 1929.

The War Department defined the post–World War I organization and curriculum of the AWC as directed by Secretary of War Baker, who summarized the most significant challenges the nation faced in mobilizing for the World War in his annual report for 1919:

It has been made specially apparent that General Staff officers for duty with the War Department and for larger expeditionary forces should have broader knowledge, not only of their purely military duties, but also a full comprehension of all agencies, governmental as well as industrial, necessarily involved in a nation at war, to the end that coordinated effort may be secured from all these agencies, and that they may be employed economically and efficiently both in the preparation for and during war.[3]

Secretary Baker recognized that most of the War Department's challenges associated with mobilizing for and fighting World War I stemmed from economic and industrial issues related to mobilization for war and the logistical requirements associated with changes in military technology. Tactics and doctrine also posed significant challenges of their own, but the War Department could deal with these more quickly and easily. The War Department sought to resolve the more significant challenges Baker identified by emphasizing them in the education of the army's future senior officers at the AWC.[4]

Baker also asserted that the prewar officer education system had proven "inadequate and duplicatory in many respects." Therefore, he directed a comprehensive review of the entire army officer education system, aiming to improve school curricula and reorganize the school system as required. Thus, the first AWC commandant after the World War, Major General James W. McAndrew, reviewed the school's entire curriculum. Upon reflection, he realized that he could best achieve the goals Secretary Baker identified by reorganizing the faculty and rewriting the curriculum based on the staff organization of the AEF, rather than that of the prewar organization of the War Department. Fortunately, the 1920 National Defense Act (NDA) established a new war department based on similar logic, resulting in a post–World War I War Department organized much like the AEF staff and closely aligned with the new AWC curriculum and faculty as redesigned by McAndrew and his advisers between 1919 and 1921. Historian George Pappas has asserted, "McAndrew's visionary decision enabled retention of the core curriculum of the Army War College basically unchanged from 1919 to 1941." However, the AWC, while faced with the same fiscal constraints affecting the rest of the military during the interwar years, changed the organization of the course and updated the curriculum during this period, particularly during a major restructuring that the faculty completed the year before McNair's arrival there.[5]

Evolution of the Army's Officer Education System Before 1928

General of the Armies Pershing, desiring to keep military education current and relevant despite budget constraints, convened a board of officers in February 1922 to assess the organization and mission of the army's entire senior officer education system. Pershing appointed Brigadier General Edward F. McGlachlin, who had replaced McAndrew as commandant of the AWC in July 1921, to chair a board of officers appointed to determine how to restructure a school system designed for an army of 280,000 (as specified in the 1920 NDA), when Congress ensured that the army never achieved that actual strength. With regular army numbers falling below 150,000 by midyear, Pershing wanted to optimize the army schools for actual army officer strength, reducing wasteful spending to increase efficiency. As historian Harry P. Ball asserted, "Fundamentally, the problem was money."[6]

The McGlachlin board convened on February 20 to assess the organization and curricula of the army schools at Fort Leavenworth and the AWC and the relationship between them. The debate among members of the board soon devolved into a struggle between two competing priorities. Although budget cuts and personnel caps pointed to a need to seek efficiencies, existing war plans called for a minimum number of trained officers, which the army could not produce under some of the recommended courses of action. Colonel Hugh A. Drum, commandant of the School of the Line at Leavenworth, proposed significant reductions, including disestablishment of the AWC by combining it with Leavenworth's General Staff School. Drum envisioned a consolidated school that provided instruction on subjects applicable to echelons ranging from army corps through theater army, while the School of the Line would teach topics pertaining to army divisions through corps. For those aspects of the AWC curriculum dealing with matters of mobilization relating to industry, war plans, and the Zone of Interior, Drum suggested the War Department could teach these subjects to thirty-five officers detailed annually to their headquarters for a work-study program.[7]

Arguing against Drum's proposal, Brigadier General William Lassiter, of War Department G-3, reminded Pershing that the approved mobilization plan required 1,650 general staff trained officers: 800 from the School of the Line, 500 from the General Staff School, and 350 from the AWC, based on the specific topics covered at each school. Lassiter asserted that the War Department's mobilization plans justified retention of all three schools with no reductions in the established numbers of graduates, regardless of reductions in overall army personnel strength. Further, he (speaking for the entire AWC faculty) advised against expedients such as Drum's "understudy" program of officers detailed annually to the War Department.[8]

When McGlachlin submitted his board results to Pershing on March 30, they included a minority report from Colonel Harold B. Fiske, chief of the War Department G-3 training branch, a dissenting opinion from McGlachlin, and several less contentious dissenting views as alternatives to the recommendation contained in the majority report. Despite this lack of consensus, the board did agree on one key point: it did not recommend closing the AWC. In fact, against Hugh

Drum's recommendation, the majority report recommended leaving the AWC in situ while combining the two schools at Leavenworth into a yearlong Command and General Staff School that would provide instruction in command and general staff duties from the brigade through corps levels.[9]

Fiske, who had served as Pershing's G-5, chief of training (and McNair's immediate supervisor) on the AEF staff during World War I, focused his report on the nature of the education that officers should receive at the AWC. Fiske wrote in 1922 a highly critical assessment of the performance of officers at every level of command during the World War. In this report, he expressed an Uptonian view that America simply could not mobilize an army made up primarily of untrained civilians and expect it to meet the demands of modern warfare after only a few months of training.[10] On the basis of this view, short of maintaining a large standing army, Fiske believed Leavenworth should retain the responsibility for tactical, division-level-and-below command and staff officer training. However, he argued that the AWC should provide two paths, one focused on branch-specific staff duties for the majority of future senior officers and another reserved for the truly elite subset of those officers to prepare them specifically for the responsibility of high command. Ball argued, "Fiske's concept was original and on the surface seems to have much to commend it." However, his minority report did not persuade the board, which remained committed to an officer education that would "delineate the mission of its officer schools by branch of service and tactical echelon."[11]

McGlachlin also opposed the majority recommendation, but he took a different tack than Fiske, emphasizing the need to find a solution that would generate enough trained officers each year to lead an effective mobilization should the need arise. He argued for retention of both schools at Leavenworth, with the School of the Line focused on the division and the General Staff School on the corps and field army. As for the AWC, he advocated retaining its branch- and echelon-specific focus, but he believed it should prepare not only senior officers but also leaders in government and industry for the demands of leadership in a future war. As historian George Pappas put it, McGlachlin's influence gave the course "a distinct flavor of what today would be termed 'international relations and political science.'" Pappas also noted that these concepts of McGlachlin's "were carried on long after his departure from the War College."[12]

McGlachlin also raised a significant pedagogical issue by pointing to the similarities and differences that existed between the two schools' teaching methods. For example, instructors at both schools used the applicatory method of instruction, although their approaches varied. Historian Peter Schifferle has defined the applicatory method at Leavenworth as "the use of large lectures, smaller conferences that engaged students in dialogue with instructors, formal committees of ten students and two instructors, and graded problem-solving exercises."[13] The faculty's use of the applicatory method at the AWC differed in two key ways. First, although instructors did use faculty-approved school solutions in grading students' practical work, they used them differently than their counterparts at Fort Leavenworth, where most practical work was done by individuals, as opposed to using committees and boards at the AWC. This necessarily led to a different method of grading solutions to practical problems and more openness at the AWC to critiques of standing plans and policies.

The Leavenworth schools also differed from the AWC in that the mostly individual completion of their practical work meant that the students at Leavenworth had fewer opportunities for team building or learning from peers. The faculty intended the students to master doctrine, primarily through lectures by and discussions with instructors. This practice undoubtedly led to a more rigid program of instruction than one that emphasized team building, group learning, and individual study and creativity.[14] However, it also suited the needs of the Leavenworth schools, where many students received their first formal education for service at division and higher echelon units. Given most Leavenworth students' lack of experience in large units or general staffs, they needed to learn the basics before attempting to engage in group discussion and committee work to write critiques of doctrine or war plans and recommend changes to the War Department General Staff. In short, the Leavenworth schools served an entirely different purpose than the AWC.

Although both schools used curricula that emphasized military history and logistics, AWC assistant commandant Colonel H. B. Crosby noted the fundamental difference in the school's approach in his orientation lecture to the 1924–1925 class:

> I believe I speak the truth when I say that no one helps his rating by blindly accepting the views of the faculty on any subject. This is distinctly a college— where we learn from an exchange of ideas and not by accepting unquestioned either the views of the faculty or the views of the student. At Leavenworth we accepted and should have accepted the principles and doctrines laid down by the faculty of that school. Here we reach our own conclusions, faculty and student, following a full and free discussion of the subject.[15]

Crosby grasped the fundamental difference between the Leavenworth schools and the AWC: at Leavenworth, students needed to learn and demonstrate their understanding of basic army doctrine. Functioning as the army's common language, doctrine provided the foundation for how units would operate, ideally leading to a common understanding that provided the essential ability to anticipate friendly units' and fellow commanders' actions while communicating in a common language. Before one can diverge from doctrine effectively, one must understand it. Officers developed the latter skill at Leavenworth, preparing them to develop the former skill at the AWC. Perhaps Matheny put it best: "Leavenworth was about training; the War College was about education."[16]

Historian David E. Johnson criticized the interwar army officer education system in his book *Fast Tanks and Heavy Bombers,* but he did not clearly differentiate between the mission and educational methods of the Leavenworth schools and those of the AWC. Johnson argued, "The Army school system, rather than serving as an agent for change, focused almost completely on accepted doctrine." After describing the echelons on which each school focused, Johnson claimed: "Collectively, the schools focused on developing officers who could supervise the mobilization, fighting, and supplying of a mass army along World War I lines." He continued, "Although the Command and General Staff School at Fort Leavenworth, was generally viewed as the 'source of Army doctrine and procedure,' it was clearly a captive of the Army's sanctioned doctrine. Instruction remained riveted on conservative doctrines, largely ignoring emerging, competitive perspectives such as mechanization and air power."[17]

The flaw in Johnson's argument resulted from lumping together several distinct army officer educational institutions in his assessment rather than distinguishing between them. Johnson did not address the need to establish a common understanding of the army's accepted doctrine among the tiny core of regular army officers that would oversee the rapid expansion and training required during a future large-scale mobilization—the primary mission of the Leavenworth schools. Understanding this doctrine provided the army's field-grade officers with an essential common professional language and foundation on which to build their understanding of military art and science. Nor did he acknowledge the significant differences in the mission and instructional methodologies of the AWC compared to those of the Leavenworth schools. In particular, as he sought to prove that the army neglected emerging technologies in its officer education system, he did not mention the many lectures AWC students heard and committee work they took part in that focused on those topics. Specifically, research shows that by the 1920s, the curriculum covered air power, mechanization, and motorization in both lectures and practical exercises—the very subjects he claimed the army school system neglected.[18]

In May 1922, having weighed the various recommendations and dissenting views produced by the McGlachlin board, Pershing made his decision. He concurred with the consolidation of schools at Leavenworth into one institution—the Command and General Staff College (CGSC)—with a selective entrance process that would enable 250 officers per year to attend. The CGSC would instruct its students on matters pertaining to echelons through the army corps, and the AWC would focus on the field army and other elements making up the theater of operations. A fundamental shift underpinned these decisions. Reflecting the 1907 curriculum redesign, Pershing shifted the focus of the AWC from preparation for war to a curriculum that devoted at least equal attention to conduct of campaigns. As Ball argued, "After Pershing's decision, the study of the totality of the phenomenon of war had to compete with study of the combatant phase. Pershing's decision was not necessarily wrong, but it was limiting. To use Elihu Root's terms, Pershing moved the AWC away from the study of the great problems of national defense and toward the narrower problem of military science."[19] The education system focused on the doctrinal lessons derived from the AEF's World War I experience and sought to correct perceived problems arising from that experience.

By 1922, the AWC had adjusted its curriculum and reorganized its faculty to align with the consolidation of the Leavenworth schools and to match the organization of a wartime general staff, with G-1, G-2, G-3, and G-4 courses that focused on the functional responsibilities of each staff section in turn. The curriculum culminated in a course on war plans followed by a lengthy one on large unit command.[20] In each course, student committees used the applicatory method to review and propose updates to existing war plans for the War Department.[21]

During McGlachlin's tenure as commandant, he launched a fundamental shift in focus, rejecting his predecessor McAndrew's view that the AWC should focus on preparing its graduates to serve as general staff officers, instead emphasizing their preparation for large unit command while still covering the functions of the various general staff sections. In historian George Pappas's words, McGlachlin adjusted the curriculum in an "unremitting attempt . . . to impress the College with the idea that Command is the great thing in war, the true determinant of success or failure, and that the General Staff officer, while a part of the command, is but an adviser, an agent, a subordinate coadjutor of the Commander."[22] Thus, recent graduates of the CGSC encountered at the AWC a pedagogical philosophy that bore little resemblance to that of the faculty at Fort Leavenworth, and therefore they achieved complementary but different educational outcomes. Although the American populace recoiled from the notion of another war, these institutions, each in its own way, prepared a generation of officers for what most viewed as inevitable, whether the next war took place in the near or more distant future.

Interpreting Pershing's guidance somewhat loosely, McGlachlin led an evolution in the AWC curriculum. He included civilian representatives of the government and leaders of industry in the student body. He sought to eliminate the perceived overemphasis on competition among students by adopting a pass–fail grading system and encouraging cooperative work. McGlachlin also sought to reduce traditionally high attrition rates by convincing the War Department to cease issuing age waivers and by applying more stringent selection criteria.[23]

McGlachlin achieved a great deal during the 1922–1923 class. His initiatives led to the selection of a student body that possessed a wider variety of experience and background than previous classes. He also shifted the nature of the education further from the Leavenworth-style applicatory method, establishing a learning environment more like that at contemporary graduate schools, characterized by individual study and research, periodic gathering in seminar ("committee work"), and a supporting guest lecture program. Although the college still lacked comprehensive examinations and the requirement to write a thesis, groups rather than individuals worked together to find solutions to problems.[24]

Historian Michael Matheny has stressed that the consolidation of the two schools at Leavenworth into one meant that, "the overlap between the two institutions [the CGSC and the AWC] in operational art virtually ceased." Although the CGSC and AWC faculty used the same doctrine and texts dealing with large unit operations, the AWC "persisted on its own path of educating students through exercises, lectures, and conferences on joint and combined operations." The CGSC produced more graduates, but it did not encourage critical thinking or innovative group work. Instead, the CGSC focused on ensuring its graduates possessed a common foundation in army doctrine as a common language and way of thinking. The type of education required to create practitioners of operational art awaited those officers selected to attend the AWC—the future senior leaders of the army.[25]

The officer education system continued to evolve even as McGlachlin implemented Pershing's guidance and applied his own philosophy as commandant of the AWC. Soon after approving the modified recommendations of the McGlachlin board, Pershing appointed Harold Fiske to review their manner of implementation, focusing on the elimination of overlap between the CGSC and AWC curricula. After a detailed review of the AWC's new curriculum, Fiske recommended no significant changes. However, the Fiske board did delineate the boundary between the CGSC and AWC along unit echelon lines rather than functional ones. The board recommended the following AWC mission statement: "To train officers for (a) high command and staff to include units higher than army corps, (b) the War Department General Staff duty and duty in the office of the Assistant Secretary of War, (c) Corps Area Command and General Staff duty." Pershing approved this mission, which also made clear the echelons in which graduates would serve by adding to the board's recommendations the following statement: "The War College course will include the tactics of a typical army, acting independently or within an army group, covering phases of concentration, advance, deployment, combat and pursuit, with the general details of supply incident thereto."[26] Thus, the AWC assumed responsibility for all matters related to preparation for war, including the tactics and logistics of several echelons of army organizations, army–navy operations, and the complexities of economic and industrial mobilization.

Pershing ordered the AWC commandant to implement this new mission during the 1924–1925 academic year. The new commandant, Major General Hanson E. Ely, would oversee its implementation. According to Ball, "It was Ely who had convinced Pershing that the War College should teach field army operations, and that time for this instruction could be provided by reducing the time devoted to the G-1 and G-4 courses. Ely now had the opportunity to prove his thesis." However, based on the timing of Ely's appointment as commandant, the AWC curriculum for 1923–1924 remained essentially the same as McGlachlin planned it. Ely would have to wait until the following year to implement his desired changes.[27]

Ely's new curriculum added instruction related to field army and army group operations. The resulting increased focus on tactics led to deletion of much instruction related to industrial mobilization. Therefore, although Michael Matheny correctly noted that the CGSC served more for indoctrination while the AWC provided instruction in operational art, neither school gave officers adequate preparation for the demands of national mobilization. This increased the risk of a slow and incomplete mobilization in the future, like that of the AEF during the World War.

In his four years as commandant, Ely adjusted the curriculum each year to cover all of the topics he deemed essential while only briefly addressing the issues related to industrial mobilization. The creation of the Army Industrial College in 1924, considered a CGSC equivalent that produced about thirty-five procurement branch officers per year, helped seed each AWC class with a small number of students with some background in mobilization issues. Meanwhile, the AWC continued to narrow its focus on mobilization. By 1927, mobilization-related curricula dealt almost exclusively with personnel issues. In committee work, officers continued to analyze actual War Department plans, although the faculty oversimplified strategic considerations by telling these committees to begin work on the assumption, in Ball's words, "simply that a war had begun and that the object of war was obviously, victory."[28] Ely left the AWC in a state of flux and with a curriculum that neglected key strategic issues a mobilizing and expanding expeditionary army would face. Therefore, Ball asserted, "It was Ely's successor who finally articulated the role of the War College in a way that brought an end to experimentation and set the War College on a bearing that remained relatively constant."[29] Ely's replacement also created a stable and balanced curriculum the year before McNair's attendance, ensuring that several cohorts of future senior officers benefited from a common and effective AWC education.

Major General William D. Connor of the Corps of Engineers replaced Ely as commandant in November 1927. Army chief of staff Charles P. Summerall, who had replaced Pershing's successor, John L. Hines, in November 1926, made no changes to Pershing's guidance during Ely's tenure as commandant.[30] However, in 1927 he began to direct changes at both Leavenworth and the AWC. To resolve several problems caused by compression of the School of the Line and the General Staff School at Leavenworth into the single-year Command and General Staff School, Summerall directed lengthening of that course to two years beginning in 1928. He left responsibility for instruction in field army operations at the AWC. However, he approved a new AWC mission statement, which included a fundamental shift that differentiated between two basic types of activities: training and instruction. This distinction recognized that certain duties related to conducting army and joint operations on a general staff required specific skills, and the AWC bore the responsibility of providing the necessary training to ensure its graduates possessed those skills. By contrast, other duties (for example, those related to War Department or Assistant Secretary of War staff duties) required more than simple proficiency in certain skills, and Summerall understood that the AWC must provide broad and diverse instruction to help its graduates develop the necessary intuition to serve effectively in such positions.[31]

Connor received Summerall's instructions in December 1927, one month after assuming duties as commandant. With the 1927–1928 class nearly halfway to graduation, Connor focused on deciding how to implement the necessary adjustments before the next class reported. Two faculty members in particular, Colonels Troup Miller (a G-3 instructor) and Walter C. Sweeney (head of the G-1 department) provided Connor with detailed and influential advice. Miller wrote a succinct history of the curriculum since 1919, using it to support his argument that war-planning instruction had gradually grown into the primary topic in the curriculum at the expense of instruction in both field operations and command. Sweeney made the important point that, as Ball put it, "past rhetoric about 'command versus staff' and 'operations' tended to obscure the fundamental problem facing the War College. That problem, as Sweeney saw it, was that the War College had two related but nonetheless distinct fields of interest. One field was the preparation for war; the other was the conduct of war." On the basis of these officers' advice, Connor pursued a curriculum redesign founded in a Clausewitzian conception of war, and he intended the redesign to lead not just to a rational curriculum but also to a balanced one founded on logic that students could easily understand.[32]

According to Ball, Sweeney probably drew this insight from the War College Library's translation of Carl von Clausewitz's *Vom Krieg* (1832), in which Clausewitz distinguished between the two fundamental activities related to war: preparation for war and war itself. Thomas Bruscino, in "Naturally Clausewitzian: US Army Theory and Education from Reconstruction to the Interwar Years," provided additional support to this assertion by demonstrating that US army officers studied Clausewitz during the interwar period—much earlier than sometimes asserted. He also explained why, as Americans, these officers naturally gravitated toward the Clausewitzian view of war.[33]

The updated curriculum that Connor approved for the 1928–1929 class benefited primarily from both a streamlined curriculum and faculty organization. This included a clear division of the course into two phases: preparation for war and conduct of war. The changes also included reducing the number of faculty sections from seven to four: G-1, G-2, G-3, and G-4 (eliminating the command, assistant secretary of war, and war plans divisions). Connor adopted this structure because it more closely resembled that of operational unit headquarters (based on the original French model). Connor eliminated the command section confident in his conviction that the same education would prepare an officer both for service on a general staff and as a commander of a large unit. He believed that the characteristics required of a commander stemmed more from natural qualities than anything instructors could teach in a classroom. He believed army schools should produce competent officers; it fell to the officer selection process to ensure the army's best commanded its large units.[34]

McNair and the Army War College Class of 1929

The changes Connor put in place during the 1927–1928 academic year enabled him to restore balance to the curriculum by adding more industrial mobilization instruction and increasing the length of the war plans course by six weeks to facilitate more group instruction. Thus, McNair attended a revamped and much improved AWC with a new curriculum that included both lecture-based instruction and a great deal of practical application in student committees, in which students rotated through peer leadership positions. These committees worked on actual war plans that involved not just military but also industrial and political planning considerations.[35] The AWC assistant commandant, Colonel J. L. DeWitt, summed up the school's purpose in simple terms during the class of 1929's orientation briefing. He told the incoming students that the faculty sought to prepare officers of proven potential for service on the General Staff of the War Department, or in senior staff positions or in command of large units, and to conduct effective joint planning and operations with their fellow officers in the US navy.[36]

DeWitt also told the incoming class, "The work of the Faculty and the students should be so intimate and closely interwoven that all will get the benefit of the experience of his fellows. Apart from the course, the bringing together of so many men from all the activities of the Army and Navy is in itself most beneficial." DeWitt made it clear that the faculty considered the students "selected officers of proven efficiency, as demonstrated by their records." Therefore, the school was not concerned with testing or weeding out of the students—its sole focus was to educate and train them so they could reach their maximum potential.[37]

DeWitt addressed the use of the two terms, *train* and *instruct,* in the AWC mission, demonstrating that he, like Connor, understood that differences in interpretation of these terms existed among US military officers. As DeWitt put it,

> Exception may properly be taken to the words *train* and *instruct,* they being synonymous as used, because the course here can hardly be expected to actually *train* an officer, but rather to give him an opportunity to gain a fundamental knowledge of the basic principles essential to the performance of Command and General Staff duties. The education of a General Staff officer must embrace a familiarity with what is necessary to qualify an officer for high command, for the education of the higher leader and of the General Staff officer must be along the same lines: the *suitability,* however, of an officer so educated for either duty is dependent on his temperament and his natural qualities.[38]

DeWitt also emphasized the importance in an institution like the AWC of encouraging initiative and original thought so long as individuals based their ideas on sound reasoning and mastery of the relevant facts. He described the instruction the students would receive as indirect rather than direct with the faculty planning courses and supplying references while giving the students full latitude to reach their own opinions, conclusions, and recommendations.[39] He said this same philosophy applied to the students' individual study projects as well. The faculty only expected that each study dealt with a topic that required "General Staff action in that it is of interest to the Army or Navy, or both," and offered a "solution of its questions [that] should contribute something of value to the betterment of national defense."[40]

DeWitt's comments about committee work highlighted the freethinking nature of the educational environment at the AWC and demonstrated its similarity to today's best professional military education institutions. DeWitt emphasized the criticality and challenging nature of this type of work, highlighting the role of the chairman, who must lead the committee while "lacking the powers of command"—a role typically referred to today as peer leadership. This required "tact, judgment, patience, and forbearance." By providing all students opportunities to serve as either committee or subcommittee chairmen or leaders of staff sections, the faculty would teach its students the similar but distinct skills of coordination and cooperation.[41]

McNair's AWC education began with the preparation for war course, organized in a structure similar to a general staff. The first subcourse, the operations and training division (G-3), began with ten days of lectures on a wide range of topics. These included "The Development of the War Department General Staff and its Relation to other War Department Agencies," "The Joint Army and Navy Board and the War Plans Division of the War Department General Staff," "Naval Organization," and the "War Department General Mobilization Plan." Committee work began on September 14, 1928, with eight committees running concurrently, culminating in committee presentations to and assessments by the entire class. The committees analyzed a wide variety of topics, to include plans and preparations for the Franco-Prussian War and the Russo-Japanese War; US War Department plans and preparations for the wars it had fought since the Revolution; German, British, and French land forces' plans and preparations for the World War; and British and German naval war plans and preparations for the World War. Finally, one special committee analyzed the development of rules, regulations, and procedures for map maneuvers and field exercises.[42]

During the two weeks students spent in committee, they held a variety of conferences that included students from a wide cross section of the class. This provided each committee with important insights that strengthened the findings they included in their final reports. The conferences addressed topics including the future organization and use of air forces; War Department mobilization and concentration plans; peacetime American military policy and defense requirements; and the organization, equipment, and use of mechanized forces in future wars.[43]

McNair served on Committee 3, which the faculty directed to study "rules, regulations, and procedures for the conduct of Map Maneuvers (War Games) and Field Exercises at the Army War College." This committee served a unique purpose. Given the commandant's intent to increase the emphasis on the conduct of war course, Humphrey directed the committee to conduct its work with the intent of improving the quality of war games and exercises the class would participate in during that course later in the academic year.[44] The committee considered both the particular needs and facilities of the AWC and observations from students and faculty who had participated during previous assignments in maneuvers and war games. This led to its preparation of a lengthy report laying out recommendations specific to the AWC but also applicable to the general role of map maneuvers and field exercises in military education.[45]

The committee report included a description of the "Place of Map Maneuvers and Field Exercises in Military Education" that read: "The committee's conception of the place of map maneuvers and field exercises in military education is that they serve best as a means of giving practice in the application of the principles of strategy, tactics, and logistics to the solutions of concrete military problems, and also that they serve as a means of testing proposed military operations, thus determining the soundness and adequacy of the plans for said operations."[46] The report covered nine common observations, many gleaned from student comments at committee conferences, but its primary emphasis revolved around umpiring techniques. The committee observed that the productivity of war games and exercises depended primarily on the selection and effective preparation of a well-prepared senior umpire who possessed individual authority over similarly well-prepared subordinate umpires. Adequate umpire preparation required both effective exercise design and umpires' familiarity with the situation. This enabled umpires to make fair and consistent decisions based on commonly understood rules and deliver their decisions rapidly to avoid artificial delays in execution.[47]

The committee highlighted its most significant observation in the first paragraph of the section summarizing the conference findings: "The success or failure of an exercise depends largely upon the personality of the umpire. Careful selection of umpires is essential." This insight stemmed from both the committee's experience and observations made by other officers during conferences. Various observations centered on umpiring, particularly the chronic shortage of well-trained umpires. Officers also observed that friendly forces often lacked intelligence about the enemy, even when they acted appropriately to obtain it, leading the umpires to inject unrealities into the exercise scenario to stay on schedule, creating "unsound situations, due usually to a failure to carry the preliminary play far enough" for operations to end in their logical conclusion.[48]

The committee concluded that Leavenworth's "Methods of Training (Provisional)" of 1925 covered the basic guidelines for war games and exercises adequately, and it advised the faculty to use it in future AWC war game and exercises. To correct the deficiencies in execution noted by the committee, they recommended several changes, all involving umpiring procedures. These included ensuring umpires possessed adequate knowledge of the situation to make logical decisions, assigning a single umpire with the authority to render timely and final decisions, and ensuring umpires conducted sufficient preliminary play to ensure the war game would not devolve into an unrealistic situation based on lack of preparedness or rigid adherence to a timetable. Finally, the committee recommended assigning umpires directly to the various supporting units, rather than organizing them along functional lines (that is, G-1 or G-2), a method that inevitably led umpires to make poor decisions in situations for which they lacked the appropriate expertise.[49]

By the end of the G-3 course, McNair had heard lectures on a wide range of current operational topics, including the likely impact of emerging technologies on future warfare. Most significantly, he served on a committee that completed a highly detailed study of the conduct of war games and exercises. This added to McNair's already significant expertise in training by giving him a chance to study the root causes of common problems across the army, based on the experience of his AWC peers. In addition to the main committee report, McNair helped prepare a guide to the conduct of maneuvers, focusing on the training, procedures, and data necessary to facilitate effective umpiring. This detailed study made McNair particularly qualified to serve as a senior umpire in future war games and maneuvers.[50]

McNair and his classmates next moved on to the G-1 (personnel) course, where they studied subjects primarily dealing with personnel-related mobilization issues. These centered on the question of procurement (whether voluntary or through some form of conscription or selective service), the role of the reserves and the National Guard in time of war, and the issue of personnel replacements and morale in expeditionary situations. The initial lecture series included a diverse range of speakers in addition to AWC G-1 instructors. A representative of the navy personnel office spoke about naval personnel mobilization plans. The chief of the militia bureau discussed the federalization of National Guard forces in time of war. The judge advocate general explained the legal relationship of the War Department to the other departments of government. Finally, Mr. C. R. Dooley, a representative of industry, discussed America's civilian wartime personnel concerns; the World War had highlighted the competing priorities of mobilizing men to fight and keeping men on the production lines so industry could produce adequate war matériel. Dooley anticipated America would face this challenge again in any future large-scale mobilization.[51]

The students then began their committee work and supporting conferences. Although each committee reported on a significant issue related to personnel acquisition and retention (in both the military and industry), two of them stand out as particularly interesting. The first, Committee 5 on "Reserve Systems for the Regular Army and National Guard," bears particular significance because McNair served as its chair. The second, Committee 7, analyzed the issue of replacements, a topic the AWC faculty deemed a major problem that the War Department had never solved satisfactorily and must solve before undertaking any future large-scale mobilization.[52]

Following the G-1 course committee directives, McNair's Committee 5 conducted "a study of reserve systems which might be adopted to make up deficiencies in the present peace strength and organization of the Regular Army and National Guard and thus provide more adequate forces for immediate and effective employment in the outbreak of an emergency." The directive pointed out that reductions in the size of the regular army and curtailment of the development of the National Guard meant the nation would suffer "an acute shortage of trained men available for active operations at the outbreak of a war." Therefore, the committee should determine whether the army could overcome this challenge through a system of reserve forces "obligated to join the organized forces when emergency requires." The directive also highlighted that the "G-3 is greatly interested in this study also, and the G-3 viewpoint should not be lost sight of in reaching conclusions."[53]

In his *History of the United States Army*, Russell Weigley provided a succinct explanation of the problem McNair's committee confronted. He wrote, "America in the 1920s was dedicated not only to the dream that wars had ended forever, but even more strongly to the more prosaic fetish of economy in government. The goals of the National Defense Act of 1920 broke down because Congress and the executive gave them lip service but little practical support." Therefore, not only did the regular army receive funding adequate to support only slightly more than half of its authorized strength but the National Guard and organized reserves suffered as well. Limited appropriations meant that the National Guard also only reached about half its authorized strength throughout the 1920s. Further, while the Reserve Officer Training Corps (ROTC) system provided a pool of trained reserve officers, they conducted no mandatory periodic training after graduation, and the Organized Reserve Enlisted Reserve Corps, as Weigley observed, "was practically nonexistent because there were no means of recruiting it."[54] McNair's committee faced a daunting challenge because personnel who served during the World War remembered the challenges associated with personnel mobilization and the competing demands with a quickly ramped-up industrial effort— challenges the army did not have the authority to overcome. McNair set out to provide reasonable solutions for the War Department to recommend to the secretary of war by organizing subcommittees to study the reserve systems of foreign armies, the US navy, and the National Guard. A fourth subcommittee used the findings of the other three and insights gleaned from student conferences to "develop a system which will provide an enlisted reserve for the Regular Army, including a draft of necessary legislation and an estimate of the annual cost involved."[55]

The first (and shortest) subcommittee report found that of several foreign nations' reserve military systems studied, "the reserve system of Great Britain is the most nearly applicable to the needs of the United States, since it is based on voluntary recruitment. The various categories are based on state of training and degree of availability. Most categories receive training annually. All are paid."[56] Perhaps most significantly, the subcommittee found that all of the eight major powers it analyzed had some form of organized reserve; however, only Great Britain's system included voluntary participation. These systems all involved a period of active service, followed by a longer period (in most cases several years) on inactive reserve status during which members conducted mandatory periodic training. This meant of nine major world powers, only the United States lacked a sizable and regularly trained pool of reservists available for service in the ground services in time of war.[57]

The second subcommittee found that the US navy had a system of reserves only marginally better than that of the army, with a fleet naval reserve of approximately 18,700 men required to perform some period of ship duty annually (for pay). These men remained ready to augment the active navy if required. The merchant marine served a commercial function but remained prepared to augment the navy's transport fleet if required. Formed under the same law as the navy's reserve system, the marine corps reserve system also proved to be marginally effective. Although its 500 officers and 8,400 enlisted men did not perform any annual training, they did have to pass a physical examination to join. The subcommittee concluded, "The Naval Reserve System is sound and workable." They found it had produced sizable numbers of men ready to augment the active navy and marine corps in time of emergency. Its members recognized "some of the features of the Naval Reserve system are not desirable for the Army" but concluded that the navy and marine corps reserve systems provided suitable models on which to base an army reserve system.[58]

The third subcommittee found itself tackling the quite contentious issue of the reserve system for the National Guard. It quickly identified two significant issues. First, the National Guard recruited personnel to serve as National Guard reservists to augment guard units in the event of mobilization, but no army reserve system existed to enable a similar augmentation of regular army units—an issue that seemed to the subcommittee to be a poor prioritization of assets. They also learned that the National Guard Bureau either aligned most of these reservists with an existing unit or simply left them unaligned. These seemed to be far less logical options than using these reserves to form many of the 368 units (out of 3,894 total units in the National Guard) that remained unformed.[59]

The subcommittee identified three additional weaknesses of the system of National Guard reserves. National Guard unit commanders lacked the time to recruit active personnel and reservists, the lack of pay often deterred recruits from entering the reserves or from participating in training after induction, and "The enrollment of reservists has not been pushed from above as no trouble is anticipated in filling up units in case of emergency."[60] Although lack of pay appeared to be the most significant of these issues, the subcommittee did not recommend that the War Department provide funding for National Guard reserves until it had created and funded a regular army enlisted reserve system—a far more significant priority, in the committee's estimation.[61] The subcommittee ultimately concluded, "The value of a National Guard reservist over a new recruit is very small," and it therefore recommended "that no change be made in the present provision of law or regulations for an Enlisted Reserve for the National Guard until an enlisted reserve for the Regular Army has been provided."[62]

McNair's fourth subcommittee, directed to design a proposed compulsory reserve system for the regular army, first reviewed the army's five congressionally mandated missions. It found that "all of the missions . . . are of vital importance and no single one of them can be safely neglected."[63] It went on to state that as a result of the realities of fiscal constraint and isolationist influence, "the present strength is entirely inadequate for the fulfillment of the peace-time missions of the Regular Army." Therefore, the whole system rested on a false fundamental assumption. Instead of possessing a regular army capable of its peacetime role and needing reserves only for augmentation in the case of a national emergency, America required a system of reserves that could also account for those routine missions for which the regular army currently found itself unprepared in peacetime.[64]

The subcommittee found that the army was at a disturbing level of unpreparedness, mostly because of personnel shortages and no trained regular army reserves. Of the 17,728 officers and 280,000 enlisted men currently authorized, the regular army only consisted of 12,000 officers and 115,000 enlisted men assigned. Despite these shortfalls, the subcommittee observed that a recent War Department decision to increase the strength of the air corps by 15,000 men "is now being made at the expense of the other branches of the army." This meant that any crisis that required the regular army to reach its initial war strength of 450,000 would require an increase of 223,000 men, rather than the 153,000 it would require if operating at its authorized peacetime strength. Further complicating matters, of its authorized force structure of nine divisions, three of the regular army's divisions existed only on paper, and the other six lacked a significant percentage of their authorized personnel. Thus, mobilization would not simply involve reinforcing understrength divisions. Rather, it would require the much more daunting task of bringing six divisions up to strength while forming three new divisions—a third of the total force.[65]

This led the subcommittee to a logical but disturbing conclusion. At its current strength, the War Department could not use any significant portion of the regular army to fight while receiving and training new recruits; their sheer number and lack of training would require the entire regular army to act as trainers and cadres around which to form new units. Therefore, the subcommittee argued that any system of reserves must provide for at least 91,000 fully trained personnel, ready to join their designated units immediately to help train new recruits. Any viable system of reserves must enable the regular army, at whatever strength it currently existed, to respond to the national emergency that prompted mobilization while simultaneously training new recruits and forming new units. This meant that any acceptable system of reserves would have to bring the regular army up to the strength of 450,000 designated in the 1920 NDA at a minimum. Given the severely limited active force structure of the regular army since the World War, even if Congress approved such a massive system of trained reserves, the entire regular army would have to serve in time of war as "merely a training machine for turning out reservists."[66]

McNair provided a detailed and unanimously approved report of his committee's findings to the director of the G-1 division and briefed the whole class on the report. McNair and his fellow committee members had gained a particularly detailed understanding of the problem of establishing a system of enlisted army reserves in the United States. However, it remained outside of the US army's control to do any more than merely identify the problem, which remained unresolved even though the systems currently used in both Great Britain and in America's own navy and marine corps provided proven and affordable models on which to base a system of army reserves made up solely of volunteers.[67]

Although McNair did not hold a leadership position in the G-4 course, which immediately followed the G-1 course and covered a broad range of logistics issues during a month of lectures and committee work, he did lead a subcommittee in the last of the staff section–aligned courses, the G-2 (military intelligence) course. The faculty placed the G-2 course last in the staff section sequence on the basis of the logic that the students required the education and training they received in the other courses to prepare friendly staff estimates before attempting to anticipate an enemy's estimate of the situation and most likely courses of action. The faculty expected the students not only to master the duties of a G-2 staff officer but also to learn to think like the enemy—a key to developing realistic and comprehensive war plans.[68]

Interestingly, in his orientation to the G-2 course, DeWitt referred to the curriculum's having a cultural motive in that it aimed "to stimulate interest in world politics, economics and social conditions, beyond a bare superficial knowledge of those subjects."[69] This highlights the significant shift that the AWC sought to create in its graduates' worldviews, enabling them to develop original, creative solutions to the problems they studied based on a sound understanding of world events and the ability to see a military problem from a perspective other than their own.

The students first received a series of detailed briefings on the military, economic, political, and social status of the world's major powers, including Russia, Great Britain, Mexico, Japan, and China. They next formed into committees that analyzed the contributions to existing war plans by the War Department G-2. This required the class to consider a wide range of factors including international law and American foreign policy, comparative military power and resources among potential enemies of the United States, and intelligence estimates of foreign military capabilities and propensities. McNair served on Committee 8, G-2 "Studies on the British Empire." He chaired one of two subcommittees, which updated the existing military estimate of the British empire, including Great Britain's likely intentions involving use of military force and the most dangerous coalitions that it might join.[70]

After the G-2 course, the students transitioned to the six-week-long war plans course, during which McNair served in the G-3 division of Group 5, "War Plans—Green," which dealt with possible hostilities between the United States and Mexico. In his course orientation, DeWitt described its three primary goals. The faculty sought to provide instruction in development of war plans by allowing the students the opportunity to analyze and recommend updates to real-world colored plans. Simultaneously, the war plans course highlighted the necessity of coordinating army and navy plans—an important developmental opportunity. Finally, the faculty used much of the analysis prepared by the committees to develop exercise scenarios for the conduct of war course, executed near the end of the academic year.[71]

Each of the six student planning staffs prepared four component parts for each plan they updated: the joint plan, the army strategic plan, the army concentration plan, and the army mobilization plan. This gave the students experience dealing with issues related to interservice cooperation, planning military operations that would achieve strategic objectives, preparing detailed troop movement tables to support those operations, and orchestrating the mobilization of the required personnel. Although the faculty did not expect the student groups to develop complete, executable plans in the time allotted, they did expect them to address the required areas based on detailed research of all information available. They required of each student staff a "simple, flexible, and practicable" plan that "definitely set forth the objectives upon the attainment of which it is counted to win the war and the operations to be undertaken initially to that end," which would "form the basis of the initial concentration and strategic deployment."[72]

Immediately after the war plans course ended, the second half of the AWC began: the four-month-long conduct of war course. This course focused on practical, hands-on application through map maneuvers, map problems, terrain exercises, and field reconnaissance. Students assigned to various general staff positions studied the strategy and tactics of field armies, and they addressed both army and joint considerations in their practical exercises. They relied on both actual War Department plans and historical case studies to achieve the four course outcomes. These included training participants for positions of high command, testing the soundness of the war plans prepared in the preceding course, familiarizing the class with the mobilization-related features of certain areas of the United States, and training officers in the conduct of map maneuvers and command post exercises.[73]

During the first period of the six-phase course, McNair served as the chairman of Command Group 3, which analyzed French operations on the Western Front in 1914 from mobilization through the First Battle of the Marne. His committee's final sixty-page report provided a thorough assessment of French mobilization, operational plans, and combat operations, providing an insightful critical analysis of French decisions and their outcomes. For example, McNair's group highlighted the illogical French decision to assume the offensive—a choice they made despite their lack of any advantage in mobilization or troop strength. In the report, McNair's Command Group 3 perceptively linked this decision with the post-1871 "military renaissance" that led to the French "creed of the offensive."[74]

During the second period of the course McNair served as a recorder for the "Assistant Umpire Group for Historical Studies." The students conducting the historical study analyzed the attack of the British Fourth Army in August 1918 by conducting map maneuvers, facilitated by umpires who executed each side's plan for the day. The umpires rendered decisions and provided updated information to the staffs overseeing the Red (Great Britain) and Blue sides conducting the map maneuvers. This gave McNair a bird's-eye view of the umpire process for a map maneuver. It also led to an opportunity for McNair to gain further insight regarding umpire procedures. This occurred during McNair's involvement in a study of the AWC's internal procedures for the conduct of umpire duties during maneuvers.[75]

A lengthy debate had ensued during the second period maneuver between Major General Connor and his staff regarding the quality of execution of the map maneuvers. This prompted Connor to order a comprehensive review of the AWC maneuver procedures, including detailed and honest critical input from one of the student command groups. On the basis of guidance he received from Connor, the assistant commandant, Colonel DeWitt, directed each subcommittee of Command Group 3, the one that conducted the Green map maneuver, to submit a set of written recommendations for improving maneuver execution procedures two weeks after the maneuver ended.[76] Writing for the command group's umpires, McNair authored a three-page memorandum consisting of the umpires' observations and recommendations, providing valuable insight that improved procedures specific to the conduct of map maneuvers at the AWC.[77]

Many of McNair's comments applied not only to AWC map maneuvers but also to the conduct of umpire duties in any exercise. For example, McNair advised giving ample time for participants to familiarize themselves with the situation before execution began, and he pointed out the problems associated with appointing partisan umpires, or umpires with an attachment to one side and therefore often biased when rendering decisions. He also advised providing more time for deliberation, coordination, and staff conferences by having the command groups work through fewer situations, but more deliberately and in more detail. Finally, McNair expressed doubt that map maneuvers could replicate the actual functioning of a staff, but they did offer value in teaching command and staff duties, as well as testing war plans.[78]

During the third period, the course focus shifted to a Blue–Orange scenario, in which both sides fought without allies. For this period, McNair served in the G-4 (services of supply) staff section on the Blue side. During the fourth period, McNair found himself in the Blue forces' G-3 section, facing a "special situation" involving an Orange invasion of Blue possessions in the Western Pacific Ocean, followed immediately by Red and Maroon (Italy) naval force operations against Blue shipping in all other oceans. Although seeming rather unlikely in retrospect, this particular contingency shows the comprehensiveness of the War Department's various colored plans by the late 1920s, which covered a wide range of potential threats. This variety provided significant diversity in the training opportunities that they provided for AWC students.[79]

The last two periods of the conduct of war course involved a significant change in activity for the class. Instead of another map maneuver, the student staff groups first conducted a command post exercise in field conditions and then a reconnaissance of America's Northeast theater. As described in the command post exercise instructions, the exercise differed significantly from a map problem: "(a) *Actual terrain conditions* will govern in all plans and orders; (b) All headquarters will be operated under field conditions, as far as it is practicable to do so; (c) Signal communications and message centers will be installed and operated by the Signal Corps. These facilities will be used exclusively in the exercise." The faculty provided cars and airplanes to enable command group reconnaissance and brought in faculty from the Quartermaster Corps, Air Corps Tactical, and Signal Corps Schools to serve as assistant umpires and provide technical advice. As in the map maneuvers, staff groups studied both historical cases and existing War Department plans, only under field conditions and on real terrain.[80]

For his individual graduation requirement, McNair prepared a seventeen-page paper, supported by seven highly detailed tables and graphs, offering a recommendation for how the War Department should use the limited funds available each year to maximize the level of preparedness among all arms of the US military—active, National Guard, and reserve.[81] He concluded the report with fifteen recommendations. These included establishing a more specific national military objective, continuing development of the regular army while either slowing or suspending expansion of the National Guard, increasing use of ROTC graduates as officers in the National Guard, expanding the organized reserves and improving their officer development programs, and providing pay for all personnel serving in the reserves. These conclusions supported his overall recommendation "that the Regular Army as a whole and the War Department especially, with broad vision, continue their efforts, so notably successful to date, to the end that there may be a maximum of military preparedness with the total resources available from year to year."[82]

Although he could not control national-level decisions regarding appropriation of funds, this research study reflected McNair's continued concern about reliance on a national guard over which the federal government held little authority, limiting the regular army's ability to affect its training readiness or officer education. It also demonstrated that he believed limited defense dollars would provide a greater return if spent on a federally controlled and monitored army reserve—a capability the nation currently lacked.

Two days after the end of the final command post exercise and reconnaissance, Major General Connor gave a brief closing address to the soon-to-graduate class. Having interacted daily with the students, faculty, and War Department staff for the past academic year, Connor said he would limit his address to only two subjects, one general and one personal. First, Connor reminded the class that the demand among officers to attend the AWC far exceeded the school's capacity. He told the class,

> I mention this at this time merely to bring out the fact and impress upon you that while the Regular Army itself is a nucleus in our National Army, that you and the other graduates of the Army War College are a nucleus within a nucleus, and remembering that to whom much is given, much will be expected, and obligation rests upon you and that obligation is to use the things you have learned here in regard to the doctrines of national defense and the principles of military training, not only in your ordinary military duties but, what is of more importance I think, that you should spread them to the Army at large and by the "Army" I want to use the word in its full sense, its legal sense, and it is just as important that you should spread sound doctrine to the civilian components of the Army as it is that you should spread sound principles to the Army itself.[83]

On a more personal note, Connor discussed the topic of aging. Here he touched on a particularly relevant issue in an army that often retained officers in their current grade for well over a decade and that had no system for moving aging officers aside to make room for the upward mobility of their more youthful and energetic subordinates. He urged the soon-to-be graduates to stay young, explaining,

> Youth means vigor, enthusiasm and receptivity. Without health, which is vigor, a man can neither take advantage of the opportunities that a kind fate or his own ability may give to him, nor can he enjoy any measure of success that may come to him for any reason. Without enthusiasm you cannot hope to inspire in others that will to do, that belief in your projects, which is half the victory in the battle toward achievement. Without receptivity to new ideas and methods, you are living in the past, you are a tale that has been told in this world of today where new marvels spring into being with startling frequency.[84]

In his brief remarks, Connor had addressed two of the most critical challenges the graduating officers would face in the aging, underresourced army that they would soon reenter. He stressed the need to seek continual self-improvement while passing on their education to the army at large, and the challenge of remaining youthful in mind and body amid an aging cohort of regular army officers. Connor understood what these future senior leaders needed to do so that they could cope with the intellectual and potentially physical challenges of the future.

In a 2011 *War and Society* article, Grant W. Jones emphasized the value of the AWC education to future senior leaders of large units like armies and army groups—a particularly valuable educational opportunity at a time when the US army possessed no such units on active duty. Writing about one of McNair's classmates, Dwight D. Eisenhower, Jones highlighted the value of the AWC in developing "professional mastery of the military art."[85]

Upon graduation, McNair received an efficiency report for the academic year in which Major General Connor rated him "superior," with no noted deficiencies, and recommended him to hold peacetime command or staff positions at the brigade, division, or War Department General Staff level. Connor judged McNair to be "an officer of high professional attainments, able, energetic and of sound judgment, quiet but forceful." He also rated McNair's potential for high command or a senior position on the War Department General Staff "superior," and evaluated him fully qualified for duty with civilian components. This exceptional efficiency report also included a letter of commendation for the superior nature of McNair's individual research project, which Connor forwarded to the War Department, calling it a "study of exceptional merit made at the Army War College."[86]

McNair departed the AWC having completed a challenging curriculum intended to prepare graduates for high command and senior general staff positions. He also attended at a time when the curriculum, having just undergone significant changes as part of the reorganization of the army's officer education program, included a particular focus on both military and civilian–industrial mobilization for war. McNair prepared in the summer of 1929 to embark on a new stage of his career. He had set himself apart as a superior officer even among the select subset of officers chosen to attend the course while receiving an education that prepared him for duty as a commander or general staff officer in an upper-echelon army unit. As a select member of Connor's "nucleus within a nucleus" of well-educated senior officers, McNair soon put his AWC experience to use in demanding jobs where he would foster innovation and improve army organization, despite the increasingly constrained resources available during the years of the Great Depression.[87]

6
Getting Over the Hump

Upon his graduation from the Army War College (AWC), McNair returned to his basic branch, serving as the deputy commandant of the Field Artillery School for the next four years. Although McNair served in a largely administrative position, he contributed significantly to innovative efforts the gunnery department pursued during his tenure there. A longtime believer in the superiority of observed fires and the need to provide forward guns and observers to support attacking infantry, McNair strongly supported the gunnery department's effort to find ways to provide faster, more accurate, and more effective fire support in open warfare conditions. He contributed most significantly to the innovative methods the gunnery department developed by shielding the department from the resistance of traditional-minded senior field artillery officers. These officers opposed the work younger gunnery department personnel undertook to update fire direction methods because many of their ideas involved establishment of centralized control at regimental or higher headquarters over guns traditionally controlled by battery commanders.

Innovation at the Field Artillery School, 1929–1933

The 1923 *Field Service Regulations* devoted more pages to the issue of artillery support to the infantry than any other topic. Although artillery might arguably be the king of modern battle, unreliable communications and difficulty observing and adjusting fires remained a major challenge to the realization of artillery's full potential. The field artillery branch devoted significant effort to finding solutions to these problems, particularly at the Field Artillery School, located at Fort Sill, Oklahoma. After graduating from the AWC, McNair reported for duty on July 23, 1929, to serve as the assistant commandant of the Field Artillery School.[1] Long known as an outstanding officer in his branch, subordinates acknowledged the new energy McNair brought to the position and to the Field Artillery School as a whole. Major Carlos Brewer, chief instructor in the school's gunnery department,

Lieutenant Colonel Lesley J. McNair, Field Artillery School Assistant Commandant, Fort Sill, Oklahoma, 1929. Courtesy of Fort Sill National Historic Landmark and Museum

Field Artillery School Gunnery Department, 1929 (seated left: Major Carlos Brewer; seated right: Captain William A. Campbell; standing left: Captain Russell G. Burkalow; standing right: First Lieutenant Edwin L. Sibert). Courtesy of Fort Sill National Historic Landmark and Museum

later said McNair "could get an awful lot out of people" and called him "extremely thorough and very, very capable."[2]

McNair put these qualities to use overseeing all activities of the Field Artillery School and in particular supporting the gunnery department's efforts to develop and instruct students in new fire direction techniques. The school had already made progress in the delivery of fires by the time McNair arrived at the school, but it achieved perhaps the most significant advances during his four years there. Although McNair served in an administrative position and appears to have had little direct involvement with the gunnery department personnel who actually developed, tested, and trained new fire procedures, he oversaw all training activities, and all memoranda and reports produced by any of the school's departments passed across his desk. In retrospect, the progress made at the Field Artillery School in modernizing gunnery procedures proved truly remarkable, particularly since interwar conservatism and lack of funding for weapons technology hindered the efforts of the dedicated personnel assigned to the school. Nevertheless, McNair saw the potential in their efforts and lent essential support to the officers of the gunnery department. The advances achieved by the Field Artillery School during this period served as the foundation for the development of incredibly effective, devastatingly powerful artillery support over the coming years.[3]

In an unpublished article titled "Fort Sill and the Golden Age of Field Artillery," Russell A. Gugeler of the US Army Center of Military History described the process of postwar artillery innovation that had already begun in the school's gunnery department and continued with McNair's support during his tenure as assistant commandant. In the first several years after the end of the World War, regular army officers recognized the need to overcome limitations in the artillery support available during that war. Limited mobility of guns, inadequate means of communications, and laborious fire direction techniques greatly reduced the effectiveness of American field artillery during the war. Furthermore, only a few years after the war, many artillerymen already recognized that machine guns mounted on newly developed tanks made a future scenario in which war consisted primarily of static fighting between entrenched forces highly unlikely. Therefore, officers in the Field Artillery School's gunnery department sought ways to adapt artillery to the more fluid, mobile form of warfare likely in a future scenario. However, despite sporadic efforts to improve fire techniques, Gugeler argued, "there was less agreement on the direction of the changes than there was resistance to changes of any kind."[4]

The Field Artillery Center finally began to make progress upon the assignment of Major Jacob L. Devers, McNair's former platoon leader, as director of the gunnery department in 1925. Described by one historian as "a man of action and decision," Devers commenced a deliberate effort to make fire direction procedures both less complicated and more effective. Realizing that forward observers possessed the most current and accurate understanding of the battlefield situation, Devers began experimenting with letting them control artillery fire from their positions—a method of conducting observed fires that McNair had strongly advocated since the World War. Devers also directed his department to begin updating regulations adopted from the French during the World War. The aim was to simplify procedures for firing the 75mm howitzer while retaining the main strength of that doctrine: increased artillery effectiveness through the simultaneous delivery of massed fires.[5]

When Major Carlos Brewer reported as the new chief instructor of the gunnery department in 1929, he took charge of an organization already infused with an innovative spirit. Brewer agreed with Devers's assessment that achieving effective fires required relying on observed rather than timed fires. He also supported the concept of massing fires by placing fire direction responsibility at the battalion rather than the battery level, even though this ran contrary to long-standing field artillery branch tradition. Traditionalists believed battery commanders should retain full control over their batteries, including execution of fire missions, and they appeared unlikely to change their minds about this principle as long as no senior artillery leaders embraced these new ideas.[6]

Several technological limitations hindered both Devers's and Brewer's efforts. No method existed for the battalion to control the individual batteries in open warfare because batteries were typically emplaced 1,000 yards apart from each other, relying on wire communications or large radio sets, which seriously limited mobility. Calculation of fire data also depended on accurate knowledge of the location of the firing battery and the target, which in turn required accurate and detailed maps (relatively easy to obtain on the stabilized fronts of the World War but harder to come by in open warfare). Unobserved fire also required detailed surveys to determine the location of each individual battery and the positions of planned or likely targets. These surveys could take hours to complete. Radio operators still communicated in Morse code, adding delays in transmission of target location data to the battery to an already laborious process. Finally, no method existed to calculate fire missions at the battalion level for each battery to execute in concert.[7]

Brewer made it his goal to find a faster way to prepare batteries to fire and a feasible method of engaging targets of opportunity with massed fires. The capability to provide timely and accurate fires, mass fires effectively, and provide mobile artillery support to maneuvering units had eluded America's artillery throughout the World War and still required the development of improved techniques and new technology. Significant breakthroughs finally began to emerge in the early 1930s, just when McNair arrived at the Field Artillery School and provided the impetus required to overcome traditionalism and turn new concepts into formal doctrine.[8]

An article Carlos Brewer wrote for the July–August 1931 edition of the *Field Artillery Journal* described "Flash-Sound Ranging," one method the gunnery department used to overcome the laborious methods the field artillery had relied on during the World War. Flash-sound ranging showed potential as a way to estimate the range to an enemy battery and conduct counterbattery fire without relying on accurate maps. Brewer pointed out that flash and sound ranging equipment had improved since the war and required only six hours to set up (it had taken up to forty-eight hours during the World War). Brewer still considered this an excessive amount of setup time, but he saw potential in combining flash and sound systems and using calculations devised by the gunnery department to derive a more accurate position estimate by combining information from the two systems. Brewer described the method's pros and cons and admitted it remained experimental, but he emphasized the value of developing innovative means to prepare the field artillery for motorized warfare.[9]

Brewer also made strides in developing new methods for adjusting observed fires. Several years' experimentation with using aerial observers highlighted the difficulty of relaying map coordinates over the radio using Morse code. Frustration with this system led Brewer and his gunnery department to develop a new adjustment technique in which observers transmitted basic corrections rather than detailed map coordinates to the firing battery. The aerial observer estimated the distance between a round or barrage's point of impact and its intended target, and he simply transmitted the observed error—for example, "200 left, 400 over"—to the fire control personnel, who used this information to calculate adjustments and transmitted them to the gun crews. This significantly reduced time between barrages and allowed spotters to guide rounds progressively closer to targets using real-time information without relying on detailed maps. First Lieutenant Edwin L. Sibert, one of Brewer's instructors, found ways to teach ground observers the same technique. This method initially showed great promise and proved so easy to use "that untrained soldiers could adjust fire after only a little instruction."[10]

These new techniques sped up the process of transmitting adjustments to a battery, but pinpointing the battery's fire on target or achieving accurate and timely massed fires still proved problematic. Because no procedure yet existed for centralized calculation of fire data for multiple batteries firing from separate locations, massed battalion fires still required each battery to rely on its own observer and to calculate its own fire data. Individual observers had to adjust their battery's fire onto the correct target and do so quickly and in a coordinated manner to achieve a battalion "fire for effect." In practice, the gunnery department and its students found this challenging. Observers often incorrectly identified targets or took too long—usually twenty to thirty minutes, if not more—to adjust fire onto them. In fact, accurate adjustment of individual battery fires proved so difficult for students that most did not even advance to the point that they could attempt to coordinate efforts with other observers to mass battalion fires. In 1931, when Major Orlando Ward joined the gunnery department, he soon found himself swept up in the faculty's enthusiasm and added new energy into the quest for innovative methods to overcome the deficiencies in the support the field artillery provided the infantry during the World War.[11]

McNair shared this enthusiasm, as demonstrated by the annual reports he prepared for the commandant. In his first report, submitted on June 11, 1930, McNair addressed the importance of the instruction students received in the school's advanced course. In particular, he emphasized the gunnery department's work to modernize fire direction techniques:

> There has been and will be a continuing effort to shape the courses so that the instruction in the methods peculiar to the World War will not be unduly emphasized at the expense of methods which would be more appropriate for a war under other conditions. It is contemplated to lay greater stress on artillery fire against tanks, and it is expected to improve the gunnery methods and practical execution against such targets. The use of the range finder demands greater emphasis in view of conditions where maps would not be available or when there would be insufficient time to use them in connection with the preparation of fire.

Further, McNair emphasized the importance of field artillery officers attending the advanced field artillery officer's course. In his first year at the school, he noted cases of officers missing that opportunity because they received orders to report to Fort Leavenworth, where, per Army Chief of Staff Summerall's direction in 1928, the course once again consisted of two years of instruction. McNair argued,

> It is to be regretted that it has been found necessary in some cases to detail officers of field artillery as students to the Command and General Staff School without their having passed through the advanced course at this school. If the necessity continues, it clearly would justify a return to the one-year course at the Command and General Staff School. In other words, as far as the field artillery is concerned, the advanced course at Fort Sill is far more essential than a second year at Fort Leavenworth.

Having completed less than a year of his tour of duty, McNair already saw the potential in the new techniques under development in the gunnery department and their importance to future field artillery commanders. Beginning with his first annual report, he urged the Field Artillery School commandant to support both the modernization efforts and field artillery officers' opportunities to receive training in the new methods under development, even if it meant not attending the second year of instruction at Fort Leavenworth.[12]

McNair further supported this recommendation by pointing out the need for the assignment to field units of more artillery personnel who were qualified to provide unit training—an ability that required the education received at the various advanced courses at the Field Artillery School. These included not only the field artillery officer's advanced course but also advanced courses in horsemanship, motors, and gunnery. During the preceding year, the school had completed and gained War Department approval for the full set of base texts for the extension course of the Field Artillery School—a first since the World War. Therefore, educational materials existed to support training in field units, but shortages in experienced personnel to lead the training would persist unless more artillery officers attended the three advanced courses at the Field Artillery School.[13]

McNair devoted the second half of his 1931 report to the results of a survey given to students of the previous year's advanced course. The faculty had observed a wide range of field artillery expertise among attendees of the battery officer's course, despite all students' reporting for attendance at approximately the same point in their careers. In particular, the gunnery department observed among its students a significant lack of experience and ability adjusting observed fires, demonstrating the neglect among field units in this type of training. Therefore, the school required attendees of the course to fill out a survey before graduation to try to determine why their skill levels upon arrival at the Field Artillery School varied so much. McNair believed the results of the survey would reveal ways for the branch to increase the quality of artillery instruction in the field. This in turn would enable the Field Artillery School to begin instruction at a more advanced level, improving the output of the battery officer's course. Combined with the War Department–approved extension course materials and a larger pool of advanced course graduates to lead instruction in the field, this initiative would increase the quality of training in units and the proficiency of battery officer's course graduates, raising overall proficiency across the branch.[14]

The survey included eighteen questions to determine each officer's time in commissioned service, experience in field artillery units, service in gun batteries, type and quality of unit instruction received, specific tasks trained, and whether their level of experience upon reporting for the battery officer's course affected the difficulty they experienced completing it. McNair reported ten conclusions and several additional observations from the answers to the survey, with the overall finding unsurprising: many common tasks went untrained in most field artillery units, and rarely did unit training meet the minimum acceptable standard established by field artillery training publications and regulations. The answers also indicated problems already suspected through informal observations at the school—in particular a general lack of experience in the field conducting observed fire missions. The overall results led McNair to call for remedial action. This included several steps, but they came down to two basic remedies. The first involved revision of the army regulation that covered unit training, because in many instances it either set unreasonable or unsupportable training requirements, or it simply did not specify the standards that training should meet. The second involved leadership—in short, ensuring that commanders from the troop all the way to the corps area level possessed the knowledge and took the action necessary to participate in and oversee quality unit training. McNair summed up his conclusions with two salient points: "Means should be devised to bring home to battery and higher commanders their responsibilities in connection with the training of junior officers," and "in assigning officers to duty with troops, special attention should be given to providing suitable instructors in the various subjects."[15]

The additional energy Orlando Ward brought to the gunnery department, and McNair's efforts to support innovation at the Field Artillery School while finding ways to improve proficiency across the branch, ensured progress continued during the 1931–1932 academic year. In particular, Gugeler highlighted two events that helped the gunnery department in its efforts to improve fire direction procedures that year. First, Brewer discovered a recently arrived book in the school library titled *Field Guns in France*, written by Lieutenant Colonel Neil Fraser-Tytler, a French officer who served as an artillery observer during the World War. Brewer found Fraser-Tytler's account quite compelling. It made him rethink just how much the US army field artillery branch needed to change the way it supported the other arms, and he made the book mandatory reading for all of his instructors. The book described Fraser-Tytler's efforts to accompany the infantry and remain as far forward on the battlefield as possible, so he could see the targets they needed the field artillery to neutralize as they advanced. Using a telephone system he developed that simplified communications with the gunners, Fraser-Tytler could direct their fire onto point targets, quickly shifting from one to the next, to enable the infantry to keep advancing past machine gun nests or other strong points. Although Fraser-Tytler used a fire correction method similar to the one under development in the gunnery department, he described a manner of employment much different from the one Brewer envisioned. As Gugeler put it, "Tytler-Frazer's [sic] concept of moving the artillery fire from point to point on the battlefield, and shifting it rapidly as the infantry needed help, went well beyond the artillery's accepted role during the World War." It also went well beyond what Brewer envisioned accomplishing at the Field Artillery School. The book made both Brewer and Ward rethink just how much they could accomplish by improving American artillery fire procedures.[16]

McNair highlighted the other significant event for gunnery innovation that year in his annual report of June 15, 1932. He closed the report by noting the receipt of new radio equipment—the SCR 131, 161, 171, and 163 radios—in sufficient quantity to begin giving instruction in their use, as well as experimenting with them during the traditional Saturday morning gunnery department tests. McNair described excellent results with the radios, particularly during the end-of-year field exercise. To McNair, their performance indicated that "a greatly enlarged sphere of usefulness for radio communication is at hand. It appears entirely probable that definite steps may be taken conservatively, looking toward the progressive substitution of radio for wire. It is proposed during the coming school year to exploit the possibilities of the new equipment to the utmost."[17]

By late 1932, the larger field artillery community started paying attention to the new developments at the Field Artillery School. The November–December 1932 issue of the *Field Artillery Journal* included in its "Field Artillery Notes" section a short article titled "Gunnery Liaison Methods." The article begins with a pointed statement: "The advent of the SCR-161 short wave radio set has introduced new possibilities in liaison between the field artillery and infantry. Practical work already has shown that the artillery's response to calls for fire from the infantry can be speeded up materially." The author wrote the article to summarize the recently issued "Field Artillery School note No. G-47, 'Gunnery Liaison Methods.'" However, the final paragraph of the introduction to this short article reminded the reader, "These notes are authorized by the Chief of Field Artillery for use at the Field Artillery School only. Where in conflict with TR 430–85 they are to be considered as experimental, being tested at the Field Artillery School, and unorthodox until embodied in the Field Artillery Manual or other regulations." After this introduction, the article merely described the new fire adjustment methods based on transmitting error corrections rather than lengthy map data, highlighting the potential of the new generation of radios to increase the ability of the field artillery to provide flexible fire support in fluid situations. Although considered experimental, this brief article demonstrates the Field Artillery School's efforts to foster its innovative spirit throughout the branch.[18]

The new radios, like their wire-based predecessors, still only transmitted and received Morse code, but the advantage they offered in mobility alone gave them great potential for changing the way field artillery personnel directed fires. Similarly, Brewer's efforts to change fire direction procedures achieved progress but the gunnery department still had much work to do. Brewer understood the shortcomings of unobserved fires—one of the biggest limitations in America's artillery employment during the World War—and he reminded McNair that they had long shared this understanding in a memo he sent just before his departure from Fort Sill:

I remember reading a report during the progress of the war of a staff inspection made by Brig. Gen. L. J. McNair in which he described a certain engagement which he observed from a good OP [observation post] near the front line. In this report the failure of the artillery to utilize available observation was criticized in terms somewhat as follows: "If I had had command of a single battery I believe I could have inflicted greater damage on the enemy with observed fire than an entire regiment did with the rolling barrage."[19]

Brewer may have recalled "Extracts from 'Notes on Recent Operations,' by Brigadier General Leslie [*sic*] J. McNair, General Staff, GHQ, AEF," from the April–June 1919 issue of the *Field Artillery Journal*. Reporting on an attack he observed in which American forces broke through the enemy trench system and attempted to transition to mobile warfare, McNair lamented the American forces' reluctance

to cease the extravagant methods of map firing and utilize direct observation. The terrain afforded excellent observation posts and battery positions. Observed fire was used barely—if at all. It must be inferred either that artillery commanders do not appreciate the immense advantage of adjusted fire, and the waste and loss of effectiveness in searching areas, or that they lack confidence in the ability of their battery commanders in the rapid preparation and conduct of observed fires. It is conservatively estimated that of the ammunition fired during the first two days of this operation, 50 per cent was wasted.[20]

Brewer used his memorandum, written to a like-minded senior field artilleryman that he obviously respected, to both summarize the work of the gunnery department that he supervised and make recommendations for the way forward. He had a capable successor in Orlando Ward, but he also recognized the important role McNair would fulfill by providing the continuous support of a like-minded senior officer, particularly in shielding the personnel in the gunnery department from the interference of traditionalists who objected to their innovative efforts.

An article McNair wrote based on his experiences in the World War, published in 1921, further illustrated the similar views he held with Brewer regarding the superiority of observed fires. In this article, McNair displayed a deep understanding of combined arms attacks in both trench-to-trench and mobile warfare conditions. He also made a passionate and well-argued case for the need to provide attacking infantry with mobile accompanying guns, and he explained that the artillerymen operating these batteries must learn to transition from precalculated to observed fires upon penetrating the enemy's initial defenses and continuing the attack to secondary positions. McNair argued that this required close proximity of supporting guns to lead infantry elements because battery commanders must remain close enough to the front to observe fires and close enough to the guns to provide adjustment instructions to overcome the limitations of communications technology. In short, McNair made an early and powerful argument for combined arms training of observed fires—a key element of mobile warfare, but an unpopular one among many field artillerymen who believed it ceded too much control over artillery to infantrymen. Both during and after his tour with the American Expeditionary Force, McNair remained a staunch advocate of combined arms operations and training, in particular mobile, observed, responsive artillery fires. McNair's innovative spirit and concern for the effectiveness of the army over the needs or wants of the branch set him apart even at this stage of his career from the traditionalist majority in the field artillery. The army could not have assigned a better-suited artilleryman to oversee the training and innovative efforts taking place at the Field Artillery School in the early 1930s.[21]

Brewer's seven-page memorandum focused on his strong desire to find ways to enable the field artillery to provide more effective fire support in a future, probably motorized, war than it did during the World War. He lamented the time lost since the war merely seeking ways to refine the laborious and ineffective French methods that the American Expeditionary Force adopted during the war (the unobserved map-calculated and highly orchestrated rolling barrages McNair so highly criticized) and summarized the advances his department achieved in just a few short years. Brewer did realize, however, that the new fire direction techniques his division taught required a level of competence difficult to achieve and sustain in the US army of the early 1930s because of their complexity and the need for regular practice to maintain the necessary skill. As a remedy, he offered two primary suggestions. In addition to McNair's efforts to standardize fire direction procedures and improve gunnery training in the field, Brewer recommended creating a subset of artillery specialists known as gunnery officers, drawn from the best-qualified graduates of the field artillery officer's advanced course (he believed only about half of the latest classes' graduates demonstrated the requisite skill). Because they would be able to focus in training on fire direction procedures, these officers stood a much better chance to gain and retain the competence modern gunnery methods required.[22]

Brewer also recommended a reorganization of artillery units to group these gunnery officers together at the artillery battalion, coinciding with a change in gunnery procedures involving the consolidation of fire direction at the battalion headquarters. Although Brewer had not yet overcome the technological challenges of adjusting several batteries' fire from a single headquarters and relying on one observation point to provide adjustment data for more than one battery, he saw this as the only way to continue moving forward and sustaining the progress his gunnery department had achieved during his and Jake Devers's tenure there. Brewer summarized several advantages of this new organization, including easing the training of gunnery officers and their ability to share new ideas, improving staff coordination, simplifying observation post placement and security, and creating maps more quickly and accurately than when attempted at multiple battery-level headquarters. Brewer recognized the single most likely obstacle facing this recommended organization: "Probably the greatest objection of all is that this will rob the battery commander of one of his time honored prerogatives, that of firing his own battery, and tend thereby to stifle his ambition and desire to have an efficient firing battery." However, Brewer believed the branch could overcome this objection, and noted from his own observations while serving with the gunnery department that battery commanders strove to deliver the most accurate fire possible, wherever the fire direction responsibility rested.[23]

Nevertheless, Brewer had not yet developed a procedure for calculating fire adjustment data in a consolidated battalion gunnery section and then transmitting it to each firing battery.[24] The responsibility would fall to his successor, Orlando Ward, to solve this problem, while McNair fended off the resistance from field artillery branch traditionalists who believed the battery commander should fire his own guns. Fortunately, as Gugeler put it, "From the beginning, [Ward] enjoyed several advantages: Brigadier General Lesley J. McNair, then the Assistant Commandant [and serving in his current permanent rank of Lieutenant Colonel], supported all efforts to simplify or improve artillery support; Ward understood artillery techniques thoroughly; and he inherited from Brewer a group of about 15 capable and enthusiastic gunnery instructors." Describing Ward's methods, Gugeler pointed out his hands-off approach and lack of strict control. Ward encouraged new ideas, even ones that seemed impracticable, believing the officer might not only see the infeasibility of his idea, but in doing so develop a new one. Gugeler quoted one of the gunnery department officers, John M. Lentz, later a later major general, as recalling, "His methods were not obvious. There was no prodding, no laying out of objectives, only a gentle happiness with every new thought, every development. The result was a vastly greater change in every facet of our technique than has ever happened before or since."[25]

Progress accelerated under Ward's leadership. Building on the previous several years' experimentation, Ward's open-minded approach to developing new methods soon led to discovery of a rapid and relatively simple method of controlling fires and calculating fire data at the battalion. The gunnery instructors realized that the main hindrance they had experienced to date involved using several observers, each trying to adjust his own battery onto the same target simultaneously, often leading them to confuse another battery's rounds for their own and therefore miscalculating further adjustments. Not long after Ward took over as chief of the gunnery department, the instructors worked out a new fire adjustment method. A single observer adjusted one battery until it placed a round on target, at which point the battalion used a newly devised technique to calculate and send firing data to the battery that had fired and the others that had not, enabling them all to place, quickly and accurately, massed fires on the target. After seeing this new method in action during one of the department's standard Saturday morning gunnery experiments, Ward realized they could now place accurate fires on a target of opportunity in ten minutes, a process that had previously required several hours. They also could do so as a battalion, achieving accurate fires with unprecedented speed and mass. Upon returning to his office from the firing range, Ward described the results: "It was just like squirting a hose at the target."[26]

In solving the problem of calculating fire data for separate batteries at the battalion, the gunnery instructors formed a new organization that eventually evolved into the Fire Direction Center (FDC). The FDC consolidated all the complex procedures associated with adjustment of fire in a single organization. Answering directly to the battalion commander, the FDC received correction data from the forward observers, who no longer had to calculate adjustments because the FDC calculated fire data for each battery. With accurate maps, battalions could consistently achieve accurate concentrations in ten minutes; without maps, they required more time, but the procedure still worked exceptionally well.[27]

Working in this exciting, innovative organization, gunnery instructors continued to improve artillery fire direction by refining procedures and developing new techniques, some deceptively simple, like the back-azimuth technique that eliminated the need for time-consuming surveys by enabling a battery to calculate its position based on the trajectory and point of impact of fired rounds. One of these new techniques, the range fan, developed by First Lieutenant Charles C. Blanchard, enabled FDC personnel to measure range and deflection (lateral error) with a single device, rather than a range scale and protractor. The range fan consisted of a fan-shaped piece of clear plastic, connected to the map by a pin placed at the location of each firing battery. By shifting the position of the range fan on the basis of a round's point of impact, an artilleryman could quickly calculate both the range and angle of deflection adjustments. Field artillery battalions soon adopted Blanchard's range fan as standard equipment.[28]

Similarly, while the new procedures dramatically sped up fires delivered on opportunity targets or before completion of battery position surveys, Ward also sought ways to speed up surveys to improve artillery responsiveness when a forward observer had not yet reached a position where he could provide adjustment data. Captain John M. Lentz, jumped at the opportunity to work on this problem. Realizing that both the antiquated French survey equipment and the inaccurate aerial surveys they relied on created most of the problem, Lentz borrowed instruments from the coast artillery—including the far more accurate transit—and developed a procedure for testing the speed and accuracy of surveys conducted using them. Convinced that the average officer would never have allowed his experiment because the field artillery at that time did not possess the transit and because developing a procedure relying on unauthorized equipment served no use, Lentz gave full credit to Ward for allowing him to develop yet another procedure the army later adopted for widespread use.[29]

The gunnery department developed several additional new or improved methods to adjust fire, including improved fire calculation tables, map overlays, and aerial photography techniques. However, Ward's greatest obstacle remained "the resistance, by most of the artillery, particularly the Chief's office, to taking any of the prerogatives away from the battery commander." Ward argued that it made sense for a battery commander to control his own battery's fire if engaging a target it could neutralize with four guns or fewer, but larger targets required the massed fires of the whole battalion, which only the FDC, using the new procedures developed by the gunnery department, could achieve. With officers from other departments attending Saturday morning gunnery practice and seeing the amazing results the department could achieve, Ward grew confident that the marked increases in speed, flexibility, and accuracy that it achieved would outweigh traditionalist concerns, and he began to urge the school to adopt the new procedures for instruction to all students. Despite growing enthusiasm for the new techniques, he soon faced a new obstacle. Ward remained convinced that his department, rather than the tactics department, should teach fire direction. With this achieved, the sheer efficacy of the new procedures, propagated through the branch via annual classes of graduates trained in the new procedures, would eventually overcome traditionalist resistance.[30]

Ward faced a tough battle when he confronted the tactics department. However, McNair's reputation among his fellow artilleryman had grown since his arrival at Fort Sill, and in his fourth year as assistant commandant, he wielded significant influence at the Field Artillery School. An advocate of innovation for many years, McNair supported Ward and convinced the commandant to grant Ward's request, giving the gunnery department the freedom not only to continue experimenting but also to train students at the Field Artillery School in the latest fire direction techniques. Resistance among senior field artillery officers remained, and the War Department did not support immediate implementation of the FDC. However, the gunnery department now had control over fire direction instruction, and with it the freedom to influence the thinking of every young field artilleryman that attended the Field Artillery School about how much the branch could achieve using the latest procedures.[31] As these young artillerymen aged and increased in rank, they might finally hold sway over the traditionalists currently preventing the field artillery branch from exploiting these new techniques to overcome the challenges that hindered its effectiveness during the World War.

McNair submitted his final annual report at the Field Artillery School on June

7, 1933. Significantly, he did not mention the new developments in the gunnery department, probably realizing he would only place at risk his success in transferring responsibility for fire direction instruction to the gunnery department if he advertised that change to the traditionalists among the more senior officers in the branch. He did emphasize the updating of texts, a process carried forward from the previous year in an ongoing revision process, along with efforts to print enough texts for use at the school and for distribution to the field. As regular army artillery personnel gained proficiency, he recommended implementation of admittance tests to ensure students met minimum qualification standards before acceptance into the school's various courses. He also highlighted the lack of motorized equipment in the 1st Battalion, 1st Field Artillery, that prevented it from conducting motorized tactical training. McNair emphasized the need to acquire the necessary equipment at the school, arguing that in modern conditions, at least half of all instruction should cover motorized rather than horse-drawn artillery. Finally, McNair mentioned the dramatic impact on the school of the newly created Civilian Conservation Corps (CCC), a New Deal program put in place by President Franklin D. Roosevelt. Because the program relied on regular army personnel to run the CCC's many civilian work camps, most army units and schools lost many personnel. The Field Artillery School lost 60 percent of its personnel, forcing it to close the academic year early on May 22, 1933. McNair reported that the school retained sufficient personnel to maintain minimum functioning in each of its key departments and expected it to resume functioning upon arrival of the fall class.[32]

McNair's efficiency reports from his four years at the Field Artillery School invariably rated him a superior officer, qualified both for promotion to the next highest grade and for command of a regiment in peace or a brigade in time of war. In the section evaluating his suitability for duty with civilian components (required by Army Regulation 600-185), he received a similarly consistent qualified rating. After a brief seven-month period working for Colonel George P. Tyner, acting commandant of the Field Artillery School, McNair served under the new commandant, Brigadier General William M. Cruikshank, for the duration of his time there. He clearly made a strong impression on Cruikshank, who wrote the following unusually long "Brief General Estimate of this Officer" (section "R" of the form) on McNair's final efficiency report before departing the school: "A superior officer in the highest sense of the word. Extremely well informed, hard working and conscientious. Very tactful, a fine disciplinarian and gets results from all with a minimum of friction. Very pleasing personality, liked and respected by all. I cannot give him too much credit for the continued progress and efficiency in the Academic Division of the FA School during his four years service here."[33] Not only did Cruikshank deem McNair "suitable for civilian contact," but he also added the following handwritten statement: "Eminently qualified for any duty to which he may be assigned."[34]

McNair had obviously made quite an impression within his branch. After his excellent performance at the Field Artillery School and his overall strong record of performance since the World War, the army selected McNair for battalion command. He reported to Fort Bragg, North Carolina, on July 1, 1933, where he took nine days of leave before assuming command of the 2nd Battalion, 16th Field Artillery.

Battalion Command at Fort Bragg, 1933–1934

Like the rest of the army, the field artillery branch remained in a consistent state of flux throughout the 1920s and 1930s. Largely as a result of the greatly understrength and budget-constrained condition of the army, units frequently reorganized, redesignated, and shifted from the control of one higher headquarters to another. McNair experienced this situation firsthand when he received orders to report to Fort Bragg upon his selection to serve as a battalion commander.

Per Special Orders No. 112, dated May 15, 1933, the War Department relieved McNair of duty at the Field Artillery School and reassigned him to the 16th Field Artillery at Fort Bragg, effective June 30, 1933, "for assignment to duty." Although these orders did not specify that duty as battalion command, McNair's efficiency report for the period July 1, 1933, through June 30, 1934, listed nine days of leave en route, followed by service as battalion commander for the rest of the upcoming year. However, the report indicated he commanded the 2nd Battalion, 83rd Field Artillery, not a battalion in the 16th Field Artillery.[35]

The two-volume set on field artillery in the Center of Military History's Lineage Series helps to clarify the situation. The War Department constituted the 16th Field Artillery Regiment in the regular army on July 1, 1916, and the regiment organized on May 21, 1917, at Camp Robinson, Wisconsin. After service with the 4th Division during the World War, the War Department inactivated the regiment on September 21, 1921, at Camp Lewis, Washington. The following year, it activated the 1st Battalion at Fort Myer, Virginia, assigning it initially to the 4th Division. However, the War Department reassigned the battalion back and forth between the 4th Division and the 8th Division several times over the next twelve years. Concurrent to one of these reassignments, the War Department activated the 2nd Battalion at Fort Bragg on September 5, 1927, as a subordinate unit to the 83rd Field Artillery Regiment.[36]

The 83rd Field Artillery Regiment also formed before the World War. Constituted on July 1, 1916, in the regular army as the 25th Cavalry, the unit organized on June 5, 1917, at Fort D. A. Russell, Wyoming. It converted from cavalry to field artillery, and the field artillery branch redesignated the unit on November 1, 1917, the 83rd Field Artillery, assigned on December 17, 1917, to the 8th Division. The War Department inactivated the regiment (less the 1st Battalion) on January 7, 1922, at Camp Benning, Georgia, and disbanded it (again, less the 1st Battalion) on February 28, 1927 (the 1st Battalion concurrently reorganized and was redesignated as the 83rd Field Artillery Battalion). The War Department reconstituted the 83rd Field Artillery Regiment on March 17, 1930, and assigned it to the 8th Division. (The War Department simply reorganized the 83rd Field Artillery Battalion as the 1st Battalion, 83rd Field Artillery, reforming the rest of the regiment on paper; the other battalions remained inactive.) The War Department relieved the regiment on October 1, 1933, from assignment to the 8th Division and assigned it to the 4th Division, concurrently activating the 2nd Battalion (a horse artillery unit) at Fort Bragg, North Carolina.[37]

Thus, McNair apparently commanded the 2nd Battalion, 16th Regiment, from July 1 through October 1, 1933, when his command changed from the inactivated 2nd Battalion, 16th Field Artillery, to the newly activated 2nd Battalion, 83rd Field Artillery Regiment (records do not reflect whether this merely consisted of reflagging an existing unit). Although this is all clarified in the lengthy Field Artillery Lineage Series volumes, McNair's efficiency reports make no mention of this turbulence, probably as a result of regulations governing the generation of such reports on the basis of how long an officer served in a unit or for a particular supervisor. His first efficiency report as battalion commander mentions only the 2nd Battalion, 83rd Field Artillery, while his second, covering the brief period from July 1 to September 1, 1934, includes command of the same battalion plus a short period of detached service at a civilian military training camp. These efficiency reports do reflect consistently superior performance, as judged by the regimental commander, Brigadier General Manus McCloskey. In particular, the first endorser on his second evaluation, the newly assigned IV Corps area commander, Major General George Van Horn Moseley, added the remark, "Colonel McNair is one of the outstanding officers of the Army," and he signed his name to this endorsement above his official signature block.[38]

Thus, although no other information appears to be available on McNair's battalion command, these efficiency reports indicate that he performed as well in this assignment as he did in previous positions, drawing the attention of yet another senior officer who singled him out for particular commendation. Further, as a result of the turbulence in the field artillery community, McNair probably faced significant administrative challenges during his command, reorganizing and reflagging the unit after only a few months. Nevertheless, he performed yet again in a superior manner and soon found himself reassigned to another high-profile command, although one of a very different nature.[39]

District Command with the CCC, 1934–1935

McNair departed Fort Bragg in August 1934, having received orders to serve as commander, CCC District "E," VII Corps Area, at Camp Beauregard, Louisiana.[40] McNair began this tour of duty at a time when America was continuing to suffer the financial debilitation caused by the Great Depression. The army officer salaries and annual raises enacted by Congress in 1922 placed regular army officers in a better financial position than many Americans, but federal employees of the other branches of government reaped the greatest benefit. They had already earned higher annual salaries than regular army personnel had, and the 1922 legislation included pay raises for other federal workers that more than doubled those of army officers. When Franklin D. Roosevelt won the presidency in 1932 and implemented his New Deal policies, the situation for members of the regular army only worsened, including implementation of a 15 percent annual pay cut and one unpaid month per year from 1933 through 1935.

Roosevelt established the CCC to put young, unemployed civilian men to work, but the program significantly affected regular army personnel as well. Almost all regular army officers served a one-year assignment as a commander or leader in a CCC district over the life of the program. Most contemporary accounts about the CCC emphasized the role of the military in establishing the organization, but they also emphasized the absence of any military training at the camps. The administration turned to the army to establish and command the camps and equip and organize the individuals joining the CCC because the army possessed the capacity to mobilize a large number of people quickly and effectively. However, aware of the prevailing sentiment against widespread military training of civilians in early 1930s America, the administration ensured (and publicized) the conscious avoidance of militarization in the camps.[41]

The regular army answered the call, but reluctantly, given the massive personnel demands with no apparent benefit to the army. The army still lacked an organized reserve, and the CCC program seemed to some the ideal opportunity to create one. Most army officers also saw their support of the program as a diversion of an already skeleton force away from its primary mission of national defense. Nevertheless, despite the reduction the regulars experienced in their own military readiness, the army did derive some benefit from the program. As Charles Johnson put it:

The Army benefited from the CCC in a variety of ways. The Corps provided a valuable training experience for a large number of reserve officers, the Army utilized CCC labor to perform badly needed conservation work on military reservations, and 2½ million enrollees acquired skills that were potentially useful to the War Department. The Army was in a position to misuse its authority over the enrollees, but it did not abuse its power because of its awareness of the probable public response to anything resembling the militarization of the camps, its knowledge of the Administration's hostility toward such action, and its clear understanding of the proper place of the military in a democracy.[42]

The army provided an irreplaceable capability to establish and run the program, but it did not approach the mission as a military one or view the CCC personnel as military trainees or reservists. Only time would tell if the army would derive any significant long-term benefit from the program.

In preparation for his reassignment to command of CCC District "E," Lieutenant Colonel McNair received orders on August 18, 1934, to report to Fort McPherson, Georgia, for a meeting with Major General George Van Horn Moseley, commander of the IV Corps Area. Two days later, after his meeting with McNair, Moseley wrote Brigadier General Manus McCloskey, commander of the 83rd Field Artillery Regiment and McNair's immediate supervisor, to inform him of his decision to reassign McNair. Moseley, who took particular notice of McNair during his assignment at the Field Artillery School, wrote, "I know you will be sorry to lose McNair, but I also appreciate that you are willing to cooperate with us fully so that we may keep up a fine record throughout the whole Corps Area in handling these important activities." The CCC program, a major initiative at the forefront of Roosevelt's New Deal, attracted a great deal of attention from the War Department and political leaders; corps area commanders experienced significant pressure to assign quality officers to district commands. District "E" in particular presented significant challenges to the commander.[43]

As Moseley explained to McCloskey in his letter of August 20, unlike all other CCC districts, no regular army post existed to serve as the headquarters for District "E." Although General Fleming, adjutant general of the Louisiana National Guard, offered the use of Camp Beauregard as the district headquarters, this atypical arrangement required particular effort both in establishing and maintaining the district headquarters and in coordinating CCC activities with Louisiana National Guard and state government officials. Moseley wrote, "I have been searching for a highly desirable man to relieve Packard [the outgoing commander], and I hit upon McNair. I have known McNair for many years and I look upon him as one of the very best officers in the Army. It will be a great relief to us to turn over that command to such a fine leader." Moseley's meeting with McNair apparently reinforced his confidence that he had selected the right man for the job: he immediately arranged for McNair to visit Camp Beauregard and familiarize himself with the district and its thirty-four camps before departing Fort Bragg permanently for his new assignment. McNair departed Fort McPherson by train the next day for Shreveport, Louisiana, and from there he proceeded to Barksdale Field for air transport to Camp Beauregard.[44]

McCloskey's response to Moseley revealed both McNair's fitness for the complexities involved in the District "E" command and the immense pressure the regular army experienced in its rush to establish the CCC camps and receive the massive civilian workforce. Writing on August 24, the day McNair returned to Fort Bragg, McCloskey assured Moseley he understood the challenges McNair would face, largely due to the "immense distance between our eastern and western companies of about 600 miles." He had compiled for McNair all the necessary background information and regulations to help him in the transition to his new command. McCloskey's letter only reinforces the fact that the regular army understood it must assign quality officers to CCC commands: "Like you, I regard Col. McNair as one of the outstanding officers of the Army and I know that he will handle his District most successfully."[45]

McNair officially assumed command of District "E" on September 5, 1934. He immediately began dealing with the wide array of responsibilities associated with managing the CCC camps spread out over Louisiana and Mississippi. In addition to ensuring property accountability, coordinating with various state government and Louisiana National Guard officials, securing necessary equipment, ensuring safe work and living conditions, and answering many requests for employment at a CCC camp, McNair's personnel file contains temporary duty orders demonstrating that he spent a great deal of time conducting inspection visits to various camps. For example, between January 21 and February 18, 1935, McNair made seven trips by car to camps in his district, usually visiting two or three camps per day. His senior subordinate officers maintained similar travel schedules, usually to provide their individual expertise when called for by a particular problem.[46]

McNair highlighted one of the CCC's key areas of emphasis in his introduction to a pamphlet entitled "Progress in Education in District 'E' CCC." Acknowledging the enormous challenges initially facing the program, including lack of facilities and educators as well as the need to develop an academic curriculum, McNair wrote, "Camp educational advisers have been improved and will be improved still further, and the young men themselves are learning that the instruction affords them a fine opportunity for self-improvement." McNair emphasized the relevance of the educational program within the CCC's overarching goal of "building young men for better and more useful and successful citizenship," which involved both physical and mental development. He wrote, "This education rounds out his camp life; his daily work, his recreational activities, and his educational efforts blend to make a rational and healthful whole."[47]

Like all of the officers who participated in the CCC program, McNair received valuable practical experience in mobilizing, housing, supervising, and building the mental and physical toughness of young inductees. Reserve officers in particular benefited because the lack of an organized reserve meant that before the creation of the CCC, few Reserve Officer Training Corps graduates received any annual training after receiving their reserve commissions. Regardless, McNair soon moved on to a new stage in his career. Like many AWC graduates, McNair began ascending into the ranks of the army's senior leadership, meaning accelerated promotions and positions of greater responsibility. The first indication he might soon leave the CCC arrived in November 1934 in the form of orders to report to Fort Benning for a special physical to determine his fitness for continued active service and promotion.[48]

McNair had passed his annual physical in January 1934 with his long-standing hearing loss noted but no treatment or administrative action recommended. Nevertheless, promotion boards required a special promotion physical, so McNair received orders on November 19, 1934, to travel to Fort Benning, Georgia, to undergo his second physical examination that year to determine his fitness for continued active service and promotion. He proceeded to Fort Benning as directed and underwent the physical exam (annotated "promotion" on the first page) on November 27.[49]

Interestingly, the examination revealed significantly improved numerical scores for hearing sensitivity, but the examining doctors still noted defective hearing in his left ear and physical damage to his eardrums. Just as in previous exams, his doctors assessed his hearing loss "not considered a disqualifying condition." A medical board composed of three infantry colonels and two medical corps majors found him fit for continued active service and promotion. On December 11, 1934, the secretary of war approved the board's results, and on February 1, Moseley wrote McNair to inform him he would soon change duty stations, having made the colonel's list (presumably to move McNair to a colonel's assignment pending promotion).[50]

McNair remained in command of District "E" through April 1935 while awaiting the arrival of his replacement, Colonel Thomas Osborne. During his final months with the CCC, McNair continued his busy travel schedule and maintained a huge administrative workload. On March 14, 1935, a few days before he began the process of transferring responsibility for District "E" to Osborne, McNair received a letter from General Moseley regarding the establishment of educational programs in the CCC camps. Noting the Roosevelt administration's emphasis on these programs, Moseley commended McNair for his achievements in District "E" and directed that he send a copy of the letter to all his subordinate commanders to ensure they sustained the CCC's educational program after Mc-Nair's departure.[51]

Moseley also indicated his continued respect for McNair in his April 1935 efficiency report, in which he wrote the following "Brief General Assessment" of McNair: "An able, even-tempered officer with outstanding talents. Possesses great tact in leading human beings. One of the very best field artillerymen in the Army." Regarding his potential for service with civilians, Moseley wrote, "Ideally suited for duty with the civilian components. Colonel McNair was specially selected to command District 'E,' Civilian Conservation Corps, containing 34 camps. In the performance of this duty he fully measured up to my expectations."[52]

7
Rise to Prominence, 1935–1940

As a result of the attention he gained for his excellent performance in key positions at the Field Artillery School and as a district commander (and periodically acting corps area commander) serving with the Civilian Conservation Corps, McNair had developed throughout the early 1930s into one of the army's up-and-coming officers. His service with CCC District "E," in particular, drew attention from senior officers in his branch, leading to his selection to serve as the executive officer to the chief of field artillery—a position that exposed him to many senior commanders and gave him a taste of high-level officer leadership. His performance in the late 1930s led to further progression in authority and responsibility as well as participation in key innovative and organizational efforts that led to his serving as a key individual in the modernization of the army in the final years of the decade.

Executive Officer to the Chief of Field Artillery, 1935–1937

McNair departed Camp Beauregard on April 20, 1935, en route to his new assignment in the office of the chief of field artillery in Washington, DC. He soon found himself in one of the key positions in a high-level headquarters: executive assistant to Brigadier General Upton Birnie Jr., chief of field artillery. Unlike an aide-de-camp, an executive assistant performed various administrative functions for the senior general officer in a headquarters—managing his calendar, keeping records, handling correspondence, and serving as the gatekeeper for people seeking to meet with the general. In addition to the heavy administrative burden associated with this position, Birnie wasted no time in taking advantage of McNair's expertise with experimentation and testing of new and innovative military equipment. At Birnie's direction, McNair traveled to Aberdeen Proving Grounds in Maryland just days after he reported for duty, on May 17, 1935, to observe the results of a test of field artillery material, including a Hotchkiss 25mm gun. On the same day that McNair traveled to Maryland to observe these firing tests, notification arrived at the office of the chief of field artillery of his promotion to the permanent rank of colonel. McNair executed the required oath of office after his return to Washington on May 20, with an effective date of rank of May 1, 1935.[1]

McNair returned to Aberdeen Proving Grounds in March 1936 to observe further field artillery tests, but few records exist describing the other duties he performed while serving as the executive to the chief of field artillery. However, detailed records McNair kept in his personal files demonstrate the significant effort he expended learning about and studying the potential of an emerging technology, as demonstrated in an article in the *Field Artillery Journal* published in January–February 1937 entitled, "And Now the Autogiro." The article describes the potential for the autogiro, a hybrid aircraft combining the characteristics of the airplane (for speed) and the helicopter (for low-speed takeoff and landing) to transform the practice of aerial observation of artillery fires. Unlike a helicopter, the autogiro relied on both a powered propeller and unpowered rotor blades for flight. Looking much like a typical airplane with a rotor system attached above the pilot and observer seats, the aircraft possessed significant advantages over a standard airplane, primarily as a result of the constant autorotation of the rotor blades, which enabled the autogiro to maintain flight at speeds as low as twenty to thirty knots. Any typical airplane at that time stalled at much higher airspeeds. Thus, the autogiro possessed obvious advantages over the balloon as a result of its maneuverability, enabling it to avoid enemy threats. However, it also offered significant advantages over the airplane, including the ability to take off from and land on very short fields and fly low and slow, enabling artillery commanders to perform detailed aerial reconnaissance for siting batteries and aerial photographers to capture much clearer images than those taken in airplanes flying much faster and higher.[2]

The field artillery began evaluating the potential uses of autogiros in 1934, when it planned to purchase three of these experimental aircraft—one for the Field Artillery School, one for the Infantry School, and one for the Cavalry School. Major Edwin P. Parker Jr. described the autogiro's potential for field artillery support in the *Field Artillery Journal* in 1934, while reminding his readers, "It must be borne in mind that the autogiro is in its infancy, and great development thereof is to be expected." Parker wrote his short article about the Kellett KD-1, the model under evaluation by army personnel, primarily to provide a brief description of the aircraft's characteristics and to describe its potential for replacing the observation balloon, which proved extremely vulnerable to enemy fire during the World War. Parker described the short takeoff and near-vertical landing ability of the aircraft, along with its minimum airspeed, which enabled a runner on the ground to keep up with it long enough to hand a bag to a courier in flight. He also described the aircraft's ability to use wired communications when operating over a small area or radio at longer distances and its potential for field artillery reconnaissance and observation.[3]

Despite the potential Parker described, by 1935 the army still had not procured any autogiros, although various tests continued. In its May–June 1935 issue, the "Field Artillery Notes" section of the *Field Artillery Journal* contained a description of the sixth annual field artillery dinner, which took place shortly after Mc-Nair's arrival in Washington as the executive to Brigadier General Birnie. At the dinner, hosted by the McNairs and the Birnies and attended by 164 guests, the decorations included place cards with hand-drawn illustrations of children playing with various toys, including a rifle, an artillery piece, a bridge section, and an autogiro. Later in this section of the journal, the reader learns, "For various reasons the purchase of autogyros anticipated in the FIELD ARTILLERY JOURNAL of July–August 1934 has not yet been made. It is hoped that these will be procured in the near future." However, the notes described the ongoing testing of these aircraft, not just in America but also in France and Russia, including a demonstration at Bolling Field in Washington, DC, for General Birnie "and numerous other officers." General Birnie rode in an autogiro during this demonstration and supported continued efforts to develop and procure the aircraft through the direct involvement of his new executive.[4]

McNair clearly took great pride in the various equipment tests he led and the boards he presided over because his notes and reports from these projects make up the majority of the personal papers that he left behind. His work on the autogiro remains preserved in one of the largest of these records, detailing a lengthy period of research, including trips to visit the manufacturer of the army's autogiros, the Kellett Autogiro Corporation. The records include correspondence with pilots and field artillerymen involved in testing earlier models, the results of later field tests, and many other letters providing information to McNair and commending him on his efforts.[5]

McNair captured the results of more than six months' research in his thirteen-page article "And Now the Autogiro." This article focused on the latest autogiros in production: the Kellett YG-1 and YG-1A. The army air corps had recently purchased one of each model, placing the aircraft and pilots at the ground forces' disposal to conduct service tests. He began the article by describing the many technological advances in various forms of aerial transport since the World War. As McNair pointed out, the American Expeditionary Force (AEF) used an earlier version of almost every piece of the equipment the army possessed in 1937. He described the autogiro as one of the few truly unique technological advances available for military application, largely because of the same features Parker described in his 1934 *Field Artillery Journal* article. As McNair explained, by 1937 the newer models demonstrated improved performance in every major performance category. They could fly as slow as sixteen knots without stalling, and they could hover over a point if facing a sixteen-knot headwind. They could land nearly vertically, with a forward roll of no more than fifty feet upon landing, and take off over a fifty-foot obstacle only 300 feet away.[6]

McNair credited the invention of the autogiro to a Spanish engineer, Juan de la Cierva, who built the first operational prototype in 1920. Cierva sought to create a safer alternative to the traditional airplane, with its tendency to stall at low airspeeds, by making use of the autorotation capability of the autogiro's rotor system. Ironically, as McNair pointed out, "at the age of forty-one and after bringing his brain-child through the most trying period of its development, he met death recently in a modern transport airplane." However, other aeronautical pioneers continued Cierva's work, including a Purdue alumnus, R. H. Prewitt, chief engineer of the Kellett Autogiro Corporation. By 1937, Prewitt had worked out the aerodynamic principles for the jump takeoff—an initial vertical climb of 200 feet before beginning forward flight—although many credited this concept incorrectly to Cierva. Although this capability remained under development, the autogiros of 1937 offered a much more versatile alternative to the airplane, and now that the army finally owned two of the aircraft, McNair sought to help his readers understand the potential they held for use by the field artillery.[7]

Perhaps because the autogiro looked so strange in comparison to the airplane, or perhaps simply because he found the technology fascinating, McNair provided his readers not only with a description of the aircraft's flight characteristics and potential for field artillery use, but he also wrote a detailed yet accessible explanation of the general aerodynamic principles of rotary wing aircraft. This remains a highly complex topic that still proves challenging to student helicopter pilots today. In particular, McNair focused on the concept of autorotation, the main characteristic that made the autogiro unique.

Unlike the modern helicopter, which relies for normal flight on a powered rotor system, the autogiro pilot used a clutch to provide power to the rotor system before takeoff. The pilot released the clutch once the rotors reached the desired speed, thereby transferring engine power to the propeller. This gave the aircraft forward motion, which in turn maintained the spinning of the rotor system via autorotation and provided the lift necessary for flight. This mode of operation differs significantly from that of the modern helicopter, in which the pilot only relies on autorotation in an emergency involving the loss of engine power. As the helicopter descends unpowered, the upward airflow through the rotor system provides the energy to maintain the rotation of the blades—thus autorotation—as long as the aircraft retains sufficient forward velocity. As the helicopter approaches the ground, the pilot can use the kinetic energy in the spinning rotor system by changing the angle of the blades to create one brief, life-saving reduction in speed of descent, enabling a safe landing with little or no forward movement. This provides the helicopter its enhanced safety compared to an airplane, which must land at much higher forward velocity and therefore in a much longer and smoother field or airstrip. Because of the autogiro's rotor design, its forward speed enabled the rotors to remain in a constant state of autorotation. This supplemented the power provided by the propeller and kept the aircraft aloft at airspeeds well below those at which an airplane would stall. McNair used photos provided by Prewitt of a miniature model of a rotor and a standard desk fan to demonstrate the principles of rotor aerodynamics (in addition to complex and surprisingly modern-looking engineering drawings).[8]

McNair emphasized the autogiro's distinct flight characteristics from those of the helicopter, another new form of aircraft in development at the time, despite their visual similarity. At the time of writing, the autogiro had advanced much further than the helicopter, which had not yet achieved any notable success. Helicopter prototypes at that time combined a propeller and a (powered) rotor system, so they looked similar to autogiros, although they operated according to different aerodynamic principles. However, McNair realized the helicopter also possessed potential, mentioning one engineer's concept of a helicopter with no propeller, relying solely on a powered rotor system that the pilot could tilt forward to gain airspeed—a concept not yet developed into a prototype. Perhaps more importantly, McNair did not exaggerate the autogiro's potential, despite its unique characteristics. Rather, he provided an objective analysis of the strengths and weaknesses of the balloon, airplane, and autogiro in various scenarios, and he emphasized the need for further development: "Does the giro offer something worthwhile which the airplane has not? If the answer is yes—or even possibly yes—then the Federal government should put its might squarely behind this struggling infant, and push its development." He ended on a cautionary note: "We must not forget, however, that the giro is only a boy, and we should neither expect nor demand that a boy do a man's work."[9]

Like the reports of many of his previous equipment tests and experiments, the detail and clarity of McNair's article attracted a great deal of attention and earned him numerous accolades. Alexander Klemin of the Daniel Guggenheim School of Aeronautics called it "a splendid article," and various business leaders and politicians commended both Birnie and McNair on the article's publication. Prewitt wrote McNair a particularly gracious letter, congratulating him on his ability to communicate such a complicated topic with admirable detail and clarity and stating that his article "warrants all the praise that anyone could give." Prewitt thanked McNair for mentioning him as the originator of the jump-off autogiro concept and mentioned that the Kellett Autogiro Corporation received an order for six more autogiros from the army (model YG-1B) after publication of the article. Once again, McNair demonstrated his fine intellect, innovative spirit, and influence not just within the field artillery but also within the army and the defense industry.[10]

The cautionary note McNair included regarding the potential of the autogiro proved insightful. By the mid-1930s, air corps engineers determined that the giro lacked sufficient power to lift a pilot, observer, and service radio into the air. However, they remained hopeful that an aircraft that possessed greater power while still offering the benefit of the autogiro's short takeoff and landing capability would emerge and offer practical military application. This led them to experiment with the helicopter—which used a powered rotor system—after two Frenchmen, Louis Bréguet and Réne Dorland, achieved the first successful helicopter flight in 1935. The helicopter increased in reliability and power as engineers developed new models, but within a few years, the light airplane emerged as the most useful field artillery observation platform. The autogiro quickly faded into obscurity, as did any recollection of McNair's participation in the army's experiments with it.[11]

Throughout McNair's tour as the executive to the chief of field artillery, Major General Birnie rated him consistently superior, writing in his final efficiency report, "An officer of preeminently outstanding ability and high attainments; especially clear headed in thought and sound in judgment." This final report, dated through December 31, 1936, preceded McNair's promotion to the permanent rank of brigadier general, which the War Department announced on December 22. Having reverted from brigadier general to his permanent rank of major after the World War in 1919, McNair finally earned back his star, with an effective date of January 1, 1937. Also on New Year's Day, the War Department issued Special Orders No. 1, both announcing McNair's promotion and relieving him of duty in the chief of field artillery's office. These orders identified his next assignment as commander, 2nd Field Artillery Brigade, at Fort Sam Houston, Texas, with a report date of March 1937. McNair took the oath of office as a brigadier general on January 4, 1937, and promptly requested a leave of absence from January 10 to March 5, with permission to visit Cuba. McNair had finally made it over the hump, rising in rank and authority rapidly since graduation from the US Army War College (AWC) in 1929. His hard work, competence, and noteworthy achievements had paid off, and he requested a well-deserved vacation, receiving approval from the War Department on January 3 for leave, including his request for travel to Cuba.[12]

Redesigning the Infantry Division, 1937–1939

Newly promoted Brigadier General McNair reported for duty at Fort Sam Houston on March 7, 1937, to take command of the 2nd Field Artillery Brigade. McNair's assignment to the 2nd Division represented a conscious decision to place him where the army could once again make use of his particular experience and talent in unit organization and equipment testing. Concurrent with McNair's notification of his imminent promotion and change of duty station, General Malin Craig, who had replaced General MacArthur as army chief of staff on October 2, 1935, decided to test the recommendations of the Modernization Board, formed in January 1936 to examine the organization of the army.[13]

When Malin Craig, described by Russell Weigley as "a Pershing protégé," took over as army chief of staff, he immediately sought to correct what he saw as troubling flaws in army plans, organization, and equipment. Many of Craig's concerns revolved around mobilization issues that McNair and his fellow students had studied at the AWC, recommending solutions that the War Department could not implement because it lacked the resources. AEF veterans remembered the significant problems the US army faced while attempting to mobilize forces to fight in support of the Allies in France, many of which traced back to economic issues. These included shortages of personnel, equipment, and money in the stunted prewar army, and a flat-footed economic stance that severely hindered the effort to transition to a war economy. The lack of clear plans or processes to enable the administration to break the deadlock resulted in an embarrassingly slow mobilization. Only the French and British coalition made possible America's intervention in the war in time to make a difference. America's coalition partners invited the unprepared AEF to deploy to France in 1917, where the Allies provided American units the weapons and training they needed to achieve a state of combat readiness. The Allies also solved the AEF's most significant problem. As Robert Ferrell pointed out, "In January 1918 the British government offered shipping to bring the divisions over, and [. . .] Pershing gratefully accepted." Without this assistance, one can only guess how long it would have taken to deploy the AEF, much less in a combat-ready state.[14]

Historians of this period have found that America possessed greater potential to respond to the demands of economic mobilization than capability or willingness. One would think that the nation's plentiful raw materials, its Industrial Age economy and mass production methods, and its large and motivated labor force should have made the shift to a war economy relatively easy. In reality, applying the nation's industrial might to the war effort proved to be a much more difficult task than it needed to be. The challenges centered on poor planning for the sort of mobilization required, the complexity of shifting from a capitalist to a managed economy, halting leadership by both national level leaders, and leading industrialists and economists working within the new government organizations created to oversee the transition. A few common problems created the greatest difficulties: the reluctance of capitalists to accept centralized management of their businesses; the harmful influence of greed and profit motivation; and the military leadership's inability to provide clear requirements to industry. The struggle to establish an economic war footing wore on for two years, and it nearly caused the collapse of the national economy before regulatory measures finally took hold.[15] Personnel who served in the AEF learned a great deal from this experience, but awareness of a potential problem does not always lead to the ability to plan for it adequately and find a solution, particularly when military plans rely as much on civilian-provided funding as operational skill and foresight.

Upon his appointment as army chief of staff in late 1935, Malin Craig found the army in disturbingly similar circumstances. In particular, he found a massive divide between the existing war plans that would theoretically guide the mobilization and employment of the military in a contingency, and the actual capability of the army in its current atrophied state to accomplish the tasks specified in the existing plans. Craig understood that an army required years, not months, to design, build, and field new equipment, and he desperately wanted to avoid the AEF's mobilization challenges should the nation again require its army to deploy overseas and fight a major war. Lacking the ability to control the nation's industrial mobilization plans, Craig did his best to improve the army's readiness within the limits of his authority. He worked doggedly to convince Roosevelt to wrest budget and personnel increases from the legislative branch, where members of Congress expended the bulk of their intellectual energy on efforts to forestall the ever-worsening Depression, paying little attention to foreign policy or military affairs. Roosevelt managed to convince the legislature to begin a slow increase in military expenditure in 1935, but his preference for all things naval led him to funnel most of the new funds to the navy. Although the army did receive some additional funding, it was not enough to resolve the gap between army capability and war plan requirements. Craig did manage, however, to convince the president that this gap existed, making existing war plans essentially theoretical in nature.[16]

As the international situation grew increasingly tense, the president began to support some of Craig's recommendations, although he still devoted the majority of military spending to the navy for the development of an improved blue-water combat force. As for the army, following the advice of his G-4 and deputy chief of staff, Craig recommended in October 1936 reductions in spending on weapons research and elimination of any nonessential programs. He argued that in his experience, procurement programs required at least two years to advance from concept to prototype production, at which point further delays accompanied the ramp up to full production, depending on the complexity of the systems in development and the nation's economic readiness to support these programs. Therefore, Craig advocated focusing the limited funds available on development of critical items while reducing funding for research. With ongoing procurement programs at various stages of completion, competing for the limited funds available, many fell idle. Craig saw the wisdom of maintaining existing stocks of aging but still functional, noncritical weapon systems; he used scarce funds wisely by shutting down all but the most promising or critical weapon development programs. He secured Roosevelt's approval for this plan.[17]

As army historian Mark Watson has written, "The dominant purpose, it is clear, was to get the existing Army re-equipped without further delay with the best equipment currently available. . . . Prolonged research undoubtedly would produce better weapons five years hence. It would not provide any immediate betterment of a force currently handicapped by obsolete weapons and, in some cases, possessing none at all." Watson mentioned one shortfall in particular: "the lack of antitank weapons adapted to use against post–World War I armor." Halting an ordnance department antitank weapon development program, the War Department staff instead supported the field forces' request for the fielding of a weapon system as early as possible to fill an "imperative need." This led to the army's purchase of a 37mm gun of German design that army arsenals could quickly replicate and produce, but it delayed the fielding of an improved version, of a design recommended by McNair, to some future date several years after resumption of a development program. In the 1930s, just like today, currently fielded equipment represents the outcome of choices made years earlier, and even high-priority procurement efforts last for years between initial concept and fielding.[18]

Much like his concerns about obsolete equipment, Craig believed the army's World War–vintage organizations had not kept up with emerging technology—and the resulting potential for a future war that would be quite different from the last one. This motivated his effort to reevaluate the organization of the army, particularly the infantry division. Military personnel had argued over the organization of the infantry division in a debate that had raged on and off since the end of the World War. As historian John B. Wilson described, "January 1929 marked the beginning of a ten-year struggle to reorganize the infantry division. The assistant chief of staff, G-3, General Parker, reported that European countries were developing armies that could trigger a war of greater velocity and intensity than anything previously known." The major powers in Europe, each searching for a way to increase mobility and minimize losses in a future war, had already begun to use increasingly sophisticated motorized and mechanized vehicles as a solution. Although each arrived at different conclusions regarding the specifics, Great Britain, France, and Germany all reorganized their military units to exploit these new technologies in the late 1920s. In particular, Parker pointed out that some European militaries had restructured their divisions into smaller, more maneuverable units, compensating for reduced mass through enhanced firepower and mobility.[19]

Concurrent with its imminent acquisition of semiautomatic rifles and air-cooled machine guns, Parker believed the US army should make similar changes, starting by streamlining its cumbersome square infantry division—an idea considered but rejected after the World War. The 2nd Division tested various forms of triangular divisions in 1929, but in the end, Army Chief of Staff Summerall, perhaps as a result of his experience during the World War, saw no need to change the square division structure.[20] Therefore, the infantry division retained essentially the same structure it had used during the World War for another six years, when Army Chief of Staff General Malin Craig decided to revisit the issue.

Noting the increasingly nonstandardized organization of existing American infantry divisions, all of which relied on a variety of foot, animal, and motor transport for mobility—none of which he deemed suitable for modern warfare—Craig polled senior commanders in 1935 for solutions. No consensus emerged, even among senior infantry branch leaders, so Craig formed a Modernization Board to make an objective assessment of the situation. The board, led by Major General John B. Hughes, War Department assistant chief of staff, G-3 (operations), focused its efforts on a study of the infantry division to make the task manageable, because the infantry division served as the cornerstone for the organization of all army units. Hughes submitted the board's first report to Craig on July 30, 1936. It recommended abandoning the massive square division for a smaller and more versatile triangular division. Much like Parker's efforts in 1929, the board's report reflected many commonly held views, in particular a guiding vision of open warfare as the fundamental nature of a future war and therefore a key organizational principle guiding the board's efforts. The board also sought to comply with Craig's guidance to equip the new division with the best equipment available, leading to the adoption of the recently approved Garand semiautomatic rifle and even the inclusion of 105mm howitzers, still only in the prototype stage, in the division's authorized equipment. Despite many dissenting opinions regarding specific recommendations, the board report served as the primary guidance for the conduct of the tests that would lead to the new division organization.[21]

In particular, open warfare thinking dominated army personnel's conception of the modern battlefield. Often attributed only to certain leaders, particularly McNair, key aspects of the open warfare view influenced the organization of the proposed division and the design of test division maneuvers well before McNair's involvement in the process. These ideas included the image of a fluid battlefield, characterized by rapid maneuver and the existence of gaps between adjacent enemy units, offering opportunities for reconnaissance and raids against enemy rear areas where headquarters and supply organizations resided. These ideas appeared in a two-page summary of the Modernization Board's findings, dated July 30, 1936, and included in the guidance for design and conduct of the Proposed Infantry Division (PID) test issued to the division before McNair's assignment as chief of staff. This guidance represented the thinking of a generation of military personnel influenced by the AEF experience and post–World War I motorization and mechanization. In particular, this summary enumerated many guiding principles for the upcoming division tests and capabilities that the new division should possess for evaluation during those tests. A few warrant particular mention:

Acceleration of operations in open warfare requires that the number of command echelons be reduced to the minimum.

Weapons, services, personnel, and equipment not always required but needed only under certain contingencies should be pooled.

Antiaircraft defense of combat units of the separate arms by those units, and of other units and installations by A-A units. Extended field test with reference to A-A units.

Division organized on basis of its operating as a part of a larger force, under open warfare conditions. Gaps between divisions.

Team-served weapons pooled in the machine-gun battalion—the .30 caliber machine gun and the .50 caliber machine gun.

The cavalry squadron has the primary mission of reconnaissance and security, not combat. Its principal weapon is the .30 caliber machine gun, auxiliary armament the semiautomatic rifle and pistol.

This guidance illustrates the influence of open warfare thinking on the foundational concepts that guided the PID test. Review of the voluminous correspondence, reports, and orders related to the new division design reveals many varying ideas regarding the specifics, particularly equipment by type and quantity that should exist in divisional units, units organic to the division versus pooled at higher echelons, and specific methods of employment of division assets. Despite the debate over such details, one common thread ran through the planning documents and test reports: an open warfare view of the modern battlefield. The army inculcated this thinking among the ground forces through its doctrine, military educational institutions, and unit training.[22]

Upon reviewing the board's recommendations, Craig directed a test of the PID, both to determine the effectiveness of the triangular organization and to quell discontent among the interested parties, and he selected the 2nd Division to conduct the tests beginning in the fall of 1937. It was not until June 1937, three months after his arrival at Fort Sam Houston to command the 2nd Artillery Brigade, that McNair's division commander, Major General Parsons, selected Mc-Nair to serve as the chief of staff of the PID over many other possible appointees. No reason would exist to make the appointment of a specific brigade commander a foregone conclusion, and all things being equal, one would expect such an assignment to go to an officer on the 2nd Division staff. It seems likely that Parsons selected McNair for this duty on the basis of his previous experience in equipment tests and organizational redesigns. In this role, McNair oversaw the implementation of the PID redesign based on Craig's guidance, which included the findings of the 1936 board, enclosed in the order directing General Parsons to conduct the PID field service test. On the basis of this guidance, McNair oversaw the planning and conduct of the maneuvers and equipment tests, post maneuver boards, and preparation of reports for the War Department.[23] Once again, the army needed someone with a talent for objective experimentation and innovation, and its senior leaders called on McNair. However, McNair did not exert full control over this process. Instead, he acted as directed by Craig and on the basis of the recommendations of army school instructors and branch representatives from across the army.

The infantry division proposed by the 1936 board satisfied the intent of Upton's "rule of fours" concept, intended to facilitate task organization in the square division, at least to the regimental level, and actually improved on it with a "rule of threes" basis. Each division would consist of three infantry regiments, and these regiments would in turn consist of three subordinate units at each echelon—battalion, company, and platoon. Similarly, the division would have one field artillery regiment, but it would break down into three 75mm battalions, plus one 105mm battalion. The sum of all subordinate units, including the addition of the first divisional cavalry squadron since before the World War, the PID as initially designed consisted of only 13,512 men. More importantly, the triangular structure meant the division could easily reorganize into three independent regimental task forces, each with its own 75mm field artillery battalion. The division would retain control of the 105mm (and eventually the 155mm "Long Tom") howitzers, along with the heavy machine guns and mortars, as well as various support elements, allocating them to the task forces as the situation dictated.[24]

The triangular division in its wartime organization also possessed adequate vehicles to motorize its troops fully; however, the army lacked the resources to motorize all its divisions should it adopt the new organization, despite its congressionally capped personnel level that remained well below 200,000. In fact, the War Department had to arrange for the reallocation of adequate trucks and other vehicles from various units to 2nd Division—equipped before the PID test at peacetime levels, like any other division—to facilitate examination of the benefits of complete motorization of the division and performance of the division with its full wartime allotment of equipment. Thus, in theory the division benefited from greater agility and mobility, simplified logistics sustainability, and the ability to reorganize easily into regimental task forces when required. The PID organization tables reflected all of these modifications, intended to enhance the infantry division's capability to conduct open warfare. The War Department intended the PID tests to verify these advantages while determining what capabilities the division might have lost in the reorganization.[25]

Recognizing that unit training, receipt of equipment, and consolidation of units to form the PID at Fort Sam Houston would require several months of preparation, the War Department issued its initial guidance in a memorandum dated March 26, 1937, directing the 2nd Division to conduct the test in the fall of that year. A second memorandum, dated April 2, 1937, authorized 2nd Division to coordinate directly with the various organizations that would provide additional personnel and equipment necessary to form the PID and facilitate the tests. In this memorandum, the War Department, through Headquarters, VIII Corps Area, placed responsibility for the tests "directly under [2nd Division] control." However, the War Department issued guidance to all participating units for activities they should undertake pending conduct of the tests in the fall of 1937. For example, the War Department directed the various branch schools to submit lists of questions and current issues they wanted the PID test to explore. The War Department also issued its own list of "Secondary Questions" in topic areas, including maneuverability, fire power, frontage, ability to sustain combat, and command and staff.[26]

McNair also received his first efficiency report since his promotion to the permanent rank of brigadier general before the first PID test began. The report covered his first three months in brigade command, from March to June 1937. His commander, Major General Parsons, evaluated McNair superior overall, with excellent physical activity and endurance and superior knowledge of his profession. In the event of war, Parsons recommended McNair for duty as chief of staff of a corps or army, and, in an evaluation specific to reports on general officers, Parsons ranked McNair second among the thirty general officers personally known to him. The VIII Corps Area commander, Major General H. J. Brees, concurred with Parsons's evaluation. On the basis of this report alone, Parsons and Brees obviously considered McNair one of the best general officers they had worked with. They selected him to serve in the critical role of chief of staff, PID, both for his competency in general and his previous experience, which made him particularly well suited for the position.[27]

Upon his assignment as PID chief of staff, McNair oversaw all aspects of the upcoming division test, as evidenced by his signature on almost every document generated by the division after the early spring. One of these, a memorandum he distributed on June 4, 1937, projected the tests taking place in six phases. These included the following: (1) organization and preliminary training at home station, (2) training and tests of company and smaller units, (3) training and tests of battalions and regiments followed by movement of supporting units to Fort Sam Houston, (4) assembly of the division, (5) combat team tests, and (6) division tests. McNair projected phases 4, 5, and 6 taking place no earlier than September 1937. By July 13, McNair identified the date for the start of the fourth phase as September 15, 1937, and issued a tentative schedule with a more detailed breakdown of events in the final three phases, including the specific tests the PID would undergo during phases 5 and 6, during the five weeks from October 11 through November 15. These included strong attacks and defenses, envelopments, division counterattack in support of a corps defense, wide front advances to test the daily range of the motorized formations, night attacks, and pursuit operations. On September 3, McNair identified the umpires.[28]

On September 20, McNair appointed a board of review comprising two infantry colonels, one infantry captain, and one field artillery captain to develop a process that they would use during the latter phases of testing to receive, standardize, and consolidate the test results. He also studied the many issues the branch schools (including the Leavenworth schools) and the supporting units sent the War Department in anticipation of the tests, using them to help develop appropriate scenarios and umpire rules. Although these are far too numerous to list here, several common themes and particularly interesting comments deserve mention. Perhaps the most common concern, whether from a combat arms or support unit perspective, dealt with the consequences of motorizing the infantry division, good and bad. Various organizations wanted the tests to identify how far the division could move in a day and with what limitations in terms of various support elements' ability to reposition and prepare for combat operations after a long road march. Map maneuvers at Fort Leavenworth identified the potential for the division to move as much as seventy miles in a day and then conduct a deliberate attack or defense. However, these maneuvers also revealed that this rapid advance often led to thin dispersal of units over excessively large fronts, the formation of a salient the enemy could exploit, and challenges for combat support and logistics units trying to maintain the same pace as the combat units.[29]

Some of the more specific comments involved particular capabilities, limitations, and employment recommendations for specific units and types of equipment. For example, map maneuvers at Fort Leavenworth revealed significant difficulty keeping mortars supplied over long road marches preceding an attack.

Because mortars served as the backup method of fire support for attacking infantry that maneuvered outside the range of field artillery support, this represented a significant problem. The infantry school at Fort Benning echoed this concern while recommending the use of light machine guns primarily for support to attacking rifle squads and .50 caliber machine guns for antimotorized and antimechanized defense. The Field Artillery School also identified challenges keeping artillery in supply when supporting infantry formations conducting envelopments, indicating that in both attacks after long marches and enveloping maneuvers, infantry would likely operate without field artillery or 81mm mortar support. The coast artillery school's primary concerns revolved around motorized units' vulnerability to mechanized and air attack when on the march, leading them to recommend movement by motor only at night. Finally, cavalry officers at Fort Leavenworth emphasized the proper employment of the reconnaissance squadron, highlighting their conviction that "reconnaissance and security [are] its primary roles." Therefore, they recommended equipping and using the reconnaissance squadron in a manner that would prove unlikely to lead to prolonged fighting, discouraging the unit from engaging in sustained combat, and ensuring the squadron handed off the fight to infantry as soon as possible so it could continue its reconnaissance mission.[30]

The final phases of the PID test commenced in early October and ended in late November 1937. Following McNair's directive of September 20, standardized reports of the various tests identified the scenarios undertaken, resulting friendly and enemy actions, and recommendations stemming from the observations of the participating units and umpires. Despite the widespread equipment shortages throughout the army, the PID received the weapons that it needed to conduct the test from various army units or used suitable alternatives where necessary. For example, the heavy artillery battery used 155mm howitzers because the 105mm models had not yet been issued, and the tripod-mounted Browning automatic rifle replaced shortages in .50 caliber machine guns. In addition, General Craig ordered augmentation of the division by antitank and antiaircraft artillery battalions and an observation squadron, to give it capabilities it would normally receive via reinforcement from the corps reserve, enabling a more realistic test (including evaluation of the organization of these nondivisional units). Therefore, in terms of organization, equipment, and execution, the test represented a valid and thorough examination of the capabilities of the PID, as reflected in the report that McNair provided to the War Department on February 24, 1938.[31]

McNair organized the final report into four sections. Three recommended changes in the PID, the antimechanized battalion, and the antiaircraft battalion. The fourth section provided information specifically requested by the War Department. Seven appendixes contained the PID test data that elaborated on the findings and justified the division's recommendations. Some highlights from the findings include recommendations to eliminate several positions and units, including the infantry advisor and the commander of service troops (both brigadier generals) and their staffs, the reconnaissance squadron, the machine gun battalion (including a machine gun company in each rifle battalion instead), the quartermaster service company, and the band. The report included recommendations to remove the 81mm mortars from the artillery regiment and place them directly under each infantry battalion commander, to reduce the size of the rifle and light machine gun squad to seven men, and to reduce the size of the engineer organization from a battalion to a company, all enabling reductions in transportation equipment. It also described several advantages of the 155mm howitzer compared to the 105mm, including greater power, "abundant tactical mobility," availability (with the 105mm not yet fully fielded, few of these howitzers existed in the army inventory), and the field artillery's overall preference for the larger gun. From this early date, McNair expressed a preference for the 155mm howitzer.[32]

Parsons signed the report, but McNair served as its primary author, and it bears the same stamp of quality and detail as his many previous such reports. His efforts during the first PID test earned McNair great respect, demonstrating his capability not just as a field artilleryman but also as a general staff officer well versed in all aspects of army doctrine, organization, and equipment issues. One can see this in the efficiency report McNair received just two weeks before publication of the final PID test report, in which Parsons once again rated him superior as a field artillery brigade commander and expert in his profession, and also rated him superior in the performance of his duties as chief of staff of the PID. Parsons ranked McNair second among the forty general officers he knew, citing daily interaction with McNair during the rating period, and included the following optional remark: "An officer of outstanding ability. He will go far in the Military Service if given the opportunity." Malin Craig also recognized McNair's work on the PID test with a letter of commendation that read, in part, "As you are aware, I consider the results of this test of great importance to the entire Army. You have personally contributed a great deal toward a correct reorganization of the Army. I wish to express to you my personal appreciation of your constant and untiring work and the splendid results thereof."[33]

Despite the success of the PID test and the accolades received by McNair and the other participants, a multitude of individuals and organizations sent to the War Department objected to various details of the proposed organization as soon as they had a chance to review the test report. The PID therefore served as a first step in a lengthy reorganization process, during which many participants lost sight of a basic consideration: to make the division smaller and easier to deploy and employ, yet more powerful. Because of his involvement from the start, Mc-

Nair never lost sight of this intent. His involvement in the PID test and preparations for the Provisional 2nd Division (P2D) test gave him particular insight regarding the significant increase in size and shipping weight of the new division. Greater mobility and firepower significantly increased shipping requirements for overseas deployment, even for a division with significantly reduced numbers of personnel, making efficiency and pooling of resources at a higher echelon key considerations in unit organization thereafter. The PID test did not include overseas deployment considerations specifically, given the general view of the army at this time as a national defense force. However, the test report and comments referencing it frequently addressed the size and shipping demands of the division. For example, the PID test division used 2½-ton trucks for motorized transportation of infantry between engagements rather than half tracks, which would significantly reduce shipping demands for a division deploying overseas.[34]

McNair also underwent another annual physical examination on January 3, in the interim between the end of the PID test and submission of the test report. This physical revealed the long-term nature of his hearing loss, which had gradually worsened since first noted in 1908, the lack of potential treatment options, and his otherwise excellent health. The surgeon general recommended a second inpatient medical exam, this time at Fort Sam Houston, which the War Department endorsed, probably because of the accelerated rate at which the condition had worsened in recent years. McNair underwent this exam from January 31 through 4 February. Weighing in at 151 pounds, with "few teeth missing" and "no dentures," the examining doctors judged McNair physically fit, with no significant health problems other than his degraded hearing. In his final statement upon McNair's discharge, the lead examining doctor, Lieutenant Colonel S. U. Marietta, noted the existence since 1908 of information on McNair's hearing loss in his medical records. He also wrote in the clinical record that McNair remained "very frank about the condition. He states that the onset and progress has been so insidious that he scarcely recognizes it except when he compares his hearing now with a period of some years ago. He has no difficulty in using the telephone or in transacting the business incident to his duties except that, on occasions, he is impelled to request the repetition of remarks made to him. A further physical survey, including 6 ft. plate of chest, urine concentrations, blood picture, blood chemistry (urea and sugar) urine concentration test, and electrocardiogram was negative."[35]

Despite his otherwise excellent health, the surgeon general, upon receipt of this report, recommended further examination at Walter Reed Hospital, followed by a medical board to determine McNair's fitness for continued active duty. At this point, the army chief of staff intervened, seeing no need for yet another medical board, given McNair's demonstrated capacity for excellent performance in a wide range of tasks despite his hearing loss. In short, common sense prevailed.

Overruling the surgeon general, Craig's replacement as chief of staff, General George C. Marshall, refused to order another medical exam or board and ordered the issuance of a waiver for hearing loss, effective June 1939. McNair would no longer have to worry about a medical board or possible early retirement due to his hearing loss because several of the most senior officers in the army personally observed his ability to perform in a superior manner during the PID test despite his condition. Later physicals merely noted his degraded hearing, although the surgeon general continued to include an endorsement that indicated the condition warranted a medical board, but that this would not take place because of the chief of staff's waiver.[36]

Long before the conclusion of this final chapter in the long history of McNair's service-connected hearing loss, the War Department began its analysis of the PID test report, with some staff officers criticizing certain recommendations and suggesting changes. However, more troublesome opposition to the PID organization emerged even before the 2nd Division completed the field tests. Major General George A. Lynch, chief of infantry, wrote the War Department in late 1937, after observing a portion of the PID tests, to voice his objections to the proposed organization. For example, he opposed the creation of machine gun companies, which separated the machine gun—a critical asset—from the direct control of the rifle battalions, and the inclusion of signal detachments and mortar batteries in rifle battalions, which Lynch saw as a threat to unity of command. He also argued against the presence of a commander of service troops—a general officer—within the division because it further complicated command and control. He pointed out that the movement of supply trains remained a tactical matter, depending on the division's combat situation. Therefore, the decision remained the division commander's to make, not one he should delegate to a commander of service troops. Because logistics trains operated to the rear of combat units, Lynch saw no need to burden the division with their presence or the division commander with a subordinate intended to control them. In short, Lynch proposed an even leaner division, resourced for fighting only, with corps organizations tailored to provide logistic support.[37]

To address Lynch's concerns, Craig appointed a committee to design a new division based on the results of the initial PID test. Craig chose Major General Fox Conner, Colonel George C. Marshall, and McNair to serve on this committee—men who all supported the idea of a leaner triangular division and who would make an objective assessment of Lynch's concerns. However, the committee never convened because General Conner took early retirement for medical reasons.[38]

Meanwhile, the War Department General Staff began to discuss its own modifications to the organization of the PID presented in the 2nd Division report. Unlike the comments received from Lynch and other senior infantrymen across the army, who supported the idea of a leaner infantry division, differing only in the details of its modified organization and employment, the War Department General Staff recommended overruling some of the streamlining and other modifications recommended in the test report. For example, it argued for retention of the infantry advisor and the commander of service troops and their staffs, and lowering the rank of the chief of staff to colonel and relieving him of his duty as division second in command. It also recommended retaining a separate service company rather than consolidating the division's service and headquarters companies, and allocating 81mm mortar companies to each infantry regiment, rather than assigning two 81mm mortars (each manned by a squad) directly to the infantry battalion headquarters, as recommended in the PID test report. However, these discussions soon came to Parsons's attention, provoking a preemptive rebuttal, which he wrote to General Craig on June 13, 1938. In this terse but respectful letter, Parsons wrote,

> The test showed that if the 81mm mortars were to be included in an infantry regiment, they would be in the battalion and directly under the battalion commander. Changing the organization proposed as a result of the test cannot be based upon any data in the War Department as valuable as that obtained during the test, and this recommendation can only be considered as the personal opinion of the General Staff officers making it.

Parsons dismissed another possible rationale for the recommended changes:

> I hear that the principle [sic] reasons for the changes recommended . . . are because of the effect on the National Guard; I know it well and appreciate its value in our plan of national defense, but I think it is a mistake to make major changes in an organization that has been built up as a result of a thorough field test because it might adversely affect the national Guard, and I am sure that the National Guard will neither expect nor ask that this be done.

Instead, Parsons noted that all the senior National Guard officers he spoke to merely asked for adequate time to adjust their division organization to match the approved PID structure.[39]

While the division organization proposed in the PID test report answered many of Lynch's concerns, the main point of contention centered on the logistics capability within the division. Lynch advocated removing all logistics from the division and assigning service support responsibility to corps headquarters, allowing the division to streamline even further into an organization tailored purely for fighting. This conflicted with the recommendations in the original test report, which advocated the retention of a limited logistics capability within the division, but it proposed an even smaller organization than that originally designed by the 1936 Modernization Board. Upon receipt of the PID test report, the Modernization Board reconvened to analyze it and the various responses it provoked to this and other points of contention over division capabilities and specific equipment and weapon systems it should possess. Soon the board put forward a new division organization (designated the Provisional 2nd Division, or P2D) that retained the triangular structure of the PID but that sought compromise between the many recommendations and concerns expressed by various schools and corps area headquarters across the army. In doing so, the board created a new division structure that satisfied no one—and worse, one that overlooked recommendations made as the result of months of field tests and intense work within the 2nd Division in favor of the opinions of a few men reviewing the test results from their offices in the War Department.[40] These dissenting views came from individuals who did not participate in the tests; they also did not reflect the basic organizing principle: creating a smaller yet more powerful division, easy to deploy despite mechanization.

The new division organization the board proposed retained the band and a service company within each infantry regiment headquarters and assigned a weapons company to each rifle battalion armed with heavy mortars and machine guns, despite the PID test findings regarding the difficulty of keeping 81mm mortars supplied with ammunition when moved forward to support infantry attacks. The board did not assign the rifle battalion an antitank unit, believing the weapons companies' .50 caliber machine guns and the regiment's 37mm guns provided adequate antitank defense.[41] The board reduced the size of the field artillery regiment on the basis of command and control concerns expressed by various branch school and corps area commanders, even though the PID test showed no evidence of such command and control difficulties. It also retained the two general officer advisers that the PID had found worse than useless but removed them from the chain of command (apparently thinking this would mitigate the problems identified in the PID tests). Finally, the board disregarded Lynch's recommendations concerning logistics, redesigning the division's supply system instead of assigning logistics responsibility to army corps. Under the revised organization, combat arms units bore the responsibility for ammunition resupply and baggage transportation. This led the board to eliminate the motor battalion in favor of a quartermaster battalion that combined transport and some maintenance capability (the division would handle any repairs requiring three hours or less). Finally, the newly organized division retained responsibility for evacuating their sick and wounded to corps medical facilities.[42]

Upon reviewing the board's new division design, Craig realized it would attract criticism, and he ordered a yearlong test, to begin in February 1939. After a brief two-month break serving solely as commander of the 2nd Field Artillery Brigade, McNair found himself once again serving as the test division chief of staff and taking the lead role in the preparations for an extensive test of the newly proposed division organization. McNair planned for the second round of tests by developing a series of scenarios for the P2D headquarters to oversee, each describing the day's timeline of events and the orders the division staff would issue to its subordinate units. Each day's scenario comprised a detailed schedule, including orders for the headquarters to issue and missions that the division would conduct, all focused on evaluating the division's mobility, flexibility, and combat effectiveness. The scenarios reflected meticulous planning, including detailed movement rate calculations and timings for issuance of movement orders to coordinate the arrival of march columns originating from both Fort Sam Houston, Texas, and Camp Bullis (about thirty miles to the northwest), at the desired time and place and in the correct sequence. The scenarios also included plans for movement of divisional headquarters, timed to ensure the staff would complete movement and resume full function before each key event began. The scenarios considered reconnaissance plans and orders, supply and other logistics requirements, and command and control processes, including the preparation and distribution of orders and overlays to facilitate coordination.[43]

Guidance for the new division organization test included many specific details, two of which stand out as particularly significant. The guidance document noted that

> it should be continuously borne in mind that the division under test is designed to function as part of a larger balanced force. Consequently, the determination of its ability to function as one of the divisions of a corps is important. However, our situation and the necessity for reinforcing the overseas garrisons may frequently call for the use of a single division. It is recognized that for independent missions, it will have to be reinforced by at least some reconnaissance, antiaircraft, antimechanized, artillery, engineer, medical, and transportation units in accordance with its mission. Some of the problems for operations of the division as a whole should be drafted on the assumption that it is operating as part of a corps and some under the assumption that the division reinforced is acting alone.[44]

The second round of tests therefore differed significantly from the first, taking possible overseas deployment into consideration and specifically testing the concepts of pooling and task organization by testing the division as it would fight as part of a corps, or reinforced with pooled assets and fighting independently. The test guidance also specifically directed subjecting the P2D to attacks by "hostile aviation and hostile mechanized units," including evaluation of the "adequacy or inadequacy of the facilities provided in the organization for warning of and for defense against such attacks."[45]

Although McNair conducted most of the planning, he did not participate in the actual P2D tests, although this lengthy involvement in the design, organization, testing, debate, and redesign of the triangular division gave him an intimate knowledge of the specific organization characteristics of the new division. It also instilled in him fundamental War Department and armywide views on the nature of modern warfare (assumed to look much like the open warfare Pershing envisioned in 1918), efficiency-focused concepts like pooling, and effectiveness-focused concepts like task organization for combat. McNair also served as chief umpire during the Third Army maneuvers that took place near San Antonio—his first experience in a field unit overseeing umpire duties since the academic instruction he received at the AWC—before he departed for his next assignment.

Just before the beginning of the P2D test, scheduled for March 1939, the 2nd Division welcomed a new commander, Major General Walter Krueger, and learned McNair would leave the division for a new assignment on March 17. The previous month, General Craig selected McNair to succeed Brigadier General Charles M. Bundel as the commandant of Fort Leavenworth's Command and General Staff School (CGSS). Increasing tensions in Europe had confirmed Craig's conviction the army must accelerate preparations for war. With the bulk of the hard work associated with redesigning the infantry division done, Craig's deputy, Brigadier General George C. Marshall, advised that he take the opportunity to assign McNair to Fort Leavenworth to improve the education programs there. Craig had significant concerns about the Leavenworth schools' readiness to support officer education, particularly with the potential for wartime mobilization rising. After witnessing McNair's capability and work ethic over the past two years, he knew of no regular army officer who possessed stronger qualifications to accomplish the much-needed revitalization of CGSS. Marshall wrote to McNair on February 23, 1939, to provide some insight regarding the War Department leadership's expectations. Marshall wanted McNair to know that Secretary of War Woodring had expressed concern about the course and believed "something should be done immediately to modernize the school methods of instruction."[46] Having served on the post–World War inaugural faculty, McNair would return as the Leavenworth commandant, with the charter to prepare the school for the possibility of military mobilization.

McNair's final efficiency report as commander, 2nd Field Artillery Brigade, and chief of staff, P2D, reflected the exceptional reputation he established during his time at Fort Sam Houston. The division commander, Major General F. W.

Lieutenant Generals Ben Lear, Lesley J. McNair, Walter Krueger, and Delos Carlton Emmons at the Third Army Maneuvers, Fort Polk, Louisiana, 1939. Courtesy of US National Archives II, College Park, Maryland

Rowell, rated McNair superior in the performance of both his primary duties and ranked him first out of seventeen brigadier generals Rowell knew personally. Brees, still commanding the VIII Corps Area, concurred with Rowell's report, ranking McNair as number five out of the forty-one general officers that he knew. Each added a special endorsement to their report, congratulating McNair and commending him for, in Brees's words, "your unflagging energy, your vision, the training you gave your umpires, and to your excellent executive and organizing ability. It gives me great pleasure to make my views of record." Thus, not only did McNair develop an expertise unique among the army in the intricacies of the US army infantry division's organization, capabilities, and limitations, but he also put his AWC education in umpire procedures to practical use while serving as the chief umpire for the Third Army maneuvers in the fall of 1938.[47] At this stage of his career, McNair had risen to general officer rank and possessed a wealth of experience that extended well beyond the scope of his background in the field artillery. In short, he epitomized the general staff officer—one not only possessing years of experience but also a wide variety of skills honed in diverse and demanding positions. McNair was no longer merely a field artillery officer.

The P2D tests began in February 1939 as scheduled, but they did not last a year, as Craig envisioned. They ended early because Germany invaded Poland on September 1, 1939. Demonstrating the diverse range of opinions among senior army officers regarding army equipment, organization, and doctrine during this period of uncertainty and resource constraints, Krueger expressed concern over many of the changes that resulted from the Modernization Board's review of the first round of tests. He worried about the lack of robust logistics capability within the division, and he believed that the organization could only fight independently for forty-eight hours at its 1939 peace strength (the P2D had an authorized peace strength of 7,970 and a wartime strength of 11,485). Krueger did agree with the streamlining of the division in general, supporting the pooling of air, antiaircraft, and tank units at corps or higher echelons, although he believed the division lacked adequate antitank capability. The division still relied on 37mm antitank guns and .50-caliber machine guns for antitank defense, and with funding to purchase existing models limited and Craig's halting in 1936 of most weapon development programs, no solution to this problem appeared imminent.[48]

Although the tests convinced army leaders that streamlining divisions and reorganizing them as triangular units would lead to an optimal balance between efficiency and effectiveness, the War Department continued to debate specifics regarding unit organization and equipment long after the end of the PID and P2D tests. McNair continued to monitor these developments while serving as the commandant at Fort Leavenworth. A wholesale reorganization of the fundamental building block of the army, sure to create debate and discord, required updated doctrine. By assigning McNair to his new position at Leavenworth, Chief of Staff Craig placed him in an ideal position to modernize the teaching methods at CGSS and to play a key role in bringing army doctrine up to date, to account for recent changes in organization and fighting techniques.

Part III

World War II
The Culmination of a Career

8
Protective Mobilization

Throughout the first half of the 1930s, President Roosevelt had remained focused inward, concerned about America's struggle with the Depression and his New Deal while showing little interest in international affairs, economic or otherwise. The American people's attitudes reflected that of their government. Even in the increasingly volatile environment of the late 1930s, Roosevelt and America's legislators held dramatically different views regarding foreign affairs. Meanwhile, most of the world's powerful nations either engaged in acts of aggression or sought to contain or defend themselves from others engaging in these acts in one way or another. Despite increased media attention on these ominous international events, and Roosevelt's landslide victory in the 1936 election, the president still possessed limited influence over Congress, in part because of a significant political misstep that Roosevelt took shortly after his reelection. The Supreme Court had steadily overturned elements of his New Deal during his first term. Roosevelt realized that six of the justices that routinely voted against his policies exceeded the age of seventy. To rebalance the makeup of the Supreme Court in his favor, he proposed that Congress grant him the power to add one justice to the Supreme Court for every justice who did not resign within six months of turning seventy. Congress saw through this plan immediately and overwhelmingly refused to support it. Far worse, however, Roosevelt lost much of his influence over the legislators, not regaining it until the final year of his second term. This meant that for three years, the president saw the need to prepare for intervention in international affairs but could not convince Congress or the American people to support any such plans.[1]

During the interwar years, the War Department saw the resource-starved island nation of Japan as America's most likely future enemy, but the American diplomatic efforts to contain Japan only led its government to pursue an increasingly expansionist foreign policy. Even so, America did not take any greater action to deter Japanese aggression than it did to deter similarly antagonistic nations in Europe. In fact, the Roosevelt administration remained almost entirely uninvolved in international affairs until 1939, in part because Congress began to constrain executive branch power in 1936. The power of the executive branch grew significantly during Roosevelt's first term as the federal government led various efforts to curtail the Depression, intervening in matters traditionally handled by the states. Congress soon sought to limit the president's power, both to intervene directly in affairs normally handled by the states, and in particular, to intervene in international affairs, passing a series of neutrality acts throughout the 1930s to prevent American entanglement in increasingly turbulent global affairs. Congress sought to use the fourth such act, the Neutrality Act of 1937, to establish a permanent state of isolationism by placing the strictest limits yet on presidential power. Most of the measures in this legislation remained law well after Roosevelt finally began to convince various government officials that America would have to intervene—directly or indirectly—in the rapidly degrading state of international affairs.[2]

While America remained neutral despite Roosevelt's growing unease with the global environment, Benito Mussolini's forces invaded and established Italian control over Ethiopia, General Francisco Franco sought to establish a fascist dictatorship in Spain, and Hitler began a series of increasingly aggressive and ambitious actions to expand his power in Europe. The Japanese government pursued its own ambitions by seeking to establish resource independence, beginning its strategy of expansion by starting a war with China in 1937. Japanese troops landed at Shanghai and then marched to the Nationalist Chinese capital of Nanking, seizing control of the city on December 12. For weeks after this successful operation, the Japanese engaged in horrific acts of violence against the citizens of the capital city, including rape, torture, and murder, eventually resulting in the death of over 200,000 Chinese civilians in what historians now refer to as the Rape of Nanking.[3]

One can see the powerful hold that isolationism had over America in the 1930s with the political battle over the Ludlow amendment that took place at the same time Japan was beginning its war with China. American citizens voiced strong support for the amendment—a support that did not wane even after the Japanese committed a significant act of aggression against America during its invasion of Shanghai. The Ludlow amendment, if enacted, would have required a national referendum before any American declaration of war. Historian David M. Kennedy called the Ludlow amendment a "transparently silly idea, accurately likened by critics to convening a town meeting before authorizing the fire department to put out a blaze."[4]

During the initial invasion of Shanghai on December 12, 1937, Japanese aircraft bombed and sank an American gunboat at anchor in the Yangtze River in broad daylight, killing two crewmembers and wounding thirty. Overwhelming evidence indicated that the Japanese pilots intentionally attacked the ship, and knew it was American. To ensure pilots could identify their gunboat as American from the air, the crew displayed two large American flags (fourteen by eighteen feet each) on the upper deck. The most important evidence came from a film of the event, taped by a journalist who happened to be on board during the attack. The images on the tape disproved the Japanese claim that the pilots attacked from too high an altitude to recognize the flags. Even worse, the film clearly showed the Japanese pilots repeatedly returning to strafe the survivors as they attempted to escape. Even after this event, known as the *Panay* incident, a Gallup Poll found that 73 percent of Americans still favored the Ludlow amendment. Only the influence of a determined Roosevelt administration led to the defeat of the Ludlow amendment in the House (and this, as Kennedy highlighted, by a "narrow margin of 209 to 188") in January 1938. This event did, however, give Roosevelt resolve to act, a desire he had declared in a speech the previous October, saying, "The epidemic of world lawlessness is spreading. . . . There is no escape through mere isolation or neutrality. . . . There must be positive endeavors to preserve peace." By the end of the year, Roosevelt requested funds from Congress to enable expansion of the armed forces. He argued for this expansion on the basis of the Japanese threat and also because an increasingly aggressive Germany posed the threat of potential invasion. Both justified the need for a larger defense force—in particular the creation of a huge air force and an expanded navy.[5]

At this point, Japanese aggression against China, and whatever strategic aims Japan intended to pursue next, remained America's primary concern. Still, the president's remarks demonstrated that those paying attention to Europe saw the tension building there as well and recognized the threat to America's traditional European ally, Great Britain. Financial crises and ideological clashes set the conditions for armed confrontations, raising the specter of another Great War. During the first half of the 1930s, Hitler secured his power over the Nazi Party, the German government, and the German army. He made great strides in reasserting German power in Europe. In 1933, Hitler withdrew Germany from the League of Nations and from the Disarmament Conference in Geneva. In 1935, he renounced the disarmament requirements in the Treaty of Versailles. On March 7, 1936, he ordered over 30,000 troops from his rapidly growing army to occupy the Rhineland, regaining control over this industrially vital territory, which also served as a buffer zone between Germany and France. The German troops completed the occupation without meeting any resistance. By 1936, Hitler negotiated both the Rome–Berlin Axis agreement and the Anti-Comintern Pact with Japan.[6]

These initial successes emboldened Hitler, who grew increasingly aggressive, annexing Austria in April 1938 through an enforced plebiscite that, through various means of coercion and mischief at the polling stations, resulted in a 99 percent "yes" vote in support of the annexation. Cleverly, Hitler ensured that Austrian citizens understood a "yes" vote for the annexation included an affirmation of their personal support of Hitler and his policies as the leader of Germany. Hitler's forces next occupied the majority of German-speaking Czechoslovakia, one of Europe's few remaining democracies, after a long military buildup and significant political maneuvering. When German troops marched into the Sudetenland on October 1, 1938, the well-equipped Czechoslovakian forces withdrew from their hardened defensive positions. The Sudeten Party, German speakers who formed a majority of the population in this region, had driven out most non-Germanic Czechs before the occupation. It looked much like a repeat of the annexation of Austria. Many Czech and German Jewish refugees fled as Germany incorporated other nearby Germanic regions into the Reich, and Hitler planned for the takeover of Czechoslovakia proper. Over the next several months, Germany applied increasing pressure on the Czech government, ultimately compelling the cowed and elderly president to submit to the establishment of Czechoslovakia as a Reich protectorate on March 15, 1939.[7] Those paying attention heard reports of anti-Semitic policies emerging from each new area that the Nazis occupied. These racist policies reached a boiling point in Germany on November 1, 1938—the *Kristallnacht,* or the night of broken glass.[8]

An increasingly concerned Europe continued to take no decisive action to prevent the spread of Nazi power, convinced by leaders like Great Britain's prime minister, Neville Chamberlain, to continue the impotent policy of appeasement. Under political pressure to do something more than merely negotiate, however, the leaders of Britain and France agreed to guarantee retaliation if Hitler violated Poland's sovereignty. Therefore, when Germany invaded Poland on September 1, 1939, the policy of appeasement finally took its last rattling breath. Ironically, while the invasion prompted a formal declaration of war by Great Britain and France against Germany, the unprepared French and British armies mobilized so slowly that the campaign in Poland ended in another German victory before they could oppose Hitler's aggression. This marked the beginning of the period now known as the Phony War, during which France and Britain stood by while Hitler prepared for his next move.[9]

Throughout this period, despite general American disinterest in international affairs, Roosevelt sought ways to take action by working around the limitations presented by America's nonaggression policy. By the fall of 1939, he had only managed to initiate a halting move toward a war economy, put forward a plan for a relatively small-scale military mobilization for defensive purposes, and gain congressional approval to begin providing raw materials to Great Britain in the fledgling period of lend-lease. Although at this point the lend-lease program offered the greatest potential for the American government to influence the course of events, Roosevelt found his hands tied by the cash-and-carry policy still in place after the passage of the Neutrality Act of 1937. This required the British to pay with cash for any materials America provided and to transport these materials from America to Great Britain purely with British transport ships—both requirements soon beyond the means of a cash-strapped Britain relying on its navy for defense against the threat of a German invasion.[10]

With no formal government decision to mobilize or take action, Roosevelt began to act, but in a way that demonstrated his discordance with his senior military leadership regarding American strategy, as war appeared increasingly imminent. As Mark Stoler described, Roosevelt "launched a series of major initiatives in both Europe and the Far East. These included the extension of material aid to Great Britain, the application of early economic sanctions against Japan, and the maintenance of the Pacific Fleet in its new and exposed position at Pearl Harbor." Yet Roosevelt would only go so far, refusing to take actions that his key advisers considered mandatory, such as transferring a significant portion of the Pacific Fleet to the Atlantic. Meanwhile, he ignored advice to avoid acts of provocation, such as his trade of 50 obsolescent destroyers to Great Britain for 99-year leases on British bases in the Western Hemisphere—a largely symbolic gesture but one that gave Churchill assurance that he could count on American assistance in the difficult struggle to come against Germany.[11] Still struggling with a seemingly endless economic crisis after two decades of isolationist foreign policy, America finally seemed determined to become a player on the world stage—but it remained uncertain to what degree the nation could prepare effectively for the events on the horizon, and with what means.

Leavenworth Commandant, 1939–1940

The army's education system represented one of the most important of these means, given the widespread impact it could have even in a budget-constrained environment. General Craig, at the recommendation of General Marshall, selected McNair to serve as commandant of the Command and General Staff School (CGSS) at Fort Leavenworth, counting on him to update the teaching methods at Fort Leavenworth and to prepare this critical educational institution for the possibility of mobilization. McNair's new position would require him, among other things, to update doctrine and instruction to cover the latest improvements in military technology, and to design a curriculum that would enable a small cadre of regular army officers to oversee large-scale mobilization while effectively yet rapidly training civilians to serve as soldiers. To prepare McNair for this responsibility, Craig provided him airplane transport to Barksdale, Langley, and Maxwell fields en route to Fort Leavenworth. On this trip, Craig intended McNair to familiarize himself "as to the principles and theories being taught at the Air Corps Tactical School." Shortly before his departure, McNair requested the addition of Fort Knox to his itinerary so he could observe the newly created mechanized force as it conducted experiments with armored vehicles. Craig approved this request.[12]

Marshall expounded on his intent for McNair's assignment as CGSS commandant and the preparatory tour of other training installations in a letter he wrote to Brigadier General Asa L. Singleton on February 27, 1939. Marshall anticipated that McNair would have only one day on his itinerary to spend with Singleton, who had served as commandant of the infantry school at Fort Benning since July 1936, and Marshall wanted to ensure that Singleton took maximum advantage of this opportunity. Marshall scripted the discussion by writing:

> I hope that in that brief time, you can give him a good idea of the practical tactics and techniques taught there. I think it very important to have brought to his attention any apparent differences between Benning tactical techniques and that at Leavenworth. For example, during my period, a Leavenworth Infantry battalion order would be two or three pages long, where a similar order at Benning would be less than a page in length. The same applied to G-2 summaries, supply details and so forth. The one was ponderous and cumbersome, while the other at least showed struggle towards simplicity. Benning used geological survey maps and Leavenworth was more inclined to the Gettysburg variety. Benning's procedure suggested more of contact with soldiers and the soil, than did the Leavenworth procedure. I am writing you most informally to give you some idea as to why McNair is being sent to Benning. Times have changed and maybe there is not the difference today that there was in my day.

Marshall closed this letter like many he wrote to general officers late in his career: "Please treat all that I have said here as confidential."[13]

On March 4, 1939, with McNair still on his tour of training installations, Marshall wrote another letter to McNair in which he elaborated on his concerns about CGSS. Marshall believed that the course had adopted an overly rigid and laborious staff procedure, and in particular one not optimized to the nature of the forces on which the army would rely in the event of mobilization for war. Believing the army would have mere weeks, not months or years, to mobilize for a future war, Marshall worried that Leavenworth improperly focused on training officers to lead the professional regular army rather than preparing them to lead partially trained troops activated from the National Guard, not to mention a potential horde of untrained conscripts. Marshall believed that

> regular officers should be experts regarding every consideration involved in the training and the leadership of partially trained troops; they should be intimately familiar with the employment of organizations below war strength and

lacking in artillery and similar components, as well as supply echelons. They should be most familiar with the technique involved in working on poor maps of the Geological small scale variety—rather than the Leavenworth fourth-year-of-a-war-type.[14]

He based these views on three years' experience working with National Guard units and his participation in two army maneuvers, which had left him "horrified by the methods taken by Regular officers in handling these partially trained troops."[15]

Marshall also lamented the "laborious stabilized command post technique and procedure" he regularly witnessed. He cited the frequency, length, and detail of orders; the number of highly detailed reports headquarters demanded from their subordinate units; and "the absurd amount of G-2 information supplied." All this led Marshall to believe a "stabilized or siege warfare" mentality still governed regular army officers' views of warfare. Writing, "Now, we know what kind of an army we are going to have on M-day, and we must presume that open warfare will be the rule rather than the exception," Marshall wanted McNair to refocus CGSS on the tactics and leadership methods appropriate to lead inexperienced troops in that demanding environment.[16]

This letter seems remarkable in retrospect. It preceded Germany's invasion of Poland by almost five months but predicted the mobile nature of warfare that would result from motorization and mechanization of modern armies. It showed the lasting impact of the two generals' American Expeditionary Force (AEF) experience, both in the use of language Marshall knew McNair would understand ("open warfare" versus "stabilized or siege warfare") and in the desire to avoid the mistakes that the army and the nation made in its preparations for and operations during the World War. Finally, it demonstrated that like McNair, Marshall continued to struggle intellectually with the impact of the increasing technological sophistication of modern armies and with the challenge of how to prepare the US army for modern warfare despite the limitations posed by the economic constraints and the isolationist sentiment that had dominated America throughout most of the previous two decades. This letter, representative of the content of a long-term correspondence between Marshall and McNair, indicates that at least these two US army officers, and probably others who had served with the AEF, recognized the changing nature of warfare, particularly because of the potential for motorization and mechanization to change the complexion of the future battlefield.

Upon the conclusion of McNair's preassignment tour of training installations, he wrote to Marshall to describe the great benefit that he accrued from visiting the various installations and witnessing their current training systems and modernization efforts. Two months later, after Marshall learned of his selection to succeed General Craig as the army chief of staff, he wrote to McNair, "You at the head of Leavenworth are one of the great satisfactions I have at the moment in visualizing the responsibilities of the next couple of years." As Stephen R. Taaffe noted, "Marshall had countless responsibilities as chief of staff, but he believed that his most significant and difficult task was recommending officers for the president to nominate as generals and assigning them to their posts." Therefore, the fact that Marshall placed so much trust in McNair at this early stage in his rise to the highest position of responsibility in the army speaks volumes about Marshall's respect for McNair's competence and character—traits Marshall valued above all others in an army officer.[17]

Russell Weigley has pointed out the irony that Marshall's replacement of Craig as chief of staff in August 1939, while placing the ideal officer in this key position at a pivotal historical moment, obscured the significance of Craig's influence on the army's preparedness for war. Although the army remained far from ready in 1939 to fight a war in modern conditions, it had made great strides under Malin Craig's leadership. Craig oversaw a massive effort to update the organization of the infantry division, the first step in an overhaul of army organization as a whole. Despite the limited means available to the budget-constrained army, he managed to equip units with the best weapon systems available at the time. Most of the army's limitations in 1939 stemmed from long-standing funding shortages and personnel caps. The infantry division's two authorized strengths—one for peace and a much larger one for war—serves as just one example of these limitations. However, the army did possess far more equipment, if somewhat dated, than before Craig's tenure, and the significant organizational modernization effort that he oversaw—particularly the conversion of infantry divisions to the triangular structure—enhanced the army's ability to use those weapons that it possessed more effectively. Craig also accelerated the War Department's study of the challenge of industrial mobilization and led the army to investigate the impact of motorization and mechanization, both in the officer education system and in unit field tests. Nevertheless, Marshall overshadows Craig in most historical accounts of the period. This leads to misunderstandings, like the widespread belief that the army's reliance in the early years of Marshall's tenure on the 37mm antitank gun represented a choice made while Marshall was chief of staff, rather than a downstream effect of Craig's decision to halt most weapons development programs in 1936, many of which did not resume until 1939 or 1940.[18]

McNair faced significant challenges upon his reassignment to Fort Leavenworth. Marshall expected him to oversee a significant modification of the curriculum while preparing the minds of Leavenworth graduates to cope with the complexities of contemporary motorized and mechanized warfare—and to do so as America's involvement in the war loomed on the horizon. In his graduation address, made only a few months after his arrival as the new commandant, McNair described some of the changes made necessary by the demands of modern warfare—a significant factor that the graduating class must never forget as the graduates had learned applicatory methods to solve concrete cases. He warned them, "You have applied principles and, in many cases, definite procedures. . . . It may be possible that Leavenworth was wrong." Furthermore, "changes in organization, armament, and transportation are ahead. Aviation is coming into the picture more and more, and leading us to no one knows just what and where." He admonished the graduating class, "Do not use horse-and-buggy methods in a motorized age."[19] As these comments reveal, the applicatory method might have suffered from imperfections, but McNair recognized them and encouraged Leavenworth graduates to avoid applying the principles they learned there blindly, instead applying them in a manner appropriate to the situation in which they found themselves.

Thus, McNair arrived at Leavenworth well aware of both the benefits and the flaws in the school's pedagogical approach. Historians have often taken Leavenworth to task for its use of the applicatory method, but others have found it both appropriate to the school's mission and reasonably effective. Peter Schifferle demonstrated the essential role that the Leavenworth schools played in maintaining the preparedness of the interwar US army, while Michael Matheny emphasized the role of the Army War College (AWC) in the development of American operational art. These historians have written detailed assessments of the interwar army's professional officer education system, each concluding that officers received an excellent and appropriate education at both the Leavenworth schools and the AWC.

Schifferle's account pointed out key gaps in the education that officers received at Leavenworth in the 1920s and 1930s, particularly the lack of focus on logistics and army air forces. Further, he observed that flawed mobilization estimates exaggerated these problems because they "grossly underestimated the need for large headquarters to form, train, deploy, and sustain ground forces, grossly underestimated the needs of service forces, and nearly completely failed to understand the needs of the burgeoning army air forces for senior officers and staffs." However, Schifferle argued that the school's contributions far outweighed its shortcomings. It benefited from a particularly talented faculty, mostly selected from the top graduates of each class, who served a tour with a field unit and then returned to Leavenworth to teach. Many of these officers also possessed experience serving with the AEF during World War I.[20]

The school provided many officers during this period their only opportunity to study large-unit operations, even if funding constraints prevented field maneuvers and limited this instruction to the classroom. Most importantly,

Although students were not always encouraged to be innovative, student solutions that did not mimic the instructors' rote answers were possible and did not necessarily result in a lower grade. What every graduating class gained at Leavenworth were not cutting-edge technological advances or new, doctrine-shaking ideas about combat. They gained the three essential elements of the Leavenworth educational system: skills in problem solving, the principles and techniques of handling large formations in combat, and, of inestimable value, the confidence that they could manage these large formation command and staff tasks that had so greatly challenged officers in the AEF.[21]

Matheny pointed out that many of the men who attended the staff school at Leavenworth went on to graduate from the War College, which produced by 1939 the vast majority of the officers who served as the army's most senior commanders in the 1940s. Graduates of the AWC also practiced large formation operations through map maneuvers and command post exercises, filling many of the gaps in their military education that remained after their studies at Leavenworth. Matheny argued,

> The lessons of World War I, as distilled in the curriculum of the War College in the twenties, continued to be studied and taught into the thirties. The emphasis on logistics remained evident in virtually all of the exercises and map maneuvers. The scale, scope, and detail in campaign planning became more refined and more sophisticated, particularly as war clouds gathered at the end of the decade. More than anything else, the specificity of war planning . . . helped to develop meaningful and modern solutions to problems in operational art.[22]

In the end, the rapid acceleration of America's preparation for war had an unforeseeable impact on McNair's efforts at Leavenworth. It arose from the curtailment of his assignment there to just one year and the decision to abbreviate the course near the end of his tour as commandant. Rather than revising the curriculum of the existing one-year course to bring it more in line with the methods Marshall and McNair had discussed, events led the War Department to direct the creation of a significantly abbreviated course in hopes that it could produce the number of graduates necessary to support large-scale mobilization should the need arise. Nevertheless, McNair did not merely lead the reorganization of CGSS into a short course; he made great strides in updating the teaching methods and grading system used by the faculty and contributing to the army's ongoing modernization efforts.[23]

For example, in 1939 the army still relied on a core doctrine developed by assessing the AEF's performance during the World War, which several postwar boards judged as generally adequate and based on valid doctrine. This led to the publication of the 1923 *Field Service Regulations* (*FSR*), a document that served as the army's overarching operational doctrine, on which it based all other doctrine and procedures. This manual governed army operations for over a decade, and despite various efforts to rewrite the army's core doctrine throughout the intervening years, the updated *FSR* remained unapproved and in a state of flux upon McNair's arrival at Fort Leavenworth.[24]

As Walter Kretchik has argued, the 1923 *FSR* grew increasingly outdated as technological and organizational changes took hold in the army throughout the 1920s and 1930s. The 1923 manual, fundamentally unchanged from its 1914 predecessor, stressed mobile offensive operations—open warfare—above all else, although it did add some specificity to the concept by defining tactical actions like meeting engagements and attacks against stabilized fronts. As seen in the 1929 curriculum of the AWC, the year McNair and Dwight D. Eisenhower graduated, students analyzed both their own doctrine and that of other armies as they reviewed and suggested changes to existing war plans that anticipated many possible scenarios that might lead to war with other nations. Nevertheless, halfhearted congressional implementation of the 1920 National Defense Act meant the army lacked the resources to effect change on the basis of the insights gained from lectures and practical exercises at the War College or the vibrant discourse that took place in the various professional branch journals like the *Field Artillery Journal*.[25]

Although doctrine writers incorporated other changes in the 1923 *FSR* that were based on the army's postwar review of the World War's lessons, Kretchik argued that the content of the manual mattered less than its effect on the army's approach to thinking about modern warfare. Kretchik described the 1923 *FSR* as the "intellectual core of the Army." The War Department not only approved the content of the *FSR* but also took on a new role in its influence on the content of the various branch doctrinal manuals: "Through doctrine, the War Department had furthered its authority over the service as a whole. Yet, without a war to test it in battle, the 1923 *FSR* was obsolete by the mid-1930s."[26]

In 1939, the army remained undermanned, equipped with aging or obsolete equipment, and slow to adopt new doctrine and operational concepts compared to the armies of some of the world's powerful—and dangerous—nations. Even though many officers in army schools and operational assignments studied new concepts of warfare emerging in other parts of the world, these ideas only gradually worked their way into the US army's discourse on war. Only Japan lagged behind America in the major powers' mechanization efforts, and America's first experiment with a mechanized force ended in disappointment after only a few months, serving only to highlight America's slow adoption of mechanized weapons, particularly armored units. Even in the development of infantry, the US army did not appear to learn from its European counterparts' experiments with machine guns and armor support, and the United States was the last of the major powers' armies to adopt the triangular division structure.[27]

This fundamental change in organizational structure formed the main catalyst for the eventual approval of a new *FSR* in 1939. Although various efforts took place beginning in the late 1920s to update the doctrine, they did not result in a new *FSR*, although they did lead to creation of a series of supporting manuals. However, lack of consensus on these manuals only added confusion to the effort to update army doctrine. Between 1935 and 1939, the War Department stepped up efforts to update the official doctrine in the *FSR* and gain approval for the unofficial doctrine contained in the supporting manuals, which had drawn much criticism since their creation, in part as a result of their early foundation in French doctrine. By 1937, the War Department staffed an updated draft *FSR*, broken down into three volumes (*Operations, Administration,* and *Large Formations*). As Walter Kretchik described,

> The responses ranged from detailed analyses to total apathy. . . . The drafts eventually made their way into the hands of Brigadier General Lesley J. McNair. . . . McNair and his staff [at CGSS] painstakingly reviewed everything chapter by chapter. McNair was involved to the point where he authored many changes himself. His personal comments also took shape in a formal reply to the War Department. The general staff adopted most of his ideas.[28]

Thus, the man individually most involved in the development and adoption of the triangular division also led the final push to develop a doctrine to bring the army up to date with the technological and organizational changes it had undergone over the preceding decades. He also did so from an ideal position. As commandant at CGSS, McNair could monitor ongoing developments in the organization of the triangular infantry division, contribute to the army's new operational doctrine, and ensure the Leavenworth curriculum covered these topics, keeping the students up to date with the latest changes to army organization and doctrine.

After only two months in his new position, Marshall wrote to McNair on August 7, 1939, to inform him of the imminent approval of the *FSR*. He also lauded McNair on the positive effect he had already achieved as commandant: "I hear on every hand the most flattering comments regarding your effect on Leavenworth. You apparently—to use a hackneyed word—have vitalized the place and yet in a most harmonious manner."[29]

In his recent study of US army doctrine, Kretchik observed, "These draft manuals were subjected to far more scrutiny than any previous *FSR*." However, he pointed out the process of buy-in among the War Department staff, army schools, and operational units made for a slow but inclusive process. Finally, in September 1939, George C. Marshall approved the new doctrine while putting in place a fundamental change in the organization of doctrine by dividing the 1939 *FSR* into three field manuals (FMs): *FM 100-5, Operations, FM 100-10, Administration,* and *FM 100-15, Large Units.* This subdivision of the army's core doctrine accounted for the significant differences in the three functions the FMs described by creating a separate manual for each. The creation of the new manuals meant that the army's overarching doctrine now existed in the form of an FM (*FM 100-5*) rather than its longtime predecessor, the *FSR*.[30]

Perhaps most significantly, the 1939 *FM 100-5* contained significant changes regarding how the army should view and conduct combined arms operations on the modern battlefield. As Walter Kretchik put it, the new manual "contained a warfighting philosophy that considered national strategy, not just operations and tactics. Acknowledging the influence of Clausewitz, the manual was the first to link the political objects of government in waging war with the army's role in achieving them."[31] The doctrine also accounted for the dramatic effect of modern technology on the nature of warfare. While maintaining the army's traditional offensive mind-set, the manual identified a key implication of the size and dispersal of modern armies in achieving their destruction. Wars would no longer end as the result of a single decisive battle; rather, planners would need to identify a series of intermediate objectives leading to the enemy's destruction. This new concept of linking tactical actions in campaigns designed to achieve the strategic objective now serves as the basis of today's operational art. Given the manual's inclusion of many other new and important topics, ranging from sociological and psychological factors to the centrality of combined arms operations in maximizing combat effectiveness, it represents a more significant departure from its predecessor, the 1923 *FSR,* than some historians have asserted.[32]

However, tentative approval of the 1939 *FSR* by Chief of Staff Marshall—a decision endorsed by Secretary of War Craig—did not create consensus across the army regarding its contents. Although Marshall gave the manual his tentative approval, he also directed commanders of large units to provide feedback on its contents. This prompted an armywide review process in which the new provisional manual drew considerable criticism from field units, particularly regarding branch-specific roles, missions, and procedures. For example, the Army Air Corps (AAC) rejected the manual because it did not identify the AAC as an independent force—a debate that now ranged well into its second decade. Despite the length of time since the last revision, the 1939 *FSR* contained more similarities with its 1923 predecessor than differences. It still highlighted the primacy of the infantry while relegating the other arms to support roles when many believed they could accomplish more if given greater autonomy. This also attracted criticism because it led many reviewers to see a traditionalist adherence to the past.[33]

On closer inspection, the manual contained changes that reflected the incorporation of new thinking into traditional army fighting methods while adhering to many of its core principles. This new thinking reflected changes in army organization and equipment, such as the reorganization of the infantry division and the advent of mechanization and motorization. Gaps in the new doctrine remained, however, leading some reviewers to question why the army had not incorporated more ideas gleaned from the study, particularly at the AWC, of military developments in other countries. The 1939 *FSR* included the somewhat vague and contradictory ideas that not only through the combined efforts of all arms could the army win wars, but also the infantry retained the primary role in combat. The manual also lacked adequate descriptions of innovative ways to exploit the potential of mechanization and air power. To a certain extent, these gaps in the new *FSR* reflected the inconsistency of views across the army on these topics, resulting, for example, in confusing descriptions of air power's role, at once emphasizing the need for air and ground coordination while providing no guidance describing how units would use close air support.[34]

Kretchik pointed out another, more fundamental reason for the varied reception of the new doctrine. As the army's keystone doctrinal publication, in theory, the *FSR* should have served as the guiding manual for the subordinate doctrine of the various arms. However, service schools still developed the tactics that their own branches would use. With no formal War Department review and approval process, the arms and services could simply ignore the War Department–issued doctrine and continue developing the methods they deemed appropriate, leading to a divergence of views that publication of a new *FSR* could do little to curtail. This meant that the concept of the manual serving as an overarching guide for army operational doctrine did not match reality. Kretchik observed, "Given differing priorities within the War Department and the schools, the various doctrinal manuals were not 'nested' with FM 100-5. The result was a keystone doctrine that failed to integrate the needs and missions of branch schools." William O. Odom provided a similar assessment, emphasizing choices that the army made regarding how it spent the limited funds available to it, which in turn limited its ability to experiment with new technologies and combined arms concepts. Like Kretchik, Odom pointed to the lack of a systematic means for developing new doctrine as the real problem.[35]

Despite its flaws, the army made progress with the publication of the 1939 *FSR,* updating a sixteen-year-old manual while bringing army doctrine more in line with organizational changes and technological advances since the World War.

However, leaders did not initially make use of the new funds slowly finding their way into army coffers to develop new, significantly updated US army operational doctrine. Once they experienced the army's rejection of the 1939 *FSR* and then learned of Germany's rapid and successful invasion of Poland on September 1, 1939, army leaders sought to update the doctrine to reflect changes in technology and describe a modern combined arms approach to warfare. Marshall once again called on McNair and his faculty to oversee the doctrinal update, setting January 1, 1941, as the due date for a new draft.[36]

Meanwhile, McNair achieved a great deal of change at CGSS in a short period, and his efforts benefited the entire army. By late summer 1939, the pace of War Department preparations for mobilization accelerated to the point that senior army leaders began to realize that CGSS must develop the capacity to produce graduates at a much faster rate, requiring abbreviation of the course. In addition, the rapid pace of change indicated that the school leadership must begin to tailor the curriculum, optimizing it for the many National Guard officers expected to attend in preparation for mobilization, along with the many reserve officers who had received no military training since completing Reserve Officer Training Corps (ROTC). A mobilization of any significant size would result in the attendance of far more National Guard and ROTC officers than regular army officers, and the curriculum would have to account for this because students would begin the course with different baseline levels of knowledge. The faculty first had to overcome the chaos and find a short-term solution before it could optimize the instruction at Leavenworth to meet its objectives in such significantly different conditions.[37]

Further, concurrent with changes enabling CGSS to increase the number of graduates, the curriculum required modification to prepare those graduates for the particular challenges of transforming mobilized guardsmen and civilians into combat-ready military personnel. Marshall first addressed this topic with McNair in a letter dated August 16, 1939:

There is also another matter I want to suggest to you. That is the great advantage which would result from a shortening of the course at Leavenworth for National Guard and Reserve officers. It is always very difficult to get the type of man we want when he has to give up his business for three months. *Confidentially,* under the present system at Leavenworth, at Benning, and at other schools, a three months' course is too apt to produce what might be termed "bread-ticket" people. I know that your instructors will say that three months is the minimum time in which a satisfactory course of study can be given. Confidentially, for your eye alone, I'll bet I could do everything they do and only take two months to do it in, if you wipe out certain unimportant details, and if the preparatory material sent in advance is carefully arranged toward the desired end.[38]

McNair's ongoing correspondence with Marshall and many initiatives to improve CGSS placed the course on a path toward preparedness for mobilization.

The War Department implemented protective mobilization in the spring of 1940 as ordered by Roosevelt, who realized the significance of Germany's recent victory in France. An order soon followed to abbreviate CGSS to make more officers available for mobilization. This required graduation of the 1940 class four months early, after which the faculty, unprepared for the rapid and dramatic changes required to meet the demand for CGSS graduates, worked through the summer and fall of 1940 to design and implement an abbreviated version of CGSS. As Peter Schifferle described it, a frenzy of activity eventually resulted in the adoption of a focused short course designed to produce competent staff officers. The first abbreviated class, which began on November 30, 1940, consisted of ninety-seven students—but the high demand for graduates led to a steady increase in class size. The final wartime class graduated 1,080 officers, and the twenty-seven mobilization classes completed between 1940 and 1946 produced more than 18,000 graduates, nearly tripling the total output of the school from its first class in 1881 through 1939.[39]

McNair began the process of transforming CGSS, and although he departed Fort Leavenworth before the commencement of the first abbreviated course, he prepared the faculty for the transition and oversaw the development of the short course with confidence.[40] McNair's reorganization of the curriculum by staff section simplified the process of shortening the course, which in its first form greatly resembled the staff school at Langres, France, that McNair and Marshall remembered from their service in the AEF. Organized along staff section lines, only a small percentage of the curriculum consisted of general instruction, and all applicatory work placed the attendees in positions in the specific staff section in which they would most likely serve in combat. Although the abbreviated course lacked the comprehensiveness of the full-year version, which prepared officers for service in any of the various general staff sections, it proved far more effective than it might have been because of the energy and focus McNair instilled in the faculty. Further, as Marshall pointed out to McNair in a memo he sent on April 12, 1940, "Regular Army methods of training take little account of the economy of time." Thus, in some ways the abbreviation of the course benefited its graduates, who learned specific duty-related skills and how to complete staff officer tasks under time pressure.[41]

Significant obstacles still stood in the way of forming a well-trained and properly equipped army guided by an internally consistent doctrine. The abbreviation of CGSS limited Marshall's ability to address one of his particular concerns. He remained convinced the AAC could not provide effective aerial support to ground forces as prescribed in current doctrine unless its officers thoroughly understood land operations.[42] Marshall wrote to McNair on January 24, 1940, after visiting the western maneuvers and the air corps tactical school, to describe measures he intended to take to resolve this problem:

> I was again impressed with the importance of developing every means to give the Air Corps an understanding of the ground army. I completed the tentative arrangements while en route to have the class of 300 flying cadets who finish at Kelly Field in the first of April attached for six weeks to the headquarters of companies, batteries, battalions and regiments of all the troops which are to participate in [future large-scale] maneuvers.

Marshall also mentioned "trying to make a similar arrangement for the class at the Air Corps Tactical School" and seeking to modify the future AAC officer's career path so they served at least one year in a large unit of the ground forces before beginning service in the AAC. With the basic structure of the triangular infantry division worked out, he believed that reports of German combined arms effectiveness in Poland, including the highly effective use of integrated close air support to ground maneuver units, made settling the dispute over air power's support to ground forces one of the highest priority issues the army faced.[43] At this point in his career, Marshall saw close air support as a critical role for the AAC.

Beginning in the 1920s, the AAC had increasingly sought independence from the ground forces, which it believed did not understand or support the full development of air power's potential. A significant divergence took place in the late 1930s, when the AAC abandoned the development of purpose-built ground support aircraft. AAC personnel had experimented with such aircraft for most of the decade, equipped between 1932 and 1936 with 156 single-engine attack aircraft armed with weapons ideal for the support of ground forces. However, the AAC began in 1939 to phase out single-engine ground support aircraft in favor of twin-engine light bombers while devoting the majority of its resources to strategic bombers—ironically just as Germany prepared to use ground support aviation as an integral element of its combined arms team with great success in its upcoming campaigns in Poland and France.[44]

Despite the benefits that this education exchange program between the ground forces and the AAC offered in solidifying the integration of the combined arms team, the acceleration of the mobilization effort and the abbreviation of CGSS prevented the implementation of Marshall's concept. Instead, US army doctrine continued to describe a significant ground support role for the AAC at the same time that its modernization efforts and operational focus throughout the 1930s widened the gap between the concept of close air support and the capability or intention of the AAC to provide such support to the ground forces.[45] As Richard Muller noted,

> Far from increasing the efficiency of ground attack aviation, the strides made in aircraft technology during the 1930s virtually expunged close air support from the air corps' roster of capabilities. [. . .] While the development of the medium bomber was in many ways a successful and worthwhile endeavor, it did little to provide reliable air support to the ground forces. Proponents of attack aviation embraced the broader definition of their mission as a means of preserving attack's distinct identity. This development coincided with the emphasis on the long-range bomber and the air superiority mission within the staff of GHQ [General Headquarters] Air Force.[46]

McNair remained skeptical and more conservative in his thinking regarding the potential of air power to change the nature of war, focusing on its use as a close air support platform as his preferred means of employment. As the new decade dawned, Marshall also remained committed to the idea of close air support and believed that the AAC should seek a balance between the three primary roles of strategic bombing, medium-range interdiction missions, and close air support to ground forces.[47]

Marshall had similar concerns about the lack of progress in the development of both armor and antitank defense capability. Chief of Staff MacArthur had disbanded the experimental mechanized force in 1931, after only a single year in existence, to allay fears among the infantry and cavalry that armor might gain autonomy as a separate and coequal arm. Therefore, throughout the 1930s, the infantry and cavalry each independently experimented with armor (which the cavalry called combat cars to circumvent the provision of the 1920 National Defense Act that infantry retained full control over tank development). Complicating matters, the chief of ordnance retained authority over technical design and production, meaning that ordnance could modify either branch's requested design specifications as it saw fit before producing and delivering prototypes. Therefore, by 1939 no consensus existed either on the role of the tank or on its optimal design, although the infantry and cavalry did agree on one issue: American tanks' primary mission would not involve direct engagement of enemy tanks. The former viewed the tank as an infantry support vehicle, while the latter viewed the combat car as a system that enabled the cavalry to conduct its traditional missions of reconnaissance, pursuit, envelopment, and exploitation on the modern battlefield. They also agreed the army should develop light, fast tanks—although to serve very different purposes. Only direct War Department intervention broke the logjam by centralizing tank design, organization, and doctrine development under one headquarters.[48]

This meant the ground forces needed an effective means of antitank defense, but the army had made even less progress by 1940 in this area than it had in tank development. In fact, at this point the army still relied primarily on the 37mm gun—its only antitank weapon other than the .50 caliber machine gun—drawn from the pool of German 1936-model guns reproduced in 1937. In addition to the lack of an effective weapon system and development having remained idle since 1937, the army also still used antitank guns in a passive, cordon defense method in 1940, greatly limiting the ability to respond to the speed and mobility of modern tanks.[49] During his tour at Fort Leavenworth, McNair remained one of the few army officers devoting significant intellectual effort to this capability shortfall. This probably came as a result of his involvement in the Proposed Infantry Division tests when he convinced the War Department that the redesigned division's infantry regiments required antitank companies, and he developed a keen interest in antitank doctrine and gun design. Upon his assignment as commandant at Fort Leavenworth, McNair directed a faculty review of antitank methods, which led to the publication of *Antimechanized Defense (Tentative)* in 1939. This instructional manual filled a significant gap in the CGSS curriculum, although the topic remained a focus of debate for the next several years. This study formed the basis of McNair's thinking in 1940 regarding antitank defense.[50]

As McNair instituted change and generally raised the level of activity at CGSS, he also continued to develop the vital skills needed in a general officer. His roles as CGSS commandant and post commander required him to interact with local community leaders, visiting dignitaries from foreign armies, and particularly the media, who sensed the increasing pace of army preparations for mobilization and sought any information they could get, particularly from senior leaders like McNair.[51] Peter Schifferle summarized a few of McNair's key accomplishments during his year at CGSS, pointing out that McNair

set Leavenworth on the road to a wartime instruction system. McNair changed the basic system of instruction from exposure to command and general staff concepts to a focus on staff skills. This focused system of instruction had been the hallmark of Langres, which McNair understood from his service in the . . . AEF headquarters. And, because McNair had also been a member of the inaugural faculty in 1919–1920, discussions about the form of instruction at Langres were undoubtedly one of the topics debated among the instructors. After mobilization, McNair's consultations with the War Department, coupled with the mobilization of National Guard divisions, resulted in combining the regular army course with the reserve component courses, shortening the course length to nine weeks, and organizing students and instruction by specific staff section. By the time of McNair's departure in October 1940, the system for the first special course was in place.[52]

McNair met Marshall's expectations for his service as commandant, but surprisingly, this remains another little-known period in McNair's career. When historians do mention McNair's year at Fort Leavenworth from 1939 to 1940, they sometimes underestimate the impact that McNair had on the army as war loomed on the horizon. Some accounts can leave the reader with a negative impression of McNair's effectiveness as commandant, perhaps unintentionally. For example, David E. Johnson somewhat vaguely asserted that "McNair accomplished little" in his year at Fort Leavenworth.[53]

Army Chief of Staff Marshall, at least, seemed quite satisfied with McNair's performance, calling on him once again in the summer of 1940 to serve in a critical position. As the Roosevelt administration tentatively began the process of protective mobilization, Marshall expanded the War Department in anticipation of the new responsibilities it would shoulder. He ordered McNair to report to General Headquarters (GHQ), a new organization established at the home of the recently closed AWC to oversee the mobilization training of new recruits and the units that they formed around a nucleus of regular army cadre. McNair's imminent reassignment meant that he could not oversee the revision of the 1939 *FSR* through to the end, but he would remain intimately involved in the development of the army's operational doctrine because his new position involved training the army—including hundreds of thousands of new recruits—to use this doctrine to guide their actions in combat.[54]

Within one year, McNair managed to revitalize Fort Leavenworth and design a significantly modified curriculum that changed CGSS into an abbreviated short course. On the basis of his extensive experience in military education and staff officer duty, McNair gained approval for a course tailored to provide an education in the branch and staff section skills that would prepare each student for the specific duties he would perform in the event of war. McNair's achievements during his year as CGSS commandant illustrate Marshall's foresight in assigning a first-rate officer to Fort Leavenworth in 1939. McNair did not fail him, instilling the renewed vitality at the college that Marshall spoke of while placing it on a wartime footing, overseeing updates to the curriculum, and modifying teaching and grading methods as changing circumstances dictated. Such vitality did not exist in all elements of the national apparatus that would mobilize, equip, and deploy an army should circumstances require it.

The Difficult Transition to a War Economy

During the first half of McNair's tenure at CGSS, while he and other forward-looking senior military leaders like George C. Marshall and Malin Craig worried about the storm clouds on the horizon, most of the US government remained focused on the turbulence in America's backyard. Caught in the middle, Roosevelt and some of his advisers recognized the need to reestablish American influence in international affairs, even though the American people still largely demanded that their representatives continue to support only government programs intended to end the Depression and revive the economic prosperity that America had once enjoyed. Although nobody could predict the success of America's return to the arena of international affairs, one could certainly anticipate significant repercussions based on the success or failure of his efforts—repercussions not only related to Roosevelt's political standing or the US army's combat readiness but also connected to America's economic welfare. Roosevelt's lend-lease program finally initiated economic recovery in 1940—something none of his New Deal measures had accomplished—but further involvement in foreign affairs offered both risks and opportunities, as many industrialists remembered from America's role in the Great War. Despite the difficult initial transition to a war economy, Americans by 1919 drew specific and somewhat surprising lessons from the war. Schaffer argued, "Potentially the most important result of all was a lesson deposited in the historical record: overseas wars can be beneficial to American business—for profits they generate and for the security and stability a war welfare state affords to those in a position to take advantage of it."[55]

Although industrialists and laborers in 1940 happily grasped the opportunity that war production offered them, most American citizens remained thoroughly opposed to direct American intervention in the war. Roosevelt reassured them in a campaign speech in October 1940: "I have said this before, but I shall say it again and again: Your boys are not going to be sent into any foreign wars." As Kennedy pointed out, "Conspicuously, Roosevelt omitted the qualifying phrase that he had used on previous occasions: 'except in case of attack.'"[56]

Renewed American prosperity in 1940 contributed significantly to Roosevelt's reelection. By the end of 1940, war production put 3.5 million more Americans to work than at the low point of the recession of 1937–1938, and unemployment dropped to its lowest level in the past ten years. Roosevelt famously referred to America as the "great arsenal of democracy" during protective mobilization, but years of neglecting military readiness compounded the difficulty of living up to this promise. In Kennedy's words, "Time was the most precious of military assets, and America had already squandered much of it." On the other hand, the government had access to more money than it had since the beginning of the Depression. Senator Henry Cabot Lodge Jr. told General Arnold, "It is the general feeling of the Congress, and as far as I can gather, among public opinion throughout the country, to provide all of the money necessary for the National Defense, so all you have to do is ask for it." The administration did just that, requesting $7 billion for lend-lease and $13.7 billion by the end of 1941 for military acquisitions—a dramatic increase over the $2.2 billion defense budget of 1940.[57]

The dramatic change in the global situation during the second half of McNair's tenure at Leavenworth made it clear that American forces must prepare for war, whether purely for defensive purposes or to fight another overseas war after a long and arduous mobilization process. In Europe, further Nazi aggression seemed almost inevitable. In the Pacific, American efforts to contain Japan's expansionist policies pushed the Japanese government to pursue increasingly aggressive means to establish the resource self-reliance it craved. These means included the seizure of resource-rich territory in the south Pacific, but the Japanese military would have much work to do to prepare itself to hold its gains if the Americans retaliated. Facing these threats, Roosevelt and his military advisers began to focus on the effectiveness of America's preparation for war, which soon overtook domestic affairs as Roosevelt's primary concern.[58]

Germany's defeat of France in yet another rapid campaign in the spring of 1940 significantly increased the Roosevelt administration's concerns about military readiness. Unlike its previous worrisome but relatively minor acts of aggression, Germany's defeat of France left Great Britain isolated in its effort to defend itself from a German attack. Roosevelt understood that America must do everything in the nation's power to prevent a British defeat, but a reluctant public still resisted the idea of direct intervention, so the president nudged America ever closer to war while providing economic support through the lend-lease program to its beleaguered ally. He managed this by taking advantage of a loophole in the Reorganization Act of 1939. Although aimed at combating the Depression rather than preparing for war, the Reorganization Act gave the executive branch the authority to create new organizations as needed to oversee New Deal programs. One of these, the Office for Emergency Management (OEM), required only a presidential order to take shape as a centralized coordinating agency that reported directly to the executive branch in case of national emergency. Because no emergency had taken place to justify its activation, this organization remained on standby. Roosevelt recognized the opportunity this provided for him to centralize mobilization activities under executive branch control.[59]

Historian Paul Koistinen described the OEM as particularly significant—and the nexus of debate for the next six years—because it enabled the consolidation of US government agencies responsible for various aspects of economic mobilization under the president's direct authority. Merely the possibility of its activation caused friction with staffers in the War Department who knew of the existence of this legislation. The War Department saw the OEM as a direct threat to the War Resources Board, which in 1939 had begun to seek support from the Roosevelt administration for the Industrial Mobilization Plan (IMP). Military leaders viewed the IMP as an imperative in the event of mobilization because it placed the war economy under their control. Although War Department leaders argued that the IMP rested on a solid foundation of processes proven effective during the mobilization for the World War, Roosevelt and civilian industrial leaders chafed at the thought of placing the national economy in the hands of the War Department. Military planners believed the mobilization for World War I proved the validity of the IMP, and they had viewed it throughout the interwar years as a central element of War Department mobilization plans. Others who saw the terrible friction and inefficiency of economic mobilization for World War I knew that the validation of the IMP came only after years of debate, military leaders' inability to project requirements, and business leaders' hesitancy to submit to a managed economy while quietly looking for ways to ensure they profited from the coming war. This left the validity of the IMP for oversight of a future mobilization an open question.[60]

New Deal supporters within the administration opposed the War Resources Board and the IMP that would provide its operational logic, seeing them as the basis for a military and big business takeover of the economy. Recent analysis that looks back at the amazing industrial output the United States achieved, and the somewhat counterintuitive effects this industrial output had on the nation's wartime and postwar economy, emphasizes the need to view peacetime and wartime production models through distinct lenses of economic theory. New Deal supporters who opposed economic plans and organizations because they saw them as a means for military and big business control of the economy did not see the larger issue. The socialization of the nation's economy under federal control for the duration of the war made the existing models that economists used for measuring industrial output and gross national product unsuitable for assessing the health of the wartime economy. As it turned out, the military made demands but had no ability to take control of the economy in the coming years, and big business did profit, mostly at a level considered acceptable within the larger context of achieving wartime production goals. However, the key issue remained the radical change in a very short period from a substantially free market to a controlled economy, followed by a rapid transition back to the free market model after the war. This created dynamics that economists debated during the war, and that continued to influence the economy in the ensuing decades.[61]

Roosevelt ultimately chose to leave the OEM on standby, ready to take control of the economy if the situation required it—an idea military leaders opposed. To appease them, he agreed to delete the specifics of the OEM's organization and authorities from the legislation, giving the military more room to maneuver in the inevitable power struggle that would ensue in the event that the OEM made the transition from theory to reality. This led to the beginning, in Koistinen's words, of "a running battle . . . within the administration over mobilizing the economy for war." Events in Europe led Roosevelt to bring the OEM into existence by administrative order on May 25, 1940, and although the OEM itself soon faltered, some of its subordinate organizations served as hubs of power and friction in equal measure as the government began to transition to a war economy. This national-level inefficiency did not bode well for McNair and his fellow army leaders as they sought to prepare the army for war. Lack of national preparedness had made the mobilization for the World War much harder than it should have been; it appeared the United States might find itself in the same position soon if the nation needed to mobilize large numbers of troops for combat duty.[62]

Beginning in 1940, key military and political leaders also began to see flaws in the nation's primary strategy for a modern war that added to the complexity of the mobilization process and led to changes in GHQ's mobilization training plan. The long-standing strategy, developed and refined over the previous two decades and encapsulated in War Plan Orange, envisioned a Japanese attack on US territories in the Pacific or against the American West Coast, requiring a response primarily by naval forces with the main effort in the Pacific. As Jim Lacey described, War Plan Orange did not fit the actual situation in which America found itself in 1940. After Germany defeated Poland in 1939 and France in 1940, American strategic planners anticipated that Germany would next set its sights on Great Britain. This made Europe and the Atlantic a far more significant strategic concern than the Pacific. Both General Marshall and the chief of naval operations, Admiral Harold R. Stark, grasped the inapplicability of War Plan Orange to the current situation and realized that the defeat of Britain by Germany would leave the United States in an extremely vulnerable strategic situation.[63]

By June 1940, Marshall asked at a strategic planning conference, "Are we not forced into reframing our naval policy, into one that is purely defensive in the Pacific, with the main effort in the Atlantic?" This matched Stark's viewpoint, and by November, he sent a plan to Marshall who concurred and forwarded it to the president, recommending this adjustment in national strategy, to which President Roosevelt gave his tacit approval. This new plan, known as Plan Dog and later integrated into both the Navy Rainbow 5 Plan and the Joint Rainbow 5 Plan, included one particularly relevant insight: defeat of Germany would require, in Stark's words, "military success on shore." This led to the logical conclusion that because Great Britain did not possess the strength to defeat Germany on land, ultimate victory would require the intervention of US ground forces.[64]

This shift made decades of strategic war planning obsolete while highlighting the fact that existing mobilization plans lacked a realistic analysis of the demands the military would place on industry if called upon to deploy forces to fight a war in Europe. Therefore, America did not merely have to change its military strategy—a challenging task, but one for which the development of the rainbow plans had prepared army planners to accomplish. Instead, American strategists faced the far greater challenge of creating an integrated industrial mobilization plan based on an unanticipated strategic situation. Without the information that they would normally glean from an approved war plan, industrial leaders could not develop supporting plans to equip and supply the army, or even project how soon the army could feasibly begin to undertake ground combat operations in Europe if necessary.

Michael Matheny highlighted the increased emphasis on logistics considerations in the AWC curriculum throughout the 1920s and 1930s, making a strong case for the improvement of senior military leaders' appreciation for the importance of logistics in the execution of campaigns—a key element of operational art. However, this did not improve these leaders' ability to anticipate the likely characteristics of a future war or the requirements that the military would place on civilian industry if war broke out. Lacey pointed out that even in 1940, members of the National Defense Advisory Commission, created by executive order to oversee industrial support to protective mobilization, found that "the military would not even hazard a guess as to what any future conflict would look like." Robert Nathan, the lead commission member responsible for studying military requirements, "found that assignment to be nearly hopeless" because of the refusal of military leaders to provide the data necessary to anticipate industrial requirements in the event of war.[65] This seems particularly inexplicable after twenty years of detailed contingency planning at the War Department, augmented annually by the AWC class.

Not even the Industrial Staff College, founded in 1924, prepared its students adequately for the scale of the industrial mobilization required to support a large-scale war—particularly one involving the possibility of offensive operations—despite graduating more than 1,000 officers by 1941. James Lacey has argued that both schools failed in this mission for a common reason: their instruction rested on the assumption that the nation would implement the IMP developed after World War I and updated periodically ever since. The IMP placed all responsibility for leading the nation's industrial mobilization effort in military officers' hands. When the time came to begin industrial mobilization, President Roosevelt scrapped the IMP, primarily because he refused to consider placing such responsibility in the hands of military officers rather than the civilian leaders of US industry and economic development. Therefore, when protective mobilization began in 1940, the Roosevelt administration struggled to create a proficient and well-equipped expeditionary military force in the absence of a feasible national strategy or industrial mobilization plan—a shortfall unrecognized for months and one that delayed army readiness significantly.[66] Frequent requests from civilian production chiefs for military requirements finally prompted Roosevelt to direct Secretary of War Stimson and Secretary of the Navy Frank Knox on July 9, 1941, to "explore the munitions and mechanical equipment of all types which in your opinion would be required to exceed by an appropriate amount that available to our potential enemies." Thus, Roosevelt did not ask until the summer of 1941 for a coordinated civil–military plan that addressed the nation's requirements to conduct offensive operations rather than simply its needs to defend the United States.[67] This led to rapid and significant change in the nation's economic structure and the national government's role in economic management.

Lacey assessed ammunition production—one of the earliest of the government's efforts in this economic program—as "not flattering to the United States. With 2.5 times the combined population of Britain and Canada, America's installed munition production capacity lagged far behind both its potential and the relative production levels achieved by the other two nations. The stark numbers clearly demonstrated that the United States did not contribute as much as it could have as the 'arsenal of democracy.'"[68] Lacey also revealed that by late 1941, initial plans existed that described the industrial requirements to support an eight-million-person American army and the manner in which the military would use that combat equipment, but it still remained an open question when industry could actually provide that equipment. Two economists, Robert Nathan and Simon Kuznets, provided an answer to that question in November 1941 that "led to some of the fiercest and nastiest military–civilian debates of the war." Nathan and Kuznets based their calculations on army projections of requirements for, in Koistinen's words, "major finished products, components, and raw materials broken down by months according to military objectives from October 1, 1941, to March 31, 1943. The army was able to provide rough general data on scheduled end items, but it made little headway with materials and components." The navy also could not provide timely projections of requirements.[69] On the basis of this information, Nathan and Kuznets calculated that production of the required material by the fall of 1943, including lend-lease projections, would rely on America increasing its expenditures on the defense program by over 200 percent. This would require both a massive increase in gross domestic product (GDP) and commitment of half the target GDP to defense spending to meet its production goals.[70] Economic analyses of the nation's war and total production throughout the war years demonstrated the infeasibility of these targets, particularly because America's program of production expansion was complete by 1942—the point at which the nation transitioned from industrial mobilization into steady-state production of munitions and logistical services.[71]

Civilian industry leaders also could not meet the military's production requirements without accurate estimates of those requirements—something Lacey revealed that the military could never provide with any reliability. The military still suffered from the same unclear relationship that had long existed between the combat personnel who employed military equipment and the ordnance personnel who designed and procured that equipment. It also lacked the unity of effort that would have resulted from appointment of a single agency or individual to oversee the various organizations involved in military industrial production. In his usual manner, President Roosevelt attempted to resolve the impasse by forming committees and boards of men who did not see eye to eye or even work well together (in Lacey's words, "chosen with typical political astuteness by Roosevelt"), believing lack of consensus led to original thought and insightful solutions.[72] However, the dysfunctional process that emerged only served to demonstrate the ineffectiveness of this practice when a national crisis required quick and decisive action. It also identified one key military individual as primarily responsible for the military's inadequate, even counterproductive, contribution to the process: Lieutenant General Brehon Somervell, commander of the Army Service Forces (ASF).[73]

Reviewing the minutes of the many boards responsible for various aspects of industrial mobilization, Lacey recognized an ongoing trend between November 1941 and the fall of 1942 in which the military consistently questioned the civilians' production estimates and economic analyses while insisting they increase material production to infeasible levels. Lacey highlighted the October 6, 1942, War Production Board (WPB) meeting to demonstrate the severity of the civilian industrialists' frustration with Somervell by this point in the war. All parties arrived at the meeting already in intense disagreement regarding the feasibility of the 1942 and 1943 production plans, about which Somervell remained far more optimistic than the civilian industrialists and economists who would have to meet their demands. Somervell had consistently criticized the civilians' reports and estimates before the meeting, and he continued to do so once it began. The civilians provided detailed analyses that demonstrated why American industry and GDP simply could not support the military requirements provided by the Joint Chiefs for 1942 and 1943. At a seeming impasse, it appeared the meeting might end with these issues still unresolved. Somervell and Undersecretary of War Robert Patterson refused to accept the civilians' recommendation for formation of a new production strategy board, asserting that they saw no need for civilians to concern themselves with strategy. Instead, they insisted the civilians should focus on finding ways to meet military requirements rather than questioning their feasibility.[74]

At this point, Leon Henderson, head of the Office of Price Administration, finally lost his patience with Somervell, who continued to insist that the figure Nathan identified as the nation's maximum potential for production of munitions, construction, and other military expenditures was both overly conservative and insufficient for the conduct of the war. Lacey recounted,

> "The amount in question, 90 billion dollars, was interesting," said Henderson, "because it exceeded by far the value of our entire national product both for 1933 and 1934." Then, as if a great light were dawning, he said, in substance, "Maybe if we can't wage a war on 90 billions, we ought to get rid of our present Joint Chiefs, and find some who can."[75]

This brought the meeting to dead silence. As Lacey's research revealed, this pause "allowed Henderson to turn to Somervell and proceed to make the most violent personal attack ever heard in a meeting of the WPB." Henderson stated that "he found himself disgusted with Somervell's repeated obstinacy, overbearing manner, and ignorance of production problems. He stated flatly his belief that Somervell had always padded his requirements, and that the general had no idea of the disastrous implications of infeasible goals."[76] This last point highlights the central issue with the entire war production process. In a planning effort based on flawed assumptions and unrealistic requirements, leaders lacked the ability to make informed prioritization decisions.

Just a few months earlier, in a characteristically positive manner, *Time* reported on the challenges that the problem of supply posed to the American war effort, describing what it referred to as two great miracles by which the nation would overcome them. Credit for the first of these miracles, the establishment of war production, went to "US Industry [which] in six months had worked it." A second miracle remained necessary, the article continued, "a greater miracle still: to the problem of dispersed supply in both hemispheres the US must add the problem, of vast concentrated supply for a second front in Europe." This miracle required the army "not to walk on water, but to sprint," and one man would ensure it achieved that goal: Brehon Somervell.[77]

The *Time* article poured effusive praise on Somervell, presenting the problem, and his vaguely described plan for solving it, in much the same light in which he and Patterson presented it to the civilian industrialists that they expected to do the work. The article went on:

> It took a lot of nerve, a lot of dead-aim calculation, a fine disregard of precedent to give the answers he had made to the questions which were posed him. In WWI the Allies, with a pool of about 20,000,000 tons of shipping, drew 60%

of their supplies from France, Scandinavia, and Spain. They threw their 100% largely at Germany on the Western Front. This time the Allies have only about 3,000,000 tons afloat. But the world is their battlefield. Vast stores of fuel oil, rubber and other riches once available are in the hands of the enemy. So are the resources and shipping of Scandinavia and, for practical purposes, of Spain. Moreover, the requirements in mechanized tools of war, model 1942, have shot up until supply is a fearsomely different art from the supply of 1917.[78]

Once again, the press understood the challenges the nation faced, but some military personnel chose to ignore them, or believed they could overcome them by sheer force of will.

Given the long-standing dysfunction associated with the production planning effort, President Roosevelt had simply continued to insist that the industrialists meet military production goals as determined by Somervell and Patterson, regardless whether the nation's economy could support them, while simultaneously refusing to impose significant sacrifice on the American people. Numerous historians have pointed out this last important yet often forgotten fact. As Lacey argued, "The myth that in the pursuit of total victory the American people sacrificed so that consumer production facilities could convert to war production is demonstrably untrue. Consumer spending in America went up (as a percentage of GDP) every year of the war, and virtually all wartime munitions production can be accounted for by GDP growth and not by limitations placed on consumer production."[79] In fact, as Koistinen revealed, civilian production companies began hoarding essential raw materials needed for the mobilization effort to instead support their increased output of consumer durables. Koistinen noted that "between April and May 1941—within months of Pearl Harbor—automobile output had grown by 27 percent over the same months in 1940, and that pattern was continuing. This situation was breaking down the entire priority system."[80]

As David Kennedy put it, "In Britain personal consumption shrank by 22 percent [during the war]. In the Soviet Union, a crash mobilization program [included] harshly regulated scarcity rather than the Americans' loosely supervised abundance." Adding the Axis to the equation, Kennedy pointed out that "over the course of the war, civilian consumption fell by nearly 20 percent in Germany and 26 percent in Japan. Only in America was it different. The United States, alone among all the combatant societies, enjoyed guns and butter too—and both of them in unrivaled quantities."[81] Whether by choice, political necessity, or rampant inefficiency and corruption, America never applied its full industrial potential to the problem of war production. One can only wonder whether greater consumer sacrifice or effective management of war production might have enabled an American mobilization for war that met, or at least came closer to meeting, military material requirements.

The blowup at the October 6, 1942, WPB meeting finally led to the realization among most members of the board that America's military strategy required major revision. Only Somervell remained obstinate in his conviction the civilians must find a way to meet military production demands. To break the impasse, Nelson formed the Production Executive Committee, placing Charles E. Wilson of the General Electric Corporation in charge of the committee and charging him with the responsibility of developing and enforcing realistic production schedules. Nelson formed this new committee specifically to backpedal from the cooperative spirit in which the WPB had theoretically operated, realizing that Wilson (described by historian John Kennedy Ohl as "a crackerjack production man . . . who was thought to be sympathetic to the civilian outlook") would reassert civilian control over the production process. In essence, this represented a reversal of the original WPB arrangement, in which the military determined requirements and the civilians found ways to accomplish them.[82]

By November 1942, Somervell recognized the implications of Nelson's actions and engaged directly in conflict with Wilson, attempting to retain military control over development of production requirements. At this point, even navy and Maritime Commission representatives had accepted the need to turn over production requirements and scheduling to the civilians; only Somervell remained in opposition. This led to further debate, prompting President Roosevelt to invite Nelson to the White House to hear the WPB's case, which Nelson summed up as the need for "proper, orderly scheduling." Roosevelt offered to help, but Nelson declined, asking only that the president not help "the other fellow" (that is, Somervell). From this point on, Nelson dealt directly with Secretary of War Stimson, enabling him to bypass Somervell, who remained belligerent even after Roosevelt called a meeting between Nelson, Stimson, and Secretary of the Navy Knox, at which Roosevelt told them to work together to resolve the production debate quickly. Ohl argued that Somervell's futile attempts to influence the negotiations between Nelson and Stimson suggested that "if Roosevelt and Stimson had not entered the picture, there probably would not have been an agreement at all."[83]

After months of bureaucratic squabbling, the civilians had finally gotten through to the military leaders—and President Roosevelt—that America had been pursuing an infeasible troop basis (goals for military unit mobilization by date and type, requiring both the personnel and material required to form the units) and military strategy. As reported in *Time*, the "WPB certainly had the impression that for the first time—'the very first time'—it knew exactly what the military expected to be done in a given span. For the first time—'the very first time'—WPB considered that it had a specific, intelligible, practicable schedule of requested production, reasonably keyed to the actual production capacity of the US. The men in charge of war production were even able to visualize an overall, master plan for 1943." Although the article did not describe the ineffectiveness and personality clashes within the WPB up to that point or illuminate just how severely the nation's personnel and industrial mobilization goals had exceeded realistic estimates, it did express the most significant point: "The decision apparently had to do with the intricate, vital, all-inclusive problem of US manpower (*Time*, Oct. 5)—a problem which goes to the roots of global strategy, because the number and kind of fighting men the US elects to place on the battle lines will determine what must and can be done by those remaining in the home arsenal."[84]

This key insight helps explain why the material superiority narrative, to whatever degree it might accurately portray America's industrial potential in the early 1940s, does not explain the success of America's ground forces on the battlefields of World War II. The ground forces felt the effects of the manpower crisis of 1942 to a far greater degree than the navy, the air forces, or the service forces. Roosevelt's recognition of the severity of this crisis led to two significant military consequences. First, the Joint Chiefs reduced spending projections for 1943 by $12 billion, $3 billion of which came from the navy, and $9 billion from the army (all from the ground forces), along with a reduction in troops of 300,000—further demonstrating the War Department's consistent prioritization of Army Air Forces (AAF) and ASF mobilization requirements over those of the Army Ground Forces (AGF).[85] Second, senior American military leaders not only finally accepted that America could not pursue a cross-Channel attack in the summer of 1943, even if Britain would support one. They understood that "the crooked timber of humanity, not scarce critical materials, was [...] the principal obstacle to efficient production." This revealed the significance of America's unsynchronized and logically unsound personnel mobilization policy, and the fact that those responsible for managing the mobilization did not recognize the full impact of these problems until three years after protective mobilization began.[86]

In fact, the US army proved more ready in a sense than the nation's political leadership or its industrial system to engage in modern mechanized and motorized warfare. The army's effective interwar officer education system and the vibrant discourse that took place in military schools and journals enabled a small core of regulars to develop a sound understanding of modern warfare and prepare, at least intellectually, for mobilization. This foundation of competency in sound doctrine and modern war-fighting methods eventually enabled the army's ground forces to overcome the severe constraints placed on them during the manpower crisis of 1942. In contrast, Roosevelt handed responsibility for the IMP to civilian industrial leaders without warning after America's strategic war plans had for two decades rested on the assumption that the War Department General

Staff would manage the wartime economy. Having unexpectedly adopted this responsibility on the eve of war, civilian leaders of industry therefore confronted protective mobilization flat-footed and lagged behind the army's tactical and operational training for several years, struggling to produce adequate war matériel in time to meet the army's needs. The demands caused by the breakneck pace of both US army mobilization and lend-lease programs to Great Britain and Russia upon the nation's awakening in 1940 pushed the United States to the limit of its production capacity by 1942. The nation still managed a vast output from this point on, but maintaining the levels of production expected by Roosevelt and the Allies that depended on America's support through lend-lease soon led the nation to its production breaking point. Mismanagement by leaders like Somervell and Patterson only exacerbated the problem. America hardly possessed a limitless pool of personnel, shipping, or production capacity. Contrary to longstanding myth based on various historical interpretations since the war, only the army's interwar education, doctrine development, reorganization, and extensive training processes enabled the ground forces to make up for these deficiencies.[87]

Still, as the industrial base struggled, the US army, too, began a rapid but flawed program of mobilization. The army's rapid expansion in the absence of a viable national strategy created innumerable difficulties for those military personnel who bore responsibility for the various requirements associated with military mobilization. As McNair's AWC experience demonstrated, officers during the interwar period prepared, reviewed, and updated a wide range of war plans annually, and War College students reviewed these plans, identifying shortfalls and recommending remedies, such as implementing an organized reserve system to augment the regular army in a crisis. Nevertheless, in 1940 America still lacked an organized army reserve (beyond a list of ROTC graduates who had received no mandatory training since graduation), relying instead on an inconsistently trained and organized National Guard. This situation remained the same as the one McNair studied and commented on while a student at the AWC.

The first step the nation undertook to increase the size of the army, the Selective Training and Service Act of 1940, suffered from lack of standardization and limited national-level oversight, resulting in inconsistent implementation at the state and local level. The act required counties and parishes to create local draft boards, where local leaders would decide where individuals could best serve the nation—whether in the army or through service in industry, agriculture, or other nonmilitary activities. The act required all male citizens and aliens between the ages of twenty-one and thirty-six to register for the draft, but depending on their classification, determined by local boards to fill quotas set by the services, men received deferments from military service on the basis of occupational status, dependents, legal restrictions, or any condition that made them unfit for service. As

David Kennedy argued, "Contrary to much later mythology, the nation's young men did not step forward in unison to answer the trumpet's call, neither before nor after Pearl Harbor. Deferments were coveted, and their distribution traced a rough profile of the patterns of political power, racial prejudice, and cultural values in wartime America."[88]

Because no opportunity existed during the interwar years to serve in an organized reserve and receive military training, many men who might have possessed excellent potential for military service had instead worked to develop a civilian skill now considered indispensable to the mobilization effort. With no guidance from the federal government for prioritizing these skills, local draft boards could only subjectively weigh potential for military service against the board's perception of the criticality of an inductee's particular civilian skill. This greatly limited the army's ability to influence the quality of men inducted into military service and resulted in significant variance from one draft board to the next in decisions to draft potential inductees or leave them in their civilian trades. The act also allowed individuals to bypass selective service by volunteering for a military enlistment, but again, it set no clear standards for implementing the policy, forcing some local draft boards to meet their selective service quotas by enlisting men from deferred classes.[89]

Making matters worse, competition began almost immediately between the service arms for the highest-quality recruits, leading to another form of the self-destructive behavior that military leaders had engaged in throughout the interwar period in the competition for scarce resources. Further enabling this behavior, the Selective Service Act initially allowed volunteers to choose the specific arm or specialty in which they would serve, leading to slogans like the navy's "Choose While You Can." Recruiters soon developed various methods of reserving the best recruits for later enlistment. The army placed 140,000 young men in its special training program, a supposed cadet-training program that merely made these men unavailable for the draft so that recruiters could later funnel them to the most critical positions. Similarly, the navy used its V-12 program to send seventeen-year-olds to college for up to two years, achieving the same result. Remarkably, as David Kennedy pointed out, "The air corps cadet program by war's end held some two hundred thousand young men who never left home."[90] Unsurprisingly, few volunteers requested to serve in the ground combat arms. As late as 1942, just before the Roosevelt administration put a stop to the practice of volunteering near the end of the year, only about 5 percent of volunteers selected to serve in the infantry or armored force.[91]

The small pool of regular army officers from the ground combat arms who had studied and prepared for modern war recognized that the increasingly complex, mobile form of combat they were likely to experience in the future would require physical strength, endurance, and high mental capacity. As Robert R. Palmer, Bell I. Wiley, and William R. Keast noted, "The intelligence, skill, and stamina of semi-isolated riflemen and small-unit commanders were to determine not only individual survival on the battlefield but also in many cases the outcome of battle. Although these facts were appreciated increasingly as the war proceeded, they were recognized [by leaders in the ground forces] from the beginning."[92]

The provisions of the Selective Service and Training Act of 1940 resulted in the placement of the lowest-quality men—as determined by physical and mental tests in use at the time—in ground combat units. Palmer, Wiley, and Keast asserted, "The net result was that men having established trades or skills in civilian life tended to be assigned to the noncombat elements of the Army. The problem of technical training in the Army was thereby simplified, but the problem of tactical and combat training was rendered more difficult."[93] Ironically, experience in even relatively simple skills that the army could easily have taught average or even below-average recruits qualified them for exclusion from the draft. Conversely, the skills necessary in an infantryman required advanced physical fitness and mental acuity that the typically low-quality recruit assigned to the combat arms rarely possessed. Therefore, in the implementation of the Selective Training and Service Act, the War Department did not recognize those characteristics that would make new recruits suitable for service in the ground combat forces. Flawed assumptions about the nature of duty in the ground forces and the type of individual best suited for this duty contributed to an already flawed procurement process, leading to placement of the least qualified personnel in ground force positions. This significantly added to the challenges McNair already faced in planning and conducting mobilization training of new recruits and units in a rapidly expanding army.[94]

As Palmer described, "There were various reasons for the relatively inferior quality of the human raw material made available to the ground combat arms. One was the absence of a central system of personnel classification and assignment for the armed forces as a whole. Another was the Army's own system of Classification.[95] Soon after the end of the World War, as rapid demobilization gutted the regular army, the War Department found itself forced to relax physical and mental recruitment standards to attract enough new soldiers to maintain the regular army's personnel strength, even at its greatly reduced interwar low. Few men wanted to experience another war like the one that had just ended, leading to widespread reluctance to serve in either the regular army or the National Guard. This, combined with America's tradition of maintaining a large army only in time of war, as well as a generally low regard for military service as a career, low pay, and poor quality of life led the army to reduce personnel standards significantly after the war.[96]

From 1919 to 1926, volunteer recruits did not have to pass any form of intelligence testing, and by 1927, a man only had to achieve a ten-year-old intelligence level on entrance tests to pass (and the recruiter could even waive this requirement). The onset of the Great Depression increased the number of volunteers, allowing for greater selectivity, but by 1932 a man still only had to demonstrate an eighth-grade intelligence, and as a result of widespread food shortages, recruits could weigh several pounds less in each height range than those volunteering in the 1920s. This placed significant responsibility on the officer corps because of the significant challenges these reductions in quality created for the officers who would have to train these men and lead them into battle.[97]

After twenty years of relaxed physical and intelligence requirements for men seeking to enlist in the regular army, when the government finally began to induct new recruits through Selective Service in September 1940, it lowered the standards for new recruits even further. This occurred largely because of the effects of the Depression, when most Americans had little opportunity to receive a high-quality education, and many poor families subsisted on severely restricted diets, leading to a reduction in the average size and weight of young men. To account for these changes in the male population, the administration modified national induction policy accordingly, lowering the existing height restriction from sixty-four inches to sixty inches. The lower average education level of Depression-era recruits posed the knotty challenge of identifying a specialty appropriate to each inductee's intellectual level. As Theodore Wilson explained, this led the adjutant general's office to adopt in 1940 the Army General Classification Test (AGCT), developed by a group of psychologists as a means to measure what the army referred to as mental alertness. Wilson pointed out that "the AGCT was never officially labeled an intelligence test, but the vast majority of those who administered the test and those who took it perceived the AGCT to be an 'IQ' test. [. . .] Its educational and cultural biases are immediately apparent."[98]

The army personnel who determined the need to measure an inductee's potential to learn did so out of the conviction that the technologically advanced army required soldiers with the potential to use the army's new high-tech equipment. In short, intellectual capacity trumped physical characteristics when placing recruits in jobs. This required some means of matching a soldier with the characteristic the army called high mental alertness to jobs perceived as requiring that trait. Wilson described a group of 925 men inducted in June–July 1942, representing an above-average sampling of typical recruits at that time. These men "averaged 65.2 inches in height and 124.9 pounds in weight." After two or three months of service, these physical characteristics remained essentially the same—years of dietary deficiency led to weak bone structure that could not support a substantial increase in muscle. As for AGCT results, these 925 men performed extremely poorly. With grade I the highest and grade V the lowest, 0.1 percent scored grade

I, 0.7 percent grade II, 12.5 percent grade III, 39.8 percent grade IV, and 46.9 percent grade V.[99] The poor physical characteristics and low learning potential, as assessed by the AGCT, did not bode well for the technology-centric army that national leaders envisioned.

Nor did it bode well for the army's ground forces, which consistently received a disproportionate number of low-quality recruits. A number of policies, each in different ways, diverted high-quality recruits away from the AGF. For example, the AAF benefited from a preferential assignment policy based on its perceived need for a majority of the inductees with the highest learning potential. With more than half of the top scorers on the AGCT taken out of the pool, other criteria applied to the remaining recruits that tended to divert them from ground combat duty. For example, soldiers possessing a skill in civilian life similar to one required for military service usually found themselves in the ASF or AAF service troops, even though recruits could have easily learned many such skills, like operation of trucks or other equipment in mobilization training. In addition to these and other assignment policies, until the end of 1942, volunteers earned the right to choose their field of service. Throughout this period, the AGF remained by far the least popular choice. Ultimately, the relaxation of physical standards necessary to enable rapid army expansion, combined with various assignment policies, resulted in a disproportionately low number of physically or mentally high-scoring inductees ending up in the AGF. Army historian Robert Palmer noted, "One commander observed in a moment of exaggeration, his hardest problem was to find competent enlisted men to act as instructors, because 'everybody higher than a moron' was pulled out for one reason or another."[100] This made the interwar training and education of the regular army's ground combat forces even more critical, given the challenge of training the lowest-quality recruits for wartime service in the infantry, armor, artillery, and other ground combat arms.[101] As Palmer observed, "General McNair felt very strongly on this matter. He came increasingly to believe . . . that American soldiers were sustaining avoidable casualties . . . because average or subaverage young men were thrown into front line combat while their natural leaders (of course with exceptions) sat at desks or tended machines well behind the lines."[102]

Several issues added to the basic problem of the limited time the army faced in its effort to replace obsolescent weapons, now that Congress finally started to appropriate additional funds. Throughout 1940 and most of 1941, those funds remained limited in part because Roosevelt could not afford the political fallout that would result from a public statement advocating intervention in the war. This, however, did not prevent Roosevelt from requesting appropriations from Congress for spending on his favored military capability: a large and powerful air force. As David Kennedy wrote, "Ever receptive to novelty, Roosevelt had easily succumbed to the seductive logic of aerial warfare. At the time of the Munich crisis he had mused that 'pounding away at Germany from the air' would crack the morale of the German people. 'This kind of war,' Roosevelt claimed, 'would cost less money, would mean comparatively few casualties, and would be more likely to succeed than a traditional war by land and sea.'"[103]

Meeting with his military advisers in November 1938, Roosevelt described his ambitious plan to create an American aircraft industry capable of equipping the British and French while creating an American air force of 10,000 airplanes. He argued that if America had 5,000 planes that summer and had the capacity to build 10,000 more each year, "Hitler would not have dared to take the stand he did." With the exception of the exultant AAC commander, General H. H. "Hap" Arnold, this belief in the strategic bomber's assumed war-winning potential greatly disturbed most of Roosevelt's advisers, who preferred a balanced force. They also protested the president's intentions to equip foreign air forces when they still had only a tiny budget to spend on the American military. Army Chief of Staff Malin Craig asked angrily what the military was supposed to do with that many airplanes. When Roosevelt asked Marshall, Craig's deputy, what he thought of his plans for an airplane-centric strategy and production effort, Marshall answered Roosevelt, "I am sorry, Mr. President, but I don't agree at all."[104]

Therefore, Congress appropriated only enough funds to create a defense force—funds that had to pay for new recruits and weapons in addition to infrastructure upgrades such as barracks, dining halls, parade grounds, and training facilities with the capacity to support hundreds of thousands of new recruits. Therefore, limited funds existed to pay for weapons, and the president preferred to spend that money buying more and newer models of airplanes. Limited resources and priority decisions affected the complex development and fielding process as well, meaning aircraft production happened relatively quickly, but no weapons development program came to fruition as soon as the War Department desired. A few documents from the War Department's Operations Division files illustrate the result.

Despite Roosevelt's service as secretary of the navy during the Great War and his continued devotion to all things naval, his belief in the potential for the airplane to change the nature of warfare overmatched his support for naval development. In a letter to Secretary of the Navy William "Frank" Knox dated January 2, 1942, Roosevelt wrote, "We simply must have more aluminum than is in sight for our aircraft. The Navy is the other great user and I am therefore asking that you make a thorough analysis of your shipbuilding plans in order that the amount of aluminum may be substantially decreased at an early date."[105]

While Roosevelt sought to divert key raw materials from the navy to airplane production, the nation remained critically short on shipping throughout 1941—a shortage long anticipated by military planners. They based this expectation not only on shortage of American shipping during the mobilization for World War I (a situation left unaddressed ever since) but also because of the significantly greater demands for shipping created by the mechanization or motorization of the entire army—demands that the officers involved in the conversion of the infantry division to the triangular structure anticipated. Demonstrating his awareness of the danger of overtaxing the limited shipping available, McNair wrote to Patton on September 28, 1942, in response to his request for additional half-tracks to ensure every infantryman moved in an armored vehicle. In his response, McNair wrote,

> I can appreciate your desire to provide for every contingency, but you now are facing one contingency which enters into the picture of the motorized division—shortage of shipping. The transportation of the infantry in trucks instead of in half-tracks saves over 200 vehicles in the division. I for one fail to share the belief that infantry must move in armored vehicles. It has not done so in previous wars, and experience in our maneuvers thus far indicates that these half-tracks are ruining our infantry as such. In the desert maneuver which I have just witnessed, I doubt that there was an infantryman in the entire problem who marched two yards. If they must fight, they must do it on foot. If they are not needed so, why have them?[106]

Building on his experience reorganizing the infantry division in the late 1930s with the lessons of the large-scale maneuvers that he oversaw in the early 1940s, McNair continued his efforts to persuade his fellow officers of the need to economize in anticipation of shipping shortages—an effort that enjoyed little success in the early years of the war.

It seems strange that McNair appears to have had little support from his peers at AAF and ASF. As early as April, 1942 the War Department ordered all three functional commands to minimize excess by eliminating all unnecessary equipment from their organizations, in part by pooling all equipment that divisions did not need on a daily basis in separate units. Evidence of the origin in the War Department of efficiency-focused initiatives to minimize the burden on limited shipping capacity exists in many sources, including the records of the War Department's Operations Division. A memorandum for record prepared on April 20, 1942, by the Operations Division captured the key points of a conference held with the War Department G-3 and G-4, with the subject: "Reduce equipment of all organizations in order to minimize demands on shipping." The memo lists as present at the conference the G-3, the G-4, and the Operations Division chief, Eisenhower. Significantly, after noting the requirement to eliminate unnecessary equipment and pool occasionally utilized equipment wherever possible, the memo includes the observation, "It is understood that all three of the Commanders mentioned are already working on the subject: the purpose of a directive is to assure immediate results and complete cooperation in the effort."[107] It does not appear that this complete cooperation happened, requiring further effort by the War Department to enforce efficiency-related policy.

Shortages of transport shipping had led Roosevelt to order Malin Craig as early as January 4, 1941, to monitor carefully lend-lease shipments and maintain a balance between space devoted to TNT and ammunition versus weapons systems. Roosevelt ordered Craig to reallocate shipping space to the latter whenever stocks of the former reached thirty days' supply, illustrating the overall shortage of shipping and the careful management it required.[108] A year later, on January 8, 1942, shipping remained in short supply, requiring Great Britain to loan ships of the Queen Mary class to America for transport of combat units to Australia. Meanwhile, Roosevelt directed Rear Admiral Emory S. Land, chairman of the US Maritime Commission, to step up transport vessel production to eight million tons in 1942 and at least ten million tons in 1943.[109] Even if the Maritime Commission could reach these goals, it remained anybody's guess whether the requested tonnages would prove adequate for the military's shipping requirements, because of military planners' inability to provide accurate requirements to civilian industrialists.

As Jim Lacey argued, "Although by early 1941 the United States had cast a new strategic conception of how it would fight a future global war, the planners had yet to match that strategy against national resources and capabilities."[110] When in July 1941 President Roosevelt finally requested information regarding the industrial requirements necessary to support offensive operations, the army could still provide industrial planners with only vague information—rough numbers of military personnel, with no numbers of specific types of equipment the US army would use and no details regarding the enemy it would face. This made detailed production planning for munitions and equipment impossible. As late as early 1942, production experts still only expected initially to support an army of two million personnel, which would increase in size according to a rough estimate of annual growth.[111] With even initial size projections creating such challenges for industry, significant increases would only exacerbate the problem. Similarly, with so much in flux—particularly a strategic situation the military had not planned for and a flat-footed economic stance that once again led to a delayed and chaotic mobilization effort—orders to build more equipment and field more units seemed like wish lists rather than viable mobilization plans.

This forced the economists and leaders of industry who actually facilitated the nation's industrial mobilization to project the amount of munitions and equipment necessary to field new units and replace combat losses based purely on their own best guess. Army officers proved unable or reluctant, after decades of operating in a climate of extremely limited funds, to provide accurate projections of equipment requirements. For example, in 1940 a leader of civilian production sought projections of textile requirements from the military. One of his manufacturers, Robert Stevens, asked a military procurement officer how many parachutes he thought the army would require during the war. The officer told him 9,000 would suffice—an estimate Stevens increased to 200,000. When the procurement officer asked him to defend this seemingly excessive number, Stevens replied, "The President wants to build 50,000 planes and they will have an average crew size of four. I simply multiplied."[112]

These mobilization issues meant that McNair faced more than the challenge of training ground forces made up of the lowest-quality subset of the army's pool of new recruits. He also had to find a way to train these recruits to fight in accordance with the army's latest doctrine and equipment. The army possessed a reasonably well-established and stable doctrine, making the training requirement straightforward. Training personnel to use modern equipment in the course of this instruction proved far more problematic. With President Roosevelt pushing the bulk of America's production capacity first to airplane development and then to shipping, availability of army equipment remained limited and its fielding unpredictable long after protective mobilization, and even combat deployments, began. These challenges, stemming from poor planning and lack of effectiveness in the nation's economic mobilization efforts, seriously hindered McNair's ability to achieve his training mission and explain his support for the army's long-standing goal of achieving efficiencies through pooling and streamlining. The army had not always concerned itself with such efficiency-focused goals, but the difficult mobilization and deployment that the army experienced—remarkably similar to that experienced during World War I—demonstrate the wisdom of seeking efficiency in unit organization while maintaining effectiveness in combat.

Given its low priority in the production effort, the slow arrival of replacements for some of the army's most outdated weapons systems, like the 37mm antitank gun, should not have come as a surprise to anyone, and it certainly did not reflect McNair's choice, or that of any other officer. Those who anticipated the challenging mobilization that the army faced simply accepted that desiring an improved weapon system had little effect on its date of receipt once mobilization began. Rather than sending an army to war lacking confidence in many of its weapons, leaders like McNair who knew the ground forces lacked optimal equipment accepted that they had to train the rapidly mobilizing army to use the weapons available as described in doctrine as effectively as possible until new ones came along.

These various challenges remained a problem for McNair throughout his four years of wartime service as GHQ chief of staff and later as commander of AGF. The foregoing summary describes the causes and initial manifestations of the most significant military and economic mobilization issues, which required a brief break from the chronological narrative in order to carry these topics through to their logical conclusion. The following chapters return to a chronological organization, describing McNair's service during the last four years of his career when he dealt with these challenges and many others as he sought to prepare the army's ground forces for combat.

McNair's efficiency reports from his year as commandant at Fort Leavenworth reflect not only the continuation of his exceptional performance but also the high level of responsibility he had reached, with a corps area commander rating his performance as post commander and the army chief of staff rating him as CGSS commandant. His first report covered the short period from April 6 to July 1, 1939, but he still received superior ratings in all categories from Malin Craig, who ranked him second out of forty-six brigadier generals he knew. Craig judged McNair qualified for corps command in the event of war, despite his hearing loss (which he did not even mention on the efficiency report), and described him as "a superior officer of superior value to the service." McNair's rater, Major General P. P. Bishop, commander of the VII Corps Area, ranked McNair fifth out of the thirty-one brigadier generals he knew at the time of this first report, and he, like Craig, ranked McNair superior in all areas and recommended him for division or corps command in combat.[113]

McNair's final efficiency report, covering the period July 2, 1939, to July 1, 1940, gives a clear indication of his impact as commandant at Fort Leavenworth—an assignment that increased his already high reputation among the army's senior leaders. By this point, War Department policy waived efficiency reports for officers directly supervised by the army chief of staff. However, Bishop, the corps area commander, commended McNair's performance as post commander in a report in which he now ranked McNair first among all brigadier generals he knew. This fit a long-standing pattern of superior performance in a wide variety of extremely demanding positions and indicated that McNair would find himself serving in positions of increasing responsibility as events in Europe unfolded.[114] Those soldiers who answered the call of Selective Service or volunteered to serve learned to fight effectively through individual and unit mobilization training based on sound doctrine—a process led by McNair and a small but dedicated staff formed in Washington, DC, in the summer of 1940.

9
Training the Army Ground Forces

Having accomplished a major transformation of Command and General Staff School (CGSS), and continuing to influence the modernization of US army doctrine, organization, and equipment, McNair departed Fort Leavenworth for his new duties in Washington, DC. In ways strikingly similar to 1917, America found itself far from prepared in 1940 to engage in the rapidly accelerating European war. Roosevelt did not initiate protective mobilization until June, so the army had to make do with limited resources as the industrialists attempted to jump-start war production. In this rapidly changing environment, the army began to prepare for war—presumably merely to defend America from foreign aggression. The regular army's attempts throughout the 1920s and 1930s to modernize in step with developments in military theory and technology had the greatest effect in its intellectual growth, as the army's leaders sought to maximize benefit from the limited resources available through education and doctrine development.

Chief of Staff, General Headquarters: Organizing a Staff to Train an Army

On August 3, 1940, McNair reported to Washington to serve as chief of staff, General Headquarters (GHQ). The War Department activated GHQ on July 26 to oversee the organization, training, and equipping of all mobilizing field forces within the continental United States. Originally conceived in the aftermath of World War I, the War Department consciously modeled GHQ after General Pershing's American Expeditionary Force (AEF) staff. Upon its formation in 1940, Secretary of War Henry L. Stimson appointed George C. Marshall as GHQ commander, a position that included the title commanding general, field forces (although the president retained responsibility for selection of an expeditionary force commander, should the need arise). Recognizing the challenge of serving simultaneously as army chief of staff and GHQ commander, Marshall selected McNair to serve as chief of staff of GHQ and initially gave GHQ responsibility for training the field forces—a role Pershing had performed when preparing the AEF for war twenty years earlier. McNair established GHQ headquarters at the former home of the recently closed Army War College, seeking both geographic distance and relative autonomy from the War Department General Staff and Marshall, who, according to the army's official history, "freely delegated authority over training to General McNair."[1]

In reality, McNair enjoyed much less autonomy from Marshall and the War Department General Staff than the official history implied. Army historians recorded the fact that Marshall did not visit GHQ headquarters until early 1941, more than six months after its formation, but they also documented the frequent and detailed correspondence between Marshall and McNair. A review of this correspondence reveals that McNair sought Marshall's approval before he made any significant decisions. He also received frequent, unsolicited guidance from Marshall regarding the conduct of his duties at GHQ, much of which dealt with relatively minor issues—ones Marshall would have left for McNair to handle, had he intended to give him full autonomy.[2]

For example, on August 16, 1939, just weeks after selecting him to serve as the CGSS commandant, Marshall wrote to McNair to express his concerns about McNair's recommended replacements for departing CGSS instructors:

> In looking over your recommendations for replacements of instructors I notice the names of former instructors included in the list. I have no intention of reneging on my assurance that you would be given a free hand in the solution of your problems, but I do want to call your attention to the fact that to recall an officer as an instructor, and not to a conspicuous key position, does serve to penalize the individual, and what seems to me of more importance, does further the continuation of old non-realistic methods to which there seems to be so much current objection. I suggest that it would be a good idea, and fairer to the officers, to ascertain informally whether they desire the re-detail.[3]

This letter demonstrates that despite his busy schedule and many responsibilities, Marshall reviewed and commented on even minor administrative issues that fell under McNair's jurisdiction—not the sort of oversight one would expect for a commander given a free hand to carry out his duties. Further, wise officers have always understood that they should not lightly disregard a suggestion from one's superior officers, much less the army chief of staff, and Marshall's correspondence with McNair included many letters like the one above. This correspondence includes many interventions by Marshall in matters within McNair's area of responsibility, beginning in the earliest days of their professional relationship during the World War II years. McNair, ever the loyal subordinate, always followed Marshall's guidance, which was often both unsolicited and related to relatively insignificant matters that McNair could (and probably should) have handled without Marshall's involvement.[4]

Early in his tenure as GHQ chief of staff, McNair learned just how significantly the War Department (and General Marshall) would influence his ability to manage affairs within his span of control. Shortly after assuming his new role at GHQ, McNair made a proposal to streamline mobilization efforts by establishing unity of command over the four field armies and eight corps areas. McNair proposed viewing the Zone of Interior as a theater of operations, with corps area headquarters taking over responsibility for all administrative functions, thereby freeing up armies, corps, and divisions to focus on organizing, training, and administering troop units. This would remove the field armies from the control of corps area commanders and place them under the direct command of GHQ, with the goal, in McNair's words, of developing "the field forces into a unified whole—GHQ troops and four armies—free to move strategically and capable of prompt and effective tactical action. Thus it would be possible to move an army when and where directed by a simple order." McNair did not develop this concept for centralizing command of the Zone of Interior by using his imagination, and no evidence exists to suggest that McNair's recommendation stemmed from a desire for more power. This plan existed long before McNair's assignment to GHQ, serving as a basic organizational concept in the color-coded plans (later, the rainbow war plans) throughout the interwar period. The beginning of protective mobilization in June 1940 should have included implementation of this arrangement by the War Department, without prompting. War planners envisioned this as a means to streamline command and coordination within the Zone of Interior. In fact, Marshall initially concurred with McNair's proposal, but during staffing, members of the War Department General Staff opposed it. His staff led Marshall to reverse himself, heeding their advice to retain War Department authority over the four field armies, rather than concurring with McNair's proposal to implement a basic element of long-standing war plans.[5]

This convoluted decision-making process soon developed into a trend in which McNair routinely worked against constraints imposed by War Department General Staff officers, who often favored the branch-specific views of various army leaders and school commandants and who benefited from quick access to Marshall when seeking his support to settle disputes. In this case, corps area commanders retained control over Zone of Interior troops, meaning McNair struggled—often in vain—to eliminate GHQ's subordinate commanders' distraction from their primary mission of unit training. This decision by the War Department enabled the corps area commands to delegate administrative matters to subordinate commands that would have remained the responsibility of senior corps area representatives had GHQ exercised unity of command. The War Department made matters worse by ensuring that unit commanders understood the limits placed on GHQ's authority once it abandoned the concept of GHQ as a theater command responsible for the Zone of Interior. As described in the army's official history,

In December 1940 the War Department found it necessary to remind the commanders of units placed under GHQ for training that only those communications which dealt with training should pass through the Chief of Staff, GHQ. "In the past," the letter ran, "the Chief of Staff has exercised his functions as commander of the Field Forces through the War Department. GHQ is the agency through which he would exercise command over such forces in an emergency. For the present, however, the recently formed GHQ will be concerned only with the direction and supervision of training of the Field Forces, exclusive of overseas garrisons. The War Department will continue to be the agency through which command, except for training, will be exercised."[6]

Marshall gave due consideration to McNair's advice, which he clearly respected and valued, but Marshall limited McNair's authority significantly, weighed McNair's advice in contrast to often conflicting advice from his staff at the War Department, and always retained final decisions, exercising his authority to settle even relatively trivial matters.

Although no military professional would question Marshall's authority to lead in this manner, some might question its wisdom, as he repeatedly undermined his own GHQ chief of staff. McNair found his authority limited from the start, and he watched it continue to dwindle as time passed. War Department staff officers soon learned that Marshall would usually support their position over the recommendation proposed by GHQ (and later the Army Ground Forces). Further, as Stephen R. Taaffe has pointed out, "Once the army began deploying overseas . . . Marshall more and more relied upon the suggestions of various American theater commanders."[7]

McNair's autonomy and influence decreased further as events unfolded over the coming years. Other organizations took on responsibility for various aspects of the mobilization process that directly affected McNair's training duties. For example, the War Department G-4 logistics section retained authority over corps area commanders with respect to logistical matters, limiting GHQ's control over the billeting, equipping, and supplying of mobilizing units about to undergo induction training. Even after the formation of GHQ, the War Department continued to serve as Marshall's primary staff, and in this role, Marshall's staff adjudicated differences of opinion between GHQ, military and civilian mobilization leaders, and later deployed unit commanders.[8] Therefore, McNair represented only one voice, albeit a familiar one, in a cacophony of views espoused by individuals and organizations attempting to influence Marshall's decisions regarding the army's mobilization process.[9]

McNair approached his new responsibilities at GHQ with the energy and determination Marshall had come to expect despite these challenges, setting high self-expectations while working tirelessly to streamline mobilization procedures and enable the exponential growth of the army. McNair faced an enormous task upon his arrival at GHQ in August 1940, beginning with his observation over the next few months of the maneuvers conducted by the First Army and the newly formed armored force under Brigadier General Adna R. Chaffee. McNair noted numerous individual- and unit-level training deficiencies during these maneuvers. This impressed upon him the difficulty he would face preparing the regular army for the stress of combat while inculcating in it the latest doctrine and training it to fight effectively as recently reorganized. Adding to his challenge, McNair also had to ensure their training prepared the regulars for the difficult task of overseeing the training of recently mobilized National Guard personnel and raw recruits. McNair's observations of these maneuvers served as the foundation for his plans for a series of large-scale maneuvers scheduled to take place in 1941.[10]

Although the regular army had tested and begun to transition to the triangular division design between 1936 and 1940, the National Guard remained in the process of reorganization during the 1941 maneuvers. This led to varying approaches to combat missions, such as relying on a variety of solutions for antitank (AT) defense. The regular army still had not achieved complete uniformity in equipment or organization during the early months of protective mobilization, and even when they began to establish uniformity, the flawed mobilization process led to more changes as the War Department sought additional efficiencies to ease the burden of fielding combat divisions.[11]

Upon the formation of GHQ, the field forces consisted of fewer than 200,000 personnel, including eight infantry divisions, one division of armor, and slightly more than one division of cavalry, all understrength and each marginally trained and equipped. Within one year, the army expanded dramatically, to 1.4 million officers and soldiers. Despite the resulting magnitude of GHQ's responsibilities, McNair remained determined to keep his staff small. GHQ initially consisted of only seven officers, augmented by several former members of the War College faculty. His staff grew to 64 officers in its first year of existence, even though the War Department authorized 156 and, in July 1941, added responsibility for planning and command of military operations in the event of an attack against the United States.[12]

The extension by the War Department on July 3, 1941, of GHQ's mission led to a great deal of confusion and friction between the two staffs. According to plans developed by the Harbord board in 1921, modified slightly in 1936 but substantively unchanged, in time of war, the War Department would establish a General Headquarters (which it had done) that would serve if the situation called for it as the command center directing the operations of the field forces. In this event, the chief of staff would transfer to GHQ to take direct command of the field forces unless the president identified a different officer to fill that role. The field armies' operational headquarters would consist of the GHQ War Plans Division augmented by representatives of other staff sections and granted command authority over operational units as needed. The War Department's extension of GHQ's mission, based on the provisions of the Harbord board, did not include these central provisions of the Harbord board's vision.[13]

The War Department assigned to GHQ various operational responsibilities (like planning for the defense of Iceland, Greenland, Newfoundland, and Bermuda base commands) but not the authority envisioned by the Harbord board. In a War Department memo establishing the basis for the extension of GHQ's powers, a staff officer wrote, "The War Department should be careful to avoid the relinquishment of that control which is essential to the execution of its responsibility for the army's function in the conduct of war. . . . The War Department must retain strategic direction of all military operations."[14] McNair and his deputy chief of staff, Major General Harry Malony, saw the problem right away: the Harbord board had created the concept for a wartime field command patterned after the AEF in World War I, a situation completely different from the one that the nation now faced. In an attempt to resolve the situation, McNair sent a memo to the War Department on July 25, 1941, requesting the authorities that he and Malony believed their new mission required, but the War Department saw that if it granted GHQ these authorities, it would simultaneously dilute its own. The Army Air Forces (AAF) objected strenuously to any such arrangement as well because this would infringe on the independence from ground forces control that it was working so hard to ensure. Marshall, considering this prospect unacceptable, decided instead to conduct a thorough review of the situation, limiting GHQ's role to its training mission until he found an acceptable solution. In the end, it came down to one of two choices: retaining a GHQ and giving it the responsibility and authority envisioned for it by the Harbord board, or retaining operational authority at a streamlined War Department by establishing a services of supply, making GHQ a redundant organization. McNair preferred the second option, and to solve the problem of redundancy, he proposed giving GHQ operational command of the four field armies, while the War Department commanded an expeditionary force, should one form and deploy overseas. This option still lacked unity of command, leading Marshall by early 1942 finally to decide to completely reorganize the War Department. In the meantime, GHQ performed two functions—training and organization—with the very small staff McNair preferred.[15]

This partly reflected McNair's belief in keeping staffs small and efficient rather than allowing bloat and bureaucracy to limit their effectiveness and keeping talented officers in high-level staff positions when they could benefit far more from professional development in combat units, simultaneously increasing the army's readiness. McNair sought to ensure that all deserving officers had the chance to serve as commanders and staff officers in newly formed units, and this required the transfer of many officers from various staffs and army schools into those units—a policy that other army senior leaders did not always agree with. This reduced the number of officers available for assignment to organizations like the GHQ staff, even had McNair desired such an increase. This also meant that many of the officers who developed and understood existing war plans left their staff positions just as the time approached to refine them and prepare for the possibility of conducting operations based on those plans. Marshall's policy of placing youthful officers in important positions, which led him to assign only officers below fifty years of age to GHQ, did help McNair keep his staff small because its members possessed high energy and innovative minds.[16] Nevertheless, the GHQ staff found itself increasingly overstretched by its growing responsibilities.[17] In the midst of these transitions, Marshall recommended McNair's promotion to the temporary rank of major general, which occurred on December 1, 1940, commensurate with his increased level of responsibility.[18]

Lieutenant Colonel Mark Clark, assigned to GHQ to serve as McNair's operations officer (G-3), arrived in Washington shortly after the headquarters' formation, only to discover that McNair had already departed Washington to observe units conducting field training. As Ely Kahn noted, although "sometimes called the most intellectual of generals, McNair preferred being in the field to sitting at a desk." Finding air transport of his own, Clark tracked McNair down at Pine Camp, New York, observing the First Army's maneuvers. Quickly establishing his position as a key member of the staff, Clark enjoyed greater access to McNair than most GHQ staff officers did during his time in the headquarters. He observed firsthand McNair's highly respected work ethic and dedication to duty, flying over 80,000 miles with him in just one year to observe unit training and oversee GHQ maneuvers across the continental United States. This lengthy and near-continuous exposure to McNair led Clark to hold him in such high regard that he described him in his autobiography as "one of the most brilliant, selfless and devoted soldiers" he had ever encountered.[19]

Mark Clark soon learned that McNair suffered significant hearing loss, probably resulting from his decades of service in the field artillery. Although McNair made up for this disability in part by reading lips, it did create challenges for him. He generally disliked attending large conferences—a responsibility he increasingly delegated to his subordinates—and he preferred to do most of his work alone, interacting with only a few trusted agents on his staff to whom he delegated the responsibility of overseeing day-to-day operations. Army senior leaders considered his hearing loss when they passed McNair over for field command during the war, but Marshall recognized the immensity of the tasks that he had assigned to McNair and praised the skill and determination with which he and his small GHQ staff accomplished them.[20] Writing to Lieutenant General Charles D. Herron on October 29, 1940, Marshall admitted: "McNair has taken a considerable load off my shoulders, but is having a pretty hard time himself. He has a ten-passenger plane and he and his staff are on the go almost constantly."[21]

John T. Whitaker wrote a series of articles profiling several of the army's most senior officers for the *Saturday Evening Post,* entitled "These Are the Generals," later compiled and published as a book. In his piece on McNair, Whitaker provided insight into McNair's character and work ethic during these early days overseeing army mobilization training at GHQ. The following passage offers key insights into the personality and work habits of the enigmatic McNair:

The mild-mannered general with the blue eyes and sandy hair is hell on "metallic generals." A "metallic general" is described as a gentleman who has silver in his hair, gold in his teeth and lead in his pants. McNair is the man who turns them in for scrap. If you have a son or husband in uniform, you may owe his welfare or even his survival to "Whitey" McNair. "It's plain murder," says the general, "to send boys into battle under incompetent officers. You can't live with your conscience and you can't win that way." Nevertheless, McNair claims that he has never sacked an officer without giving him a chance to make good elsewhere. The general can be so ruthless in making and breaking careers only because the word "favoritism" is not in his vocabulary. He has scrapped personal friends and at least one West Point classmate. On his own staff there is only one officer whom he has known or leaned on before—Brig. Gen. John M. Lentz, from the artillery, which is McNair's own service. Unlike other ranking generals, McNair did not ask for individual officers he had known and liked. He asked the engineers, artillery, Signal Corps, and the like, to send him officers with certain qualifications. The qualifications are purely military. McNair doesn't care about an officer's bridge game or his wife's social connections. He has told his own wife that during this war they can accept exactly one dinner engagement a month. "And just think," she says with a rueful smile, "of the wonderful invitations pouring in. I refuse them all. The general works every night. He is true to Elsie." "Elsie" is the name the McNairs have given the L. C.

Smith typewriter which rests on a packing case beside the general's bed. He pecks away long after taps.[22]

Perhaps McNair's consistently long workdays explain the lack of personal letters or diaries in the historical record. One must rely on accounts like those written by Whitaker and Khan, or interviews of officers who served with McNair, to gain an understanding of his personal views and the way he interacted with his staff. Fortunately, many archival records, some previously neglected or unknown, reveal much about McNair.[23]

One of McNair's most significant responsibilities upon his arrival at GHQ consisted of planning the army-level maneuvers scheduled to take place throughout 1941. Marshall and McNair shared a common vision for these maneuvers. They intended for them to increase the proficiency of regular army personnel conducting large unit operations, to test the updated *Field Service Regulations* (*FSR*) and the experimental armored and mechanized cavalry divisions, and to prepare the regular army to train the many National Guard units and conscripts that would mobilize over the coming months.

Various issues increased the challenges associated with preparing for these maneuvers. These included the ongoing debate between the army's various arms and branches over doctrine development, as well as the slow start of industrial mobilization. Most European armies possessed qualitative and quantitative advantages in military equipment compared to the US army in the spring of 1940, and even with America's immense production potential, the nation never completely made up this lost ground, particularly given the challenges of shipping equipment overseas. Nevertheless, McNair set out to prepare the rapidly expanding army for war by developing an aggressive training plan intended to achieve large-unit collective proficiency by 1941. This plan reflected McNair's basic training philosophy that emphasized tough, realistic training. Peter R. Faber described McNair's training scheme:

> The standardized phases included fundamentals, small unit operations, combined arms, and lastly, corps and army maneuvers. By adopting this gradualist approach, McNair not only promoted efficiency, he also trained combatants to perform a variety of tasks and therefore protected the US Army from overspecialization. Lastly and perhaps most importantly, McNair introduced realistic training into the American Military. He used live ammunition (more than 240,000 tons) in combat education; he turned mere obstacle courses into mock battlefields; he organized twenty-seven large-scale maneuvers in the United States, one of which involved 1.5 million people; he used the 180,000-square-mile Desert Training Center in California and Arizona to simulate the-

ater-level warfare; and he demanded "free" maneuvers, in which local commanders had to solve battlefield problems with little or no guidance from superiors.[24]

As Faber pointed out, the training reforms McNair instituted have remained core principles of the US army's combat training methodology to the present. It is remarkable that he managed to establish these enduring principles while shouldering the burden of transforming into a combat-ready force the small and unevenly trained army of 1940 and the masses of National Guardsmen and conscripts that swelled its ranks. Even as he managed these massive responsibilities, McNair remained committed to keeping his staff small and never employed the traditional services of an aide-de-camp.[25]

McNair and his seven-man GHQ staff began this process by assessing the state of army training based on their observation of the August maneuvers of 1940. McNair delivered this assessment to General Marshall in the form of a draft letter to the army commanders on September 5, 1940, seeking Marshall's guidance. Marshall directed his staff to publish the findings on January 7, 1941, summarizing the observed training deficiencies in ten points:

1. Obviously deficient training of small units and in minor tactics.
2. Faulty employment of the infantry division and of its combat teams.
3. Failure fully to appreciate the purpose of motor vehicles and exploit their capabilities.
4. Inadequate reconnaissance and lack of contact between adjacent units.
5. Inadequate support of infantry by division artillery.
6. Faulty signal communications.
7. Too passive employment of antitank guns.
8. Improper employment of horse cavalry.
9. Neglect of ammunition supply and evacuation of wounded.
10. Unreal situations due to faulty umpiring.

As official historians Greenfield, Palmer, and Wiley wrote, all but points 8 and 9 proved enduring challenges in the training of army ground combat troops. National Guard observers at the 1940 maneuvers not only concurred with these deficiencies in their divisions' training readiness but also noted other challenges, including shortages of qualified staff officers and commanders, and deficiencies in individual training that would delay the effectiveness of unit training.[26]

McNair and his staff developed a training plan for 1941 focused on correcting these deficiencies and issued it to the four field army commanders on January 15, 1941. This schedule reflected McNair's training philosophy, allowing individual and small unit training to take place in a distributed fashion, building up to corps maneuvers as the final phase of independent unit training before the armies and corps participated in one of several GHQ-level maneuvers (army versus army or corps versus corps/army). The initial target date of August 1941 for completion of the training plan and combat certification of the protective mobilization army proved overly optimistic. This led GHQ to allocate more time for training at the individual and unit level, rescheduling the first GHQ maneuver to begin in September and the final maneuver to end in November, ensuring all nine army corps completed unit training and participated in GHQ maneuvers in 1941. McNair and his staff also devoted significant time and effort to developing tough and realistic maneuvers.[27]

Given the overall supervisory role McNair would fulfill during the maneuvers, Marshall recommended McNair for promotion to the temporary rank of lieutenant general on May 28, 1941. In a memorandum to Secretary of War Stimson, Marshall noted the scope and difficulty of McNair's role at GHQ, pointing out that he had flown 43,000 miles in less than a year in the conduct of his duties, which included frequent interaction with five lieutenant generals and thirty-five major generals. He also noted McNair's involvement with the "critical and delicate matter of relief or re-classification of high-ranking officers, as a result of training inspections and of the coming maneuvers." Marshall closed the memorandum by observing, "General McNair has one of the best minds in the army. He is conspicuous for loyalty, modesty and soldierly qualities. He should have greater prestige for his arduous and highly responsible duties of the coming months, especially since I am being held rather closely to Washington. Therefore I urge his immediate advancement to the temporary grade of Lieutenant General."[28] McNair received notification from the adjutant general in a June 21, 1941, memorandum that President Roosevelt approved his promotion, effective June 9, 1941. McNair took the oath of office one week later.[29]

As historian Christopher Gabel described in *The US Army GHQ Maneuvers of 1941*, most European armies possessed a long tradition of conducting large-scale maneuvers. Gabel cited Frederick the Great as a particularly relevant example: he enjoyed a significant advantage at the Battle of Leuthen, although heavily outnumbered, because he had previously used the same ground for his annual maneuvers. In contrast, the US army had no such tradition, mostly because it rarely possessed an active duty force large enough to conduct large-scale maneuvers at anything like the scale of those planned for 1941.[30]

Remembering the AEF's costly frontal attacks and the difficulty of conducting open warfare as Pershing envisioned, Marshall and McNair intended to prepare the army in advance for the possibility of another war. Significantly, they expected the next war to take place under open warfare conditions unattainable during

World War I but made possible by the significant technological advances of the previous two decades. Congressionally authorized funds for protective mobilization resulted in an eightfold increase in the size of the army, which grew to a force of 1.2 million by late 1941. This enabled the War Department to field thirty-three divisions, providing the units needed to conduct large-scale maneuvers. However, as Christopher Gabel pointed out, "The Army that had once had the time to modernize but not the money now had the money but not the time."[31] The 1941 maneuvers revealed the impact of these time constraints in areas including individual soldier skills, leader proficiency, weapons development and availability, and gaps between doctrine and practice resulting from various unresolved debates.[32]

As GHQ chief of staff, McNair observed the performance during the 1940 and 1941 maneuvers of officers aspiring to division and corps command. This enabled him to serve as the principal advisor to General Marshall on the selection of combat commanders. Both McNair and Marshall possessed strong opinions, similar to General Pershing's when he commanded the AEF, regarding the qualities necessary to make an officer suitable for division command. They usually only saw these qualities in regular army officers, and they agreed that the officer corps as a whole consisted of many officers too old to command troops in combat.[33]

The shortage of trained and capable officers represented one of the army's most significant mobilization challenges. By late 1941, McNair had only observed two National Guard colonels he recommended for promotion, and he recommended these officers only reluctantly, writing to Marshall on October 24, 1941, "I fail to see the wisdom of promotions such as these when one ponders the welfare of the Country and of the troops commanded. I believe that a citizen officer in general should be content to reach the highly respected grade of colonel, and that the high command should be by selected professional soldiers."[34]

Accompanying General Marshall to a meeting with Secretary of War Stimson on October 27, 1941, McNair described to Secretary Stimson the stark contrast between the capabilities of regular army officers and National Guard officers—a situation nearly identical to the one Pershing faced when mobilizing the AEF. Partly due to their education during the interwar period at Fort Leavenworth—and, for some, at the Army War College—regular army officers proved far more capable than those in the National Guard, leading McNair to recommend in 1940 a wholesale demobilization of the National Guard. Marshall and Stimson knew such a decision would lead to disastrous political backlash, but Marshall had also witnessed the excessive time and effort GHQ expended attempting to bring National Guard commanders up to regular army standards, thus detracting from the overall training of their divisions. Marshall therefore sought a compromise solution that prioritized collective training over the careers of individual officers but minimized political repercussions. He advised Stimson to retain the National Guard as an organization while supporting McNair's recommendations to relieve all but two of the senior National Guard commanders after their initial unit mobilization training, replacing them with younger and more capable regular army officers.[35]

This effort to ensure officers with the appropriate youthful vigor led combat formations applied to the National Guard and to the regular army. As Taaffe pointed out,

> Marshall looked at an officer's age when making promotions and assignments, especially for combat commands. Marshall's World War One experiences convinced him [like McNair] that leading soldiers in combat was a job for younger men because they had the necessary energy, stamina, and vigor. When he became chief of staff, Marshall was dismayed that elderly officers past their prime led so many field armies, corps, and divisions. To rectify this, in 1940 a new War Department policy limited the maximum age of officers serving with troops to sixty-two for major generals and sixty for brigadier generals. Marshall applied this new rule in a tenacious and cold-blooded campaign to supplant overage officers with younger men in their fifties and even forties.

Marshall did attempt to consider officers' feelings when making these decisions, many of whom felt slighted because they missed an opportunity to lead soldiers in combat after a long period of often tedious peacetime service. Nevertheless, age remained one of Marshall's top considerations in selecting officers for troop command; McNair recommended only officers who met Marshall's age limits and who possessed youthful vigor for combat command based on his observation during maneuvers, despite resistance from both the War Department and senior commanders who petitioned to retain subordinates who exceeded age limits.[36] When necessary, Marshall definitively asserted his authority to include age as a criterion for selecting generals for troop command. As Taaffe noted, "On one occasion he bluntly told a group of officers, 'All four of you are too old to command divisions in combat.'"[37]

The relief of elderly officers in favor of their more energetic subordinates and the mobilization training these officers received improved the overall quality of the officer corps. However, the rapid expansion of the army made it impossible to place a well-trained and experienced officer in every key leadership position. Inexperienced officers thus consistently outnumbered experienced officers. Many of these young officers lacked discipline and shared little enthusiasm for combat, much like the soldiers that they would lead.[38]

Doctrine matured slowly as the army began to mobilize. Debate over the update of the 1939 *FSR* meant its replacement did not gain War Department approval until May 1941. Therefore, the 1939 doctrine guided mobilization training during most of the protective mobilization period.[39] Perhaps this explains why William O. Odom devoted only two pages in *After the Trenches* to the 1941 *FSR*. However, while the units participating in maneuvers in 1940 and 1941 either had not yet seen the final approved 1941 *FSR* or lacked adequate time to study it before the maneuvers, the manual's publication in May 1941 preceded the mobilization of most of the army's divisions. In addition, the manual's longevity (it remained in effect until publication of the next *FSR* on June 14, 1944) provided doctrinal stability for most of the war. Even of those units that conducted maneuvers before its publication, most had several months to study the new doctrine before they had to apply it in combat. Further, as Odom described,

German victories in 1939 and 1940 ended much of the debate over methods of war. With the blueprint of modern war provided by German operations, the army raced to revise its doctrine. . . . The army published *FSR 1941* based on information received from the world's battlefields and its own growing experience with large-scale exercises. The new manual was a vast improvement over its predecessor if only because it more accurately reflected current technological capabilities and represented a truly revised doctrine. The new, battle-tested prescriptions for successful combat erased doubts about trends in modern warfare and swelled the new manual to twice the size of its predecessor. The biggest difference between the 1939 and 1941 editions was in emphasis on armored and air operations. Use of air and tanks, as well as means for antitank and antiaircraft defense, dominated the work. Fire superiority, previously a function of infantry–artillery cooperation alone, now hinged on integration of combat aviation and tanks into the partnership.

Nevertheless, after describing the manual's qualities, Odom made clear why he devoted such a small section of his conclusion to it.[40]

In *After the Trenches,* Odom focused on the doctrinal development challenges the army faced during the interwar period, and, as he pointed out, "ultimately, the North African battlefield exposed the shortcomings of the army's crash course in modern warfare." He admitted, "The army would learn from its defeats, and eventually emerge from World War II as the most skilled and powerful fighting force of the war," but he emphasized "the price exacted in soldiers' blood for neglect of peacetime training, equipment modernization, and doctrine development." This led to an unbalanced emphasis on the longevity of the 1923 doctrine and the ill effects Odom attributed to it and to its marginally updated 1939 successor while relegating the 1941 doctrine, which guided the army's efforts through most of the war, to a mere afterthought in his analysis.[41]

Walter Kretchik described the 1941 manual as "the combined product of the 1939 version, service criticism, German *Blitzkrieg,* and lessons taken from the Louisiana Maneuvers." He identified significant changes from the 1939 to the 1941 versions of the manual, although both emphasized offensive, combined arms warfare. For example, the 1941 manual described two forms of attack: envelopments and penetrations. Envelopments were further broken down into three types: single envelopments, double envelopments, and turning movements. Both envelopments and penetrations sought the ultimate goals of striking the enemy's rear areas, creating disruption and exploiting the breakdown in enemy cohesion through pursuit operations. This reflected the long-standing view among army leaders that the modern battlefield, with its greatly enhanced mobility and combined arms fighting methods, would look like that conceived by open warfare advocates, with dispersed, fast-moving units and gaps between adjacent units that the enemy could exploit. This prediction emerged logically from changes in technology. If not for the unforeseeably massive scale of the mobilization, which often led to high densities of units fighting along narrow fronts, the battlefield might have looked much more like the doctrine anticipated than it did during World War II, particularly in Western Europe. The new doctrine also continued to describe a close air support role for AAF, a mission separate but complementary to interdiction of enemy air power. The doctrine acknowledged that airpower by itself would not prove decisive, but did describe air support of ground forces as an important source of firepower in mobile warfare.[42]

In contrast, Peter Schifferle argued that the 1941 manual did not reflect a significant degree of change but instead "maintained the basic conceptualization of war found in the 1923 and 1939 *FSRs.*" Schifferle did describe the numerous additions to the manual that incorporated the various aspects of branch doctrine previously at odds with or ignored by the *FSR.* For example, Schifferle pointed out that the new manual covered the different types of divisions (infantry, cavalry, motorized, and armored) as well as various types of operations not previously described in the *FSR,* such as combat in woods or towns, operations in harsh terrain like jungles and deserts, and static and mobile (retrograde) defensive operations.[43] Thus, both Schifferle and Kretchik recognized the additional detail contained in the *1941 FSR (FM 100-5, Operations)* and the manual's attempt to resolve branch and service discrepancies with overarching army operational doctrine, even if they did not agree about the degree of change from one manual to the next.[44]

Kretchik's and Schifferle's assessments of the 1941 doctrine stand out as exceptions in a large body of negative analyses. By demonstrating the efficacy of the army's interwar doctrine development process (and the professional discourse that took place in military schools and journals), these works help explain why the army proved more ready than the nation for war when protective mobilization began. Roosevelt handed leading civilian manufacturers responsibility for the Industrial Mobilization Plan without warning. This caused them to confront protective mobilization flat-footed, struggling to increase production fast enough to meet the army's needs. The demands caused by the breakneck pace of industrial effort upon the nation's awakening in 1940 revealed significant weaknesses in American preparedness for economic mobilization for war, and these weaknesses grew to the breaking point during the early years of mobilization.

As the industrial base struggled, the US army learned to fight effectively by building on a solid foundation of individual and unit mobilization training and sound doctrine that accounted for lessons learned from German success in Europe and American large-unit maneuvers at home.[45] McNair and his staff at GHQ developed one of the key processes that enhanced army effectiveness—the extensive mobilization training program that established a standard training regimen, building from individual to unit-level training, and finally to army-level maneuvers, which McNair and his staff planned and McNair personally directed and assessed. Despite the thoroughness of this training plan, however, continued turbulence in the mobilizing army—particularly debates about doctrine, organization, and equipment—made the execution of this training particularly challenging for McNair and his staff.

The Challenges of Training a Rapidly Mobilizing Army

Although some historians have criticized McNair's hands-on role in the planning of the GHQ maneuvers, Christopher Gabel identified the most logical reason for his direct involvement: "Given the smallness of the GHQ staff (only twenty-nine officers and sixty-four enlisted men as of June 1941), General McNair himself became closely involved with the myriad details of organizing the maneuvers."[46] McNair's authoring of the umpire manual, which can give the impression that McNair sought to ensure that the manual reflected his and Marshall's confidence in specific doctrinal and equipment-related issues like AT guns and tank destroyers, also has a simpler explanation. In 1940–1941, McNair's extensive experience with umpire procedures—dating back to his Army War College education, his experience as the senior umpire at the Third Army maneuvers in 1939, and his observation and critical analysis of the 1940 maneuvers—was probably unmatched by any other officer in the army.

Although the rules in the manual did credit AT guns with kills at longer ranges than the guns in use at the time simply could not achieve, McNair acknowledged

Lieutenant General Lesley J. McNair and Brigadier General E. F. Harding at the Carolina Maneuvers, 1941. Courtesy of US National Archives II, College Park, Maryland

these limitations in his critiques of the 37mm AT gun. On the other hand, he knew the potential of AT guns, and he knew that the War Department anticipated fielding a more powerful gun before the army saw combat. Despite his key role in preparing the army for war, McNair had no authority over the ordnance department, which controlled weapons development and which did field several new weapons before the 1941 maneuvers. This did not include the next generation of AT guns, however, which did not enter production until well after the maneuvers ended. This left McNair no other choice than to develop a set of rules that reflected the anticipated capabilities of the AT weapons that the War Department expected ordnance to develop and provide to the ground forces before any units deployed. He never expected the army to enter combat overseas relying on the 37mm gun.[47]

McNair also saw no value in demoralizing participating soldiers by demonstrating the limitations of obsolescent weapons that the War Department expected ordnance to replace soon. Regardless, McNair had no authority to undermine the War Department's decision regarding the use of the 37mm gun and tank destroyers (later fitted with a more powerful gun)—a decision Marshall made on the basis of his own instincts, supported by recommendations from the War Department G-3, then ordered McNair to implement. Perhaps most significantly, McNair understood the shipping limitations that required the US army to keep the weight of deploying units as low as possible, supporting the logic of AT guns. The army would field towed AT guns if he had his preference, but even configured as mechanized tank destroyers, as Marshall directed, the gun-based AT solution significantly reduced shipping demands compared to an overseas tank arms race the United States could not possibly hope to win.

In short, no other army officer possessed stronger qualifications than McNair to oversee the writing of the umpire manual for the 1941 maneuvers—the same qualifications that led Marshall to select McNair for the GHQ chief of staff position in the first place. Nor is there any evidence to indicate that McNair intentionally favored AT guns despite some foreknowledge that the army would find itself in combat still equipped with ineffective AT guns. Instead, McNair simply encountered a difficult situation, and he did the best he could to deal with it. Preparation of the umpire manual, which GHQ distributed to the field armies in February 1941, required him to develop rules to adjudicate engagements between units using weapons systems that remained either in production or, in the case of new AT guns and tank destroyers, in a preliminary design phase. This has long proven to be a challenge for army leaders who work to prepare the army of the present for the war of the future.

Throughout McNair's two years as chief of staff of GHQ, he worked to train a rapidly expanding army in the midst of these industrial mobilization challenges. Adding to these difficulties were various issues related to army equipment, doctrine, and training, which remained matters of heated debate throughout the mobilization period; many of these debates continued throughout the war and well beyond. Space constraints do not allow analysis of all of these issues in detail; however, McNair's efforts to lead the army's development of a concept for AT defense provides a suitable case study that exemplifies the sort of problems he tried to solve. It also illustrates how important details revealed in recently conducted research provide additional context related to McNair's efforts to deal with various mobilization related issues, and what historians since World War II have written about them. The AT debate serves as a particularly relevant example of the difficulties McNair faced when attempting to prepare the army to deal with the realities of modern warfare because many historians now view McNair as the main

Lieutenant General Lesley J. McNair Arriving in California to Observe Maneuvers, August 23, 1942. Courtesy of the Military History Institute

proponent of AT guns and tank destroyers. This had led some historians to depict him as the sole authority on this issue, often leading to criticism—some warranted, some not.[48]

McNair believed that guns, not tanks, should serve as the primary means of defense against enemy tanks. He supported this conviction on several grounds, generalizable as matters related to either efficiency or effectiveness. However, most histories that describe McNair's support of the AT gun as the best defense against the tank distill a long and complex debate into an oversimplified anecdote. Several key details found in the documents McNair wrote and the correspondence he exchanged with other officers shed light on this debate.

Gabel identified McNair as one of the few army officers who worked on the question of AT defense throughout the 1930s, receiving "little encouragement from his superiors." Research confirms that few army officers devoted significant intellectual effort to the question of AT defense before 1940. However, McNair wrote a letter in June 1940 to Lieutenant Colonel Bacon, a field artillery officer in the Missouri reserves, that sheds light on the origin and nature of his continued interest in the matter. Writing in response to the officer's request for feedback on his own study of existing AT gun capabilities and limitations, McNair noted that his superiors in the office of the chief of field artillery directed him in 1936 to "draw up the initial study which [. . .] resulted in the present 37mm antitank gun." Therefore, as early as 1936, McNair played a formal role in AT defense by developing a design for a modified version of the 1936 model German-designed 37mm AT gun currently in use. The timing of this project coincided with Malin Craig's cancellation of the AT gun development program in 1936; apparently the field artillery branch wanted McNair to design a variant of the existing gun for continued production in lieu of a replacement. However, illustrating ordnance's long-standing control over material acquisition and design, McNair pointed out in the letter to Bacon that "this gun is not what I proposed, in that it has insufficient muzzle velocity and its sighting apparatus is too crude for effective firing."[49] Not only did ordnance not design a gun that met McNair's recommended specifications, but the AT gun development progressed no further in the next several years. The 37mm gun fell into increasing obsolescence over the next several years, with no replacement model in production or design.

This illustrates, as some historians have pointed out, that in 1940 McNair supported an AT concept centered on the AT gun while recognizing the deficiencies in existing AT weapons. It shows that McNair's work on an AT gun serves as another example of a test or experiment senior army leaders assigned to McNair on the basis of his record of diligence and merit in such work. It also highlights the significance of America's delayed development of a realistic strategy and industrial mobilization plan—factors that drastically slowed production of many new weapons or forced the army to rely on a single "good enough" model when faster production and shipping capability might have allowed for fielding of progressively better weapons. Contrary to assertions that McNair did not recognize the flaws of the 37mm gun because he possessed a flawed view of modern mechanized warfare, research shows that McNair provided specific criticisms in this memo, and many others, of the 37mm gun. More significantly, a review of contemporary doctrine and military modernization guidance produced by the War Department shows that his view of modern mechanized warfare rested solidly on a foundation of accepted military doctrine and discourse.[50]

McNair also wrote detailed critiques of the other guns available to both the US and the British armies in 1940 that possessed the potential for use as AT weapons. McNair not only recognized these guns' limitations but also understood that inherent delays in the army's acquisition system meant that the army would have to do its best with the equipment it currently possessed for at least two years in the event of a mobilization (a lesson he learned from Malin Craig in 1936). Therefore, when mobilization began, he focused on organizing and training the army to use a viable AT concept that acknowledged the limitations of the weapons currently available, developing procedures to employ them as effectively as possible while expecting industrial leaders and army ordnance to field an improved AT gun in time to equip army divisions before they engaged in combat.

Efficiency and streamlining influenced McNair's support for an AT gun–based defensive scheme to combat enemy tanks. He remembered the shipping limitations that delayed the AEF's deployment to Europe during World War I, and his participation in the Proposed Infantry Division and Provisional 2nd Division tests had convinced him that the army would face far greater shipping challenges in the next war. Motorization and mechanization had dramatically increased the size of divisions and the number of ships required to move them, and unlike World War I, the army of the 1940s would deploy overseas with all of its own equipment. McNair did not, however, dogmatically support an AT gun–based defensive scheme. He merely wanted the army to avoid the habit it had developed of falling back on deeply entrenched branch biases and refusing to conduct objective tests and evaluations to find the most efficient and effective method to solve problems like developing the most efficient and effective method of AT defense possible. At an antitank conference at the Army War College on July 14, 1941, McNair opined:

> The antitank question, as I see it, is the largest single question facing the Army today. When responsible people in the War Department—not individuals but subdivisions—assert formally that the Army should consist essentially of armored divisions—which has happened recently—you can realize the possibili-

ties of this question. While neither the War Department nor I subscribe to such a view, there is support for it in the exploits of the German mechanized army in France on and after May 10, 1940. [...] There is great disparity among the troop units of the field forces, with reference to what has been done to date in this connection. [...] There is support for the belief that, while the armored force was not opposed with complete success [in the Second Army maneuvers recently held at Camp Forrest]—far from it—an answer can be found. I appreciate that many aspects of antitank tactics and equipment are controversial, and there is no intention on my part of attempting to indicate doctrine. [...] The question whether the tank or the antitank gun will be successful in this struggle has not yet been answered conclusively. Certain it is, however, that unless guns are equally as capable as the tank of moving rapidly, the tank will avoid the guns. You gentlemen must find the correct answer to the questions here involved.[51]

McNair did not appear to see himself as a decision maker in the AT debate; his remarks seem intended only to persuade the conference to carry out a thorough and objective analysis, indicating that he knew he could not force the issue in one direction or another.

McNair also made no effort to hide the significance of economy in his preference for the AT gun:

I do not quarrel with the assertion that the best defense against tanks is by other tanks; possibly it is correct. However, it is questionable economy to employ a tank costing $35,000 to destroy another tank of substantially the same value, when the job could be done by a gun costing but a fraction of that amount. It seems more logical to employ our guns to counter the hostile armored force while saving our own armored forces for use against profitable targets to which they are invulnerable.[52]

He understood the technical issues involved, and he knew that many remained theoretical until ordnance fielded a new-generation gun. This meant that whatever AT method the War Department decided to pursue, it would have to rely initially on inadequate weapons, making its investment in one method over another something of a gamble, mitigated only through the most realistic and objective training possible.

McNair emphasized that an effective AT gun must possess a flat trajectory to improve its odds of scoring a hit (because a flat trajectory allows for error in range as long as the firing azimuth is accurate) and high muzzle velocity combined with the proper ammunition to ensure that it penetrated the armor it hit.

No existing American or British AT gun could hit and penetrate modern German armor reliably and at an acceptable range in 1940. McNair specifically cited the inadequacy of European AT guns during the 1939 and 1940 offensives to demonstrate the need for a more powerful gun to defeat German tanks. However, McNair emphasized AT guns' various theoretical advantages, beyond simply their low cost relative to tanks. He pointed out the ease with which crews could conceal and cover their guns, giving them a significant defensive advantage over exposed tanks. He emphasized their ease of mobility, demonstrated in tests that showed a trained crew could unhook a gun and fire an initial aimed round within ten to twenty seconds, depending on the type of vehicle towing the gun. He highlighted their ability to create layered, combined arms belts to defend a position against tanks from all sides and to operate effectively on the offense as well, or to act as mobile reserves.[53]

McNair's work on AT defense in the 1930s had led to his publication at CGSS of *Antimechanized Defense (Tentative), May 22, 1939,* a manual that reflected McNair's views on modern mechanized warfare and AT defense in 1939—views that remained consistent from then on (after modification to adapt them to Marshall's tank destroyer preference). Some historians have asserted that McNair based his ideas regarding proper use of AT assets on the false notion that AT weapons would usually face masses of enemy tanks fighting independently, rather than as members of combined arms teams. Historians have also asserted that McNair believed in the necessity of usually massing AT weapons as the only way to defeat these tank masses.[54] In contrast, the available evidence reveals that McNair consistently emphasized the importance of using the combined capabilities of all of the arms and services acting in concert.[55] One can see this thinking underlying his post–World War I efforts to improve artillery support to the infantry by task organizing mobile artillery and spotters with front line infantry units. The German victory over France reinforced this emphasis of combined arms as the key to effectiveness because the Wehrmacht, in particular the Panzer divisions, fought in mechanized combined arms teams, occasionally using masses of tanks to achieve or exploit a breakthrough.

A close read of *Antimechanized Defense* reveals a concept for the use of tanks in much the same manner in which the German army used them in its recent campaigns, and in other correspondence on this topic, McNair specifically referenced these campaigns to clarify his views. Admittedly, one could easily misconstrue the meanings of certain portions of *Antimechanized Defense*, given the importance of the first section in providing clarity to his use of two key terms throughout the rest of the manual: tank and AT.

Chapter 1, Section 1, "Definition," clarifies exactly what McNair meant in the rest of the document by these terms:

1. DEFINITION—Antimechanized defense includes defense against all armored combat vehicles—scout cars, armored cars, combat cars, and tanks. The weapons and units primarily utilized for antimechanized defense usually are referred to as *antitank* weapons and *antitank* units. Throughout this text for purpose of brevity the term *tank* is used as applying to any type of armored combat vehicle or unit.[56]

This explains how McNair sought to achieve brevity in *Antimechanized Defense*. In this manual, the term *tank* could mean an individual tank; a platoon of tanks with supporting mechanized infantry, artillery, and close air support; or a Panzer division. When read with this definition in mind, one can see that the manual describes tanks operating primarily as elements of combined arms teams, while occasionally massing as independent formations to exploit their speed and mobility, but even then within the overall context of a combined arms operation.

The manual contains seven chapters, the first titled "General," followed by six chapters describing employment of AT units in various scenarios (during the advance, halts, the development, the defense, retrograde movements, and offensive operations). McNair described his concept of modern mechanized warfare, and his specific concept of tank employment, in the various sections of his chapter 1.[57]

In the section titled "Types of Interference to be Expected from Tanks," the manual lists the following:

1. Scout vehicles and armored cars "bent on reconnaissance" which might also harass or delay friendly elements upon contact;
2. "The operations of well organized tank units" conducting delaying actions, independent attacks, or attacks "in conjunction with organized attacks by elements of all arms";
3. Tanks seeking surprise by launching attacks under cover of smoke or fog.[58]

This list indicates McNair's awareness of the advantage of combined arms fighting methods with respect to tank and AT warfare, just as he described in the *Tentative FSR (1939)* the essential contribution to success provided by cooperation among the combined arms.

The AT gun also offered significant advantages in efficiency, and although McNair could not have predicted the extent of the problems that hobbled America's mobilization for World War II, he did understand the significant fuel, ammunition, and shipping demands that a fully mechanized and motorized army would place on the logistics network. His involvement in the Proposed Infantry Division and Provisional 2nd Division tests only served to reinforce this insight. It made sense to consider economy in AT defense, considering the already significant shipping and logistic support demands of the triangular division. The manual also identified the potential employment of artillery, antiaircraft weapons, small arms firing armor-piercing ammunition, and various weapons like hand grenade clusters and other track-throwing devices to serve a defensive role against tanks.[59] In short, *Antimechanized Defense* presented a reasonably accurate prediction of the future employment of tanks and a logical summary of the various means of defense against them.

The rest of *Antimechanized Defense* merely described various schemes for use of AT defenses against the three forms of attack described in the first chapter. Nothing in these later chapters indicated a belief that tanks would only fight in independent masses, would never seek out combat against enemy tanks, would not serve as effective weapon systems to defend against enemy tanks, or would usually require the massing of AT weapons in defense. In fact, the document made repeated references to tanks acting in concert with other arms, and AT weapons dispersed or arrayed in depth in the defense. For example, in chapter 5, "Employment of Antitank Units during the Defense," the manual described an enemy attack in which tanks remained out of range of artillery until the attacker selected the time and place of their employment, at which point the enemy would use the tanks swiftly and in force. Thinking of a combined arms unit like a Panzer division, this seems like a reasonable description of the manner in which the enemy would usually commit its tanks in support of a combined arms attack.[60]

In the next section, "Employment of the Battalion Platoons," the manual read, "Guns of the battalion platoons normally will be sited in prepared positions, covering natural avenues of approach into the battalion area." As for the regimental platoon, the manual described provision of detachments from the regiment "for security or other purposes," including a section of AT guns for each battalion detached. Even when the entire regiment fought intact, the manual advised "emplacing some of the guns well forward" to stop attacking tanks before they reached the main line of resistance. The manual continued, "On the other hand, if the guns are all far forward some of them may be put out of action by hostile countermeasures prior to and during the launching of the attack. There will have to be some distribution of antitank guns in depth." The manual cautions that exposed flanks or rear of the regiment will make distribution "especially necessary." Such advice appears throughout the manual, describing tanks fighting as members of combined arms teams, and AT guns dispersed or arrayed in depth to defend against them in varying ways depending on the situation.[61]

The document did highlight the specific capabilities of tanks that made them a unique threat on a modern battlefield characterized by open warfare. For example, the manual highlighted the tank's speed and mobility, which, when combined with the lack of a stabilized front, increased the need to ensure protection of flanks and rear areas against armored attacks. To defend against this wide range of threats, McNair suggested an equally wide range of countermeasures, including the use of obstacles, tanks, AT weapons, and aircraft. His descriptions of AT weapons employment varied as much as his descriptions of tank employment and included situations requiring both massed and distributed AT units.[62] Thus, nowhere did McNair's *Antimechanized Defense*—or indeed his larger body of work on modern warfare—present massed, tank pure formations as the most frequent manner in which a future enemy would use its tanks. Nor did he argue that massed, independent AT guns represented the best form of defense against them.

By comparison, anonymous faculty at the Leavenworth schools published in 1936 a document entitled *Principles of Strategy for an Independent Corps or Army in a Theater of Operations*. Michael Matheny pointed out that this document emphasized the criticality of achieving overwhelming mass at the decisive point to achieve victory through annihilation, achieved in the age of mechanization, radios, and improved road networks by using wide envelopments. Contemporary Soviet writings emphasized deep battle beginning with penetrations of the enemy's line, relying on a combined arms formation to breach the enemy line, enabling exploitation of the breach. However, German and British theorists, like the authors of *Principles of Strategy*, emphasized the wide envelopment. This text demonstrates American familiarity with European ideas of modern warfare and emphasizes the unique capabilities of the tank—ideas attributable to authors other than McNair (because it predates his arrival at Leavenworth by three years) as well as more extreme than those he described in *Antimechanized Defense*.[63]

In his correspondence of June 1940 with Lieutenant Colonel Bacon, McNair described a different method of AT employment than he advocated in the variety of situations in *Antimechanized Defense*. He responded to a lecture that Bacon had written and sent to McNair for feedback, which included a specific scenario that differed from those in *Antimechanized Defense*. McNair wrote that Bacon's scheme for a "highly echeloned antitank defense" would scatter the guns too widely. Using the example of an attacking Panzer division, McNair wrote that the enemy would most likely attack such a scattered position with concentrated tanks, like the Germans had in France, where excessive dispersal had created a weak French defense. He argued that an attacking mass of tanks required an equally concentrated mass of AT and antiaircraft guns to form a viable defense. Although in this case McNair did describe enemy employment of tanks in concentrated masses, requiring AT guns to also fight in mass, he wrote this in response to Bacon's specific scenario, not as a description of a typical or prevalent combat scenario. McNair also tempered his advice regarding massing of AT guns even in the situation Bacon described, agreeing with him that the infantry should have "some antitank protection, to sustain their morale if not for material effect."

Placed within the context of McNair's other written views on AT defense, this letter stands out as an exception. The great majority of examples that he used described reliance on distributed but mutually reinforcing AT fires, with guns arrayed to improve survivability, prevent tanks from reaching the friendly front line, and protect one's flanks and the rear.[64]

Interestingly, the self-propelled (SP) gun or tank destroyer (TD) has come to represent in historical memory McNair's inaccurate views of modern war and his support of flawed concepts of AT defense. However, as historian Harry Yeide pointed out, McNair initially opposed the idea of SP guns, viewing towed guns as easier to conceal and less vulnerable to enemy fire, and understanding the additional shipping and logistics demands that mechanized AT vehicles would create. By May 1941, the army had made no significant progress on the issue of AT defense, largely because differing views between the branches created a seemingly unbreachable impasse. The stalemate finally forced General Marshall to take matters into his own hands. This resulted in the army's development of AT weapons and doctrine based primarily on Marshall's preference for SP guns juxtaposed somewhat awkwardly with McNair's views, implemented in accordance with organizational decisions Marshall made from necessity because of incessant interbranch debates. This led Marshall to order the creation of the Tank Destroyer Center at Camp Hood, isolated from the other branches both physically and intellectually. Both Marshall and McNair understood the limitations of this approach given their desire to develop the army's ability to fight in combined arms formations, but they saw the isolation of the tank destroyer as necessary simply to break the deadlock and prevent any one branch from imposing its views on the training and development of tank destroyer units and doctrine.[65]

On May 14, Marshall ordered the War Department G-3 division to study the issue, writing, "One of our urgent needs is for the development, organization and immediate action on the subject of defense against armored forces, to include an *offensive weapon and organization* to combat these forces." Alluding to the inertia caused by the ongoing interbranch debate, Marshall wrote, "at the risk of placing G-3 in the operating field, I believe that for the solution of this problem you should take energetic and positive steps to push this matter as fast as humanly possible." He also emphasized that the matter must remain a War Department responsibility, writing, "I do not want the question of another branch or arm brought up at this time." Instead, Marshall wanted his G-3 to organize a subgroup within his division focused on

> thinking and planning on improved methods of warfare. Our organization and methods should not lag behind developments abroad. You should organize in your division a small planning and exploring branch, composed of vi-

sionary officers, with nothing else to do but think out improvements in methods of warfare, study developments abroad and tackle such unsolved problems as measures against armored force action, night bombardment, march protection and the like. Such a group should be divorced of all current matters and should work closely with the National Defense Research Committee, Inventor's Council, G-2 and the development people in G-4.[66]

This memo serves as a vital document for understanding GHQ's role in relationship to that of the War Department.

It also reveals the fact that giving McNair credit for decisions that led to the creation of new war fighting methods and concepts, like the army's World War II AT doctrine and weapon systems, does not take into account the War Department's control over such decisions, particularly since the 1942 reorganization. It demonstrates that McNair, although responsible for training the army, did not make decisions regarding how it would fight. Like any staff officer, he made recommendations; Marshall decided. Marshall made his decision in this instance on the basis of his experience and judgment, informed both by McNair's recommendations and by those of other officers within the War Department. Once Marshall made a decision, whether or not he agreed with it, McNair always supported it without question—and this case proved no different.[67]

Historian David Johnson presented a much different account of the decision to adopt the tank destroyer. Johnson began his short discussion of AT defense at the end of the 1941 maneuvers, naming McNair alone as the source of the army's AT defense concept. He mentioned Marshall only to describe his trust in McNair, asserting that Marshall gave McNair the authority to do as he saw fit. He did not mention the War Department General Staff's role, or that of General Craig or General Marshall in the armywide AT debate that began at least five years earlier during the initial discussions of the division redesign. At this early stage McNair was not yet involved in the broader discussion, instead studying the problem in isolation, more out of personal interest than an attempt to influence army doctrine. Even after formalization of his role, McNair lacked the decision-making ability that Johnson referred to regarding matters of AT defense, apparently not realizing that McNair lacked this authority. Johnson even wrote, "The tank destroyer was the artilleryman's solution to the problem posed by a mobile, armored target." (Marshall was an infantry officer.) In fact, none of the key individuals involved in AT defense development other than McNair was a field artilleryman.[68]

During the same month that Marshall sent the above memo to the War Department G-3, both the *Field Artillery Journal* and the *Infantry Journal* published articles that significantly added to the discourse on German armor operations and highlighted the need to find a method to combat the threat posed by modern

Lieutenant General Lesley J. McNair Visiting the Tank Destroyer Center, Camp Hood, Texas, January 1943. Courtesy of US National Archives II, College Park, Maryland

tanks. The article, simply titled "Antitank Defense," by Major Albert C. Wedemeyer, received a resounding endorsement from the editors of the *Field Artillery Journal* thanks to Wedemeyer's two years as a student at the German Kriegsakademie, followed by two years working as an instructor at the infantry school. The editors pointed out that this assignment gave him "unusual opportunities for securing data on antitank employment." Wedemeyer provided a description of tank employment similar to the one McNair wrote in *Antimechanized Defense*. In particular, he pointed out that German tanks were used both as members of powerful combined arms teams and as a "tank mass" used to penetrate enemy defenses and exploit their mobility to continue the attack in depth against rear areas, supported by aerial bombardment once beyond the range of supporting field artillery. In training, the Germans went to great lengths to achieve surprise by disguising the intended point of attack and preceded the commitment of the tank mass with heavy preparatory fires (high explosives and smoke) to neutralize static AT defenses. Therefore, Wedemeyer argued that an effective defensive scheme would require—in addition to towed AT guns—mines, artillery, medium tanks, and a highly mobile "tank chaser," pooled at GHQ to provide a flexible and mobile AT reserve that could quickly concentrate and defend key terrain against attacking enemy tank masses as needed.[69] This article presented a far more definitive argument for the concept of massed tank attacks and the resulting requirement of pooling AT assets than McNair's earlier writings on the topic.

Wedemeyer's article on "Antitank Defense" included a photograph of an early German tank chaser that revealed surprising similarities with contemporary American designs. This tracked vehicle, adapted from a captured British Bren machine gun carrier, had an open turret, thin armor, and an approximately 47mm AT gun. Taken together, Marshall's memo and Wedemeyer's article provide useful insight into the manner in which these individuals built on the foundation of McNair's work, modifying it to serve as the concept that guided the US War Department's creation of AT doctrine and equipment. With this concept in place, Marshall assigned responsibility for further War Department development to the G-3, who appointed Lieutenant Colonel Andrew D. Bruce head of the new G-3 planning branch, formed the day after receipt of Marshall's memo. Bruce led a conference on AT defense eleven days later, leading to a War Department order issued on June 24, 1941, directing activation of an AT battalion in each division in time to participate in the upcoming GHQ maneuvers. This gave the triangular division both a divisional AT battalion and AT companies in each regiment, similar to what McNair originally envisioned and described in *Antitank Defense*. However, the SP design added significant shipping demands to an already overtaxed system, and the term *tank chaser* gave the system an offensive, rather than defensive, flavor that McNair never intended.[70]

The 1941 GHQ maneuvers in Louisiana and the Carolinas served as immensely valuable training events for the US army. McNair and his small staff planned and oversaw these epochal maneuvers, providing the protective mobilization army with invaluable experience in combined arms fighting while enabling the War Department to test new doctrine and equipment, and identify issues the army still needed to resolve. The above analysis focuses on two particular issues commonly identified with McNair—AT defense and the development of the umpire manual used in the 1941 maneuvers—to clarify his thinking, emphasize his qualifications for involvement in these matters, and reveal the complex nature of War Department decision making, over which McNair had little influence. The tank–antitank debate remained in 1941 perhaps the most hotly contested issue of army doctrine and equipment. As Gabel pointed out, "McNair summarized the upcoming Louisiana maneuver as being ' . . . a test of tank warfare and antitank defense . . . we are definitely out to see . . . if and how we can crush a modern tank offensive.'" During the lull between the Louisiana maneuvers and the Carolina maneuvers that took place later that year, this question remained unanswered, but Marshall's faith in the AT gun and tank destroyer, as well as McNair's support for Marshall's views, remained unshaken, even though modernized weapon systems remained in development, with uncertain fielding dates.[71]

Commanders used AT weapons more aggressively in the second set of maneuvers than in the first, leading to greater success against armored forces and seeming to Marshall, McNair, and members of the War Department G-3 to vindicate the weapons and justify their continued development. Despite the protests of Major General Jacob Devers, the new chief of the armored force, who blamed armor's poor performance in the later maneuvers on biased umpire rules, the War Department accelerated AT development—particularly SP guns. Bruce's special planning branch of the War Department G-3 recommended creation of a massive independent AT arm of 220 battalions, but GHQ disagreed with various aspects of Bruce's proposal, prompting Marshall to hold an AT conference on October 7, 1941, to resolve the remaining issues and set this aggressive plan in motion. The participants, including McNair and Clark, agreed that the War Department should establish a separate force of GHQ AT battalions.[72]

On November 27, 1941, the War Department issued an order activating the Tank Destroyer Tactical and Firing Center at Fort Meade, Maryland, and a tank destroyer board, placing both under the command of Colonel Bruce and giving him the initial task of activating fifty-three new GHQ AT battalions. A War Department order of December 3, 1941, solidified the independence of AT units, redesignated tank destroyer battalions, and ordered the inactivation of AT units in cavalry divisions and field artillery battalions. Further, this order required infantry divisions to drop the name "infantry" from their AT battalions and renumber them, although they were allowed to retain the units as divisional tank destroyer battalions. Despite later criticism of the tank destroyer concept, the official history concluded the War Department shared GHQ's ideas concerning AT policy in late 1941 and had developed "an organization well fitted to meet future demands."[73]

Many other issues remained unresolved after the maneuvers, including the role of the AAF, which had reversed itself and provided aircraft to support the maneuvers shortly before they began. Close air support remained a hotly debated issue throughout the war, perhaps first attracting McNair's ire upon the official establishment of air forces' complete independence from ground force commanders' control, even when conducting close air support for a ground unit in contact. Early war visions of conflict fought and won with airpower made the ground forces seem more like an auxiliary force. The ground forces consistently found themselves low priority for scarce material resources and high-quality personnel, significantly reducing the quality of the inductees into the ground combat arms and delaying their access to much of the quality equipment they would need to fight and win. McNair had to continue the mobilization training effort despite the War Department's inability to resolve various ongoing branch disputes or to commit resources to updated weapon systems, fielded only after excessively long delays because of prioritization decisions. He also found his training mission jeopardized by debates among the ground forces, particularly those dealing with the employment of armor and reconnaissance units, and the most effective means of establishing a viable AT defense.[74]

Further, the difficulty of adjudicating air–ground and artillery attacks during the maneuvers left the effectiveness of these key sources of fire support open for debate. Although the War Department, GHQ, and the army's various branches and arms worked to resolve these issues, the Japanese attacked Pearl Harbor on December 7, 1941, prompting America to declare war on Japan and Germany to follow suit by declaring war on America. This led to a dramatic increase in the rate of mobilization and a shift in the focus of planning from continental defense to expeditionary operations overseas. The sudden strategic shift prompted by the declaration of war highlighted the continued limits on GHQ's authority and a more general need to improve War Department organization. Since its formation in the summer of 1940, GHQ had shouldered a broad range of responsibilities while lacking the authority to make any significant decisions. Instead, General Marshall retained ultimate authority, and despite his trust in McNair, he never granted McNair the degree of autonomy or authority implied in many histories. Further, Marshall retained a full War Department General Staff, even after adding war planning to the list of GHQ's missions. After receiving McNair's July 1941 memo requesting the enlargement of GHQ's authority commensurate with its responsibilities, Marshall formed a board consisting of the chief of the AAF and representatives from GHQ and the five divisions of the War Department General Staff. This board determined that only a complete reorganization of the War Department would resolve the issue, and planning throughout the remainder of the year led to the reorganization of 1942 that, among other changes, elevated McNair once again in rank and responsibility.[75]

10
The Army Ground Forces at War

The reorganization of March 1942 elevated McNair to Army Ground Forces (AGF) command, the highest level of responsibility that he held throughout his forty years of service, but ironically, at least initially he possessed even less ability to influence the decision-making process within the War Department than he had as General Headquarters (GHQ) chief of staff. After the reorganization, McNair served as one of three functional commanders. In theory, these three commanders shared power and responsibility on a coequal basis. In reality, both of his peers possessed much more personal ambition and influence than he did. In an army fighting an industrial war, the AGF seemed to represent the old school, made up of knuckle-dragging warriors. In contrast, the Army Air Forces (AAF) seemed to offer the promise of a quick and clean victory, assuming one did not look too closely at the destruction on the ground. The AAF's pilots arguably operated the most advanced weapons used in the war, and as the aviators saw it, this meant they needed a large budget, the highest-quality recruits, and complete independence from ground forces control. The Army Service Forces (ASF), although not as glamorous as the AAF, claimed a monopoly on the technological expertise needed to make America's highly advanced army function. Even if McNair possessed the nature of an empire builder, it seems highly unlikely that he could have competed with his peers at AAF and ASF, given their temperament and the nature of their commands.

McNair struggled with these dynamics and other inefficiencies created by the reorganization of 1942 for the duration of the war. This compounded the problems inherent in the troubled economic mobilization that created a logjam between military war planners and civilian industrialists. These dynamics had a profound effect on the course of the war and the AGF's ability to prepare for it. Senior leaders in organizations other than the AGF did not feel the impact of these issues as much as he did, and he tended to obey higher command's orders to the best of his ability rather than debate them, even when he knew that they would probably create significant challenges for the AGF.

These dynamics have influenced the way historians have interpreted McNair's leadership during the final two years of his career. According to army tradition, a commander takes full responsibility for everything that goes wrong under his command, and McNair exemplified tradition in an American officer. One can therefore understand why one sees decisions attributed to McNair that he did not make or even did not have the authority to make—once his commander gave an order, he carried it out as though he had issued the order himself. Historians, however, should avoid simple causal explanations for complex events; to learn from history one must examine it objectively. As historian John Lewis Gaddis pointed out, this involves identifying continuities (threads of similarity running through the past and possibly continuing into the future) and contingencies (unique, unexpected actions or events that led to surprising outcomes in the past, which make it difficult to predict future events). Leaders with powerful effects on an organization or nation—people like Roosevelt, Craig, Marshall, Eisenhower, and McNair—stand out as easily recognizable sources of contingency. Although attributing historical events to the choices and actions of individual leaders, along with other contingencies (luck, cryptanalysis, or the atom bomb), is tempting, it leaves out the other part of the equation. A balanced analysis also considers the continuities—those trends that tend to remain consistent as one looks back in time, and therefore seem reasonably likely to continue into the future. In this case, America's slow and inefficient industrial mobilization and friction within the upper echelons of national policy and strategy stand out as continuities from World War I to World War II, as does traditional American isolationism, which led to postwar military reductions, limiting the interwar army's ability to train and modernize.[1]

Still, McNair exerted a great deal of influence over America's war effort, including significant contributions to interwar innovation, confident leadership as the army mobilized for war, and, as this chapter will show, unerring dedication to the ground forces as they encountered various obstacles on the road to victory. McNair remained the imperfect man and officer that he had always been, and sometimes he had a pessimistic view regarding America's prospects in the war. As the war moved into its final stages, flaws in various concepts that he supported or programs that he oversaw began to appear, while in other areas the AGF benefited from new equipment, combat experience, and battle hardening, learning to conduct combined arms mechanized warfare as an effective combat force. He displayed increasingly introverted behavior despite the demands of his position, including more media exposure from 1942 to 1944 than throughout the rest of his career combined. Meanwhile, debates McNair engaged in and initiatives he put in place while GHQ chief of staff, while taking a toll on him, also helped the AGF turn the tide and begin its steady march to victory in the summer and fall of 1944. During this period, the AGF began to reach its potential, conducting operational art while winning successive campaigns in theaters of war around the world. This illustrates the strength of the foundation in the profession of arms that McNair developed during his first thirty-six years of service. Above all, it illustrates the US army's development of a uniquely American approach to operational art and Mc-Nair's role in that achievement—an often unrecognized role that directly contributed to America's ultimate mission success during World War II.

The vitality of American military professionals' discourse on war in the 1920s and 1930s—which McNair participated in through articles, speeches, and assignments in officer education positions—casts doubt on the idea that inactivity and stagnation defined the army's interwar years. Perhaps the War Department did not pay enough attention in the interwar years to affairs in Europe. America's increasingly isolationist stance as the Depression wore on explains the military's apparent inattentiveness to European affairs, if not excusing it—although one should note that the War Department did make various attempts, within the means available, to keep up with military developments in Europe. For example, Major Albert Wedemeyer attended the Kriegsakademie, or German War College, from 1936 to 1938, where he learned about German instructional methods, staff procedures, and development of new technologies and doctrine.[2] Many officers traveled to Europe to serve as observers with the French and British armies as well, bringing back numerous observations but noting effects on military activity in post–World War Europe similar to those the army dealt with at home.

Despite efforts to maintain awareness of European military affairs such as these, the army did not optimize for a future war in Europe primarily because America's political leaders did not intend to involve it in one. Japan remained the focus of American war plans and foreign policy for most of the interwar years, and during the Depression, most government leaders looked only inward in search of economic recovery. Roosevelt broke ties with America's World War I allies entirely, strengthening the nation's long-standing isolationist stance. From 1936 to 1940, American policy makers left Europe to its own fate, remaining disinterested until German aggression led to the unexpected and rapid fall of Poland and France. American strategists realized that the nation must come to Great Britain's aid, but public opinion still limited the Roosevelt administration's options to indirect ones like the provision of supplies to Great Britain and Russia through the lend-lease program.

The absence of adequate funds to pay for the large army, organized reserve system, and modern equipment that made Germany such a formidable military power by 1939 delayed the US army's ability to achieve parity and eventually gain the upper hand on the battlefield. Nevertheless, interwar leaders did manage to establish a foundation of clear doctrine and extensive individual and unit mobilization training. This prepared the army to learn from its difficult early experience of war, learning while battle hardening, and gradually developing into a highly effective combat force. As AGF commander, McNair managed to overcome many of the constraints he faced as GHQ chief of staff or find reasonable workarounds. He sought to prepare the AGF for war and remained committed to improving the AGF's fighting effectiveness after units began to engage in combat, even though his command authority did not extend beyond the borders of the continental United States.

The army doctrine and organization that McNair helped develop before the war proved effective in practice, as soldiers and their leaders gained combat experience. Combat revealed the success of many interwar modernization programs, like the effectiveness and flexibility of the triangular division and the longevity of the 1941 *Field Service Regulations (FSR) (FM 100-5, Operations)*, which the War Department did not update again until June 1944. This illustrates the quality of the 1941 version that served as the army's operations doctrine for most of the war, providing a stabile foundation for combat operations in the midst of much turbulence. Even less successful programs like the tank destroyer and the individual replacement system improved significantly in the later years of the war, after the War Department fielded new equipment, leaders learned to use various combat systems as intended, and revised procedures took effect. Despite some setbacks in the midst of the terribly destructive industrial warfare of the 1940s, the AGF fought as envisioned, and fought effectively—success to which many leaders contributed, including Lesley McNair. The effectiveness of the AGF seems particularly remarkable given the speed with which it had to mobilize and deploy new divisions around the world, combined with the adjustments required by the personnel and production crisis of 1942 that forced the War Department to modify its mobilization plan, leading to a significant disruption of US army strategy and policy. This required revision of the troop basis in 1943 and new procedures like the individual replacement system, using new inductees to replace losses in existing divisions since the nation's industrial capacity could not keep up with the production demands of the new divisions originally forecasted. This meant that the forces that fought each successive campaign included a sizable number of personnel individually trained and entering combat for the first time. The overall quality of the system of doctrine, organization, and training to which McNair contributed before the war and oversaw during his AGF command enabled these units to win against a professional, determined, combat-hardened enemy in one campaign after another.

During his service as AGF commander, McNair built on the experience he gained in his early career to create a foundation of guiding principles and an innovative spirit that prepared him for senior leadership during World War II. He often faced uphill battles, but his persistence enabled McNair to find solutions to deficiencies in organization, doctrine, and policy that hobbled the AGF from 1940 to 1942, transforming it into an effective fighting force as the war continued, often while working against significant institutional resistance. This resistance increased in 1942, ironically largely as a result of a War Department reorganization intended to increase its effectiveness and efficiency.

The War Department Reorganization of 1942

When the reorganization of March 8, 1942, eliminated GHQ, simultaneously creating three new functional headquarters subordinate to the War Department—the Army Ground Forces, the Army Air Forces, and the Services of Supply, later renamed the Army Service Forces—McNair faced the task of expanding the AGF from 780,000 to more than 2.2 million personnel by July 1943. McNair's duties grew significantly upon the formation of the AGF, encompassing all boards, schools, training centers and camps, and special activities having to do with the combat arms. The commanders of the other functional headquarters—Brehon Somervell of the ASF and Henry H. "Hap" Arnold of the AAF—held (or, in Somervell's case, would soon hold) the same rank as Lieutenant General McNair, emphasizing their (at least theoretical) equivalent level of authority.[3]

Upon disbanding GHQ, the reorganization gave overall command and control of all theaters of operations, including the four continental defense commands, to the War Department General Staff while delegating responsibility for Zone of Interior functions to the new functional headquarters. Therefore, in his new role as AGF commander, McNair took direct responsibility for the four traditional ground force arms (infantry, artillery, cavalry, and coast artillery), which no longer had their own chiefs. The newly formed combat arms—armored, tank destroyer, and antiaircraft artillery—also fell under McNair's command, but in accordance with the reorganization, they either remained or became distinct commands, simply consolidated under AGF rather than falling under one or more of the four traditional arms. Somervell's headquarters took control of the technical services and the two combat support services—the engineers and the signal corps—along with several other nonsupply-related army functions. Arnold's AAF controlled all air force functions in the Zone of Interior.[4]

This reorganization did not achieve its primary goal of improving army command structure and function, largely as a result of self-interest, competition for resources, and struggles for power and autonomy among the various organizations and their staffs. The different approach each commander took in forming his staff and exercising power further limited cooperation both within the War Department and among the various elements of the combined arms team, which mobilized under the supervision of three separate organizations even though they would have to operate as an integrated force upon deployment. This new arrange-

Lieutenant General Lesley J. McNair, Commander, Army Ground Forces, March 1942.
Courtesy of US National Archives II, College Park, Maryland

ment, intended to streamline the War Department functions, violated the traditional principle of unity of effort while enabling empire building by those so inclined. It also led to more overhead, or noncombat troops, in the less
efficiency-focused commands. Overhead and excess in general frustrated McNair
perhaps more than any other challenge the army faced as it fought the war. It frustrated him so much that the official history of the AGF included a table enumer-

Lieutenant General Lesley J. McNair and the AGF Staff, March 19, 1942 (first row: Colonel Alexander R. Bolling, Brigadier General Mark W. Clark, Lieutenant General Lesley J. McNair, Colonel Rowell W. Rooks, Lieutenant Colonel Floyd L. Parks; second row: Colonel James T. Duke, Colonel Willard S. Paul, Lieutenant Colonel Lyman L. Lemnitzer, Major Robert A. Hewitt). Courtesy of the Military History Institute

ating the numbers of personnel in overhead positions, by percentage and in each functional command, as of March 31, 1945: 32.2 percent of AAF personnel served in overhead positions, compared to 22.9 percent of ASF personnel, and only 4.1 percent of AGF personnel. Greenfield, upon completing an exhaustive review of McNair's wartime correspondence, analyzed his research notes to determine those items that concerned McNair the most while at AGF. This revealed that Mc-Nair commented on organizational issues three times as often as any other. Greenfield found that these comments fit into four central themes, one of which he described as follows: "Lean headquarters—his horror of overhead was intense, and was intensified by the drain which the demands of 'overstuffed headquarters' made on the limited supply of first-rate combat commanders."[5]

McNair soon identified a key flaw with the new arrangement. He wrote to Marshall on March 17, 1942, about a personnel authorization change that troubled him, both in its fundamentals and in how staff officers handled it under the new structure:

> One of the three components asks the War Department to approve or actually issue certain instructions that affect the entire Army. The War Department approves the action proposed by the one component without consulting the other components. In this case, this headquarters [AGF] would not have concurred in [instructions ordering the creation of] so elaborate an organization, and the burden of furnishing these officers will fall on the AGF. It certainly is a fact that Headquarters AGF needs no such quota as 11 officers for this purpose. I understand well that you are determined to correct the unsatisfactory condition of motor vehicles, but I believe also that the measures being taken by Colonel Shugg, under General Somervell's supervision, go far beyond any demonstrated necessities. They are establishing a military and civilian overhead, and a mass of paper work and ritual, which I know from personal experience are unwarranted.[6]

Some of the rationale behind the reorganization of 1942 remained unclear to many of the personnel that it affected until senior military leaders made statements to the press.

Secretary of War Stimson told the press on March 5, 1942, three days before the reorganization took effect, that it would "create an organization to fight this war and not any past or obsolete wars." In addition to this primary purpose, Stimson emphasized, "the second objective was to give to the Air Corps its proper place, to recognize that this war is largely an air war and to put the Air Corps to proper relation to the function it will fill."[7] Further reducing unity of effort, the onset of American combat operations overseas added the voices of many theater, army group, army, and naval commanders to the din, and given their proximity to the front, their advice carried more weight than that of any staff officer.

The official history acknowledged in *The Organization of Ground Combat Troops* that the AAF "took the lead and applied the drive" that made the contemplated reorganization a reality, largely because the authority delegated to GHQ under the previous organization had overlapped the authority that "the Air Forces had gained as an autonomous entity on 20 June 1941." This explains why the air forces had joined those who opposed the expansion of GHQ's power to that of a true theater command over the Zone of Interior, and why they strongly supported the reorganization of 1942, which clearly delineated the authority of each command, thereby protecting the AAF's independence while increasing its power.[8]

Kent Roberts Greenfield's interview of Major General Harry Malony, conducted while Malony served as commander of the 94th Division on January 10,

1944, provides an insider's view of the perceptions at GHQ headquarters regarding the reorganization of 1942. Malony served as the GHQ deputy chief of staff and oversaw the headquarters' operational and planning functions before returning to the War Department General Staff after the March 1942 reorganization. In his interview with Greenfield, Malony highlighted the challenges created by the lack of a realistic strategy or industrial mobilization plan in 1940. Malony argued that this violated the principle that all planning must start with an assessment of means available. To illustrate his point, Malony described a brief meeting he had with Mr. Harry Hopkins in England in 1940, during which they discussed resources required for the ongoing mobilization effort. When Hopkins asked Malony what primary things America needed to wage war, Malony replied simply, "Personnel and materiel."[9] This reflected a significantly different view than that found in many histories of the American war effort during World War II, which asserted that faulty training, flawed doctrine, poor leadership, and inadequate equipment posed the main challenges to the US army during the war. These histories typically credit the near-limitless personnel and material resources that America supposedly possessed as the real reason for the army's success.

Malony also stated that upon the reorganization of 1942, when he served as deputy chief of staff of the War Department Operations Division (OPD), the staff made no effort to adopt or glean lessons from the planning processes that GHQ had put in place during the second half of 1941, when Malony headed GHQ's operational planning section. Nor did the War Department move GHQ's operations section personnel to the War Department to form the core of the new OPD—something Malony believed would have significantly improved the division's effectiveness. He argued, "The War Department should have utilized the valuable experience of GHQ in setting up the OPD. This transition threw the defense commanders into great confusion." Malony saw this as an unnecessary problem given the highly effective planning process that GHQ had developed and OPD could have adopted and built upon.[10]

Malony explained that the OPD's reluctance to embrace GHQ personnel or procedures probably resulted from frustration within the War Department General Staff caused by the expansion of GHQ's authority in 1941, which resulted, according to Maloney, in the War Department General Staff believing that it "had virtually lost the power it was supposed to exercise. The GS [General Staff] Divisions were 'dead on the vine.' Yet they refused to relinquish the right to interfere." Malony saw no difference after the reorganization of 1942: "That is the situation now. Look at WD G-1: it plays around with replacements. . . . What does G-3 do? OPD directs operations; AGF directs training. Who is G-4? Gen. Somervell." To illustrate Malony's point about Somervell, on April 3, 1943, the ASF commander sent a seven-page memorandum to Marshall pointing out several areas where he believed the War Department staff duplicated efforts that fell under ASF's purview. This led Somervell to recommend that General Marshall abolish the War Department G-1 and G-4 divisions, and transfer all of their personnel, records, facilities, and authority to the ASF and to the logistics group in OPD, splitting it, as appropriate between the ASF and AAF. Somervell sent this memo on the same day that he sent a four-page memorandum directly to Assistant Secretary of War John J. McCloy, recommending establishment of a "Joint Economic and Political Council" and a "North Africa Economic Board," including detailed considerations for the composition and function of each—which naturally included participation of the ASF. Marshall directed OPD to respond to Somervell's reorganization recommendations; they replied by recommending an increase in the War Department's logistics capability in all three sections. As he normally did, Marshall accepted OPD's recommendation, increasing overhead, duplication of effort, and infighting between Somervell's ASF staff and the War Department's logistics staff sections.[11]

Malony believed the optimal solution would have been to expand GHQ's power in 1941 by making "a little man Commander in Chief of the Field Forces" (Greenfield's handwritten notes on the interview transcript indicate that Malony referred here to General McNair). Even though Marshall refused to take this step, his staff continued to complain about its loss of authority, although, as Malony observed, "it was ridiculous to say that the interposition of GHQ was interfering with effective action. The WDGS was dead and didn't know it. It had no conception of the demands of the war we were about to wage."[12]

The reorganization of 1942 appears to have had as much to do with the desire to reestablish centralized control at the War Department as it did with achieving the goal of clearly dividing Zone of Interior responsibility between AGF, AAF, and ASF. The reorganization fell short on both counts. Responsibilities overlapped significantly between the three functional commands, leading to continued debate over matters long in contention, only made worse by the "stovepipe" nature of the new arrangement. War Department staff officers had to contend with and attempt to coordinate the frequent recommendations and requests from these three subordinate commands within the Zone of Interior, whereas previously they had only to coordinate (and argue) with GHQ.

The official history recorded the haphazard process by which the War Department attempted to centralize operational control:

In the reorganization as announced no explicit provision was made for centralized control of operations in widely scattered theaters, specifically, for "an executive group" within the War Department which "would in reality be a command section." The absorption of the operational element of GHQ into the War Department as a means of meeting this need had been rejected and the officers composing that element in GHQ were not utilized to form a new group in the War Department. But a new group was formed in WPD [War Plans Division], which, under its later title of Operations Division, became, in effect, the command post of General Marshall in Washington. GHQ, in its executive activities, had forecast and confirmed the need for such an agency, but was not made that agency. It is evident from the foregoing study that the motives and circumstances that led to its rejection were complex. They included organizational and personal interests and rivalries which inevitably attend the development of a new and forceful institution.[13]

The reorganization of 1942 simply created two new power brokers in the Zone of Interior—Arnold and Somervell—to compete with McNair for preeminence in the various areas of overlap between their functional responsibilities. Each of these men proved more ambitious and clever than McNair in the power politics that ensued. Further, numerous problems stemmed from the War Department's inability to establish centralized command and control over the various combat theaters, relying on the informal assignment of that role to OPD. This responsibility remained purely an OPD staff oversight function rather than a formalized source of centralized control with the requisite authority to establish true unity of command.

The reorganization led to several areas of conflict between AGF, ASF, and AAF in which McNair simply chose not to engage or pointed out to Marshall and his staff with limited results. As a rule, McNair simply followed orders and tried to accomplish his mission as efficiently and effectively as possible, and he expected (with some degree of naïveté) that Arnold and Somervell would do the same. McNair's drive to accomplish the mission without caring who got the credit (an important virtue in army officers to this day) significantly disadvantaged him—and by extension the effectiveness of the War Department—in the competition that emerged between the three functional commands.

In particular, the poorly executed reorganization led to a massive expansion of the overhead that McNair found so disturbingly inefficient and harmful to the ground forces. Although the reorganization problem of overhead justifiably bothered McNair, within months of the creation of the AGF, AAF, and ASF, it had expanded to outrageous proportions. In one of the AGF staff studies—feeder documents for the official histories eventually published in the ten years or so after the war—the author revealed the true extent of the expansion of overhead. Most of the staff studies used more direct language and less diluted analysis to convey their message than the carefully edited official histories, which avoided controversy and rarely singled out individuals for blame, but "AGF Staff Study

No. 2: A Short History of the AGF" surpassed even the most direct and critical of the staff studies in its findings. The concise but thorough study mostly provided a dispassionate summary of the information indicated by its title. One can find the controversial analysis in the final third of the study, which contained a comparison of the sizes of the AGF, AAF, and ASF staffs that reveals the extreme disparity in personnel numbers between the three commands initially—particularly relative to each command's number of personnel—and how this disparity grew over time.[14]

The first half of "AGF Study No. 2" described the changes in the scope and nature of McNair's headquarters' responsibilities, as it transitioned from GHQ to AGF. As McNair summed up the AGF's mission in an address at West Point in May, 1942, "Briefly, it is to create ground force units and train them so that they are fit to fight." The study then described the pervasive sense of urgency in the AGF. McNair insisted on "prompt and concentrated effort," leading to a focus on the fundamentals and McNair's rejection of any tasks assigned to the headquarters that did not support its primary mission, unless received in the form of a direct order from the War Department, signed by Marshall. It also emphasized McNair's recognition of the shipping problem, and the need to train deploying units as effectively as possible to minimize the demands on shipping caused by the need for personnel replacements.[15]

The final part of the report contained a very detailed comparison of the size of the three staffs. It described McNair's continued insistence on keeping his headquarters lean despite having responsibility for the largest of the three commands, projected to grow from the 243,095 that GHQ oversaw in July 1940 to a force of approximately 2,200,000 by March 1942.[16] The report also emphasized continuing limitations on McNair's authority, which still did not match his responsibility. He had to accomplish his mission despite War Department policy that limited his authority over doctrine to the ability to develop, review, and recommend new or modified doctrine, while conducting all training as described in War Department G-3 training directives. McNair also had to accomplish his mission with a consistently lean staff—the smallest of the three functional command headquarters, overseeing the largest organization. The study revealed the extent of the problem with overhead in the other functional commands in two tables, each footnoted heavily with War Department reports and data to ensure the reader could see the objective nature of the analysis presented. The first table listed the strength of each of the three headquarters in commissioned officers on three successive dates. On April 30, 1942, 212 officers worked at AGF, 885 at AAF, and 4,177 at ASF. On December 31, 1942, 240 officers worked at AGF, 2,210 at AAF, and 5,360 at ASF. On December 31, 1943, only 270 officers worked at AGF, while AAF's complement of officers had grown to 2,595 and ASF's to 7,227.[17]

The second table accounted for all personnel in the three headquarters, broken down by officers, warrant officers, and a third category combining all enlisted personnel plus civilians. On April 30, 1942, the total figures were 724 at AGF, 4,194 at AAF, and 37,244 at ASF. By December 31, 1943, these numbers had climbed at a highly disproportionate rate, with 1,234 total personnel at AGF, 12,591 at AAF, and an incredible 46,474 at ASF. These numbers included only personnel working directly for the three functional headquarters; they did not include any personnel serving in field units. With these extremely bloated headquarters serving as a constant reminder of the dangerous inefficiency of excessively large staffs, it is no wonder that McNair struggled to minimize overhead in operational units. The onset of war and the mobilization of the first units to deploy overseas in 1942 coincided with the recognition of the looming personnel crisis that led to the revision of the troop basis for 1943. That this drastic reduction in the projected number of divisions to be mobilized, combined with diversion of resources to build airplanes rather than divisions while delaying the Allied invasion of Europe, made such inefficient use of valuable personnel proved particularly frustrating to McNair. He understood better than most the direct correlation between efficiency and effectiveness, and attempted to lead by example among the functional commands. In the end, however, he had no ability to influence the bloat within those headquarters, and could only minimize overhead in combat units to the degree specified by the War Department.[18]

The Japanese bombing of Pearl Harbor, followed by a declaration of war by Hitler against America (which saved Roosevelt the trouble of having to convince the American people that their army would have to fight both Japan and in Europe), led to the commencement of American combat operations in the Pacific and later in North Africa in 1942. Given the frequent reliance by historians on comparisons of the German and the American armies to demonstrate the American army's inferiority, the following narrative will concentrate on those theaters where the Americans and Germans engaged directly in combat. This does not imply a greater significance of the war in Europe (in the Mediterranean and later on the continent); in fact, the whole complexion of the war changed when Admiral Stark and General Marshall recognized the need to rewrite American strategy, developing the "Germany First" approach to protect Great Britain while simultaneously reversing Japanese gains in the Pacific. This division of effort made the task in the Pacific significantly more difficult for the American forces, which fought there with relatively little Allied assistance, making their achievements in a brutal combat environment all the more notable.[19]

The British convinced the Americans that a strategy focused on attacking Germany through the Axis underbelly in the Mediterranean provided the fastest way to get American soldiers into the war and engaged in combat with the Germans.

Although Roosevelt and senior American military leaders did not agree with the British regarding the effectiveness of this strategy, preferring instead a direct assault on Germany in Europe, Marshall's planners had to admit that the US military could not make itself ready in time for an invasion of Europe in 1942. Marshall therefore reluctantly agreed to the Mediterranean strategy, but he insisted from the start that the Allies must attack across the English Channel into Europe as early as possible—as he saw it, summer 1943. While this debate continued for all of 1942, events eventually led to a delay of the cross-Channel invasion by an additional year, but more for economic reasons than pursuit of the best military strategy. In the meantime, from November 1942 through early 1943, the Americans pursued campaigns in North Africa, Sicily, and Italy before sending the main body of US troops to England to prepare for the D-Day invasion—Overlord—while operations to clear Axis forces from Italy continued.

James G. Lacey devoted particular attention to American strategists' sudden realization that the nation could not support a cross-Channel attack in 1943, because this reveals the flaw in another long-standing historical interpretation regarding the war effort:

> Sometime between Torch and the Casablanca Conference, however, Marshall abandoned his single-minded crusade for a second front in 1943 and supported a major post-Torch diversion of resources to further Mediterranean operations. In this, too, the remainder of the Joint Chiefs joined him. The Americans were not overawed or overwhelmed by superior British negotiating skills or staff procedures, as historians have often suggested they were. Rather, they had simply changed their minds about the wisdom of a major 1943 invasion, though they do appear to have been more than a bit reticent about announcing their change of heart and thereby admitting that British strategists had been right from the beginning.[20]

Lacey argued it was not simply the realization after the amphibious landings of Operation Torch that a cross-Channel invasion would present far greater challenges than previously assumed (illustrated by the war planners' doubling their estimate for the number of divisions the Allies would require to accomplish the invasion) that led to Marshall's change of heart. Rather, the Joint Chiefs admitted that the civilian industrialists had finally convinced them they had pursued highly unrealistic goals for military material production for nearly a year. This proved instrumental in changing Marshall's mind. Lacey provided numerous examples from the transcripts of the Casablanca conference that demonstrated that Marshall had given up on his hopes for a 1943 invasion. In these transcripts, Marshall's acquiescence to or lack of comment on British demands demonstrate that he no longer fought them over the issue, indicating that he knew upon his arrival at the conference that America did not possess the personnel or industrial capacity to participate in a 1943 invasion of France.[21]

This whole episode demonstrates the significance of America's halting economic mobilization and its effect on American strategy for conducting the war. Modern warfare required an army's effective employment of operational art for success, meaning in the case of World War II the ability to support a protracted war. Since the nineteenth century, tactics in the form of a single decisive battle could no longer lead to the desired strategic outcome, changing the nature of warfare as it had been waged for centuries. Michael R. Matheny traced the US army's awareness of operational art to its experience in the Meuse–Argonne offensive—the last major offensive the American Expeditionary Force conducted in World War I, which lasted forty-seven days and cost 122,000 casualties. In Matheny's words, "This seminal experience provided the Americans an understanding of the reality and the problems of modern operational art for the coming decades." While the requirement for conducting war in accordance with operational art might have resulted from the advent of modern warfare, at least one military theorist understood the need for an intermediate process to tie successive tactical actions to a strategic aim. Carl von Clausewitz drove this point home in his description of what theorists at the time called strategy, writing, "The strategist must therefore define an aim for the entire operational side of the war that will be in accordance with its purpose. In other words, he will draft the plan of the war, and the aim will determine the series of actions intended to achieve it: he will, in fact, shape the individual campaigns and, within these, decide on the individual engagements."[22]

In this case, the Allies agreed on the ends but disagreed on the ways, and the Americans reluctantly accepted that the decision was not theirs to make. The means—or their lack—required a significant modification of the Victory plan. At Casablanca, the Americans finally realized that they did not possess the means required to support their preferred strategy, forcing them to defer to their British partners. Lacey demonstrated how the slowdown of American mobilization to a snail's pace in late 1942 directly affected long-term Allied strategy, forcing a significant change in the Victory plan and the American troop basis for 1942–1943. Dysfunction in the War Production Board and associate agencies, largely the result of Somervell and Patterson's inability to provide realistic military production goals or work with civilian industrialists on a coequal basis, led to dramatic changes. The late-dawning awareness of the manpower crisis of 1942 prevented either military leaders or civilian industrialists from averting or even mitigating the crisis. America could not avoid the drastic changes to come in the period of scarcity—changes that had a profound impact on the difficulty the AGF faced in the following years.

In the short term, the crisis fundamentally altered the mobilization plan, reported in *Time* in March 30, 1942, as the activation of thirty-two more fighting divisions during the remainder of 1942 (three in March, two in May, three in June, and four on the 15th of each month thereafter of 1942). Less than a month later, on April 27, 1942, *Time* reported a somewhat rose-colored but still disturbing alteration of this mobilization schedule. The War Department canceled the army-level maneuvers planned for 1942, citing—as *Time* reported—the immense burden such maneuvers placed on the transportation infrastructure as the main reason for shifting to local unit training in task forces. The author of the article then described 1942's "little maneuvers" as "crack, postgraduate exhibitions" because only "a sprinkling" of new troops would join existing units of trained personnel to form the participating units. Not one of the thirty-two new divisions activated would "get in on the show."[23]

Acknowledging the mobilization crisis of 1942—rarely explained in detail in the military histories of World War II—fundamentally alters the historical understanding of America's contribution to the Allied war effort. Although America certainly possessed vast resources and managed to sustain an incredibly optimistic economic mobilization plan for two years—including the provision to Great Britain and Russia of huge quantities of war matériel while simultaneously attempting to mobilize a 200-division American army—even America simply could not sustain this level of industrial activity for very long.[24]

In late 1942, the War Production Board finally imploded, revealing the full extent of the production crisis and confronting America's strategic leaders with the requirement to economize. Something had to give, and true to form, Roosevelt decided to trade ground forces for airplanes, specifically bombers. He directed his advisers to fund an increase in expenditures for the AAF by reducing personnel allocations to the AGF, reducing by 330,000 men the numbers of recruits originally intended to form additional combat divisions. David M. Kennedy, quoting official army historian Maurice Matloff, noted:

"The strategic basis for this conclusion [. . .] was in part the demonstration by the Soviet armies of their ability to check the German advance. Another significant factor brightening the strategic picture was the improving prospect of gaining air superiority over the Continent. These developments finally made obsolete the initial Victory Program estimates of 1941." The economic basis for that conclusion was the sense of economic limits that the Feasibility Dispute had imposed. With the so-called 90-Division Gamble the logic of Roosevelt's

'Arsenal of Democracy' strategy had finally matured. American military planners now irrevocably embraced the concept of a war of machines rather than men. [. . .] Building a smaller army would be compensated by the construction of a gigantic, heavy-fisted air arm: bombers in fantastic numbers that would ultimately carry bombs of unimaginable destructive power.[25]

This changed the whole complexion of the war, particularly for McNair, who now, weighed down by massive economic constraints, could field only half the number of divisions originally planned. Somehow he had to create from those divisions a force that could win the war on the ground if the bombers did not manage to finish it from the air—a scenario predicted as unlikely in the final report of the President's Aircraft Board in 1925. Further, he had to create a force that could fight in the desert, in support of the new Allied strategy of attacking the Axis powers' underbelly in the Mediterranean before attempting an invasion of Europe, which the mobilization issue delayed by a year to the spring or summer of 1944.

Perhaps synthesis of economic and military strategy rarely appears in histories of the war because the War Department sought to keep the impact of the 1942 troop basis change quiet to save face. Marshall had insisted for months on a 1943 cross-Channel invasion based on logic that would not have gone over well with the American people or their army. As Kennedy described, in a January 7, 1943, meeting at the White House, Marshall urged Roosevelt to support the desired cross-Channel invasion timeline by describing the limitation of shipping losses as more important than minimizing human casualties. Marshall admitted that the cross-Channel attack would cause severe losses, but "he chose to underscore instead what was still the greatest single constraint on all American actions. 'To state it cruelly,' [Marshall] said, 'we could replace troops whereas a heavy loss in shipping . . . might completely destroy any opportunity for successful operations against the enemy in the near future.'"[26] It would also cast doubt on the image of a powerful and skillfully managed American economy to admit that the administration had only just learned before Casablanca that America could not support an invasion in 1943, even if the coalition would support this timeline.

Lacey explained this consideration in detail, concluding his analysis of the Victory production plan debate by explaining why Marshall changed his mind about the timing of an Allied amphibious invasion of mainland Europe. Lacey argued that once the industrialists had made it clear that Marshall would not have the size force originally anticipated for the summer of 1943 until a year later, "the decision was made for him." Further, Lacey argued, "the blame must fall squarely on Somervell's shoulders."[27] Paul A. C. Koistinen arrived at similar conclusions regarding Somervell's intransigence through the spring of 1943 but apparently did not find Somervell's disruption of the mobilization process as severe as Lacey did.

Referring to Somervell as Marshall's "attack dog," Koistinen recounted Marshall's postwar statement regarding Somervell's ambition, in which he acknowledged, "Of course I had to fight Somervell down or he would have taken the whole damn staff." He also noted that the desire to avoid "any future development of a man like General Somervell" played a key role in postwar reorganization. However, Koistinen also quoted Marshall's observation: "If I went into control in another war, I would start looking for another General Somervell the very first thing I did"—leaving the reader with a much more positive interpretation of Somervell's participation in the mobilization process than Lacey did.[28]

This demonstrates one reason why misinterpretations of McNair's contributions to the mobilization effort have gone unchallenged for so long. McNair had to perform his mission despite severe constraints caused by factors outside of his control, and these factors mostly related to the nation's inefficient personnel and economic policies that led to the manpower crisis of 1942—a crisis of a severity and leading to repercussions rarely acknowledged at the time or in histories of the war for several decades. This also indicates that it might be time to reevaluate Marshall's leadership of the War Department. While he was unquestionably a great leader and motivator of those around him, the war-long inefficiencies in War Department organization and interaction with civilian industrialists beg the question of whether Marshall managed these critically important functions of the War Department General Staff as effectively as he could have. This topic deserves further research in light of recent studies that point to War Department inefficiency, prioritization choices, and convoluted command structures that created challenges for the subordinate functional commanders, particularly the AGF.

The effects of the haphazard progress of industrial mobilization on McNair's role as AGF commander extended far beyond determination of the date when the Allies could first attempt a cross-Channel invasion. In short, during a period when the AGF, AAF, and ASF commanders should have worked closely together to arrive at a feasible, integrated, and unanimously supported plan to support the mobilization effort, Somervell consistently hindered McNair's efforts to mobilize and equip the AGF. Along with the various impacts described above, Somervell's stubborn refusal to listen to the industrial mobilization experts or give them realistic military matériel requirements delayed the entire process of producing necessary weapons and other equipment needed to mobilize, train, and deploy AGF units to combat. Further, Somervell's refusal to accept the advice of industrialists and economists meant that the army pursued an unrealistic mobilization plan for over a year. It also made many military leaders doubt the significance of shipping shortages and other limitations that McNair clearly understood from the start (along with other senior leaders like Marshall, who told Roosevelt that the army could replace personnel casualties more easily than lost shipping in January of

1943). McNair's awareness of the criticality of shipping capacity, probably based on his experience with previous mobilizations (particularly during World War I), led him to advocate for design of the AGF that maximized both efficiency and effectiveness—a conviction for which he drew criticism from combat commanders during the war and military historians ever since.

McNair remained consistent regarding the need to balance efficiency and effectiveness from the late 1930s, during his work with the Proposed Infantry Division (PID), through his leadership of the AGF. He saw the value of motorization and mechanization, but he opposed giving every soldier a seat in a mechanized vehicle unless the mission required it. Given the great advantage of the truck over the half-track in efficiency, requiring infantrymen to conduct the final movement to battle on foot seemed a small price to pay to significantly reduce shipping and logistics demands. McNair also imbued the doctrine to which he contributed throughout his four-decade-long career, and which the American soldier executed successfully during World War II, with this awareness of the need for efficiency. He understood long before many of his fellow officers that the American military would face shortages of key resources if they had to deploy overseas, so he ensured that ground combat units went to war trained, organized, and equipped with doctrine that combined efficiency and effectiveness in a manner appropriate to the actual combat conditions they would face. This logic supports McNair's adherence to the concepts of streamlining, pooling, and task organization—concepts also key to Marshall's thinking about mechanized warfare—which served as fundamental pillars of American doctrine and organization. This proved instrumental in maximizing the effectiveness of the ninety-division army that America planned to mobilize for World War II, after adjusting for the manpower crisis of 1942 and modifying the troop basis.[29]

Measures to gain efficiencies consumed much of McNair's attention while serving as AGF commander. This ensured that the concepts of streamlining, pooling, and task organization that had proven so important in the development of the triangular division—largely a result of motorization and mechanization and the immense burden the associated equipment would place on America's limited shipping capacity—continued to guide their evolution as the army began to employ those units in combat. While one often encounters assertions that McNair had a personal preference for pooling, streamlining, and task organization that he chose to impose on the army, these basic concepts had been in place for many years, and they increased in significance as limitations in national industrial capacity began to affect the army's mobilization plans.[30]

One of the greatest strengths of the quest for efficiency—the ability to task organize infantry divisions into combined arms regimental combat teams and armored divisions into combined arms combat commands (CCA, CCB, and so on)—emerged as a fundamental organizing principle for using the new divisions, significantly improving their combat effectiveness. Additionally, keeping the division lean and maneuverable by pooling specialized forces (armor, antiaircraft, and antitank in particular) in separate units, available to reinforce divisions as the situation dictated, proved just as important as the number and type of organic units in enabling the triangular division to task organize quickly and effectively. The pooling of transportation assets (like the venerable 2½-ton truck) provided motor transport to nonmechanized elements of the army when needed, while keeping their core organization light and freeing them of fueling and maintenance responsibilities. As Christopher R. Gabel argued, "The policy of 'streamlining and pooling' . . . underlay the US Army's organization for World War II."[31]

Gabel's assertion about streamlining and pooling—US army policy during World War II, as opposed to a concept McNair envisioned and then forced on the army—reflects a general point that is essential to understanding McNair's actions in the 1940s. His vision of future warfare was not that of a field artilleryman promoted an echelon or two higher than his level of competence; rather, it represented the prevailing army view, often as interpreted by McNair on the basis of his years of experience and the breadth and depth of insight that they enabled him to develop. Nor did McNair possess decision-making authority to impose his views on the army. In some cases, he even found himself required to support initiatives with which he disagreed, always doing so out of loyalty to General Marshall even when he knew it would detract from his ability to accomplish his mission. Given his involvement in interwar modernization efforts, his awareness of the increased demands the mechanized army would place on America's shipping capacity, and his desire, shared by Marshall, to optimize the army for the open warfare they envisioned on the basis of their World War I experience, it seems reasonable that McNair would support efficiency-based initiatives. However, one should keep in mind McNair's true level of authority when assessing his actions as AGF commander: every recommendation he made passed through the War Department General Staff, where staff officers solicited input from the field and other interested parties, using that input to support their recommendation to Marshall for decision.[32]

In keeping with his determination to achieve efficiency, McNair did not support the creation of a "type" (that is, uniquely organized) armored corps. He did support pooling large numbers of tanks in GHQ tank battalions, but this did not simply represent the outcome of interbranch debates between the cavalry and infantry, which, according to historian David E. Johnson, resulted in armored divisions performing a traditional cavalry role while GHQ tank battalions operated in an infantry support role.[33] Rather, McNair supported the War Department's concept of pooling key assets both to keep the division lean, mobile, and easy to task organize, and to maintain a large reserve of additional assets to reinforce divi-sions' combined arms teams at decisive points on the battlefield. Even Russell F. Weigley, although giving McNair too much credit as the decision maker, saw the benefits of this system:

> Perhaps McNair pruned the standard division too much, since tank and engi-neer and other supporting troops beyond those called for in the T/O&E's [Ta-bles of Organization and Equipment] had to be attached more or less permanently. But McNair's pooling system made such attachments possible with a minimum of difficulty. The shaping of the standard infantry division, before there could be much American combat experience on which to draw, was a notable achievement of American military organization.[34]

McNair built these ideas on the foundation of US army operational concepts dat-ing to the mid-1930s—but he supported efficiency-focused initiatives despite resistance from many unit commanders, as seen in his leadership during the mo-bilization, training, and deployment of units to the front. Battlefield commanders enjoyed the luxury of focusing on effectiveness, expecting support troops and in-dustrialists on the home front to ensure they had what they needed. McNair sim-ply could not indulge in such thinking because efficiency, equipment availability, and shipping demands made these concerns particularly significant to the accom-plishment of his mission.

Efficiency represented a real and constant concern that significantly influenced the army's efforts to prepare for war at the highest levels. As early as 1940–1941, American planners realized that if the president committed American forces to combat overseas, they would rely on lines of communication and logistics sup-port that crossed oceans and spanned vast distances over land. They would have to conduct numerous amphibious assaults to establish beachheads, requiring huge numbers of transport vessels and specialized landing craft to support the landing, then provide a steady flow of equipment, repair parts, and personnel as combat losses mounted. America never achieved an optimal balance between the demands of the military and industry, particularly given the lack of national strategic guidance to standardize induction policy. Demonstrating the effect of this imbalance even in the early stages of the war, before America began to lose large numbers of transport ships to German U-boats in the Battle of the Atlantic, Dwight Eisenhower included a telling remark in a diary entry on January 12, 1942. Serving as the chief of the War Department's OPD, Marshall's de facto com-mand center within the War Department, Eisenhower found himself struggling to transport adequate supplies to General Douglas MacArthur in Australia to enable him to begin offensive operations. After commenting on Somervell's success in finding boats to transport 21,000 combat troops to Australia by January 21, he wrote, "I don't know when we can get all their equipment and supplies to them. Ships! Ships! All we need is ships!"[35]

McNair's emphasis on efficiency through streamlining, pooling, and task organization—ideas he shared with the War Department and implemented for it during the lean months of late 1942 and early 1943—did not merely apply to his thoughts on ground forces organization. He understood the necessity for streamlining the deploying of combat units to use America's consistently limited shipping capacity as efficiently as possible while emphasizing efficiency in staff and services because overhead—excessively large staffs—made headquarters unnecessarily large and inefficient, and deprived combat units of much-needed leaders.[36] He continued to adhere to these core principles by keeping his AGF staff as small as possible; he did so for the same reason that he believed the ground forces should keep overhead to a minimum. McNair also simply did not possess the nature of an empire builder. He kept his staff far smaller than that of the War Department or those of his counterparts at the AAF and ASF, and he remained the loyal follower even as Arnold and Somervell competed to increase their influence over Marshall's decision making while building ever larger and more powerful staffs. McNair even refused to join the mass movement of staff personnel to the newly opened Pentagon after the reorganization, preferring to keep his intimate staff in the same location it occupied when he was GHQ chief of staff, in part because, unlike the urban environment of the Pentagon, the former Army War College grounds retained a distinctly military atmosphere. Although his refusal to engage in empire building may reveal naïveté, McNair simply did not desire to engage in such power struggles, preferring to lead by example, even if others chose to look the other way.[37]

As noted in the official history, "over pooling in principle there was little or no disagreement. Differences of opinion arose over particular cases. The most controversial of these concerned tanks, tank destroyers, and antiaircraft artillery." The inherent mobility of these weapons, their size, shipping weight, and logistics consumption rates, and their specialized nature, which meant not all situations lent themselves to their employment, made them natural candidates for pooling in large, mobile reserves. This gave senior commanders the ability to mass specialized assets where needed depending on the combat situation, terrain, and other factors, many of which commanders could not predict. The cost in the lack of formation of habitual relationships between these units and those organic to divisions did not outweigh the benefit of the flexibility their pooling gave large-unit commanders.[38]

In 1942 and 1943, the argument for pooling antitank guns, tank destroyer units, and antiaircraft artillery units seemed particularly compelling to McNair.

He did not believe air and tank attacks would only occur in independent, massed formations, as his critics have claimed. However, he recognized from observations of ongoing combat operations that the most dangerous phase of a combined arms attack began when the enemy committed his reserves of massed air and tank assets, seeking to turn the tide of the battle by creating or exploiting an opportunity. This seemingly minor difference actually represents a significant aspect of modern, mechanized combined arms combat, and McNair's awareness of it illustrates the validity of his views regarding modern warfare in the 1940s. Further, it was not until 1944 that counterarguments for inclusion of these specialized assets as organic divisional units began to proliferate. This stemmed from the recognition of the value of these weapons for performing a secondary role as additional direct and indirect fire support assets when not acting in their primary role. One of the most vocal advocates of dropping the pooling concept and providing organic tank destroyer and antiaircraft units to combat divisions, McNair's former platoon leader, Jacob Devers, began to petition the War Department directly to change the pooling policy after observing combat operations in North Africa in February 1943. McNair's own G-3, Brigadier General John M. Lentz, adopted an antipooling view around the same time as Devers, writing in a memo to McNair that he believed combined training suffered because of pooling.[39]

McNair responded to Devers via the War Department by pointing out Devers's argument for providing tank destroyer and antiaircraft artillery units to divisions could just as easily apply to GHQ tank battalions, air base defense units, and units providing command post or supply train defense. McNair argued that the question came down to whether America sought to build an offensive or a defensive army—in other words, whether the army's emphasis was in providing security to all units or maintaining the flexibility to mass capability where needed to seize the initiative and defeat the enemy's forces through offensive action. McNair, in keeping with decades of army doctrine, preferred the latter. He also pointed out that Devers's proposals would require an additional 24,000 .50-caliber antiaircraft artillery guns and 7,200 75mm antitank guns in addition to the number already fielded. McNair apparently understood better than many of his colleagues that the industrial base simply could not provide weapons in this quantity, given the strategic priorities established by the president and the War Department. The debate over Devers's proposals revealed a remarkable shortsightedness among some War Department staffers, who dreamed of such significant increases in ground forces in the midst of a major manpower crisis and shifting of resources to the AAF. The War Department ultimately supported McNair in the debate with Devers and retained the concept of pooling, and it did so again in May 1943 when the ASF proposed drastically increasing the number of antiaircraft artillery and antitank units to provide defense to logistics convoys. Given the realities of the revised troop basis, no feasible means to field these additional units existed.[40]

Pooling appeared as official policy in a War Department directive of October 2, 1942, appointing McNair to complete an armywide "downward revision of Tables of Organization." To comply with this directive, McNair formed a reduction board, constituted of "No-Men" who would accomplish the War Department's required across-the-board cut by 20 percent of motor vehicles and 15 percent of personnel, all "without lessening the combat strength of any unit or upsetting the doctrine of its tactical employment." Given the requirement to possess "exact knowledge of every item and every individual in unit tables," McNair—one of the few men in the army with this level of detailed knowledge regarding the composition of the ground forces—directed and participated in the board's efforts. As noted in the official histories, he "frequently [said] 'No' to his own 'No-Men.'" The reduction board remained in existence for eight months, from November 1942 through June 1943, reviewing almost every AGF unit and methodically removing every piece of equipment not allowed in the ground rules set for the board or determined as nonessential. "Cuts were not applied piecemeal or in a negative mood. The whole theory of army and corps organization, and hence of pooling and of inter-unit support, was undergoing constructive revision at the headquarters of the Army Ground Forces at the same time. Each unit was reshaped with an eye to its place within corps or army."[41]

Task organization dated back to the development of the triangular division, when McNair served as chief of staff of the PID. He developed the new tables of organization based on War Department guidance, planned and oversaw the tests, and prepared test reports; the regimental combat teams and combat commands that became integral components of division organizations were neither McNair's original idea nor concepts he forced on the AGF once Marshall selected him as ground forces commander. One wonders at the frequent criticism of these concepts, largely based on misrepresentations of the initiatives they actually represented, while ascribing them to McNair as ideas he conceptualized and imposed by his own authority on the ground forces. Criticism of task organization seems particularly odd when one considers the abundance of historical examples that illustrate the effectiveness of these concepts. McNair played a key role in each, including implementing War Department policy and training the AGF to fight in accordance with these principles. If anything, he deserves credit for his loyalty to Marshall, working against a great deal of resistance and criticism to train the army to fight effectively despite significant limitations in material production and shipping capacity.

Just one example serves to show how McNair managed to turn what some might have considered very limiting policy on its head and use it to the army's advantage: McNair's invaluable assistance to the gunnery department of the Field Artillery School in the early 1930s as it worked to develop more effective and faster fire direction procedures. He supported these procedures because of his strong belief in the superiority of observed fires based on his World War I experience and his inherent innovative nature, which he applied to interwar experimentation. Ironically, he also realized that centralizing control and pooling resources—typically efficiency-based methods—would make the field artillery more effective, even if it meant giving battalion commanders control over battery guns, traditionally controlled by battery commanders. Building on the concept of pooling, McNair helped to see the gunnery department's experimentation of the early 1930s through to its logical conclusion in the massed fires techniques used to such great effect in the repulse of Rommel's Afrika Korps at Kasserine Pass and innumerable other operations in every major theater and campaign of the war. The immense firepower provided by massed, observed artillery fires emerged, according to historian Frank Comparato, as "the most powerful force (excepting the atomic bomb) to come out of the war."[42]

Weigley recognized the wisdom of McNair's support of the concepts of streamlining, pooling, and task organization—reflections of his perception of the modern battlefield—a perception that Weigley acknowledged as correct. Referring to the issue of combined arms, Weigley quoted McNair in *History of the United States Army:* "An armored division is of value only in pursuit or exploitation. For plain and fancy slugging against an enemy who is unbroken or at least intact the tank battalion or group is adequate." Weigley went on to observe:

> The war proved to be much more a war of the old infantry–artillery team than the German campaigns of 1939 and 1940 had suggested. Once good antitank weapons had been developed and their tactics well planned, tanks alone could not force a breakthrough. What they could do well was to join tactical aviation in cooperating with the infantry as a sort of superartillery. In this role they did break at last the tactical deadlock which had gripped the battlefield for nearly a hundred years.[43]

In short, the tank by itself could not create significant, sustainable breakthroughs; this required combined arms, facilitated by pooling and task organizing of specialized units to achieve both efficiency and effectiveness.

The shortage of almost all motorized and mechanized equipment and the war-long persistence of shortages in transport vessels to move individual replacements, units, and supplies overseas meant that the concentration of combat power necessary to achieve McNair's vision did not simply benefit from streamlining, pooling, and task organization. The AGF's battlefield effectiveness relied on these means of balancing effectiveness and efficiency, as well as logistical supportability. McNair's investigation of these concepts during the interwar years, which later emerged as War Department policies, demonstrates the validity of McNair's vision of the modern battlefield. The roots of McNair's emphasis on efficiency, which contributed to logistical feasibility, trace back to the Army War College education and the influence of Major General Fox Connor, General Eisenhower's primary intellectual mentor during the interwar period, on the school's curriculum. As Matheny pointed out, "The faculty increasingly recognized that one of the key differences between tactical and operational art is logistics." The students learned that the responsibilities of commanders change significantly when they rose to the level of large unit command. High-level commanders paid little attention to tactical matters—the purview of junior commanders who concentrated on tactics with little regard to logistics—focusing instead on the logistical matters that enabled groupings of tactical actions to rise to the level of operational art.[44]

This led to the emphasis, for example, of tempo over speed as a key element of Eisenhower's broad front approach in the European theater. Although it might have appeared slow and unimaginative, Eisenhower's operational art ensured the logistical sustainability of Allied operations—a skill that the Wehrmacht never mastered, despite the boldness of its commanders and its impressive tactical prowess. As Robert Citino put it,

> In assessing the performance of the Germans in World War II, we can say that they did some things well, very well. Maneuver on the operational level, boldness in the assault, tenacity on the defensive, the integration and cooperation of combined arms: the German Army had no peer in the early years of the war, although it did decline in quality steadily as the war went on. The almost nine million casualties it suffered in the Soviet Union will do that to any army. The lost war, however, was the fault of the dozens of other things that it did poorly. These included items like military intelligence [...]. The entire area of supply, from battlefield logistics to harnessing of industry to the war effort, was rarely more than an afterthought. [...] Adolf Hitler ruled highly industrialized Europe, at least for a short time, and the Germans could have done much more with their conquered territories and populations than plunder the first and enslave and murder the second. Finally, the Germans once again proved, if they had not already done so to complete satisfaction in World War I, to be completely incompetent at coalition warfare. [...] Adding it all up leads to the

conclusion that the defeat was due not just to Hitler's lack of ability as a field marshal, or bad generalship on the part of the officer corps. In this great conflict, the "German way of war" took on the world and was found wanting.[45]

An excessive focus on tactical prowess has made such insights somewhat rare in histories of World War II and contributed to the view of the American ground forces as relatively ineffective. However, shifting focus to the operational level of war provides a different view.

Despite its relatively effective preparedness before entering combat during World War II, the AGF still faced many obstacles—some related to challenges with industrial mobilization and personnel procurement, others to various War Department inefficiencies. Some of these challenges approached critical levels in the later stages of the war, but within the limits of his authority, McNair continually strove to correct, or at least mitigate, the effects of these challenges, with mixed success.

The AGF, under McNair's leadership, overcame many of the key challenges resulting from the troubled economic mobilization for World War II and War Department inefficiencies that compounded those challenges as the fighting dragged on. McNair lacked the ability to break the logjam between military war planners and leaders in the military and civilian sector responsible for industrial mobilization. For many months, particularly after the great reorganization of 1942, he struggled simply to convince General Marshall of the existence of various problems that he dealt with daily or the seriousness these threats presented to American military success. For the last two years of his career, with mobilization winding down and the focus of most senior leaders on the war in the air or at sea, McNair remained an influential figure, but his scope of authority and responsibility remained limited. During his final year of service, he enjoyed a brief resurgence of influence and saw many early war modernization efforts finally come to fruition; however, many of his achievements now go unrecognized in histories of the war.

Lesley McNair made essential contributions to the military educational system and the doctrine and organizations officers studied in the army schools, ranging from his service on the post–World War I inaugural faculty at Leavenworth to his appointment as commandant there in 1940. He also benefited from his Army War College education, which gave him invaluable experience that prepared him for his wartime roles at GHQ and AGF. US army officer education stands out as one of America's greatest successes during the interwar period, and an area—like the unprecedented army-level maneuvers run by GHQ—in which America prepared more effectively before World War II than any other war.

This education and training enabled AGF personnel to recognize and over-

Lieutenant General Lesley J. McNair Broadcasting at NBC, April 5, 1942. Courtesy of the Military History Institute

come several key difficulties that hindered their mobilization and entry into combat. The vitality of the national discourse on war in the 1920s and 1930s demonstrates that inactivity and stagnation did not define the army's interwar years, even if this vibrant intellectual activity took place mostly in the officer education system and various branch journals. The absence of adequate funds to pay for the large army, organized reserve system, and modern equipment that made Germany such a formidable military power by 1939 delayed the US army's ability to achieve parity on the battlefield. Nevertheless, its foundation of clear doctrine and extensive unit mobilization training enabled the army to overcome the initial shock new units experienced in combat and develop the cohesion necessary to become a highly effective fighting force through battle hardening.[46]

McNair's leadership of the AGF from 1942 to 1944 revealed that his ideas not only represented a continuation of the evolution in his thinking during the 1920s and 1930s but also served as a key contribution to the successful fighting techniques that enabled the US army to prevail on the World War II battlefield. The army doctrine and unit organization that McNair helped develop before the war proved quite effective in practice, given the opportunity to learn, through battle hardening, how to conduct combined arms mechanized warfare effectively against a determined enemy. The stability of organizations like the triangular division and the longevity of the 1941 *FSR* (*FM 100-5, Operations*) support the validity of the organizational and doctrinal modernization effort that the army undertook (and to which McNair contributed) between the wars. This seems particularly remarkable given that progressive mobilization and deployment of new divisions after 1942, combined with reliance on an individual replacement system, meant that the forces that fought each successive campaign included a significant percentage of units entering combat for the first time. These units typically entered (or reentered) combat after receiving individual replacements to bring them up to strength, relying on many troops that had received minimal and poorly standardized individual training.

The overall quality of the system of doctrine, organization, and unit training McNair helped develop before the war and oversaw during mobilization gave these units the training they needed to achieve success against professional, combat-hardened military forces in one campaign after another. The stability of McNair's fundamental views and innovative spirit throughout the thirty-five years before World War II enabled the US army to overcome key deficiencies in interwar organization, doctrine, and policy to mature into an effective fighting force—one capable of conducting mechanized combined arms operations effectively and in keeping with the fundamentals of operational art.

The AGF at War: Learning while Fighting the German Army

Having accepted the infeasibility of a cross-Channel invasion of Western Europe in 1943, the Americans agreed at the Casablanca conference to support the British strategy of an attack against the Axis underbelly in the Mediterranean. After conducting a landing against only halting Vichy French resistance on November 7, 1942, an Allied force of primarily American and British troops headed east for the port city of Tunis on November 23. When Axis forces arrived there first and established a powerful defense, the Allies adjusted their plan. Field Marshal Erwin Rommel, having recently lost the decisive battle of El Alamein, skillfully withdrew the remnants of his Panzerarmee Afrika through Libya toward Tunisia. He preserved enough combat power to establish a defense along the Mareth Line to delay General Sir Bernard Law Montgomery's Eighth Army while taking offensive action against the newly arrived Allied troops in Tunisia. This attack, if successful, could enable Rommel to reverse the effects of his defeat at El Alamein by turning and possibly enveloping the newly arrived Allied forces in Tunisia. The American II Corps, consisting of the 1st Armored Division and elements of the 1st and 34th Infantry Divisions, having advanced southeast and attempted unsuccessfully to gain the initiative and begin offensive operations, occupied in January 1943 defensive positions in the vicinity of Kasserine Pass. The Americans expected Rommel to attack, but they did not know exactly where or when the offensive would take place. The British contingent remained farther to the north, focused on the approaches to Tunis up the coastline from the south. Ignoring orders from the Italian-led Axis headquarters to move north and join forces with newly arriving Axis troops, Rommel attacked lead elements of the American II Corps, supported by a small contingent of Free French troops at Faid Pass on January 30. Rommel's troops dislodged two Free French battalions, prompting Lieutenant General Fredendall, II Corps commander, to order a counterattack by the 1st Armored Division's Combat Command A (CCA).[47]

After unsuccessful counterattacks on January 31 and February 1, Fredendall expected Rommel to continue his attack through Faid Pass, and he issued orders to establish a defensive position to counter this expected offensive. Rommel moved elements of the 10th Panzer Division to Faid, but he also managed to move elements of 21st Panzer in position for a supporting attack through Maizila Pass while avoiding detection. Rommel attacked the Americans at Faid Pass from both directions on February 14, exploiting surprise and the weakness of the Americans' excessively dispersed defensive position to outflank and overrun the 1st Armored Division troops. Rommel attacked again the next day with similar results. By the end of the second day, American losses had reached 1,600 troops, nearly 100 tanks, fifty-seven half-tracks, and twenty-nine artillery pieces.[48]

Eisenhower grew concerned about the possibility of a major breakthrough and ordered Fredendall to withdraw his dispersed forward elements and establish a concentrated defense near Sidi Bou Zid in Kasserine Pass while employing forward elements in a delaying action to buy time. A German breakthrough at Sidi Bou Zid would have forced the Allies to conduct a large-scale turning movement to protect their rear area, seriously disrupting the Allied campaign. The Americans managed to avoid this disastrous outcome, however, by establishing a defense in depth made up of combined arms in accordance with army doctrine. On the evening of February 21, Brigadier General Paul Robinett's CCB of the 1st Armored Division joined forces with Major General Terry de la Mesa Allen's 1st Infantry Division. The two units worked through the night to establish a strong defensive position. They emplaced antitank guns alongside infantrymen and tanks in defilade in a mutually supporting, combined arms defense in depth, ensuring adjacent units could provide mutually supporting fire. They supported this defensive position with all available artillery in direct support, linking fifty guns through a Fire Direction Center, and preregistering fires in the most likely enemy avenues of advance, with forward observers prepared to mass these fires rapidly and decisively on approaching enemy formations.[49]

The attack came the next morning as expected. Robinett's and Allen's defense proved remarkably effective, quickly disrupting Rommel's attack and ultimately leading to a wholesale German retreat. This series of battles, culminating in Rommel's defeat at Kasserine Pass, can easily appear to be a decisive defeat of an American division in its first encounter with the German army in combat if one concentrates on the embarrassing defeats of the Americans' first days of combat against the Germans. One finds this interpretation of the Kasserine Pass battle in numerous accounts. This illustrates the problem of focusing on individual tactical actions rather than viewing them as an integrated series of battles, even in the haphazard organization of the engagements leading up to the fight for Kasserine Pass. Viewed as an organized series of tactical actions, one can see that the Kasserine Pass battles culminated in a decisive American victory that resulted from an effective combined arms operational approach. Gerhard Weinberg's *A World At Arms* stands out as a notable exception. Weinberg emphasized two key points, enabled by his holistic view of the event through the lens of operational art. Weinberg described how their successes and defeats in Tunisia, as well as their struggles with various complexities of modern warfare during this early campaign, helped the Americans learn how to fight effectively. He wrote: "The Americans had begun to learn the realities of fighting experienced and determined soldiers in modern war, a learning process better carried out at a distance from the enemy's main center of resistance [Germany] than closer to it."[50]

Histories of the US army's first combat encounter with the Germans at Kasserine Pass usually describe it as a decisive defeat for the Americans—or, at least, an embarrassing one. Such histories illustrate the flawed view of military history as analysis of tactics, and possibly of strategy, while neglecting to address operational art. When analyzed from a tactical viewpoint, Kasserine Pass certainly amounted to a significant, if temporary, German victory over the American II

Corps. Rommel overran the forward elements of the 1st Armored Division's defenses after two days of fighting at Sidi Bou Zid largely because commanders did not place defending units in mutually supporting positions or use their forces as effective combined arms teams.[51]

In a particularly insightful assessment of the Kasserine battles, viewed within the context of the campaign in North Africa, and emphasizing learning, not adaptation, Weinberg wrote,

> The American tactical defeat at Kasserine Pass and its two thousand casualties had three repercussions, one immediate, the other two more lasting. The immediate effect was a series of personnel changes. [. . .] The two more lasting effects were on the Americans and British thereafter. The American Army learned a great many useful tactical lessons, some applied in battle thereafter and more incorporated into the training of new divisions in the United States and the specifications for American equipment.
>
> The higher commanders of the British Army drew an entirely different and fatefully flawed lesson from this event. Both General Montgomery and Field Marshal Alexander . . . concluded that the Americans were hopelessly trained and led, made poor soldiers, and were unlikely to improve quickly in either performance or leadership. It is difficult to understand why they found it so hard to comprehend that the Americans' taking several months to learn what it had taken [the British] army and its leaders three years was a good, not a bad, sign for the Allied cause.[52]

By viewing the battles of Kasserine Pass as tactical actions in the overall Allied campaign in North Africa, as Weinberg did, one can see that they merely represent brief setbacks in a very successful campaign for the Allies. This campaign culminated in the decisive defeat of Axis forces in North Africa, the survivors ultimately departing the region from Tunis and never returning, and it enabled significant learning among the American forces that contributed to American operational art in future campaigns. As for the impact of the Kasserine Pass battles on Eisenhower, rather than leading to his relief as he briefly feared, they taught him valuable lessons as well. As Atkinson assessed, "In trying to serve as both supreme commander and field general, he had mastered neither job. The fault was his, and it would enlarge him for bigger battles on future fields."[53]

While historian Orr Kelly presented a generally negative picture of American performance at Kasserine Pass in *Meeting the Fox*, unlike many historians, he also placed the battle in the larger context of the campaign. He described the ultimate Allied reversal of the German offensive at Kasserine, although he did not directly acknowledge the nature and significance of American combined arms fighting effectiveness. For example, Kelly emphasized American superiority in numbers of howitzers but not in artillery fire procedures. However, Kelly did quote Rommel's observations of American performance after the campaign:

> Although it was true that the American troops could not yet be compared with the veteran troops of the Eighth Army, yet they made up for their lack of experience by their far better and more plentiful equipment and their tactically more flexible command. In fact, their armament in antitank weapons and armored vehicles was so enormous that we could look forward with but small hope of success to the coming mobile battles. The tactical conduct of the enemy's defense had been first class. They had recovered very quickly after the first shock and had soon succeeded in damming up our advance by grouping their reserves to defend the passes and other suitable points.[54]

Many historians have leveled criticisms against McNair for his contribution to the supposed inadequacy of American combat equipment during prewar mobilization; they often rely on Kasserine Pass as a textbook example of the early-war US army's shortcomings. As this account shows, the historical interpretation of the US army's performance at Kasserine Pass deserves further scrutiny. When one views the Kasserine Pass battles as part of a months'-long campaign, the ultimate outcomes of both the battle and the campaign provide evidence of the effectiveness of the equipment the US army used during the war. This effectiveness became increasingly evident as the campaign progressed, and the American soldier learned to use that equipment in accordance with the doctrine, organization, and procedures McNair helped develop during the interwar period.[55]

The many critical interpretations of US army performance at Kasserine Pass illustrate the pervasiveness of the long-standing accepted wisdom regarding the supposed ineffectiveness of the US army not just in North Africa but also throughout World War II. Weigley, referring to American combat operations in the final campaigns in Western Europe, wrote in the epilogue to *Eisenhower's Lieutenants*, "The German army remained qualitatively superior to the American army, formation for formation, throughout far too many months of the American army's greatest campaign. In the end, it was its preponderance of material resources that carried its army through to victory in World War II."[56] The military history community owes Weigley a great debt for not only writing some of the most comprehensive and well-researched histories of the American military, but also for helping build the foundation of professionalism on which modern American military history rests. However, the military history community must somehow break free of this deeply flawed but remarkably resilient narrative of the US army's experience in World War II.

As Weinberg pointed out, many common myths embedded within the standard historical narrative of World War II result from a focus merely on tactics, or on both tactics and strategy, while neglecting the key intermediate level: operational art. The long-standing focus on American combat equipment during the war, often dealing with technical specifications rather than how those weapons fit within the army's overall method of fighting campaigns, provides another example of this challenge. After a long and indecisive debate about antitank defense, for example, Marshall finally took direct control, ordering development of the tank destroyer in a very specific manner to avoid any branch taking control of the weapon system and morphing it into a vision that did not match the vision for the weapon that Marshall had in mind.

Ironically, Marshall's tank destroyer has long served as a key target for criticism of McNair, who initially opposed the concept. In a document summarizing the results of his review of McNair's correspondence after the war, army historian Kent Roberts Greenfield identified the tank destroyer as the equipment-related topic most often discussed. This correspondence demonstrated many complaints from the field regarding mixed performance of tank destroyers in combat, as well as efforts by McNair to influence the modification of tank destroyer doctrine and training to improve its performance.[57] Much of the weapon systems' difficult transition from concept to reality stemmed from fundamental disagreements festering since the early days of GHQ. As Gabel pointed out, "General Marshall favored experiments with self-propelled mounts. McNair acceded, but he was never really reconciled to the self-propelled weapon." Further, McNair advocated a more cautious approach to the use of the tank destroyer in combat than that reflected in the official doctrine, finally approved by the War Department and published on June 16, 1942, as *FM 18-5, Tank Destroyer Field Manual, Organization and Tactics of Tank Destroyer Units.* McNair "suggested that tank destroyer forces would 'emplace and camouflage themselves' when faced by hostile tanks," but the approved doctrine described a much more offensive-minded approach, exemplified in the Tank Destroyer Center's official motto: "Seek, Strike, and Destroy."[58]

The creation of a separate Tank Destroyer Center, an expedient deemed necessary by Marshall to prevent the infantry or cavalry branch from simply incorporating the new weapons into their existing organization and doctrine, led to significant problems in executing this aggressive doctrine. The offensive mind-set instilled in separate tank destroyer units required the ability to fight as members of combined arms teams because the open-turreted, thin-skinned vehicles remained highly vulnerable to the guns of enemy tanks. However, isolating the Tank Destroyer Center from the other branches meant that few commanders, upon receiving tank destroyer units as reinforcements, knew how to use them, even had the tank destroyers benefited from the necessary intelligence, road priority, and advantageous terrain described in *FM 18-5*—factors that rarely materialized. The new doctrine's emphasis of coordination of independent tank destroyer unit operations, rather than true combined arms integration, only added to the problem.[59]

As evidence arrived at the War Department that the tank destroyer was not meeting its expectations in the Mediterranean or European theaters of operation, McNair made it a priority for the AGF headquarters to adjust tank destroyer doctrine and training methods on the basis of guidance received from OPD. However, the late fielding of effective tank destroyers to replace the early, field expedient designs initially deployed to combat meant that much of the early criticism stemmed from the poor performance of these makeshift early designs as much as it did from flaws in doctrine. The ordnance department debated the details of tank destroyer design with Major General A. D. Bruce for months, leading the War Department to form a special armored vehicle board, chaired by Brigadier General W. B. Palmer. The Palmer board criticized the Tank Destroyer Center for inflexibility and making unreasonable demands, but it finally approved a tank destroyer design in late 1942 that met Bruce's specifications. By this time, the army was already engaged in combat in the Pacific and North Africa, and the campaign in Tunisia exposed many challenges with the existing tank destroyer expedients and doctrine.[60]

Reflecting on the combat lessons of that campaign, on April 12, 1943, McNair wrote to Bruce, commander of the Tank Destroyer Center, to pass on feedback he had received from General Patton regarding the performance of tank destroyers—and the officers who decided how to use them—during their initial engagements in combat. Patton sent his observations to General Marshall and provided a copy to McNair. In it, Patton described an attack by the 10th Panzer in which the Germans used "about 100 tanks. The initial rush carried the tanks through a gap in the 18th Infantry but before the fighting stopped we had put 30 enemy tanks out of action." This description of a Panzer division using tanks in masses to perform key tasks like exploiting a gap in a defensive line, while primarily acting in concert with the other elements of the combined arms team, bears a striking resemblance to the manner of armor employment that McNair described in *Antimechanized Defense* four years earlier. Patton continued,

> We did have what I consider unnecessarily large losses in the Tank Destroyer units. This is due to two causes, first to the absolutely open nature of the ground (there is no cover of any sort), and second to the fact that the tactics taught at the Tank Destroyer School are not applicable to this theater. Tank Destroyers cannot pursue tanks here. They must await the arrival of the tank and get in the first aimed shot at effective range. They had been warned of this be-

fore the battle but in the heat of the fighting reverted to former teachings. I believe hereafter they will do better.[61]

McNair then wrote,

I also had an interesting session with Major Cushman who is, by the way, a nephew of General Cortlandt Parker, commanding the 5th Division in Iceland. Cushman confirms reports by Fredendall and this one by Patton that our tank destroyers have been tank-hunting with guns, to their regret. These reports from the front, coupled with the observations of this staff at your problem the other day, are not interpreted by me as indicating infallibly that your instruction and doctrine are unsound, but they do indicate beyond doubt that your units and individuals have left with unsound conceptions of tank destroyer tactics. I am relying on you to take most definite and positive measures to correct this situation. Of course, we cannot have the success of tank destroyers jeopardized by remedial situations such as these. I trust you will not allow these developments to destroy the aggressive spirit. . . . It is necessary only to steer activities along proper channels.[62]

Bruce responded on June 5, 1943, that he had taken immediate steps to correct erroneous interpretations caused by use of overly aggressive language. For example, Bruce changed the name of a course called "Preparation for Tank Hunting" to "Battle Conditioning." He had also spoken to all of the trainers at the school, addressed students, and otherwise clarified the intent for employment of tank destroyers as McNair directed.[63]

The 37mm, still the primary antitank gun in use by the US army during the campaign in North Africa, attracted a great deal of criticism for its performance in combat. However, as demonstrated above, McNair had known for years that the gun lacked the power to face modern tanks, and he had believed that the Ordnance Branch would field a more capable weapon before the need arose to use antitank weapons in combat. Delays caused by debates over the details of tank destroyer design delayed this process. However, this serves as only one example of the problems caused by a system in which the AGF, whose units would actually use the new weapons systems, could only suggest the design specifications it desired. AGF relied throughout the war on the ASF's technical services to develop new weapons, and the Ordnance Branch often modified design parameters received from the personnel who would use the weapons in combat. In addition, units conducting training under AGF's supervision before deployment used training rounds, and in many cases, they apparently did not realize different, armor-piercing ammunition existed for use in combat. Upon hearing reports of the

Lieutenant General Lesley J. McNair Visiting the Tank Destroyer Center, Camp Hood, Texas, May 1944. Courtesy of US National Archives II, College Park, Maryland

dismal performance of the 37mm gun in North Africa, AGF sent a team of observers to study this and other problems. In a report prepared on February 21, 1943, these observers noted that in several instances, they found antitank gunners in North Africa unknowingly using 37mm training ammo, a factor that contributed to the gun's lack of effectiveness.[64]

Over time, many commanders developed field expedient methods for the employment of tank destroyers that improved their usefulness. In perhaps the most important lesson commanders gleaned from combat operations in both the Mediterranean and European theaters, they learned that antitank guns proved most effective when commanders placed them in mutually supporting positions, operating in conjunction with infantry and artillery as members of a fully integrated combined arms team.[65] The concentration of tank destroyer doctrine development and training at an independent center delayed the process of learning among field commanders regarding their use as members of the combined arms team. Nevertheless, Marshall believed, probably correctly, that only by shielding the nascent tank destroyer from the influence of infantry, armor, and cavalry could Bruce, supported by McNair and AGF, develop the weapon system he envisioned, rather than simply another form of tank or combat car.

Despite their flaws, Harry Yeide pointed out the ease of criticizing tank destroyers with the benefit of twenty–twenty hindsight, noting several factors worth
considering when reflecting on the overall performance of the tank destroyer in
World War II. For example, because the US army had never fought a mechanized
war before, it could only plan for one based on reports received from observers,
and these all agreed on one point: through the end of the German campaign
against France, neither tanks nor static antitank defenses had stopped German
tanks. Yeide also argued that for once, at least the developers of antitank doctrine
and weapons were not "re-fighting the last campaign." Yeide concluded, like
Gabel, that modification of doctrine and eventual fielding of effective weapons
made tank destroyers and antitank guns effective and respected members of the
combined arms team.[66] The findings of the postwar equipment review board
(also known as the Cook Board, presided over by Major General Gilbert R. Cook
after the war) support this conclusion. The board conducted a thorough review of
the combat performance of all army equipment. In its final report, the board recommended retaining the tank destroyer and antitank gun and investing more
money and effort into these weapons systems in the future.[67]

US army combat equipment of various types received criticism throughout the
war—particularly, late in the war, the M4 Sherman tank. The M4 Sherman, with
its excellent reliability, speed, and maneuverability, as well as its medium-caliber
gun, seemed well suited to commanders like Patton for various missions. These included striking enemy rear areas, exploiting breakthroughs by attacking enemy infantry and artillery units, and fighting as an integrated member of combined arms
teams with infantry, artillery, and aviation, making it effective against a variety of
enemy weapons, including armor. In December 1943 he wrote to Major General
Thomas T. Handy, chief of OPD, indicating his desire for certain capabilities in his
formation, should he receive appointment to a command in upcoming operations.
Among his requests, he mentioned his desire to have an American armored division assigned to his command: "I am quite sure that armored divisions of other
nations do not have our conception of fighting with tanks."[68] Patton wrote a mass
letter on April 15, 1944, to commanders of tank corps and smaller units containing
views that he had developed regarding the most effective employment of armor. In
the final paragraph of this letter, Patton wrote, "The foregoing notes are based
largely on the advice of Major General T. H. Middleton, who has had great success
in the use of tanks and infantry in the manner above described."[69]

In the letter, Patton began by retracting his own "slaving adherence to the pre-
cept that 'tanks should be used in mass,'" because when doing so a commander
did not gain the full advantage provided by separate tank battalions. He advised
organizing the tanks in task forces with infantry and artillery, however small, dictated by the terrain or situation, and he described the best manner of employ-

ment with either tanks or infantry in the lead, again depending on the situation. He argued that tanks could and should attack at night, and that tanks—when supported by infantry—could attack enemy tanks, even when outnumbered. He emphasized the fact that lighter tanks should not attempt to stand toe-to-toe against heavier tanks but could defeat them through surprise or withdraw under the cover of smoke, move to a new position of advantage, and strike again when the enemy tanks reappeared. He closed with the reminder that "the skillful commander uses the means at hand, all weapons, for the accomplishment of the end sought, the destruction of Germans."[70]

Later that month, a War Department ground adjutant officer, Lieutenant Colonel R. A. Meredith, advised General Marshall (and the War Department's new development division) that the army's medium tank program remained no closer to having a production-ready design for a tank superior to the Sherman. In a recent test, among other problems, the T-23 medium tank (the leading contender for production as an improved medium tank) required 112 percent more man-hours of maintenance than the M4A3 Sherman under the same conditions. This additional maintenance time highlighted several major design deficiencies that would require correction before production could even begin.[71] On March 12, 1945, Eisenhower wrote to Marshall with a general update on the situation on the Western Front. The media had started to direct its attention to Allied equipment, having heard complaints from some deployed personnel, but Eisenhower found criticisms of Allied equipment largely unfounded.

Eisenhower included a paragraph in his message in which he offered his own assessment of US army equipment, which varied considerably from the story currently gaining momentum in the media: "It is pure bosh to say that 75 per cent of our equipment is inferior to the German material. Speaking generally the reverse is true although, of course, if you take the present Sherman and the Panther and put them in a slugging match the latter will win. One trouble is that even many of our professionals do not understand that a compromise in tank characteristics is necessary if we are to meet our own complex requirements in this type of equipment." (In other correspondence, Eisenhower made it clear that these complex requirements had to do with the shipment of tanks and the fuel, ammunition, and repair parts required to keep them operational, particularly given America's warlong shortage of shipping capacity.) As for other equipment, Eisenhower wrote, "Our artillery, rifles, machine guns, airplanes (except for the jet airplane) and in general our clothing and equipage all outclass the enemy's. The jeep, the large trucks and the ducks are far ahead of him. The German 88 is a great all round gun and as a separate anti-tank weapon has caused us lots of trouble. But his artillery as a whole is far behind and the 90 mm will match the 88."[72] Nevertheless, media attention remained focused on tanks, as did many of the historical accounts of the war written in the intervening decades. This has resulted in a disproportionate focus on relatively minor issues related to the US army's combat effectiveness. While soldiers and their commanders understandably wanted the best equipment possible, the relative capability of American and German tanks played a minor role in the AGF's combat performance. The ability to conduct effective combined arms operations at the tactical level, combined with the ability to integrate those tactical actions to achieve strategic success—in today's terminology, operational art—had a much greater impact on the effectiveness of the Americans in combat.

Despite the War Department's efforts to quell the negative stories in the press and mitigate the discontent among personnel in armor units, the M4 Sherman remained a topic of debate and a target of criticism, both in combat theaters and on the home front. Eisenhower wrote to Marshall again on March 18, 1945, admitting that he had not known how serious the situation had grown until receiving several letters and telegrams from Marshall illustrating the rising tide of anti-Sherman discontent. This led Eisenhower to begin a deliberate investigation, while asking Patton to make a statement reflecting his feelings on the matter, and attempting to give objective reporters access to soldiers and noncommissioned officers who had positive things to say about the tank. After hearing from one soldier of techniques his unit had developed that enabled them to destroy "a lot more [tanks] than we have lost," Eisenhower looked up the data within Third Army. He found that it had lost about 800 tanks and had knocked out 820 German tanks since it began operations in Western Europe (through March 17, 1945). Eisenhower wrote that he planned to have a press conference during a lull in operations to clear up the issue, and he expected Bradley's support as well. Finally, he mentioned that he believed soldiers could make a more valid complaint about the winter clothing situation. Soldiers tended to discard heavy, unneeded gear, so each fall, they typically needed resupply of basic winter gear. He wrote, "Shipments of winter clothing to this Theater were subject to the same interruptions and difficulties last summer and fall as were those of every other kind of supplies." This meant that front line units often did not get cold weather gear by the time they needed it, further illustrating the constant shipping limitations deployed units had to deal with.[73]

Another news story that emanated from a noncommissioned officer in Third Army and made it to the American media finally called for a concerted effort on Eisenhower's part to assess the true severity of the tank problem. He wrote to the commanders of the 2nd and the 3rd Armored Divisions, Brigadier General Isaac D. White and Major General Maurice Rose, respectively, to ask them to answer three questions: "(a) Your own personal convictions about the quality of our tank equipment as compared to the German, and having in mind the necessity of our shipping our material over long distances to get it to the battlefield; (b) Your opinion as to the ability of the new T-23 [Eisenhower meant the T26E3] with the 90 mm gun, to meet the Panther on equal terms, and (c) A digest of the opinions of your tank commanders, drivers, gunners, and so on, on these general subjects." Rose provided a five-page answer, dated March 21, and White wrote a similar reply on March 20. Their answers reflected a general dissatisfaction with the performance of the Sherman tank, both personally and among their unit personnel, but their dissatisfaction related primarily to the tank's relative vulnerability to the German Panther and Tiger tanks, and Rose qualified his answer by writing that the Americans compensated through their superior employment of artillery, air power, and other available equipment. Both men believed the T-26 with the 90mm gun would fare better against German heavy tanks, but White wrote that he would prefer if it had thicker armor. Finally, Rose found some weapons and equipment far superior to German equivalents, including artillery and trucks, but he admitted that his soldiers preferred captured German handheld rocket launchers (Panzerfaust) to the bazooka. Neither officer mentioned the issue of shipping, despite Eisenhower's specific request for them to do so.[74]

The US army relied until late in the war on much equipment that many historians have described as inferior when compared piece for piece to German weapons like tanks and antitank guns. For example, many historians have faulted the US army for not developing a heavy tank or antitank gun comparable to the German Tiger or 88mm. However, the army did not continue to use the relatively light M4 Sherman tank and other such equipment in 1944–1945 because of a lack of awareness or imagination. When first introduced, the Sherman performed on par with most tanks used by any of the war's combatants. The longevity of the Sherman, still in use by the US army in the Korean War and by other countries even later, attests to its effectiveness. Additionally, unlike on the Eastern Front, where an arms race between the Russians and Germans led to a constant attempt to field heavier and more powerful weapons, in the theaters where the Americans fought before June 1944, the Sherman performed quite well. Complaints from field commanders desiring heavier tanks did not rise to a significant level until after D-Day, when American ground combat units began to encounter German heavy tanks more frequently. By this time the process of developing and fielding a heavy tank or even an upgraded Sherman would take a significant amount of time and overburden America's already stretched production and shipping capacity. One can only wonder what effect development and fielding of such a tank before D-Day would have had on the logistical supportability of Allied operations in Western Europe. Finally, Eisenhower reported to Marshall that one or two tank commanders wanted even more armor on the T-26, concluding, "The fact is that when a man is actually on the front line engaging a gun or a tank, he could not have, in his own estimation, a big enough gun or enough armor. While this would result in nothing but a steel pill box, it is clear that the Ordnance Department should do everything it can do to speed up production of the T-26 with the very high-velocity gun."[75]

Greenfield's February 7, 1945, interview of the AGF chief of staff, Major General James G. Christiansen, provides excellent insight into this particular aspect of the challenges McNair dealt with after the ground forces engaged in combat in Western Europe. Greenfield asked Christiansen how he responded to those who argued that the army's inferiority in tanks stemmed from the reorganization of the War Department because it placed responsibility for armor training with the AGF, while the ASF retained oversight of the technical aspects of armor development. Greenfield mentioned the contrast in the AAF's move after the reorganization to assume direct control over technical air support services and aircraft procurement, which led to improvements in the production of new aircraft and sustainment of the existing AAF, and asked how the AGF's lack of the same authorities affected its ability to procure new combat equipment. Christiansen replied,

Our position with relation to the technical services goes back to General Mc-Nair's decision when he organized the Special Staff of this headquarters. He decided to set up the Special Staff Sections solely for training purposes, leaving the initiative in developing equipment to the technical services. His object was economy of personnel. He refused to duplicate services that already existed, and believed that they must be trusted in this war, whatever the ideal set-up might prove to be. This decision may have been a mistake but it was rooted in his conviction that the enemy could be beaten only by the application of superior combat power when and where needed. With limited shipping and limited available manpower, this would, he believed, be possible for us only by the strictest economy in the services. . . . It was the principle behind his proposal, early in the war, to divide the total manpower available to the ground forces by 35,000 per division and plan accordingly. It was not followed, and we have gone to 80,000 per division. At the time of Anzio he pointed out that we were stopped dead by the 100,000 combat troops whom the Germans could put opposite our 100,000 combat troops. We had 500–600,000 [more troops] behind them; with 20,000 of these we could break the deadlock and go wherever we wanted, with lighter losses than we were suffering by attrition—the losses which our overwhelming support was designed to minimize. But we could not gain the superiority required because our troops were frozen into overhead and services.[76]

This observation reveals many challenges American ground troops faced in fighting the war—challenges McNair anticipated but lacked the authority to overcome.

The Cook Board found numerous flaws in the army's weapons development process. The board included a cover letter with its various reports on specific equipment types that addressed several points related to this topic.[77] For example, the board found that effective peacetime weapons development required that

> a weapon or a piece of equipment should be developed for a specific purpose and must represent the best possible solution to the *needs* of the *user*. [This meant] the user who is to fight the weapon in the combat zone must completely control the development of the weapon he is to employ. The complete and sole objective of the development agency must be to reflect the needs of the user. . . . Neither a development agency nor a using agency should at the same time, be a procurement agency.

These findings led the board to recommend integration of effort under a "unified Department of National Defense," with "responsibility for the development of all army ground force weapons and materiel . . . assigned directly to Army Ground Forces."[78]

This presents a striking parallel to post–World War I debates regarding equipment procurement organizations and authorities. Secretary of War Baker highlighted this very issue in his testimony before the House Committee on Military Affairs in 1919, stating that the ordnance department "makes what the other soldiers use and you have a controversy in the army all the time between the user of the weapon and the maker of the weapon. The user says that 'The man that makes it is a manufacturer and he knows nothing about what I am going to do with it and therefore he must make it the way I want it.' The manufacturer on the other hand says, 'These fellows in the field have no technical knowledge; they do not know a good weapon; my duty is to give them a good weapon.'" Nevertheless, military traditionalists did not adopt a streamlined, modernized command system after World War I, and this perpetuated various inefficiencies—including the existence of precisely the same friction between ordnance and the operational army during both world wars.[79]

Upon his retirement in 1930, General Summerall foresaw the continuing problems that would result from this persistent challenge. Summerall warned, as paraphrased by historian Daniel Beaver, of "the failure to consolidate command and control of supply and logistics under the chief of staff in the 1920 legislation [the 1920 National Defense Act] would bring difficulties similar to those encountered in 1917 and 1918." Instead, as Beaver explained, "The National Defense Act placed responsibility for procurement planning and industrial mobilization in the office of the assistant secretary of war and responsibility for military planning in the office of the chief of staff. Limited interwar funding or a specific military threat combined with the purely consultative relationship between the procurement and mobilization planners and the war planners left the army and the civilian industrialists no better prepared for World War II than they had been in 1917."[80]

Even when the War Department reorganization of 1942 gave McNair a window of opportunity to seize control of the technical services of the AGF, the major problem of excess overhead in staffs—particularly those of the AAF and ASF—provided a rationale for his decision not to do so. Two memos containing extracts from the observations of Major General George S. Patton, prepared on August 4, 1943, by Handy provide a clear and pointed description of the excess overhead Christiansen mentioned in his interview with Greenfield. Handy quoted Patton: "It seems to me that perhaps we have an exaggerated idea of the proportion of SOS [ASF] troops to combat troops. There is a tendency for the SOS to work on the eight-hour day principle. While this is o.k. in quiet sectors, in emergencies they should work 24 hours a day as do the combat troops."[81] Curiously, Handy prepared two versions of the memo, one addressed to all three functional commanders and the other only to Arnold. These memos are identical except that the above paragraph only appears in the memo addressed to Arnold. One can only speculate why Handy prepared two different versions of this memo. Regardless, the paragraph above demonstrates that at least one combat commander shared Christiansen's (and McNair's) concern over the excess amount of overhead and service troops relative to ground combat forces.[82] The War Department reorganization of 1942, while perhaps well intentioned, made it nearly impossible for McNair to solve such problems. The disparity in the size and power of the staffs of the three functional commands would only continue to grow over the coming months.

Christiansen also provided insight regarding the superiority in tanks that the Germans established in the critical phase of the war, drawing criticism of War Department armor development, particularly from armor personnel and commanders within the AGF. Christiansen remarked,

The Germans have two tanks that have outgunned, out-armored, and outfloated our M4. Our light and medium tanks are superior to anything in use by other armies, but we have nothing with which to stop, tank for tank, the new German heavies. The AGF must share in the responsibility for this. Our decision to concentrate on Shermans goes back to General McNair's concept of exploitation. General McNair was right at St. Lô and in the sweep from Normandy to the Rhine. Our tankmen there benefitted by the superior mobility, mechanical dependability and accurate fire of the Sherman. It has been argued that if the Germans had been armed with similar tanks they would have broken through in the Ardennes offensive. But because of his concept for the role of tanks, General McNair never pushed Ordnance for a gun with punch. Neither did General Devers or General Gillem.[83]

Asked by Greenfield whether the AGF caused "the lag in adjustment to the demands of armored warfare because it cut back and smothered the Armored Force, reducing it to a Center," Christiansen answered,

> The representatives of the Armored Force in the theaters—the original tank enthusiasts—have taken the same view, indeed the AGF has followed their lead. In October [1944] the AGF asked ETO [European Theater of Operations] for the proportion of 90mm guns to 105mm howitzers desired in tanks. ETO replied ⅓ to ⅔—a reflection of the same role of tanks—that their mission is not to shoot it out with tanks. Now they have reversed the ratio to ⅔ to ⅓. Similarly with regard to armor, in which the Germans have achieved superiority. Only nine months ago, when the choice between the T-25 and the T-26 was being made. The Armored Force people in ETO wanted the T-25 which was preferable on the basis of the McNair concept of armored tactics. The T-26 was adopted.[84]

Various evidence supports the "McNair concept" that the tank should not serve as the primary killer of enemy tanks. The tank destroyer did not begin to achieve significant results until the late war fielding of improved models, but the artillery proved decisive from the very beginning.

Comparato illustrated the effectiveness of the field artillery through the observations of various high-level commanders. He cited General MacArthur's praise of American artillerymen in the early spring of 1942: "On every occasion when artillery was used with audacity the Japanese were checkmated and seemed completely bewildered. The strong effect of massing artillery fire, using a fire direction center connected with all observation posts available, was proven without question. [. . .] I can make no suggestions for the improvement of the methods taught at Fort Sill." General Bradley remarked in 1943, "[The] American field artillery technique of massed fires was a major contributing factor toward the early and successful conclusion of the operation [in Tunisia]." Eisenhower wrote that battle results during the European campaign "demonstrated conclusively that the current artillery doctrines are sound and probably the most advanced in the world." Later Eisenhower reported, "In pieces of artillery, the enemy has lost eight to our one. We have knocked out twice as many tanks as we have lost." He also noted,

"The speed, accuracy, and devastating power of American Artillery won confidence and admiration from the troops it supported and inspired fear and respect in the enemy." These few remarks from field commanders illustrate the devastating effectiveness of massed, observed artillery fires directed by a Fire Direction Center—a method McNair advocated as early as World War I and directly influenced while at the Field Artillery School during the interwar years. They also demonstrate the fact that even without heavy tanks, the AGF possessed combined arms doctrine, organizations, and equipment that made it superior to the Wehrmacht in combat effectiveness, despite the threat posed by German heavy tanks.[85]

The AGF at War: Overcoming the Infantry Problem

Diversion of shipping capacity to transport heavier tanks and logistic support would certainly affect the already challenging demands of another key process designed to sustain the war effort: the individual replacement training system. This system theoretically provided a way to keep combat units at authorized strength without taking them out of combat for reconstitution, but it contained various administrative flaws that reduced its effectiveness. For example, because it used unit mobilization requirements, not combat losses, as the basis for calculation of replacement allocations, replacement training centers (RTCs) did not account for the disproportionate losses between branches and services in combat. As the official history noted,

> Hence in 1942 the Quartermaster Corps had as large an RTC capacity as the Field Artillery; the Signal Corps a larger capacity than the Armored Force; and the Medical Department half as large a capacity as the Infantry. In the Infantry the number of replacements trained as riflemen, cooks, and clerks corresponded to the number of men in each of these jobs called for in Tables of Organization of infantry units, without allowing for the fact that when battle losses began to occur the casualty rate among riflemen would be higher than among cooks.[86]

After the declaration of war in December 1941, the War Department decided not to expand RTCs in proportion to the army's overall expansion. New units would receive fillers from reception centers, while units overseas or alerted for overseas movement would receive replacements from RTCs. The War Department based its policies for RTCs on the principle that "service units, requiring a larger number of technically trained men than combat units, should receive a higher proportion of fillers already branch-trained than should units of the combat arms."[87] This put in place yet another policy that resulted in the provision of both higher-quality and better trained troops to the ASF and AAF than to the AGF, and the policies did not even allocate those troops that the AGF did receive to units where combat losses would most likely create shortages: in the infantry and other combat arms. The various War Department policies that led to steadily decreasing numbers and quality of AGF personnel made McNair's efforts to influence the war effort as AGF commander particularly difficult.

The War Department announced on March 18, 1942, that the reorganization of March 9 (to the three functional commands) would not change existing replacement policies or procedures. War Department staffers continued to view the need for replacements as a troop basis problem—an issue related to allocation of manpower within the army based on projected personnel requirements by unit type and year, not actual requirements as determined by combat losses. The flaw in this logic seems obvious in retrospect, but with no combat losses to replace at the time, it apparently did not occur to those establishing the policies (Marshall, advised primarily by his G-1 adjutant general). The War Department adjutant general remained responsible for assignment of inductees to replacement centers and of graduates of those centers to units and other organizations. The War Department established the priorities that drove the adjutant general's replacement apportionment decisions. The AGF oversaw the training of replacements conducted by the Replacement and School Command, while the ASF handled movement of replacements to theaters of operations. Thus, AGF could focus on its primary mission of activating and training units, while the Replacement and School Command oversaw the replacement system.[88]

On November 9, 1942, McNair urged the War Department to streamline the process by establishing general (rather than specialty specific) Zone of Interior replacement depots. AGF recommended this policy for various reasons, including the need to reduce the demand for quality officers to run the depots—an ongoing problem that tied officers down in administrative positions that units needed badly at the front.[89] The War Department supported this request, establishing one such depot near each coast to hold and process overseas replacements for all arms and services except the air forces. It also decentralized assignment procedures, delegating this authority to the three functional commands. Therefore, as the AGF approached the end of mobilization in 1943 and shifted its focus to replacement operations, it possessed the authority to direct AGF replacements to specific units. However, it still suffered the effects of the many other long-standing policies like volunteerism and classification testing that ensured the ground forces received the lowest-quality personnel. AGF also had no control over the movement of replacements to reception depots overseas, and from there to soldiers' gaining units. This process often took several weeks, resulting in replacements losing many of the benefits of the initial training they received before shipping out, arriving at their units out of shape, demoralized, and no longer familiar with the basic requirements of their specific duty assignment.[90]

America's entry into combat operations in 1942 revealed many problems with the army's administration of the replacement system, prompting the War Department to assign greater responsibility for its oversight to AGF.[91] Once assigned this task by General Marshall, McNair traveled to various replacement centers across America and to reception centers in Tunisia to investigate the problem personally. He saw numerous instances of individuals mismanaging or abusing the system. For example, he learned that some commanders in North Africa chose to form completely new units from personnel gathered at replacement centers rather than sending individual replacements to their intended units. Other commanders admitted they habitually traveled to replacement centers to select their replacements personally, without regard to their intended unit or even unit type. This latter practice often resulted in problems like armor-trained replacements ending up in infantry units, negating the practical usefulness of any unit-specific training those replacements received before shipping out.[92]

In 1943, the War Department gave McNair direct responsibility for the administration of the ground forces' individual replacement system and provided guidance for implementing various changes to the existing system, requesting AGF's response before making final decisions on those changes. The War Department based its guidance to McNair largely on the findings of the Committee on Revision of the Military Program. The War Department formed this committee in early 1943 to assess the state of army personnel based on the emerging manpower crisis that led to the reduction of the army troop basis to a cap of eighty-eight divisions. In its recommendations related to replacements, issued on June 7, 1943, the committee proposed an extension of the replacement-training program to six months, including unit training, and provision of well-trained replacements in the interim by moving soldiers from recently mobilized and trained units into the replacement pool. This recommendation resulted in part from field commanders' preference for noncommissioned officers promoted from within their own unit ranks, causing them to request assignment of replacements only in the grade of private.[93]

The Committee on Revision of the Military Program also suggested that AGF should consider training replacements in units rather than in replacement centers as a way to increase training effectiveness. This latter recommendation would have led to a system more like that used in the British and German armies, in which replacements trained in units and these units replaced others in the line so they could reconstitute. Given the decision to form only eighty-eight divisions, and the preference of American field commanders to rebuild broken units with individual replacements rather than replace them with new (unknown and presumably not combat hardened) subordinate units made this recommendation impractical. Further, McNair believed six months of replacement training was excessive; he recommended thirteen weeks. In August 1943, the War Department increased the replacement training program to seventeen weeks but retained the individual replacement system, assigning implementation and oversight responsibility to AGF.[94]

AGF inspectors discovered particularly troubling problems when they examined the process by which the ASF moved replacements into combat theaters. The AGF staff initially had no desire to assume responsibility for the replacement system, and until reports from deployed commanders began to indicate problems, AGF leaders believed the ASF established and oversaw an effective replacement system. However, reports of poor discipline among replacements received in theater from the ASF's Shenango, Pennsylvania, replacement center led Brigadier General Alexander R. Bolling, the AGF G-1 (assistant chief of staff for personnel) to conduct an inspection visit on May 17, 1943. The official history described Bolling and the other AGF staffers as "shocked by their findings." Bolling, "who in the past strongly favored the operations of replacement depots by the Service Forces," recommended that AGF take over responsibility for operations at Shenango.[95]

After discussing the situation with the War Department, AGF instead established two new replacement depots for its own replacements, one on each coast and both in operation by August 1943, while the ASF retained Shenango for processing and movement of service forces replacements. Thus, after August 1943, AGF managed all replacement functions for ground forces from two new depots, one at Fort Meade, Maryland, capable of handling 18,000 replacements, and the other at Fort Ord, California, with a capacity of 7,000 replacements. In doing so, AGF implemented and ensured the efficacy of functions including medical processing, equipment issue, individual training, and shipment of replacements overseas. As Palmer, Wiley, and Keast noted,

> Improvement in the quality of replacements in the ground arms was soon noted. The Inspector General reported on 30 October 1943 that since the establishment of the depot at Fort Meade replacements reached the East Coast staging areas better equipped and clothed than before, and with more confidence and eagerness to go overseas, though a few had still not qualified with their primary weapons. Reports from Italy received through the AGF Board were in general favorable. The Fifth Army found that replacements were better

than they had been in the Tunisian campaign and that infantry replacements in particular were good, though some had inadequate knowledge of their weapons. By the time of the Fifth Army reports (November and December 1943) infantry replacements had either benefited from the 17-week program in replacement centers or had come from units well along in their training. The fact that, despite all efforts, some men lacked proficiency with their weapons may be attributed to difficulties in the training and processing of certain types of specialists.[96]

To manage this new responsibility, McNair directed the establishment of a classification and replacement division within the AGF.

He also attempted to correct several systemic problems that AGF personnel identified, in part by recommending clarifications to War Department Circular 85, which described the physical and psychological requirements for overseas service. McNair and his staff found that doctors tended to apply progressively stricter medical criteria to replacements as they moved closer to the combat zone, which was based on the assumption that stateside medical personnel did not diligently hold replacements to established standards. AGF inspectors also discovered misconduct by replacement personnel. They found that some soldiers threw away issued dental appliances in hopes of avoiding overseas service by failing an exam at a replacement station further down the line. To deal with such issues, McNair recommended clarification of dental standards at a minimal and simple level: "ability to masticate the Army ration." He also sought the removal of "mental" as a medical evaluation category for replacements as a result of the subjectivity involved in assessing a recruit's mental capacity, as well as the tendency for recruits classified at the upper end of the intelligence scale to receive preferential assignment to the AAF or ASF. The War Department did not accept all of McNair's recommendations, but it did accept many, including them in a new policy document it published in the late summer of 1943: "Preparation for Oversea Movement of Individual Replacements." This document remained in effect until mid-1944, when the growing shortage of personnel forced the War Department to lower physical and mental standards for new recruits even further.[97] Significantly, once AGF established and ran its own replacement system, the quality of ground force replacements quickly improved.

These improvements, although welcomed by field commanders, could only raise the overall quality of the ground forces to limited degree. Many other long-standing personnel procurement issues continued to divert the highest-quality recruits away from the ground forces, even after AGF took over responsibility for its own replacement system and lengthened replacement training to seventeen weeks. National personnel shortages caused by the competing demands of active military service and war production made quality problems worse. This left the army short 330,000 recruits by September 1942 and led President Roosevelt to approve a recommended massive reduction in the planned end strength of the army, resulting in the updated troop basis of July 1, 1943, which allocated 500,000 fewer personnel to the army than had been projected in early 1942. Most of the resulting reductions in strength affected AGF units even though they made up less than 20 percent of the total personnel strength of the army. For example, AGF had planned to mobilize and train 125 ground combat divisions by mid-1943, but it only received enough recruits to form 90 divisions, even as both the ASF and the AAF enjoyed a net increase in personnel strength.[98]

After McNair assumed responsibility for AGF replacements, the system provided a steady stream of replacements that enabled AGF unit commanders to keep their units in the line without a break. The system still drew criticism because it provided inexperienced and marginally trained individuals to replace experienced casualties, rather than pulling units out of the line to rest and reconstitute while fresh divisions took their place (an infeasible option given the decision to cap the number of divisions at less than half of the originally planned number). Replacements arrived frequently, and units often had very little time to integrate them into their unit before sending them into combat. This meant replacements often had to learn their job in direct combat, often after a long period of inactivity while slowly making the journey from the United States to their units. The army might have had lower casualty rates using a unit rotation system, but the 90-Division Gamble made this impossible at the division level. Attempts to implement a unit-based replacement system also did not gain War Department approval. They repeatedly refused to implement the AGF-recommended creation of separate battalions or regiments of infantry to replace the hardest-hit elements of divisions taken out of the line to rest and refit.

In October 1944, AGF proposed sending eight separate infantry regiments currently training individual replacements in the Zone of Interior to the front for immediate use in a supplemental unit replacement system. AGF again made such a recommendation in November, arguing: "Our whole system of the employment of divisions for long periods and continuous replenishment of these divisions by replacements while they are in action has created a vicious circle with respect to battle fatigue which no system of individual replacement can overcome." Objections to such a system came from many quarters, including the War Department G-3; their primary basis stemmed from the fact that any such system would require increasing the authorized strength of the army, fixed since 1943. This made only an individual replacement system feasible and ensured that any significant interruption in the flow of individual replacements would greatly degrade combat units' ability to continue fighting. This left AGF in a position in which it could only seek to alleviate high casualty rates and incidence of battle fatigue and other mental strain among new replacements who had limited time to develop bonds with fellow soldiers in their units because of near-constant combat action.[99]

The Selective Service allowed the practice of volunteering, which served as the sole source of navy and marine recruits through the end of 1942. (The navy and marine corps also procured most of their officers through volunteering, usually before they had received any military training, selecting them on the basis of civilian education and experience.) This provided thousands of the best recruits, both in terms of intelligence and physical characteristics—many were well educated and highly motivated to serve—with an easy means to avoid service in the infantry, which soldiers soon identified as the least popular branch in job satisfaction surveys.[100]

Of those men who did end up in the army, many volunteered. An overwhelming percentage of volunteers in 1942 chose the AAF, while only 5 percent chose infantry or armor. These factors combined to divert the vast majority of the highest-quality recruits to the navy, marine corps, and air forces, and many of these recruits served in the technical services in noncombat roles. Intelligence testing only added to the problem. Throughout 1942 and 1943, War Department policy required diversion of an ever-increasing percentage of the army's best recruits from the AGF to either the AAF or ASF on the basis of their score on the Army General Classification Test (AGCT). After two years of reliance on the AGCT, first implemented in 1940, War Department personnel believed they had validated the test's ability to measure a recruit's capacity to learn by comparing their test scores to their performance in army training courses. By 1942, the test served as the primary tool for measuring recruits' learning ability, allowing classification of each recruit in army grades I through V ("rapid learners" to "slow learners"). War Department policy directed an even distribution of inductees by intelligence classification to the three functional commands; however, the classification system further disadvantaged the AGF by aligning civilian skills with military specialties. Because no civilian skills translated directly to service in the infantry, armor, or artillery, almost every recruit received a specification serial number below 500 (technical fields), leaving few for classification to a combat specialty (specification serial numbers above 500). Every step of the classification process incrementally reduced the pool of recruits available for assignment to combat positions.[101]

Therefore, the AGF received soldiers far shorter, weaker, and less intellectually capable (according to the classification system's standardized tests) than the average recruit. Army historians noted, "One commander observed in a moment of exaggeration, his hardest problem was to find competent enlisted men to act as instructors, because 'everybody higher than a moron' was pulled out for one reason or another."[102] As historian Theodore Wilson noted, "The AAF claimed nearly twice as many Group I and II men than the AGF, and the proportions of Is and IIs grabbed by the ASF was 30 per cent higher than that of the AGF. At the other end of the scale, the AGF contained more than five times as many Group V soldiers as the AAF and almost four times as many as the ASF."[103]

McNair began in July 1942 to use the kind of advertising the navy, marine corps, and air forces used so effectively to attract volunteers. McNair disdained publicity, but he recognized the necessity of such measures, particularly after his efforts to influence War Department policy directly had no effect. This led Mc-Nair on December 1, 1942, to make an Armistice Day address to troops of the AGF titled "The Struggle Is for Survival." Although it was directed to the AGF, the transmission of this address over national radio networks ensured that it reached a wide cross section of the American populace. In the speech, McNair noted the nation's observation of Armistice Day every year since 1918, recognizing an achievement largely stemming from the valor displayed by the American Expeditionary Force's ground forces during World War I. McNair reminded his listeners of "war-hardened enemies pouncing on green American troops, taking every possible advantage of our lack of training and battle experience. Pearl Harbor was another such case."[104]

Pointing out that Germany and Japan "comparatively speaking, both always have been at war or preparing for it," McNair described the enemy not as admirable for their military tradition but rather as formidable. He argued that America's nonmilitaristic tradition made its preparation to face this enemy in combat particularly challenging. He noted that this preparation required both personnel and matériel, and he emphasized that the latter requirement gave "even our vast industrial system a few headaches." Regarding the personnel question, McNair described the achievements of the previous year—particularly at the 1941 maneuvers—and stated the ground forces possessed generally competent soldiers and officers. However, he argued that training alone could not prepare an army for the demands it would face: "Soldiers—our kind of soldiers—must be right inside." This meant that

> our soldiers must have the fighting spirit. If you call that hating our enemies, then we must hate with every fiber of our being. We must lust for battle; our object in life must be to kill; we must scheme and plan night and day to kill. There need be no pangs of conscience, for our enemies have lighted the way to faster, surer, and crueler killing; they are past masters. We must hurry to catch up with them if we are to survive. Since killing is the object of our efforts, the sooner we get in the killing mood, the better and more skillful we shall be when the real test comes. The struggle is for survival—kill or be killed.[105]

Even today, one can imagine the immense impact of these words on the American public and on the present or future members of the army that fought the war. With American forces only just beginning to engage in direct combat in the Pacific and Mediterranean theaters, many Americans remained in a state of denial or ignorance regarding the immensity of the task the nation faced.

This speech prompted negative reactions from some members of the public, but it also gained much media attention, most either positive or soberly objective. A November 1942 *Time* article juxtaposed the joy of the American naval victory in the Solomon Islands with the mixed news from North Africa: "But there was a sobering sense of the tasks still to be done—hard and painful and bloody. If anyone did not know this, he was given a jolting reminder by the wiry, keen commander of the US Ground Forces."[106] Despite objective contemporary reporting, many oversimplifications of the speech and its impact exist in the postwar historical record. Historian Edward G. Miller summed up the content of the speech: McNair "told the public that the purpose of an army was to make skillful killers of men." Miller described the speech's impact even more simply: "The media had a field day." Although historical accounts such as Miller's rarely describe the true import of McNair's remarks, contemporary records provide a much more balanced account. A review of dozens of newspaper clippings and letters that contain responses to the speech, collected by Clare McNair in folders and scrapbooks that she later donated to the Library of Congress, revealed that the majority of both the media and individuals who wrote to McNair directly responded favorably to the speech.[107]

McNair's efforts throughout 1942 to raise awareness in the War Department of the significant deficiencies in quality caused by the Selective Service and classification processes echoed the ever-increasing number of complaints from field commanders, who, the official history noted, "protested repeatedly to Headquarters, Army Ground Forces that they were receiving men of too low a mental quality to be trained." Commanders argued it made no sense to develop expensive equipment only to entrust it to untrainable soldiers, and they said that AGCT class V soldiers posed a danger to themselves and their units when given access to lethal weapons. The air forces and service forces used exactly the same arguments to support their need for the majority of high-quality recruits, but the AAF remained the strategic priority throughout 1942 on the basis of the assumption that America's initial engagement in combat would largely entail AAF operations, requiring a significant expansion of air force equipment and personnel. Other factors worked in the ASF's favor, largely related to the technical nature of the modern army and its new equipment. As preferential assignment continued into December 1942, AGF recognized that even if the War Department initially viewed it merely as a temporary expedient, it had evolved into long-term policy. This led various branches or units of the ground forces to use similar arguments to petition McNair for preferential allocation of the best soldiers assigned to the AGF. McNair refused these requests largely out of principle, insisting that the army must take the personnel that the nation provided and employ them fairly throughout the AGF because favoring one element would only further disadvantage the others.[108]

Two additional factors added to the severity of the AGF's quality problem. Even before the reorganization of March 1942, Selective Service did not divert as many personnel to the air forces by classification as it did to the service forces. The aviation industry, still in its infancy, represented a minority of America's skilled workers. This led Selective Service boards to exclude potential recruits with aviation expertise from conscription. Therefore, the AAF convinced the War Department to institute a policy that required at least 75 percent of all white inductees assigned to the air corps to have an AGCT score of at least 100. This set in motion a yearlong battle between the air corps and McNair, who argued that the ground forces needed intelligent personnel just as badly to serve as combat leaders. Meanwhile, preferential assignment to the AAF not only continued but also grew worse upon the implementation of strategic guidance in the summer of 1942 to use air power over Europe in large numbers before commitment of ground troops. This enabled Arnold to gain War Department support in September 1942 for a new policy, extended through December 1942, which allocated at least 50,000 of each month's new inductees who scored above 100 on both the AGCT and the mechanical aptitude test to the AAF. This resulted in the assignment of a larger aggregate number of high-quality recruits to the AAF, where the majority served in noncombat roles. Before this policy ended, the War Department declared that it would remain in effect until June 1943, modified slightly to allocate to the AAF 55 percent of men scoring at least 100 on both the AGCT and mechanical aptitude tests, rather than the 50,000 previously required.[109]

Twice in 1942, McNair convinced the War Department to rescind the AAF preferential assignment policy, but in each case, it was quickly reinstated with only minor modifications. Even the G-1 and the G-3 of the War Department opposed preferential assignment unless it was a temporary expedient. In March 1942, the G-3 of the War Department General Staff even endorsed a public statement explaining the need for high-quality recruits in the ground forces:

> The increased tempo of war today, its rapid changes in local situations, and the great spaces it covers make it impossible for commanders to control the detailed action of subordinate units. Hence the accomplishment of the will of the commander depends, in final analysis, upon the ability of subordinates to make the proper decisions in unpredictable situations on the battlefield. These

decisions require sound judgment and initiative—qualities which must be carefully developed and fostered in the training of every individual.[110]

The debate continued well into 1943, to no effect. In fact, on the heels of the 55 percent rule, the War Department supported a policy that allowed any qualified enlisted man to apply for pilot training or officer candidate school. Because most chose pilot training, the AAF retained preference over high-grade personnel through the second half of 1943, when the AAF's inductees consisted of at least 50 percent in AGCT class I or II, with scores over 110, while only 30 percent of such men shipped to the AGF. By this point, the effect on the AGF had reached critical levels.[111]

In particular, the AGF supported the policy allowing any qualified man to apply for pilot or officer training, granting that such men should come from the high-caliber classes—but neither McNair nor Clark agreed with AAF's assertion that its ground personnel also needed higher mental capacity than AGF personnel. The AAF regularly assigned men who could not pass flight training to ground positions in the AAF, keeping all the higher-quality recruits allocated to it whether they ended up flying airplanes or driving trucks. The AGF chief of staff, Major General Mark Clark, argued in April 1942 for closer monitoring of volunteer transferees to ensure that the War Department reassigned any men who did not qualify as pilots to the AGF. In December 1943, the War Department still had not implemented this policy. The new AGF chief of staff, Brigadier General James G. Christiansen, observed that not one of 1,800 voluntary transferees to flight training had returned to the AGF, implying a 100 percent success rate that these individuals could not have met.[112]

Adding to the challenges posed by these various policies, a shortage of junior officers led Marshall to direct unit commanders to scour their divisions for potential officer candidates. Incredibly, once again the solution to this demand involved diverting quality personnel away from military training in units preparing for combat. By the summer of 1942, AGF personnel quality had fallen to the point that divisions resorted to examining men as potential officer candidates who had only one year of high school, and they still could not provide the desired number of qualified officer candidates. This led the War Department staff, many of whom believed division commanders simply did not want to release already trained soldiers for officer training, to seek a new solution to the shortage of junior officers. They recommend implementation of the Army Specialized Training Program (ASTP), which would remove high-quality recruits from the replacement pool and send them to college, then on to military training as officers. The secretary of war approved this program in September 1942 in anticipation of lowering the draft age from twenty to eighteen (lessening the impact of this policy by allowing a significant number of young men in this age range to attend college before entering active service). When formally established in December 1942, the policy for the ASTP looked rather different than initially conceived. Men aged eighteen to twenty-two could qualify, and even men above the age of twenty-two could apply for advanced study. Upon completion, these men might proceed to officer training, but many would fill scientific, engineering, medical, and linguistic specialty field shortages instead. The program enrollment was set at a maximum number of 150,000 men at any given time.[113] Concurrent with ASTP implementation in December 1942, Eisenhower wrote to Marshall to inform him that the number of unsatisfactory officers requiring reclassification by War Department policy had grown to the point that he had no recourse but to send them back to the states for reclassification training.[114]

McNair and other leaders at AGF opposed this program from the start. The AGF already received so few men in the class I and class II categories that the ASTP could result in the loss of the last remaining class I and class II men in the age range of eighteen to twenty-two that the AGF currently received, exaggerating the already ill-founded emphasis on vocational rather than physical factors. In particular, by focusing on inductees with above-average intelligence—personnel from whom the AAF already took a majority cut before distribution of the remainder of these inductees—the program even further devalued traits such as leadership ability that proved so critical to AGF personnel. It also diverted many men who potentially possessed leadership potential away from AGF units that were already short of officers and engaged in combat. The War Department requested on September 30, 1942, that AGF submit its plan within five days for implementation of the ASTP. Coming on the heels of the personnel crisis of 1942 and the resulting troop basis change, this led the AGF G-3 to exclaim, "With 300,000 men short, we are asked to send men to college!"[115]

McNair presented his opposition to the ASTP formally on October 4, 1942, in a memorandum to the War Department. He saw no value in sending these soldiers to college, and he enumerated a number of objections, including his conviction that the army could train men more quickly and appropriately in military units under wartime conditions—and he reminded Marshall that the AGF already suffered a severe shortage of high-quality men. McNair's memo had no effect; Marshall had already approved the program, and AGF paid the majority of its cost. Upon learning of the program's approval, McNair asked that AGF receive back at least as many class I and class II inductees as it lost to the program; this request, too, the War Department denied. Upon initiation of the program on college campuses in the spring of 1943, the War Department even drew the first participants from personnel already in training rather than new inductees. Ultimately, the ground forces provided 47 percent of the total personnel who participated in the ASTP, despite the fact that AGF already received a far smaller share of high-quality personnel than AAF or ASF, and in its entirety the AGF accounted for less than a third of total army personnel strength.[116]

With no end to the nation's personnel shortages in sight, the new, significantly reduced 1943 troop basis and the personnel demands of the ASTP halted AGF expansion for the rest of the war. The War Department capped AGF's end strength at ninety divisions, and total personnel in AGF grew from 2,471,000 at the end of 1942 to only 2,502,000 on March 31, 1945—the date the war ended in Europe. This negligible increase in aggregate numbers forced AGF to create the seventeen divisions required to grow from the seventy-three mobilized by mid-1943 to the ninety authorized by the new troop basis, mostly by using troops freed up by the disbanding of various nondivisional units. For example, many of the necessary soldiers came from demobilized antiaircraft battalions (deemed no longer necessary because the Allies had achieved air superiority in Europe by early 1944), retrained to serve in most cases as infantrymen.[117]

The low caliber of recruits assigned to the ground combat arms led to significant challenges for the AGF upon their entry into combat. As noted in a *Time* article published on March 15, 1943, McNair had warned sixteen months earlier that casualties in the ground forces' first battles would be high. This probably represents both his awareness of the low quality of the men assigned to the ground forces and the reality expressed in a marine maxim also quoted in this article: "No troops are much good in their first battle." McNair foresaw the quality problem in early 1942 and struggled thereafter to reverse the various policies that caused it. This surely added to the challenge American troops faced in their first combat experiences in the South Pacific and Tunisia, but even the best training could not prevent high casualty rates against a competent enemy until augmented by combat experience. McNair went to great lengths to increase the realism and exposure to battlefield-like conditions in mobilization training as he gained more resources in late 1942 and early 1943. Demonstrating the universality of the problem, the *Infantry Journal* even devoted several pages to review the comments made at a "What I Should Have Known but Didn't" symposium, which included marines and army ground forces recently engaged in battle in the South Pacific and Tunisia. Despite dissemination of lessons learned and the most realistic training possible, only combat experience could cement in place the learning provided by the mobilization training process.[118] Only the shockingly disproportionate casualties suffered by ground forces in the first months of the war finally convinced Marshall and the War Department to take action to correct the problem.

After struggling since the beginning of 1942 to draw the attention of War Department leaders to the various policies that funneled most quality recruits to the AAF and ASF, McNair finally appeared to get the magnitude of the problem across to General Marshall in February 1944. Marshall asked McNair on February 5 what he thought the War Department could do to find urgently needed infantry replacements. In response, McNair showed statistics to Marshall that reinforced his understanding of the magnitude of the problem. The numbers demonstrated that although the infantry made up only 11 percent of all army personnel during the campaign in Italy, it had suffered 60 percent of the total casualties incurred during that campaign. Marshall conveyed this disturbing information to President Roosevelt the next day, noting that the increased requirement for infantry sure to result from casualties suffered in the upcoming execution of Operation Overlord would only exacerbate the problem. He also sent a memo to his staff directing them to confer with McNair, then draft a proposal that would provide a means to improve appreciation of the infantry soldier. This memo read, in part,

> I am wondering just how we should go about dignifying the infantry rifleman. ... It might well be charged that we have made the mistake of having too much of air and tank and other special weapons and units and too little of the rifleman for whom all these other combat arms must concentrate to get him forward with the least punishment and losses. I don't want to discourage the rifleman and yet I want his role made clear and exalted. I don't want to unduly alarm the families of riflemen and yet it is important that some action be taken.[119]

After years of reliance on a personnel system built on flawed logic, McNair had finally convinced Marshall of the magnitude of the problem—just four months before the planned invasion of mainland Europe. The opportunity to solve the problem had passed; at this point, the only viable options involved various forms of damage control.

Meanwhile, the field commanders continued to make do with replacements that remained too few in number and of disappointingly low quality. Most of the reasons for the low quality of the infantry in early 1944 stemmed from decisions made years earlier, and neither McNair nor Marshall could do much to improve the situation this late in the war. Marshall did finally cancel the ASTP in early 1944, at McNair's urging—a decision that freed up 73,000 high-quality personnel for addition to the replacement pool. Demonstrating Marshall's awareness of the severity of the quality problem with which AGF struggled, he directed his staff to return all of these men to the army as AGF replacements (55,500 of them went to infantry divisions). Even this made little real difference at this late stage of the war, when for more than four years various policies had diverted the highest-quality troops, both in terms of physical and mental classification, to the AAF and ASF. McNair fought these processes tenaciously from their inception, but because he could not convey to Marshall the severity of their impact until early 1944, the corrective measures Marshall directed his staff to take came far too late to correct the damage they caused before execution of Operation Overlord.[120]

McNair did propose several initiatives in response to Marshall's memo to his staff of February 6 intended to improve both the morale of the infantry and the image of the American infantryman among the public—to the degree possible with the time remaining to take corrective action. His recommendations included creation of a badge denoting excellence that only infantrymen could earn, various speeches and engagements with leaders of industry, and a massive media campaign. One can see the result of these efforts in articles like one published in *Time* on April 10, 1944. This article described McNair's recent trip to Fort Bragg, North Carolina, to award the first new "Expert Infantryman" badge to Technical Sergeant Walter L. Bull, a twenty-six-year-old former steelworker from Baltimore. The article described the twelve requirements for earning the badge, including demonstrating proficiency at scouting and patrolling, field sanitation, physical fitness, marksmanship, and completion of training in "live fire" events during which bullets flew only thirty inches over the infantryman's head. The article also reported the posthumous awarding of the Congressional Medal of Honor to Private Nicholas Minue for valor in action during the Tunisian campaign the previous year. Finally, it described the respect soldiers, sailors, and aviators had for the infantry due to the arduous nature of their job.[121]

The army's push to build morale among its ground combat troops and to increase support and respect for them at home led to various civilian morale-building and fund-raising events as well. For example, Irving Berlin, already a well-established songwriter when World War II began, contacted George Marshall in 1942, seeking his approval to create a Broadway musical, tentatively titled *This Is the Army*. With Marshall's approval, Berlin proceeded with the production, with a cast consisting fully of military personnel, including black soldiers—making the unit assigned to the production the only integrated company in the army at that time. The whole cast lived and worked together, a decision both progressive and sure to generate controversy. He also took on the role of a soldier himself, even displaying sincere nervousness around army officers like many young soldiers, particularly when General Irving J. Phillipson notified Berlin that he wanted to preview the show. Despite his nervousness, his audition of the show went over well, and the production went forward, opening in 1943 as a Broadway show and eventually serving as the basis for a Hollywood movie starring future president Ronald Reagan.[122]

Although such efforts came far too late to improve the quality of the infantry before the D-Day invasion of Normandy, they did improve the infantryman's morale, and McNair hoped they would soon result in the provision of higher-

Mr. and Mrs. McNair at the Premiere of Irving Berlin's This Is the Army, *August 12, 1943. Courtesy of the Military History Institute*

quality infantry replacements. McNair's public relations efforts also appeared to have a significant impact on American leaders of industry and the media. For example, William I. Nichols, editor of *This Week*, sent McNair a symbolic check for one dollar on March 7, 1944, in payment for his "article of tribute to the Infantry," which Nichols scheduled for publication on April 2. In Nichols's words, "Having served for some time as a dollar-a-year man for the War Production Board, it gives me a certain pleasure to reverse the situation and enroll a good government man like yourself as a dollar-a-year writer for *This Week*."[123]

McNair also implemented the "Soldier for a Day" initiative at various army installations across the United States, including Camp McCoy, Camp Shelby, and Fort McClellan. This three-day series of demonstrations for leaders of industry took place June 14–16, 1944, giving them the opportunity to interact with the combat troops preparing to deploy overseas at these installations, observe them in training, and see firsthand the employment of the clothing and equipment they had produced for the army's combat troops. The program had a positive impact on the civilian industrial leaders who participated, as indicated by the many letters they sent to McNair after the event, expressing their appreciation of the opportunity to interact with mobilizing American soldiers and the admiration they held for them. These letters still exist in the AGF files at the National Archives, but evidence of this and the many other initiatives McNair led to improve the lot of the infantry during the war remain largely absent in the secondary literature on the war. McNair even reached out to Mr. Paul Gallico of the Writers' War Board and thanked him on March 18, 1944, for the letter he wrote to active fiction writers across America in connection with the infantry program, encouraging them to place "the Infantry story before a reading group which [AGF is] very anxious to reach."[124]

Despite these efforts, by March 1945, fewer than 1,200,000 soldiers served in the army's eighty-nine divisions (only eighty-seven of which actually served in combat), out of a total US army strength of 8,157,386, and most of these men had come from the lowest-classified recruits inducted into the army. McNair fought to improve the lot of the ground combat soldier, particularly the infantryman, throughout his time at AGF, but his achievements mostly remained limited to his direct area of responsibility: mobilization training of new units and, beginning in 1943, AGF replacements. He did achieve some broader successes with his infantry program, but these consisted mostly of symbolic gestures and various public relations efforts that sought to elevate the image of the infantryman both within the army and among the public. These efforts did improve morale among the infantry somewhat, and over time, they led to minor increases in the quality of infantry replacements. McNair could achieve little, however, to change the systemic problems in place since 1940. These problems led to the creation of American infantry divisions that accomplished many of the war's toughest missions, despite their formation from a pool of recruits made up primarily of men from the lowest mental and physical classification levels as determined by Selective Service. These divisions bore the majority of battle-related casualties throughout the war. The Cook board provided just one snapshot that demonstrates the severity of this problem: "In six months of combat world wide, from June 1 to December 31, 1944, the AGF suffered 83.4 percent of casualties, while making up only 35.7 percent of the force."[125]

Combat experience therefore served as the most effective method of creating high-quality infantry officers, noncommissioned officers, and enlisted men. The War Department drastically reduced the troop basis in 1942, when the poorly managed mobilization process began to reach the breaking point. One of the processes put in place to deal with the troop basis reduction—the individual replacement system—meant that large unit commanders had to leave divisions in the line for extended periods without a break. Of indirect benefit, the personnel assigned to these units received many opportunities to gain combat experience, usually very quickly after their arrival at their unit. Those personnel who survived their early experiences of combat soon learned how to fight effectively, using American doctrine and equipment that remained largely unchanged since 1941. McNair's ability to overcome the innumerable challenges caused by factors outside of his control, creating a well-trained combat force guided by sound doctrine and effective leaders, stands out as one of the most remarkable achievements of the war.

Effectiveness through Efficiency:
The AGF and Operational Art

The foregoing analysis of Lesley McNair's career demonstrates that America found itself as unprepared for industrial mobilization in 1940 as it had been in 1917. Further, the nation did not turn on a dime, achieving a remarkable transformation into a powerful militarized society in a few months or even years. In fact, despite the scale of production and the widespread impact of the war on people's lives, it would be a stretch to call American society "militarized" even by the end of the war. Only two years after protective mobilization began, the army had to adjust its troop basis, when severe personnel shortages forced a drastic reduction in military material, and the president chose to increase aviation production while reducing troop allocations and adjusting the planned number of divisions to about half the number originally intended. The American soldiers who invaded the beaches of Normandy on D-Day and then fought their way across Western Europe to defeat Germany did so in the face of disadvantages that make the material preponderance argument seem like fantasy. The army used divisions (and ground forces in general) that consisted of the nation's lowest-quality recruits, and these divisions faced a tenacious enemy in the German army that remained a competent and determined foe, fighting to protect its homeland and benefiting from shorter lines of communication and increasingly compact front lines as the war entered its final months.

This begs the question: what explains the US army's success during World War II, particularly against the Germans in the ETO? Something enabled those low-quality soldiers—at least rated as such by standard personnel mobilization tests, led by workmanlike generals and operating a mix of acceptable to outdated equipment—to defeat the vaunted German enemy. The analysis above supports the conclusion that this mysterious something existed in the doctrine developed between the wars, tested and refined in the maneuvers before World War II, and ingrained in the minds of the American soldier through the most effective individual and unit training system the army ever implemented. The army's foundation of solid doctrine and tough, realistic training helped it overcome its deficiencies in human raw material and subpar equipment (which rarely matched the quality of the German counterpart piece for piece, but which did possess the advantages of reliability and economy of shipping space). On the basis of the general principle that the specific capabilities of a new technology matter far less than one's ability to assess the advantages and limitations of that equipment to find its optimal method of employment, the American army's success almost certainly lies in its intellectual capacity rather than its physical strength and size. Developed in interwar education and professional discourse, trained extensively in peacetime on a foundation of viable doctrine, and applied in the form of operational art by commanders like Eisenhower, this capacity for learning and applying means within the construct of a sound campaign plan to achieve desired ends provided a significant advantage to the American soldier. Perhaps he was led by workmanlike generals, but the daring and panache that apparently enable a general to rise to the lofty heights of a Patton or a Rommel in the estimation of some military historians might not give that commander the intellectual tools he needs to apply his resources appropriately to the situation in which he finds himself.[126]

Eisenhower's broad front strategy provides a useful example. Seen by many critics as unimaginative, devoid of creativity or boldness, and designed more to keep the coalition together than beat the Germans, a closer look reveals that this approach formed the foundation for Eisenhower's operational art during the campaigns of 1944 and 1945 that enabled him to lead the Allied forces to victory in Germany. He did this exactly as he planned it well over a year before his assumption of Supreme Headquarters Allied Expeditionary Force command: by applying the even, concentric pressure Matheny described as the essence of American operational art in World War II. After allowing Montgomery his one attempt to win the war in the north with a thin but deep penetration into the enemy rear during Operation Market Garden, Eisenhower took direct operational control of ground combat troops in Western Europe in the fall of 1944 and ensured that the Allies attempted no further maneuvers of that sort. He did not allow his subordinate commanders to use methods that expended Allied resources inappropriately or upset the equilibrium that formed the central logic of Eisenhower's operational approach. Hitler's last-gasp counterattack through the Ardennes, later known as the Battle of the Bulge, illustrated the wisdom of maintaining a broad, mutually supporting front while steadily increasing concentric pressure on the Germans—a method that enabled the Allies to achieve their strategic aim in the Rhineland just as Eisenhower had visualized this last in a series of tough but well-executed campaigns nearly two years earlier.[127]

At a more fundamental level, just as Eisenhower's adherence to the broad front strategy demonstrated his understanding of operational art, the AGF's combat operations illustrated the army's interwar efforts to innovate within the means available to create an army and a doctrine appropriate to modern warfare. As in any war, units had to learn to use the methods they trained in peacetime in the chaotic and violent cauldron of battle to achieve success. As Weinberg illustrated, where historians have emphasized failures in first battles like Kasserine Pass, the real story revolves around the costly but necessary learning process that took place there and on many other battlegrounds—a process that came to fruition for the Americans with remarkable rapidity. Similarly, despite various challenges to interwar military weapons development, the army deployed to war with well-organized units that found an appropriate balance between efficiency and effectiveness, while accounting for the chronic shortage of American shipping and the dramatically higher consumption rates of the army's mechanized and motorized units. Some weapons performed brilliantly from the beginning, like howitzers that delivered massed, observed artillery fires controlled by a Fire Direction Center and adjusted by skilled forward observers. Others performed well until overmatched in Western Europe, where the enemy enjoyed short supply lines and no shipping problems, and suitable replacement equipment did not appear until late in the war.

Significant inefficiencies at the War Department level and among the functional commands led to further problems—personnel shortages, challenges with the individual replacement system, inefficiencies caused by empire building and excessive overhead, and the establishment of deeply flawed processes for personnel classification that greatly disadvantaged the infantry, which bore the brunt of the fighting. These and other successes and shortcomings aside, the GI deployed to combat well trained, in logically organized units, with a mechanized combined arms doctrine that proved appropriate to the World War II battlefield. McNair played a key role in all of these factors, and in the end he proved brilliant but flawed, demonstrating the appropriateness of Marshall's nickname for him: the brains of the army. He built a reputation as both a pick-and-shovel man and one of the army's most intellectual officers, making innumerable contributions to army organization, doctrine, training, and innovation over a forty-year-long career that deserves a reassessment, as does the effectiveness of the AGF that he prepared to fight on battlefields around the world during World War II.

Epilogue

Although Lesley McNair served exclusively in staff positions during World War II, he routinely visited commanders in the field to observe training and evaluate leadership directly. This desire to see the results of his organization and training efforts firsthand led him to visit combat troops at the front on two occasions during the war. In 1943, McNair traveled to Tunisia to observe Army Ground Forces (AGF) troops. While watching American soldiers conducting an attack on April 23, during the final stages of the campaign to eject Rommel from North Africa, he suffered shrapnel wounds in the arm and head. This generated a significant amount of press coverage, in which some initial reports indicated he would be "out of action" for several weeks and credited his steel helmet for saving his life (a piece of shrapnel was embedded in his skull, less than an inch from his brain). True to form, McNair spent only two days in the hospital before beginning his return trip to the United States, and in a little more than a week, he was back at work at AGF headquarters.[1]

The dozens of accounts in newspapers and magazines that covered McNair's wound and recovery mostly provided a positive account of a dedicated general officer traveling to the front to observe the combat performance of the ground troops he had been responsible for training. Some accounts mentioned McNair's admission that his wounds resulted from his failure to follow his own training principles and observe the attack from a properly covered and concealed position, but even these stories placed McNair's conduct in a highly positive light. By contrast, Steven E. Clay, in his history of the 16th Infantry Regiment, provided a rather less enthusiastic portrayal of the event as recounted through the eyes of a soldier of the 1st Division who observed it:

An incident occurred this day that is at once humorous, tragic, and indicative of how the misinterpretation of a combat situation can cause unintended consequences. After the attack began that morning, efforts to speed up the regiment's forward movement drew criticism from a high-ranking visitor to the 1st Division, Lieutenant General Leslie [sic] J. McNair. McNair arrived in the 2nd Battalion's area to personally assess its attack: "F Company was pinned down on the ridge in front of us. General McNair wanted to see the action, apparently believing we weren't being aggressive enough. By exposing himself on the ridge, our position was subjected to artillery fire during which he was wounded and our F Company First Sergeant was killed. I remember the General's aides bringing him off the hill into a jeep and speeding away to the Bn [Battalion] Aid Station. So much for him."[2]

Although this passage is illustrative of the cynical humor often identified with the American infantry of World War II, it also offers a poignant reminder of the death of a company first sergeant in the same artillery barrage that wounded McNair— an event completely overlooked by the press in their frenzy to report the injury suffered by a senior officer. No media report of the artillery barrage that wounded McNair—at least none among the dozens that McNair's wife, Clare McNair, collected from newspapers all over America, mentioned this noncommissioned officer's death. McNair also apparently never spoke of it, indicating that he probably never learned of the first sergeant's death in the barrage. Neglecting to comment on such a tragedy would not fit McNair's character, particularly given his tireless efforts to acknowledge the bravery and sacrifice of the American infantryman seen in his many other speeches and interactions with the press.[3]

McNair returned to the front a second time in 1944, visiting Normandy to observe the breakout from the beachhead during Operation Cobra before proceeding to his new assignment to relieve Lieutenant General Patton as commander of the First US Army Group (FUSAG). The Allies created the simulated FUSAG headquarters, based in Dover, England, and placed it in command of some fictitious and some real units, including the Third Army, which had not yet departed for England as the Third US Army. Through an elaborate deception known as Operation Fortitude, involving false radio messages, newspaper stories, and an increase in both real and simulated military activity, FUSAG gave the appearance of an army group preparing an amphibious assault against the Pas de Calais. This worked quite effectively, preventing the Germans from predicting and massing defending forces at the location of the impending Allied amphibious assault, or even knowing after the D-Day assault whether the Allies planned a second landing. For quite some time, the Germans believed that the Normandy landings preceded what would be the main Allied amphibious assault at Pas de Calais.[4]

The deception worked exceptionally well—in fact, much better than anticipated. Eisenhower initially hoped for the deception to keep the Germans fooled for one or two days, just long enough for the Allies to get some additional forces onto the beaches before Hitler approved commitment of the German Panzer divisions near Pas de Calais to a counterattack against the Normandy landing forces. Through clever manipulation by double agents who provided just enough additional information to heighten German concern about the supposed strength of the notional FUSAG, Fortitude achieved remarkable success. One week after D-

Clare McNair Greets Lesley J. McNair at the Airport upon His Return Home from Tunisia, May 3, 1943. Courtesy of US National Archives II, College Park, Maryland

Day, only a single German division had departed the Pas de Calais defense to reinforce German troops in Normandy. As historian Ben MacIntyre put it, "German belief in the Phantom army was unshakable."[5] On July 6, with the Germans still fooled, Eisenhower reported to Marshall, "OVERLORD cover and deception plan (FORTITUDE) has proved remarkably effective. Reliable intelligence indicates that enemy is preparing for decisive Allied effort by 1st US Army Group in Pas de Calais area under the command of Patton."[6]

At least twenty-two German divisions remained in the Pas de Calais at the end of June, fixed there by the threat of Patton and the notional FUSAG. This meant

Clare and Lesley McNair Departing for Home after Lesley McNair's Return from Tunisia, May 3, 1943. Courtesy of US National Archives II, College Park, Maryland

that Germany had far fewer combat units to deal with the Normandy invasion force—an important advantage for the Allies—but Patton had to depart for Normandy in less than a month to take command of the Third US Army, inbound from the United States. The Allies needed a replacement for Patton with a similarly recognizable name.[7] Eisenhower had originally intended to give Bradley command of FUSAG, but his early arrival in Normandy made this infeasible. As an alternative, Eisenhower gave the notional command to Lieutenant General George S. Patton, who was actually a much better choice because the German army officer corps held him in high regard, and Hitler had once described him as America's best general.[8]

The inbound Fifteenth Army also needed a commander, and Eisenhower had several options to choose from for command of both the Fifteenth Army and FUSAG. Marshall and Eisenhower had already decided to reassign McNair to France, to a position not yet determined. As a *Time* article put it, "The training of US troops for World War II had reached its Indian summer. Now the chief of the AGF, shrewd, small Lieut. General Lesley James McNair, could go overseas."[9] With all division mobilizations finished, and key matters of policy worked out, the AGF had responsibility primarily for routine individual replacement training from this point on, so Marshall and Eisenhower believed that he could serve the army more

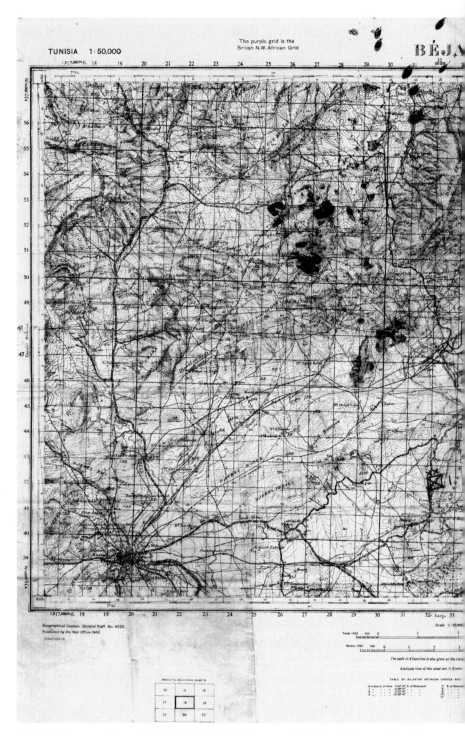

The Map Lieutenant General McNair Was Holding When Wounded in Tunisia (McNair heard artillery shells landing to his rear but did not realize he was wounded until seeing the bloodstains on the map), April 23, 1943. Courtesy of US National Archives II, College Park, Maryland

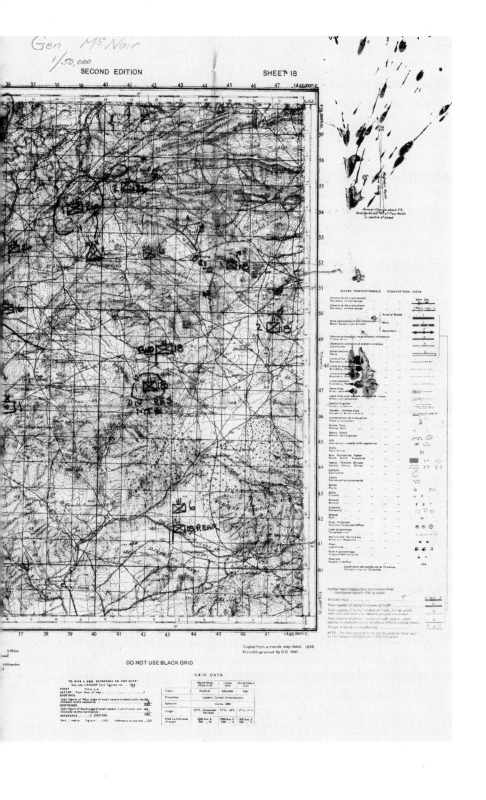

Gen. McNair
1/50,000

SECOND EDITION

SHEET 18

DO NOT USE BLACK GRID

Copied from a French map dated 1936
Photolithographed by O.S. 1942

GRID DATA

effectively at the front.[10] On July 22, Eisenhower wrote to Marshall to request that the Fifteenth Army headquarters deploy without a commander; he would select one from the officers in or soon to arrive in France. Eisenhower identified Truscott as his first choice, but this would require his reassignment from duty in the Mediterranean theater. If Marshall found this infeasible or had other plans for Truscott, Eisenhower viewed McNair and Major General Leonard T. Gerow as the next best candidates for the command of Fifteenth Army. Eisenhower wrote, "I am impressed constantly by McNair's soldierly qualities, although of course I have not seen him in actual command of a battle line and his deafness is at least a minor handicap. Gerow has shown all the qualities of vigor, determination, reliability and skill that we are looking for. If he continues as at present both Bradley and I believe he will be an excellent army commander."[11] The Fifteenth Army would not sail for France for some time, and it did not achieve operational status until January 6, 1945. As it turned out, Gerow assumed command of Fifteenth Army on January 16, 1945, and commanded the army through the end of the war.[12] Regardless, their consideration of McNair as a candidate for army command shows the high regard Marshall and Eisenhower still had for him in July 1944. In the meantime, McNair deployed to the European theater for utilization wherever Eisenhower felt he could best serve. Ultimately, he recommended McNair as Patton's replacement as FUSAG commander and received Marshall's approval.[13]

By the summer of 1944, McNair might have developed war weariness or even a dim view of the army's chances of success. For the past four years, he had struggled with uncooperative War Department staffers and with complaining battlefront commanders making requests that he had neither the resources nor the authority to provide. Perhaps most frustrating of all, he had found it surprisingly difficult to convince Marshall of the significance of the challenges that AGF faced and gain his support in resolving them—perhaps a result of AGF's low priority relative to the other two functional headquarters, AAF and Army Service Forces (ASF). Beginning with President Roosevelt, high-level political and civilian industrial leaders—along with many military leaders, including Marshall—began by 1942 to view World War II primarily as an air war. This resulted in the difficulty that McNair regularly faced when seeking support for AGF requirements if those requirements had any impact on Army Air Forces (AAF) priorities or demands. Similarly, when the manpower crisis of 1942 finally led military and civilian industrial leaders to acknowledge the obsolescence of the initial Victory program estimates of 1941, "American military planners," as David M. Kennedy put it, "now irrevocably embraced the concept of a war of machines rather than men."[14] This meant that instead of the massive army envisioned in 1941, American war planners adjusted the Victory plan to include the so-called 90-Division Gamble, intending the modern machines of war to compensate for this drastically reduced number of ground combat units. This war of machines required not only airplanes but also technicians, meaning that the ASF reached a higher level of stature than ever before achieved by service forces—a stature that perfectly suited the ambitious, empire-hungry Somervell.

The severe disparity in the quality, resourcing, and casualty rates of the AGF relative to the AAF and ASF made McNair's job particularly challenging, and probably quite frustrating. He did not establish a grip on the two most difficult problems related to these issues—the replacement problem and the problem of infantry quality—until 1943, and even after he finally convinced Marshall of their severity, so much damage had already been done that efforts to resolve them seemed more like crisis management than true solutions. Perhaps such challenges caused McNair to struggle with his own demons, although one can only speculate. He might have blamed himself for refusing to take direct control of the technical services of the AGF (like Arnold did in the AAF), thereby getting better equipment to his troops sooner, no matter how much this inefficiency and additional overhead ran contrary to his best military judgment. He might have wished that he had recognized the replacement problem and taken the initiative to resolve it for the AGF sooner than 1943, when the War Department directed him to do so (another inefficient but necessary duplication of effort). He might even have regretted not fighting harder to reduce the incredible amount of equipment that made the triangular division—with far fewer personnel than the square division—so much larger in terms of shipping space and supply requirements. This applied in particular to mechanized vehicles that trucks could easily have replaced, resulting in greater efficiency that might have delayed, if not prevented, the manpower crisis of 1942.

McNair expressed pessimism on at least one occasion regarding America's prospects for success in the war. On August 17, 1942, just after military leaders and civilian industrialists finally recognized the severity of the production shortages that the manpower crisis would cause, McNair wrote a letter to Colonel Milton A. Elliott Jr., the father of their only son's (Colonel Douglas Crevier McNair's) wife. He first informed Elliot that he should not expect the opportunity to serve on active duty because of his age, which exceeded the maximum for combat duty according to War Department policy. Then McNair wrote, as recorded in Greenfield's notes, "All is going along fairly well in these parts, except that I feel at times that we are not winning the war very fast. On the contrary, to be brutally frank, we are doing a bang-up job of losing it. Such being the case, it bids fair to be a long pull in which we should be able to crash through eventually."[15]

McNair never voiced such concerns in public or even to his close military associates, so one can only speculate whether this letter reflected a long-standing viewpoint or merely the venting of frustration to a family member on a particularly hard day. The former seems possible in light of McNair's demeanor when he bid his staff farewell, as recorded in the notes of one of his senior staff officers, who attended the brief session that took place on July 12, 1944. As the unidentified staff officer noted, the chiefs of the AGF staff sections received notice to attend a meeting in the S-Room at 11:00 A.M.:

> Gen. McNair himself appeared and sat down from us, across the table. He spoke in a low voice, and some of his words were lost to me under the roar of the air-cooling machine in the corner. He was a little pale. He may have been under emotional stress. I suspected that he was. But if he was, the only visible indication was that he seemed to be holding himself in tightly. What he said was substantially as follows:
>
> "I have not had many staff meetings. I have called this one because it is the last. I have been relieved of command of the Army Ground Forces, and assigned to a mission overseas. Where I am going, and what the mission is, have not yet been disclosed by the War Department. [. . .] We have done a big job, and its effectiveness is beginning to be seen. Our work has been criticized, as was inevitable, but I think that I can say that it has received a minimum of criticism. Much of the credit is due to you and to those who have gone before you, as members of this staff. There have been as many as two million and more men in AGF. There are now a million and a half. These figures are a measure of what has been done and what remains to be done. The task ahead is to get these million and a half ready for combat. Our training has improved and equipment is more abundant, so that the results should be better in the future than in the past. [. . .] I wish you all good luck."
>
> Gen. McNair then stood and shook hands with each of us. When he had finished, we saluted and he went out.[16]

The staff officer concluded by noting that the same group of section chiefs met with their new commander, Lieutenant General Lear, at 9:00 A.M. the next day.

This rather stiff, oddly formal farewell demonstrated McNair's discomfort with meetings and conferences (a result of his long-standing hearing loss) and indicated that he probably developed an increasingly introverted nature in the latter years of his career, when he worked long hours, mostly alone with his typewriter. His apparent emotional distress could indicate his disappointment at leaving AGF after two years of hard work, without having the chance to observe the ultimate success of AGF's labors. Perhaps not knowing what position he would next hold also concerned him. No reason exists to believe McNair feared service at the front, as illustrated by his rather impulsive display of bravery during his visit to the front in Tunisia.

From McNair's actions upon arrival in the European Theater of Operations, it seems that he still had no appreciable fear of exposure to combat. Much as Patton had done in southern England months before, McNair began a tour of Allied headquarters in France upon his arrival in the European theater, a tour that would later seem an appropriate action for the new FUSAG commander.[17] He took advantage of this opportunity to observe his beloved ground forces in action, arriving at the First US Army command post, about fifteen miles north of St. Lô, on the evening of July 23, 1944. Anxious to observe the beginning of the carefully orchestrated American breakout, Operation Cobra (already delayed for two days by weather that prevented the planned preparatory bombing by P-47 dive-bombers followed by B-24 strategic bombers), McNair went to the front, accompanied by his pilot, Colonel Jones, and his aide, Major Narramore. Although the weather once again proved unsuitable for aviation support, the air corps did not receive this information until after the bombers departed. Attempts to recall them proved largely unsuccessful, and while some bombers, upon arriving at the objective, realized the weather obscured the target area too badly to attempt the strike, others dropped their bombs. General Courtney Hodges and his party, observing the preparatory bombing from a forward observation post, could see that most of the P-47s dropped their 100-pound bombs on target, although one group struck an American ammunition truck, and another, clearly well off course, dropped its full load of bombs well northwest of the intended objective area. Otherwise, the P-47s largely remained on target for the rest of their part in the bombing—and then the B-24s arrived, about 200 of them. Hodges's party soon heard the unmistakable shrieking whistle of approaching bombs and rushed for cover. Bombs landed several hundred yards away from them. They experienced no serious injuries, but other American personnel were not so lucky. General Bradley had also already called off the ground attack, but the inaccurate bombing killed seventeen and injured eighty American troops.[18]

McNair, in his car when the bombing stopped while his aide looked for a suitable point from which to observe, did not hear the bombs approaching the friendly troops; his pilot had to push him out of the car to get him to cover. Despite this near miss in an Allied preparatory bombing mission deemed a fiasco by ground personnel and aviators alike, McNair insisted on returning to the front lines the next day, July 25. The bombing led to even worse results on July 25, but despite the number of Allied casualties, the bombing also achieved the desired effect against the German defenders, and Cobra commenced, achieving great success. The First Army's satisfaction with the ground assault lessened somewhat when Hodges returned to his command post and learned that the friendly casualties to inaccurate bombing runs greatly exceeded those of the previous day. A final accounting calculated the cost of the short bomb drops as nearly 600 personnel,

Lesley J. McNair's United States Military Academy Graduation Ring, Found on the Battlefield after His Death, July 1944. Photograph by Dr. Christopher Grant Wright

almost 100 of whom died. The 30th Division suffered 90 percent of the casualties from the errant bombs, including Colonel Harry A. Flint, a beloved regimental commander.[19] This division took more casualties from the AAF on July 25 than the enemy inflicted on it during any single day of the war. As Rick Atkinson noted, "Men screamed for medics and raged against the 'American Luftwaffe.'"[20]

Shortly after Hodges's return to his command post, McNair's aide and pilot rushed in, expressing great concern for General McNair. They thought that they had convinced him after the previous day's near miss to remain farther to the rear on July 25, but after an unidentified individual told McNair, "The troops sure like to see you up front," he changed his mind. Only several hedgerows away from the German front lines when the bombing began, McNair occupied, according to his aide, a foxhole about thirty yards from him. When the bombing stopped, the major ran to the foxhole, where he discovered a large crater. He organized a search party, but after much digging, he had still found no trace of the general, at which point he reported to Hodges. When the last of the bombing runs ended, Hodges attempted to reach the position but could not because of enemy activity. After a check of the local clearing station and evacuation hospitals in the area, combat activity in the area died down, and Narramore and Jones returned to the area where they had last seen McNair. Eventually they heard a rumor that a general had died up the road. After proceeding forward another 200 yards, they found McNair's body, thrown by a bomb blast to where it now lay, identifiable only by the shoulder patch and general's stars. McNair's West Point class ring later appeared in a search of the area.[21]

US army press officers in London initially reported McNair's death as the result of German fire; they were directed to do so by senior leaders who did not want to jeopardize the Fortitude deception. However, by August 1944, the army finally admitted that he died as a result of a poorly aimed American aerial barrage.[22] His early death prevented McNair from witnessing the eventual successes of the ground forces he worked so diligently to prepare for combat. In a final cruel twist of fate, his only son, Colonel Douglas C. McNair, died twelve days later, on August 6, 1944, in the Pacific Theater of Operations, killed by a Japanese sniper while serving as chief of staff of the 77th Division on Guam.[23]

Clare McNair learned of her husband's death while rolling bandages at the War College officers' club for the Red Cross, one of many volunteer activities in which she had engaged throughout his career. A general officer from the AGF entered the room, sat down, and spoke to her briefly, then escorted her out of the room. Among the dozens of letters of condolence that Clare received in the period after her husband's death, her correspondence with General John Pershing merits particular mention. The McNairs had maintained contact with General Pershing throughout McNair's career, and Pershing was one of the first to contact Clare directly upon her husband's death. On July 28, Clare received a letter from him that read:

> The sad news of the untimely death, at the front, of your distinguished husband has shocked and grieved me, and my deepest sympathy goes out to you. General McNair's services with the Punitive Expedition, and with the A.E.F. in France, are, of course, entirely familiar to me, and I have followed his subsequent brilliant career with particular interest and great admiration. Certainly, his contribution to the success of our present war effort has been considerable. In his passing the leadership of our armed forces has been dealt a severe blow. Indeed, the army, the country, and the United Nations have suffered a tremendous loss.

Clare replied on August 1, 1944, just five days before Doug's death, thanking Pershing for his kind letter and expressing her appreciation for his complimentary words about her husband's military service. She sent him a birthday greeting a month later, from Santa Barbara, California, where she had traveled after Doug's death to stay with Doug's widow and help care for his daughter, Clare's only grandchild, Bonnie Clare McNair. Clare described Bonnie Clare, only eleven months old at the time, as "a precious baby and so happy that she is bringing healing to our broken hearts."[24]

McNair received his only military awards earned during World War II posthumously. On August 3, 1944, Secretary of War Stimson presented Clare with two oak leaf clusters for the Distinguished Service Medal her husband had earned in France during World War I and an oak leaf cluster for his Purple Heart. Various senior military and political leaders paid tribute to McNair on May 25, 1945, at a ceremony at the Army War College. Army Chief of Staff General George C. Marshall and General Courtney H. Hodges, commander of the First Army, made remarks in remembrance of McNair's efforts as AGF commander. The ceremony

General Lesley J. McNair's Headstone and Grave Site in France. Photograph by Carol Pollard

closed with Bonnie Clare McNair unveiling a commemorative plaque that read, in part, "As commanding general of the AGF he planned, organized, trained, and equipped the ground forces of the United States for their victorious participation in the Second World War."[25]

Despite the high praise and obvious respect he had earned from many of the nation's most senior military and civilian leaders, McNair did not die a wealthy man. In fact, as *Time* reported in 1944, when McNair died at the age of sixty-one, after forty years of military service, he left behind an estate worth only $2,720. To supplement this small nest egg—typical of officers of the time who received meager pay and benefits—Clare received the pension of a retired major general (McNair had never received permanent promotion to lieutenant general), which amounted to $50 a month. Required to vacate military quarters upon his death, Clare moved out of the home where she and Lesley had recently celebrated their thirty-ninth wedding anniversary, renting a small apartment on Connecticut Avenue in Washington, DC, and accepting a job with the US State Department to make ends meet.[26]

Senate Bill 2468, first proposed in 1952, sought to secure permanent promo-

Honorable Henry L. Stimson Awarding to Clare McNair Two Oak Leaf Clusters for General McNair's Distinguished Service Medal as General George C. Marshall Observes, The Pentagon, August 1, 1944. Courtesy of the Military History Institute

tion to their highest position for the many retired and deceased officers who, like McNair, had served as high-ranking generals during the war, but because of the temporary nature of their promotions, had reverted to their highest permanent grade at the war's end. Secretary of the Army Frank Pace Jr. wrote a letter to Honorable Richard B. Russell, chairman of the US Senate committee on armed services, urging him to support this bill, which he sought to "provide suitable recognition of the distinguished services of these officers rendered in positions of great responsibility and importance. . . . The promotions to be authorized by this legislation would be in keeping with the rank accorded other Army officers who held similar wartime commands during the same limiting periods." Because Lesley McNair had served as a temporary lieutenant general but had worked directly for the army chief of staff in a command considered equivalent to an army group command, the measure, if it passed, would lead to a posthumous promotion for him to general (four star). This would also improve Clare's financial situation—a desire expressed by several supporters of the bill who were friends of the McNairs before and during the war. The Senate finally passed the bill on May 4, 1954, and it gained the House of Representative's approval on July 7, 1954. Shortly afterward, Clare McNair received a letter from the adjutant general's office notifying her of Lesley McNair's posthumous promotion to (four-star) general, effective September 10, 1954.[27] What the gruff McNair would have thought of such recognition of his contributions to America's victory, one can only speculate.

General Lesley J. McNair has long remained an enigma to many military historians. As has been noted in this study, few historians have written about McNair's service as commandant at Fort Leavenworth, chief of staff of the proposed infantry division, or chief artillery training officer on the American Expeditionary Force (AEF) staff. Even fewer (though Edward Coffman is an exception) have written about McNair's pre–World War I service, and even these historians have revealed the history of only a tiny fraction of his thirteen years of service before World War I. The history of the thirty-six years of his career before World War II has remained, until now, mostly scattered among various archives, and those aspects of his World War II service that do appear in the secondary literature consist in nearly equal measure of accepted wisdom and objective history.

McNair's relative obscurity among senior US military leaders of that era chiefly resulted from his wartime service in staff positions. Even when he served as commander of AGF, from 1942 to 1944, he led a functional command, giving him a role many historians equate to a senior-level staff position. The long-standing belief that no records of McNair's early career existed might have contributed to this phenomenon, but in the end, this seems unlikely because the records cited here were no harder to obtain than others stored at various major historical archives in the United States. Whatever the reason, many historians of World War II have analyzed General McNair's performance in his two key roles at General Headquarters and AGF based on limited knowledge of the history of his thirty-six years of service before the war.

One example serves to drive this point home. A panelist at the 2010 Society for Military History Conference demonstrated quite effectively the result of the widespread lack of knowledge regarding General McNair when he opined that, with respect to the army's mobilization for World War II, "McNair got everything wrong."[28] This statement reflects far more than one individual's shallow understanding of McNair's contributions to the mobilization effort the nation undertook beginning in 1940. It reflects the generally poorly informed view of McNair's service throughout his forty-year career held by many historians who study the early twentieth-century army. However, even lacking detailed knowledge of the history of McNair's military service, one might hesitate to dismiss so readily the efforts of a man entrusted by officers like John Pershing, Charles Summerall, Malin Craig, and George Marshall with some of the most important innovative efforts and positions of responsibility in the army.

McNair Hall—Headquarters Building at Present-Day Fort Sill, Oklahoma, Home of the Field Artillery Branch. Courtesy of Fort Sill Public Affairs Office

General Pershing selected McNair from the many officers on the 1st Division staff to serve as the senior artillery training officer in the AEF General Headquarters in 1918, rapidly promoting him to become the AEF's youngest general officer. Shortly after the war, Charles Summerall selected McNair to serve as the Hawaiian Department G-3 operations officer and to lead both the development of a new Oahu defense plan and a major experiment to test the ability of army units to defend an island from a naval attack. Chief of Staff Malin Craig selected McNair in the mid-1930s for the chief of staff position in the Proposed Infantry Division, making him the key individual responsible for designing and testing the first version of the triangular division that the army employed during World War II. In 1939, General Marshall handpicked McNair to serve first as the commandant at Fort Leavenworth to restructure the officer education system there, and later to serve first as chief of staff, General Headquarters, and then as the AGF commander—the main individual responsible for training the American ground forces that fought World War II. Even in the summer of 1944, after so much had gone poorly for the AGF despite McNair's best efforts, Eisenhower and Marshall saw fit to send him to Europe to command FUSAG, while considering him as a leading candidate for command of Fifteenth Army. It seems strange, when one considers the long-standing professional respect, based on direct, personal interaction that officers like generals Pershing, Craig, Eisenhower, and Marshall had for McNair, that later historians would arrive at negative assessments of his duty performance. McNair's subordinates and superiors held him in high regard, and he rose steadily through a series of extremely demanding jobs that elevated him to positions of significant authority and responsibility from his earliest combat service to his final years in the army.

Perhaps the lack of information on McNair's early career in the historical record left him open for criticism, even making him seem the most likely source of the various inefficiencies that plagued the AGF's performance during World War II. This study has sought, through thorough analysis of the depth and breadth of McNair's experience, combined with a closer look at the factors that created significant inefficiencies in the nation's and the War Department's management of the mobilization effort, to provide an objective assessment of McNair's performance throughout his career, including his World War II service. This analysis suggests that McNair might not deserve some of the criticism that historians have leveled against him—and to whatever degree he did err in his actions during his career, or exhibited atypical behavior and unusual personality traits, his many achievements—that easily outweigh his errors—have remained lost in archival records for too long. Historians' limited knowledge of McNair's background did not necessarily make their assessments of his actions in various positions wrong, but reassessing those actions within the context of the full span of his career, as well as the various national-level strategic and political processes that exceeded McNair's span of control, offers a new perspective on his performance. It is time to reconsider the existing historical understanding of Lesley J. McNair and simultaneously to continue the ongoing revision of the standard narrative of World War II as a story of American material preponderance overcoming the US army's inept soldiers, overmatched equipment and doctrine, and lackluster performance of its so-called workmanlike generals.

The evidence necessary to overturn this flawed narrative exists. Through the efforts of a growing number of revisionist historians, one can access much of the evidence in the secondary literature on the early twentieth-century US army. One hopes that this effort to achieve an accurate and balanced assessment will continue, and detailed searches for additional data in the historical archives will yield further evidence and prompt additional insights. Historians have made great strides in the past two decades to improve modern understanding of the US army's military effectiveness during World War II and the various innovations that enabled the army to achieve that effectiveness. These historians' work remains unfinished, however—only through a prolonged effort will they overturn the long and resilient historical interpretation that evaluates America's military effectiveness during World War II and finds it lacking.

This study contains various insights and assessments intended to contribute to this effort. The fact that an individual's archival records do not exist in a consolidated record stored at a single location does not mean those records do not exist. An officer's service primarily in staff roles should not lead historians to the conclusion that officer's career does not merit detailed historical analysis. Arguably, the addition of yet another biography of a colorful figure like George Patton to the historical literature adds little to the existing store of "great commander" histories, many of which seem to offer less original analysis than the last. Perhaps the deepest and most plentiful area in which to conduct historical research of the early twentieth-century army lies precisely in the much-neglected field of the staff officer. In an army often described as commander-centric, the explanation for victory or defeat lies remarkably often in the capabilities and actions of the staff and its degree of integration with the commander.

The foregoing analysis provides an example of the wealth of insights one can gain by developing a deeper understanding of the experience and ideas of one such staff officer. Important continuities stretch across the four decades of McNair's career. Each of these help explain his contributions in the critical final four years of his career, particularly when viewed within the larger context of the many complexities presented by America's interwar isolationist stance and economic crisis, and the dysfunction of the civil–military relationship that hamstrung the mobilization effort. Contrary to many critical analyses, McNair developed a remarkably accurate concept of modern warfare. In those areas that fell within his span of control, McNair provided invaluable service to the nation in preparing the army to fight in the conditions he anticipated they would face. In doing so, he established a model for the army training system that is still in use today. In those areas where McNair has drawn the most criticism, such as his advocacy of anti-tank guns, minimal overhead, streamlining, pooling, and task organization, the analysis offered here demonstrates that McNair did not invent and impose these concepts on the ground forces. While the war-long shortage of adequate shipping, the production crisis of 1942, and the vast overhead that limited availability of officers and soldiers to serve in line units demonstrate the wisdom of these initiatives, his efforts to adhere to them represent implementation of War Department policy and of General George C. Marshall's ultimate decision-making authority— not McNair's. At most, one can credit McNair for his early support of such initiatives and his skillful implementation of them. He did so in a manner that achieved both the War Department's desired increases in efficiency and improvement of the army's effectiveness as it learned to task organize using its pooled units and use the immense firepower it could bring to bear to facilitate maneuver by relatively light, vulnerable vehicles as members of resilient combined arms teams.

When one considers the scope of McNair's career, which includes experience in a wide range of peacetime and combat positions as a commander, staff officer, educator, war planner, and expert trainer, several threads of continuity emerge. The continuities identifiable in McNair's early career help explain how an officer steeped in the experience of World War I navigated a myriad of contingencies throughout the difficult years of the interwar period—and the significant challenges of national mobilization—enabling him to train a capable ground force despite innumerable obstacles. These continuities included high standards of officer competence and physical fitness, an emphasis on maneuver and flexibility enabled by responsive and devastating firepower and combined arms operations, a long-term dedication to professional education, an understanding of the efficiency achieved through streamlining and pooling, and a constant quest for innovative solutions to long-standing problems. One sees evidence of these continuities throughout the first three and a half decades of McNair's career and their recurrence in the final four years of his career, when he reached the height of his influence.

By recognizing and grasping the significance of these continuities as well as the relevance they provided to McNair's ideas regarding modern warfare and the combined arms doctrine and training necessary to execute it, one can see the presence of various contingencies often overlooked in studies containing broad-brush depictions of McNair. This makes possible a more balanced evaluation of his successes and shortcomings and an understanding of the many factors that limited McNair's authority and freedom of action—factors that he lacked the ability to control. These systemic issues remain the centerpiece of the largely untold story of World War II and the twentieth-century US army in general.

Ideally, the foregoing analysis not only enhances historical understanding of the career of General Lesley McNair but also highlights the need to conduct further such studies. Historians of the US army can break free of the conventional wisdom of World War II by moving beyond analyses of tactics and technology to the systemic issues that serve as the root causes of US army effectiveness. Studies in this vein remain relevant for understanding US army effectiveness not only during McNair's lifetime but also in the nearly seventy years since he died while observing the ground forces he trained as they fought their yearlong campaign to defeat the German army in the European Theater of Operations. The ground forces did not accomplish this feat because of material preponderance; in fact, logistics shortages and the 90-Division Gamble shaped the complexion of America's war effort. America's dysfunctional civil–military industrial mobilization effort ensured that the nation never achieved its production goals or synchronized its military and industrial production strategies. Despite the resulting challenges, the ground forces fought effectively even under the leadership of supposedly workmanlike generals like Eisenhower. His understanding of logistics and its effect on the conduct of operational art in Western Europe enabled him to see the logic of the broad front strategy and doggedly adhere to it despite some subordinates' desire to pursue a more aggressive operational approach. More importantly, America's ground combat troops fought effectively during World War II by relying on the fundamental ideas that McNair helped to develop throughout the interwar period. These ideas guided the mobilization training and doctrine development that provided the foundation for America's mechanized, combined arms fighting methods, instilled in the psyche of the American soldier by the most effective prewar mobilization training effort the nation has ever implemented.

Notes

PREFACE

1. "Lesley J. McNair to Andrew D. Bruce," June 11, 1943, NARA 2, RG 319, Box 129, Folder 2. Typical of his stiffly formal, professional demeanor—even with people close to him—McNair wrote, "I am delighted that Doug is with you. . . . Please make a good chief of staff out of him, for he certainly is not one at this moment."

INTRODUCTION

1. Whitaker, "Lieutenant General Lesley James McNair," 126; Herbert M. Jones to Mrs. Lesley J. McNair, September 10, 1954, McNair Papers, NARA, St. Louis; Kahn, *McNair*.

2. For example, McNair's entire personnel file still exists intact at the National Archives and Records Administration (NARA) Office in St. Louis, Missouri— hundreds of pages of data from 1919 to 1944. (His personnel file for 1904 to 1919 remains available at NARA 1 in Washington, DC.) Regardless, I have yet to encounter a book that cites any references from McNair's personnel file. Numerous additional archival sources—either unused or previously unknown—appear in the references below, many of which offer a new perspective on the prevailing views regarding McNair in existing histories of World War II.

3. Few previous secondary sources exist that focus on McNair himself and none qualify as a military life or provide significant detail on his contributions to the US army during his forty years of service. Lehner and Lehner, "McNair," 10; Kleber, "Lesley James McNair"; John T. Whitaker, "These Are the Generals—McNair," *Saturday Evening Post*, January 30, 1943, 123–126; Kahn, *McNair*, 50–54. These four works, the only previous sources containing any significant amount of biographical information on Lesley McNair, provide a narrative of McNair's career that is far from complete. The Lehners' short paper is an admirable but amateur tribute to Verndale's most famous hometown boy and contains various factual errors. Kahn's sixty-four-page essay lacks documentation and serves more as eulogy than biography. Whitaker's interview-based article consists mostly of anecdotes aimed at the general reader, and Kleber's three-page essay provides only a short biographical sketch intended to give readers a feel for McNair's personality and work habits.

4. For a rare exception, see Coffman, *Regulars*. The papers appear to be the personal office files that McNair left behind when he departed for service in Europe in 1944.

5. The Green Books, the US army official histories of World War II, did much to emphasize the last four years of McNair's career and his expertise as an organizer and trainer of troops. No other period of his career can be studied in such detail without access to archival sources. See, for example, Greenfield, Palmer, and Wiley, *Organization of Ground Combat Troops;* Palmer, Wiley, and Keast, *Procurement and Training.* Much less information exists in the secondary literature on McNair's service during the First World War, but some sources briefly address the period, including Kleber, "Lesley James McNair."

6. For McNair's thoughts on adjudicating differences of opinion between field commanders and War Department staff officers, see Lesley J. McNair to Ernest N. Harmon, April 3, 1944, NARA 2, RG 319, Box 129, Folder 2. For a particularly useful source highlighting the tension between the War Department's Operations Division and its three subordinate headquarters, see War Department Operations Division, "Operations Division Files: Office of the Director of Plans and Operations, War Department," January 1942–July 1944, NARA 2, RG 165, Entry 422, Boxes 40–48. McNair's peers at Army Air Forces and Army Service Forces held greater influence with the War Department than McNair throughout the war.

7. Blumenson, "America's World War II Leaders in Europe." Blumenson coined the term "workmanlike generals" to distinguish between what he called the bland, plodding, prudent officers that America's interwar army produced from the more daring, imaginative, and brilliant general officers that America needed (noting George S. Patton as an exception). He blamed the personal deficiencies and ill-preparedness of American officers for various embarrassing setbacks and claimed that far too many remained fixed in a World War I mind-set, leaving them surprised by and unable to adapt to the speed and dispersion of the modern battlefield of the 1940s. He credited the professional military education system for what little insight and intellectual capacity most officers developed between the wars, but he described the dull routine of service during the intewar years as the main contributor to American officers' effectiveness or lack thereof, as demonstrated by their poor record of accomplishment in the war in Europe.

8. Quoted in Kennedy, *Freedom from Fear,* 465. By Churchill's own account, he knew once he heard the news of the Japanese attack at Pearl Harbor that the Axis Powers' fate was sealed: "So we had won after all . . . !" (quoted at 523). In reality, Churchill concerned himself first with gaining assurance from Roosevelt that this change in the strategic situation would not reduce the amount of war supplies that the United States currently provided Britain through lend-lease. Given the demands of rapid mobilization that America now faced, while continuing to provide war matériel unabated at pre–Pearl Harbor levels to Great Britain and Russia, it seems remarkable that anyone believed at the time that America possessed a limitless arsenal of democracy.

9. Murray and Millett, *War to Be Won,* 428; emphasis added.

10. "Army and Navy—Lessons of Combat," *Time*, March 15, 1943, 59.

11. Coffman, *Regulars*, 233–371.

12. For two recent descriptions of the benefit of interwar discourse in preparing the US army for World War II, see Schifferle, *America's School for War;* and Matheny, *Carrying the War to the Enemy*.

13. As Matheny explained, "All the functions of operational art—maneuver, logistics, intelligence, and command and control—come together in the art of campaign planning." In all of these areas, America emerged from World War I and its interwar education system with a "modern staff system and a framework of operational art that allowed for effective campaign planning in World War II." Matheny, *Carrying the War to the Enemy*, 258–260.

14. Matheny, *Carrying the War to the Enemy*, 258–264.

15. Creveld, *Fighting Power*, 168.

16. Astore, "Loving the German War Machine," 7.

17. For critiques of Martin van Creveld's 1982 book *Fighting Power: German and US Army Peformance, 1939–1945,* see book reviews by Milan Hauner and by Patrick M. Morgan.

18. Eisenhower to Bernard Law Montgomery, *Papers of Dwight David Eisenhower,* vol. 4, pt. 8, chap. 22, "Single Thrust versus Broad Front," http://eisenhower.press.jhu.edu/.

19. Showalter, *Patton and Rommel,* back cover. For a more balanced analysis, see the main text, 372–378.

20. Colley, *Decision at Strasbourg,* 158–159. Colley also claimed that "Eisenhower lacked the hard-nosed attributes necessary for effective combat command," a surprisingly harsh criticism to level against the general who alone bore the responsibility of authorizing the incredibly risky and costly D-Day landings in Normandy, despite predictions of possible poor weather that could keep Allied aircraft from flying when the ground troops most needed their support. Eisenhower's bold leadership was never clearer than on this day, June 5, 1944, when he authorized the assault for the next day and then privately penned a letter for release to the press in the event the landings failed, assuming full responsibility for the decision and the outcome. See Ambrose, *D-Day,* 188–190.

21. Calhoun, review of Colley, *Decision at Strasbourg,* 51–52.

22. Winton, *Corps Commanders of the Bulge*.

23. Johnson, "From Frontier Constabulary to Modern Army," 192. Johnson asserted that McNair, "a powerful man," on his own authority imposed his ideas about antitank doctrine on the army and created the Tank Destroyer Command.

24. Johnson, *Fast Tanks,* 101–103, 224.

25. Although Odom remained outwardly impartial regarding McNair, his emphasis on the flawed 1939 manual and comparatively brief coverage of the much-improved

1941 version leaves the reader with a poor impression of McNair's contribution to army doctrine. Odom, *After the Trenches,* 128–131, 151–152. Regardless, just this description of McNair's direct involvement in the publication of the operations doctrine that the army used for most of the war casts doubt on Johnson's dismissal of McNair's accomplishments at CGSS.

26. Miller, *Nothing Less Than Full Victory,* 16. Research shows that letters McNair received from listeners writing in support of his remarks greatly outnumber those from listeners writing in protest of it; Various, "Folder: Letters in Response to McNair's 1942 Armistice Day Address," 1942, McNair Papers, US Library of Congress Archives.

27. Miller, *Nothing Less Than Full Victory,* 273. By 1940 McNair possessed a broad range of experience that made him much more than merely an artilleryman.

28. Weigley, *Amerian Way of War;* Linn and Weigley, "*The American Way of War* Revisited." To Linn's critique, Weigley replied, "I have to thank Brian McAllister Linn not only for the generous things he has to say about my book, but also for doing for me much of the rethinking that I have been unwilling to put on paper for myself. With a keen eye he has discerned the shortcomings that I would have to try to remedy if I reconsidered the book. I do not substantially quarrel with his critique." Linn, "*American Way of War* Revisited," 531.

29. Bonn, *When the Odds Were Even,* 52–65.

30. Doubler, *Closing with the Enemy,* 10–30.

31. Ibid., 63–86. "Doctrinal vacuum" quoted from 84.

32. Reardon, *Victory at Mortain,* 11, 85.

33. Ibid., 11–12.

34. Mansoor, *GI Offensive in Europe,* 5.

35. Rush, *Hell in Hürtgen Forest,* xvi.

36. Schifferle, *America's School for War,* 189–190.

37. Ibid., 190–191. Put simply, excessive focus on the boldness or daring of certain combat leaders distracts from the fundamentals necessary to establish true effectiveness in a combat leader. These fundamentals include both effective leadership and followership, knowledge of doctrine, loyalty to superiors and subordinates, steadiness and rationality, and a willingness to do what must be done to win without concern about personal gain or the state of one's reputation.

38. Matheny, *Carrying the War to the Enemy,* xiv–xv.

39. Robert Goldich, *The Best Defense* (blog), June 20, 2013, "Atkinson's 'Guns at Last Light': Even Better Than You Think, for These 5 Reasons," book review of Rick Atkinson, *The Guns at Last Light: The War in Western Europe, 1944–1945,* http://ricks .foreignpolicy.com/.

40. Ibid.; Jones, "Education of the Supreme Commander"; Lynch, "Supreme Allied Commander's Operational Approach."

41. Coffman, *Regulars,* 323.

42. Wheeler, "Marshall's Forgotten Men," 49–52; Taaffe, *Marshall and His Generals,* 6.

CHAPTER 1. FROM CADET TO COMMANDER:
BIRTH OF AN INNOVATOR

1. McNair, *McNair, McNear, and McNeir Genealogies: Supplement, 1950,* 833; Lehner and Lehner, "McNair," 9.

2. McNair, *McNair, McNear, and McNeir Genealogies: Supplement, 1950,* 833; Lehner and Lehner, "McNair," 9–10.

3. Lehner and Lehner, "McNair," 9–10; Adjutant General, "Summary of Efficiency Reports and Account of Services," 1917, McNair Papers, NARA, St. Louis.

4. Lehner and Lehner, "McNair," 10.

5. During McNair's four years at West Point, the curriculum only included drawing during the cadets' second and third years, and only offered ordnance and gunnery, and military efficiency in their fourth year. McNair's talent for drawing, ordnance and gunnery, and mathematics remained consistent throughout his active duty career. West Point, "Official Register of the Officers and Cadets," 1901, 17; 1902, 15; 1903, 12; and 1904, 10.

6. Lehner and Lehner, "McNair," 10.

7. West Point, "Official Register of the Officers and Cadets," 1901.

8. "Adjutant General: Consolidated Cross Reference Card, Personnel File of Lesley J. McNair (Pre-1919)," McNair Papers, NARA 1; Adjutant General, "Summary of Efficiency Reports and Account of Services," 1917, McNair Papers, NARA, St. Louis; Kahn, *McNair,* 52; Lehner and Lehner, "McNair," 10.

9. Adjutant General, "Summary of Efficiency Reports and Account of Services, 1917"; "Personnel File of Lesley J. McNair (Pre-1919)."

10. Adjutant General, "Summary of Efficiency Reports and Account of Services, 1917"; "Personnel File of Lesley J. McNair (Pre-1919)."

11. Adjutant General, "Summary of Efficiency Reports and Account of Services, 1917"; "Personnel File of Lesley J. McNair (Pre-1919)."

12. Adjutant General, "Summary of Efficiency Reports and Account of Services, 1917"; "Personnel File of Lesley J. McNair (Pre-1919)."

13. Adjutant General, "Summary of Efficiency Reports and Account of Services, 1917"; "Personnel File of Lesley J. McNair (Pre-1919)." McNair accepted promotion to first lieutenant in the field artillery on May 20, 1907, but simultaneously earned temporary promotion to captain for the duration of his branch detail. This final efficiency report from McNair's detail in the Ordnance Department makes it appear even more likely that his relatively poor evaluations by Major Wheeler probably have more to do with a personality conflict than any limited capability on McNair's part. McNair's evaluations from all the other officers he worked for, including two other Ordnance Branch supervisors, describe McNair's performance in much more favorable terms.

14. Adjutant General, "Summary of Efficiency Reports and Account of Services, 1917."

15. Ibid.; Kahn, *McNair,* 52; Coffman, *Regulars,* 153–154.

16. US Ordnance Department, *Handbook of the 2.95-Inch Mountain Gun Matériel and Pack Outfit.*

17. Lesley J. McNair, "Report of 1st Lieut. Lesley J. McNair on Ammunition Carriers for Mountain Artillery," May 17, 1912, and "Report of 1st Lieut. L. J. McNair, 4th Field Artillery on Organization and Equipment of Mountain Artillery," September 12, 1912, both in NARA 2, RG 337, Entry 58, Box 5; US Army War Department, *Drill Regulations for Mountain Artillery.*

18. McKenney, *Organizational History of Field Artillery,* 99.

19. Ibid., 101.

20. Adjutant General, "Summary of Efficiency Reports and Account of Services, 1917"; "Personnel File of Lesley J. McNair (Pre-1919)." McNair also found time while at Fort D. A. Russell to earn certificates of proficiency in field engineering, military law, the field service regulations, and military administration.

21. Major William Lassiter, "Official Extract, Report of Inspector General, Maneuver Division, San Antonio, Texas," May 6, 1911, NARA 2, RG 337, Entry 58, Box 5.

22. Ibid.

23. Adjutant General, "Summary of Efficiency Reports and Account of Services, 1917"; "Personnel File of Lesley J. McNair (Pre-1919)."

24. Lesley J. McNair, "Mountain Artillery Board Report," February 25, 1912, NARA 2, RG 337, Entry 58, Box 5.

25. McNair, "Report on Ammunition Carriers for Mountain Artillery," May 17, 1912, NARA 2, RG 337, Entry 58, Box 5; US Army War Department, *Drill Regulations for Mountain Artillery.*

26. Ibid.

27. Ibid.

28. McNair, "Report on Organization and Equipment of Mountain Artillery," September 1912, NARA 2, RG 337, Entry 58, Box 5; US Army War Department, *Drill Regulations for Mountain Artillery.* McNair provided his own detailed engineering drawings for his proposed design, demonstrating the skill he had developed in drawing and mathematics at business school and West Point, and during his four-year detail to Ordnance Branch.

29. Coffman, *Regulars,* 154; Kahn, *McNair,* 54; Collins, "Pack Saddles," 343–345.

30. Collins, "Pack Saddles," 343–345, at 344.

31. Beaver, *Modernizing the American War Department,* 60–62.

32. Ibid., 62–63.

33. Field Artillery School of Fire Commandant, "Detail of Statistical Officer," November 24, 1912; "Special Orders No. 283," December 3, 1912; and War Department, "Memo Directing Travel to France to Observe French Artillery," July 2, 1913, all in McNair Papers, NARA 1.

34. Examining Board, "Examination for Promotion, Effective Date April 19, 1914," January 13, 1913, McNair Papers, NARA 1; Adjutant General, "Summary of Efficiency

Reports and Account of Services, 1917"; Dan J. Moore, "Efficiency Report of Lesley J. McNair," January 1–September 15, 1914 (in Vera Cruz April 26–September 4), McNair Papers, NARA 1.

35. Colonel Berry, "Telegram from Colonel Berry, 4th Field Artillery, to the War Department Adjutant General," April 26, 1914, McNair Papers, NARA 1.

36. Moore, "Efficiency Report." The evaluation report indicates McNair served in the regimental supply and quartermaster sections. His rater for the period of the report covering his detail at the Field Artillery School wrote: "This officer has been on duty as statistical officer of the School of Fire for F.A. since Jan. 1913 during which period he has performed his duties in a most satisfactory and efficient manner."

37. E. F. McGlachlin, "Efficiency Report of Lesley J. McNair," January 1–December 31, 1915; and E. F. McGlachlin, "Efficiency Report of Lesley J. McNair," January 1–May 10, 1916, both in McNair Papers, NARA 1.

38. T. E. Merrill, "Efficiency Report of Lesley J. McNair," July 22–December 1, 1916, McNair Papers, NARA 1. Merrill served as McNair's rater, Allaire as his first endorser.

39. Eisenhower, *Intervention!*, 216; Grotelueschen, *AEF Way of War*, 10–25; Millett, "Cantigny," 152–153.

40. Tompkins, *Chasing Villa*, 262.

41. Merrill, "Efficiency Report of Lesley J. McNair," January 1–August 22, 1917, McNair Papers, NARA 1.

CHAPTER 2. WORLD WAR I

1. Schaffer, *America in the Great War*, xvi, 30–31.

2. Coffman, *War to End All Wars*, 20–21.

3. Grenville, "Diplomacy," 34.

4. Ferrell, *America's Deadliest Battle*, 1–11.

5. Beaver, *Modernizing the American War Department*, 64.

6. Ibid.

7. Ibid., 65.

8. Ibid., 65–68.

9. Grotelueschen, *AEF Way of War*, 14–23. This may reflect the continued influence of military theorist Henri Jomini, who in the mid-nineteenth century discounted the significance of technological developments, arguing they did not change the fundamental principles of warfare.

10. Ibid., 27–28.

11. Ferrell, *America's Deadliest Battle*, 11–17.

12. Marshall, *World War I*, 279.

13. Ibid.; Coffman, *War to End All Wars*, 43.

14. Pogue, *George C. Marshall: Education of a General*, 133–144; Millett, "Cantigny," 149–151; Grotelueschen, *AEF Way of War*, 26.

15. Kleber, "Lesley James McNair," 696.

16. Marshall, *Soldierly Spirit,* 1:109.

17. Cooke, *Pershing and His Generals,* 19–20.

18. Dastrup, *Cedat Fortuna Peritis,* 53.

19. Ibid.

20. Cooke, *Pershing and His Generals,* 21–25. After inspecting Sibert's division headquarters on October 3, 1917, Pershing wrote in his diary, "Sibert: slow of speech and of thought. . . . Slovenly in dress, has an eye to his personal interests. Without any ability as a soldier. Utterly hopeless as an instructor or as a tactician. Fails to appreciate soldierly qualities, possessing none himself." Smythe, *Pershing,* 55–56.

21. Cooke, *Rainbow Division,* 4, 20–23. Menoher also inherited Mann's chief of staff, Major Douglas MacArthur, who had served with the 42nd "Rainbow" Division since its formation in August 1917.

22. US Army War Department, *Instructions for the Training of Platoons for Offensive Action, 1917,* 5.

23. Marshall, *World War I,* 282–283; US Army War Department, *Instructions for the Training of Platoons for Offensive Action, 1917.* For a detailed analysis of the open warfare debate and resulting doctrine, see Grotelueschen, *AEF Way of War.*

24. Millett, "Cantigny," 180–182. Colonel Charles P. Summerall, serving as the senior artilleryman on the Baker Mission, insisted in 1917 that GHQ needed to double the number of guns in support of the infantry, but GHQ did not agree. For more on the artillery debate, see Grotelueschen, *AEF Way of War,* 36–37; for an explanation of how societies adapt their discourse on war when encountering the reality of warfare, see Lynn, *Battle,* 331–341.

25. Odom, *After the Trenches,* 26–27.

26. William Lassiter, "Report of a Board of Officers Convened Pursuant to Special Orders No. 289-0," December 11, 1918, NARA 2, RG 120, Entry 23, Box 3; Adjutant General, "General Order 169, Paragraph 9, GHQ, AEF," June 18, 1919, McNair Papers, NARA, St. Louis.

27. Odom, *After the Trenches,* 26–29; Millett, "Cantigny," 182–184.

28. Schifferle, *America's School for War,* 38, 87.

29. Grotelueschen, *AEF Way of War,* 355.

30. Ibid., 354–355; John J. Pershing, "Wrapper Indorsement (Forwarding Report of AEF Superior Board on Organization and Tactics)," NARA 2, RG 120, Entry 23, Box 12.

31. Grotelueschen, *AEF Way of War,* 354–363. If any consensus emerged from the early stages of this debate, it involved a common belief in the need for a combined arms approach to combat that took the human element into consideration along with technology. The exact nature of this combined arms approach remained undetermined.

32. "Estimate of Efficiency of Officers Above Grade of Captain at the General Service Schools, Fort Leavenworth, Kansas," May 22, 1920, McNair Papers, NARA, St. Louis. The assessment of McNair reads, "This officer is in robust health, has an excel-

lent military bearing and dresses well. In my judgment he has force, energy, tact and capacity combined with a good military education insofar as it relates to his own branch of the service. His general military education needs further development. He has a good organizing ability and excellent judgment. As an instructor he is clear and forceful. He is intensely loyal to his work. As a general estimate he should be classed above the average."

33. Schifferle, *America's School for War*, 15, 32, 161. As Schifferle argued, "The influence of the immediate post–World War I faculty cannot be overestimated. Officers in this group established a system of education, the subjects taught, and the methods of instruction and wrote many of the manuals and texts that would stay in use until national mobilization in 1940." Schifferle, *America's School for War*, 93.

34. "Annual Report of the G3, 1923–1924," quoted in Odom, *After the Trenches*, 36.

35. Ibid., 37–38.

36. For example, see Lesley J. McNair, "Artillery Firing: Lectures to the Staff and Line Classes, General Services Schools, Fort Leavenworth, Kansas," October 1919, Curricular Files, Box 10, 1917–1920, McNair Papers, CARL.

37. Grotelueschen, *AEF Way of War*, 356–364; Wilson, *Maneuver and Firepower*, 130–201; Odom, *After the Trenches*, 48–50.

38. McNair, "Infantry Batteries and Accompanying Guns," 135.

39. For one example of a highly critical but well-written narrative describing the debilitating branch bias that hindered combined-arms thinking in doctrine and practice, see Johnson, *Fast Tanks*. By contrast, McNair's efforts at the field artillery center to maximize the effectiveness of the artillery as a member of the combined arms team—despite the protests of asset control–motivated field artillery traditionalists—earned him commendations from both the director of the General Staff School's extension courses and the Field Artillery School commandant. See Russell P. Reeder, "Report on Visit to the School of Fire at Ft. Sill," February 27, 1930; William M. Cruikshank, "Annual Report of Commandant Wm. M. Cruikshank, Brig. Gen.," June 19, 1933. McNair Papers, NARA, St. Louis.

40. Adjutant General of the American Expeditionary Forces, "Distinguished Service Medal," March 12, 1919, McNair Papers, NARA, St. Louis.

41. Philippe Petain, "The National Order of the Legion of Honor," April 4, 1919, McNair Papers, NARA, St. Louis.

42. Kahn, *McNair*, 11; Kleber, "Lesley James McNair," 696.

CHAPTER 3. MCNAIR: WAR PLANNER

1. E. E. Booth, "Efficiency Report," December 31, 1920; Adjutant General, "Memo in Lieu of Efficiency Report: Travel Status, January 1 to February 12, 1921," January 25, 1922, both in McNair Papers, NARA, St. Louis.

2. War Department, "General Orders, No. 74, Initial General Staff Eligible List," December 16, 1920, McNair Papers, NARA, St. Louis.

3. Summerall, *Way of Duty, Honor, Country*, 178–184; William Chamberlaine, "Efficiency Report," June 30, 1921, McNair Papers, NARA, St. Louis; Summerall, a fellow artillery officer and a division and corps commander in World War I, would have remembered McNair from his work on the AEF staff, including unit visits to investigate artillery training. See, for example, Lesley J. McNair, "Visit of Colonel McNair to 37th, 2nd, 1st and 89th Divisions," August 16, 1918, National Archives and Record Administration, College Park, MD, RG 120, Entry 11, Box 1394, G5 Files.

4. "Senior Field Artilleryman"; Kleber, "Lesley James McNair," 696; Schifferle, *America's School for War*, 92–96. McNair served as the senior artillery officer in the training section (G5). See H. B. Fiske, "Personnel and Allotment of Duties in Fifth Section, General Staff," August 23, 1918, National Archives and Records Administration, College Park, MD, RG 120, Entry 11, Box 1363, G5 Files. Summerall had good reason to entrust McNair with the presidency of the McNair Board and the responsibility of updating the plan for the defense of Oahu, given the special mention of McNair in an inspector general's report from the previous month. See Eli A. Helmick, "Extract from Report of an Inspection of the Hawaiian Department," April 9, 1923, McNair Papers, NARA, St. Louis. The extract reads, "Major McNair impressed me as being an exceptionally able man and performing the duties of his office in an able manner."

5. Gole, *Road to Rainbow*, 8–13; Miller, *War Plan Orange*, 1–8.

6. Lesley J. McNair, "McNair Board: Report of a Board of Officers Convened by Special Orders No. 120, Hawaiian Department, May 22, 1923, on Powers and Limitation of Coast Artillery and Air Service," February 11, 1924, NARA 2, RG 395, Entry 6051, Box 1, 1–6 (titled as "Inclosure 1").

7. Ibid., 2.

8. Ibid., 2–6. The board report named every individual who supported the tests and made particular note of the impartiality, objectivity, and cooperation of the members of the various arms and services involved. It also described the procedures followed for each type of test in detail, including the type and size of target, as well as measurement techniques. See "Acknowledgements," 26–30.

9. Ibid., 2–27.

10. Ibid., 2–31; Charles P. Summerall, "Letter of Commendation, 8 March 1924," McNair Papers, NARA, St. Louis. Summerall wrote: "The proceedings show thoroughness of study and originality of investigation and an amount of labor that are worthy of the highest commendation."

11. McNair, "McNair Board on Coast Artillery and Air Service." See "Inclosure 8" for details.

12. Ibid., 27.

13. Ibid.

14. Ibid., 31. Despite the thoroughness of the test methodology and execution, the McNair board's findings soon drew criticism, particularly from the Air Service. One cannot help but note the irony in this criticism when one compares the diligence of

the McNair Board to Grow's haphazard and clearly biased report on bombing tests against the battleships *Virginia* and *New Jersey* conducted the previous year. In his report, Grow neglected to report on pretest preparations, did not describe the methodology used in the tests or analysis of their results, and even made unsubstantiated claims like "no conclusions could be drawn of a comparative nature. It may have been that bombers did not desire to hit the targets or to sink them at once, since it could have easily been done under existing conditions." See Grow, "Bombing Tests."

15. Johnson, *Fast Tanks*, 101. Johnson may simply have overlooked the file that would have enabled him to recount the McNair Board's activities and findings accurately because he cited a report entitled "The McNair Board and the Auxiliary Reports, Data and Correspondence, Part I, The McNair Report, the Panama Canal Report," located at the US Air Force Historical Research Agency, Maxwell Air Force Base, Montgomery, Alabama. This report may have contained only selected passages of the actual board report, but in other sections of the same book, Johnson cited records from NARA 2, where one can find the full board report of the McNair Board.

16. Ibid.

17. Lesley J. McNair, "Basic Project for the Defense of Oahu," February 9, 1924, NARA 2, RG 337, Entry 58, Box 1, 1–43.

18. Ibid., 1.

19. Ibid., 1–43 plus annexes. Only one known secondary source mentions McNair's involvement in this planning, and even this source provides very little detail. See Coffman, *The Regulars*, 356–357.

20. McNair, "Basic Project for the Defense of Oahu, 1924," G-3 Appendix, 1.

21. Ibid., endorsement by John J. Pershing, general of the armies and chief of staff, in plan front matter.

22. W. F. Hase, "Efficiency Report," February 11, 1924, McNair Papers, NARA, St. Louis; Charles P. Summerall, "Letter of Commendation for Efficiency Report, 11 February 1924," McNair Papers, NARA, St. Louis. In his letter of commendation, Summerall also made note of McNair's exemplary work establishing policies and overseeing the administration of the G-3 Section: "An even more difficult task devolved to you in studying the war plans of this Department and in preparing the Basic Project for the Employment of the Troops. In order to complete the revision required by the War Department, you have prolonged your service in the Department and you have labored unceasingly to complete the task before your departure. The Basic Project for the Defense of Oahu which you have submitted gives evidence of thorough study, masterly reasoning, and skillful knowledge of the mission of the command and of the best means to accomplish it. It is a fitting culmination of your service with the command and will remain to reflect credit upon your administration of the G-3 Section."

23. "AG 353; Chief of Air Service to the Adjutant General," February 12, 1925, NARA 2, RG 337, Entry 58, Box 5, File 321—Aviation, 2; "McNair Board: Report of a Board of Officers Convened by Special Orders No. 120, Hawaiian Department, May

22, 1923, on Powers and Limitation of Coast Artillery and Air Service," February 11, 1924, NARA 2, RG 337, Entry 58, Box 5, File 321—Aviation.

24. "AG 353; Chief of Air Service to the Adjutant General," February 12, 1925, NARA 2, RG 337, Entry 58, Box 5, File 321—Aviation, 2.

25. Ibid.

26. "AG 353; Chief of Air Service to the Adjutant General," February 12, 1925, NARA 2, RG 337, Entry 58, Box 5, File 321—Aviation, 5. Interestingly, there are two versions of page 5 included in the set of reports and endorsements. Patrick's page 5 only includes Loring's points b through g, while the second indorsement, provided by the coast artillery and signed by Coe's executive assistant, includes all of Loring's points a through g.

27. "McNair Board: Report of a Board of Officers Convened by Special Orders No. 120, Hawaiian Department, May 22, 1923, on Powers and Limitation of Coast Artillery and Air Service," February 11, 1924, NARA 2, RG 337, Entry 58, Box 5, File 321—Aviation; "AG 353; Chief of Air Service to the Adjutant General," February 12, 1925, NARA 2, RG 337, Entry 58, Box 5, File 321—Aviation, 5.

28. "AG 353; Chief of Air Service to the Adjutant General," February 12, 1925, NARA 2, RG 337, Entry 58, Box 5, File 321—Aviation, (2nd Ind.), 5.

29. President's Aircraft Board, "Report of President's Aircraft Board," November 30, 1925, NARA 2, RG 337, Entry 58, Box 5, File 321—Aviation, handwritten note on front cover of report.

30. Ibid., 3.

31. Ibid., 6–7.

32. Ibid., 8–15.

33. Ibid., 16–30.

34. Ibid., 30.

35. Adjutant General, "AG 201; Adjutant General to Major Leslie J. McNair, FA," November 20, 1925, McNair Papers, NARA, St. Louis.

36. For more on McNair's testimony in the Mitchell trial, see Davis, *Billy Mitchell Affair;* Grumelli, "Trial of Faith"; Page, "Billy Mitchell." Few sources on the Mitchell trial specifically name McNair as a witness for the prosecution.

37. Grumelli, "Trial of Faith," 234, 264n221; Davis, *Billy Mitchell Affair,* 315–319. Although these secondary sources briefly describe McNair's testimony, the full transcript seems to be available only at Lesley J. McNair, "Testimony of Major Leslie J. McNair, Field Artillery," NARA 2, RG 337, Entry 58, Box 5, File 321-F.A.

38. McNair, "Testimony of Major Leslie J. McNair."

39. William Chamberlaine, "Report of Annual Physical Examination of Officers, 1922," February 10, 1922, McNair Papers, NARA, St. Louis. Chamberlain did refer McNair to a medical board as a result of a low specific gravity reading on his urinalysis, but further tests found normal specific gravity, leading the board to certify McNair as physically qualified. E. R. Schreiner, "Report of Annual Physical Examination of Offi-

cers, 1923," April 26, 1923; and E. R. Schreiner, "Report of Annual Physical Examination of Officers and Warrant Officers, 1924," January 10, 1924, both in McNair Papers, NARA, St. Louis.

40. Today this title is simply professor of military science, and some schools might have transitioned to this shorter title earlier than others. All of the official documents available from McNair's time at Purdue (War Department orders, evaluation reports, McNair's professional correspondence, and even the title he used in published articles) refer to him as a professor of military science and tactics.

CHAPTER 4. PROFESSOR OF MILITARY SCIENCE AND TACTICS AT PURDUE

1. Matheny, *Carrying the War to the Enemy*, 45–46.

2. Trout, *On the Battlefield of Memory*, 140–141.

3. Coffman, *The Regulars*, 292–294. Congress kept army strength below 120,000 until 1936, when it approved funding for an increase to 165,000.

4. Ibid., 233–241. Personnel caps and budget cuts, combined with the economic downturn that led to the Depression, created what Edward Coffman called the hump. This ten- to fifteen-year period of stalled officer promotions occurred because of a logjam of senior-grade personnel who chose to remain in service rather than retire during an era of economic struggle, forestalling midgrade officers' hopes of gaining promotion. Those midgrade officers who remained on active duty in the interwar era often did so out of dedication to the army's mission because they possessed little hope of moving up the rank structure until the existing senior officers retired, creating vacancies for the next generation of senior army officers.

5. Ibid., 234–235.

6. Pearlman, *To Make Democracy Safe*, 187–191.

7. *The Debris* (Purdue University yearbook), class of 1927, http://earchives.lib .purdue.edu/.

8. "Reports of the President and Other Officers of Purdue University," Purdue University, Lafayette, Indiana, 1928, 111.

9. Masland and Radway, *Soldiers and Scholars*, 252; Hinckley, "How Purdue Features Military Cermonies," 187; McNair's Regular Army staff at Purdue consisted of approximately twenty enlisted men and eight officers, all field artillerymen; see *The Debris*, class of 1925. Purdue's ROTC program almost doubled in size between 1919, when it comprised one regiment of 830 men, and 1928, when it comprised three regiments of 1,369 men. See *The Debris*, class of 1928. By 1928, Purdue contributed more artillery reserve officers annually than any other school.

10. Elliot accepted in 1942 an appointment as director of the Division of Professional and Technical Employment and Training of the War Manpower Commission. See "Purdue in the Nation," *The Debris*, class of 1943.

11. Coffman, *Regulars*, 323.

12. It seems remarkable that so many talented officers stayed on active duty throughout this long period of stagnation, although the Depression gave them few options; ibid., 240. Jacob Devers and George Patton remained majors for fourteen years, while Mark Clark and Matthew Ridgeway stalled at the rank of captain for thirteen years.

13. McNair, "Military Training at Educational Institutions," 6.

14. Ibid., 6–7.

15. Ibid., 7.

16. Ibid., 7, 18.

17. Lesley J. McNair, "Letter from Lesley J. McNair to the Editor, Army and Navy Journal," January 4, 1925, NARA 2, RG 337, Entry 58, Box 1. A selective promotion system involves promotion decisions made not only based on seniority but also taking into consideration individual officer duty performance.

18. Ibid.

19. Ibid. Ironically, the inaccuracies that concerned him affected McNair's own files. Many early twentieth-century references confuse Lesley McNair with William McNair, an unrelated and older field artillery officer. The other and far more common error, seen in both contemporary records and modern secondary sources, consists of the incorrect spelling of McNair's first name as Leslie. This error proved so ubiquitous that McNair eventually gave up correcting it in erroneous signature blocks on the various documents he signed.

20. Ibid.

21. Ibid.

22. McNair, "Pacifism at Purdue University," 5.

23. Hinckley, "How Purdue Features Military Cermonies," 185–186.

24. Ibid., 186.

25. McNair, "Pacifism at Purdue University," 5.

26. Ibid., 5; emphasis in original.

27. Ibid., 6.

28. Ibid.

29. Ibid.; the quote referred to by McNair is "The Pacifist Pledge," found in Page, War, 203–204.

30. McNair, "Pacifism at Purdue University," 7.

31. Ibid.

32. Ibid., 8. Although McNair recognized and sought to defend Purdue against a very real threat, that threat remained mostly isolated during this period to small activist groups with specific targets like the ROTC; pacifism remained a minor issue at the national level.

33. "Minutes of the Purdue University Board of Trustees, 14 April 1926," Purdue University Archives, http://earchives.lib.purdue.edu/.

34. Ibid.

35. Ibid.

36. McNair, "Why Military Training in College," 5. Although the War Department no longer recognized distinguished colleges starting in 1928, Purdue earned a mark of "excellent" in every category during its inspection of May 1–2, 1928. See *The Debris*, class of 1929.

37. McNair, "Why Military Training in College," 5–6.

38. McNair, "ROTC," 172.

39. Ibid., 173.

40. Ibid., 173–174.

41. Ibid., 174.

42. Ward Surgeon, "Diagnosis Card, Walter Reed General Hospital," August 28, 1927, McNair Papers, NARA, St. Louis.

43. Adjutant General, "Orders and Oath of Office for Promotion to Lieutenant Colonel," January 9, 1928, McNair Papers, NARA, St. Louis.

CHAPTER 5. THE ARMY WAR COLLEGE CLASS OF 1928–1929

1. War Department, "Special Orders No. 198," August 28, 1928, McNair Papers, NARA, St. Louis; McNair's pre-AWC physical exam made note of his hearing loss, neither deeming him permanently incapacitated for field service nor recommending sending him before a retirement board. H. C. Fisher, "Report of Physical Examination," January 10, 1929, McNair Papers, NARA, St. Louis.

2. Matheny, *Carrying the War to the Enemy*, 57–58.

3. US War Department, "Annual Report of the Secretary of War, 1919," 27, quoted in Pappas, *Prudens Futuri*, 89.

4. Originally named the General Staff College in 1919, the War Department renamed the institution the Army War College in 1921 "to avoid confusion with the Command and General Staff School at Fort Leavenworth." Matheny, *Carrying the War to the Enemy*, 55.

5. Pappas, *Prudens Futuri*, 89–93; Ball, *Of Responsible Command*, 180–206.

6. Ball, *Of Responsible Command*, 180. The nation's celebration of the Allied victory in World War I soon turned to disillusionment, leading to congressional rejection of Wilson's goal to include America in the League of Nations and to presidential candidate (and Wilson's successor) Warren G. Harding's campaigning on the slogan "Return to Normalcy." Thus, in the 1920s America wanted peace and a return to isolationism, and it saw no need to spend heavily on what many deemed an unnecessary defense force. See Matheny, *Carrying the War to the Enemy*, 45.

7. Ball, *Of Responsible Command*, 181. Ball opined that Drum may have made sincere recommendations or may have merely sought to put forward a recommendation that protected the Fort Leavenworth schools, protecting his organizations even if at the cost of the Army War College.

8. Ibid., 182.

9. Ibid., 182–183.

10. Coffman, *Old Army*, 271–274. Emory Upton, a highly successful general during the American Civil War, emerged in the late nineteenth century as one of the army's most outspoken advocates for the professionalization of the officer corps and the retention of an adequately large and well-funded regular army to maintain consistent readiness for war in times of peace.

11. H. B. Fiske, "Training in the AEF," January 16, 1922, USAHEC, General File #118 (Training), #215–70. Fiske's highly critical and controversial report was immediately stamped "classified" by the War Department; it was not declassified until 1988. Ball, *Of Responsible Command*, 184–185.

12. Pappas, *Prudens Futuri*, 114–115; Ball, *Of Responsible Command*, 183–184.

13. Schifferle, *America's School for War*, 100.

14. Quoted in ibid., 115–116. Schifferle called this "one possible grave weakness in the curriculum at Leavenworth."

15. H. B. Crosby, "Orientation Lecture to the Army War College Class of 1924–25," quoted in Matheny, *Carrying the War to the Enemy*, 57.

16. Matheny, *Carrying the War to the Enemy*, 57. Matheny is correct in principle in that the Leavenworth experience provided a chance to learn existing doctrine, compared to the War College, which encouraged innovative problem solving; however, the War College involved both education and training.

17. Johnson, *Fast Tanks*, 223–224.

18. Ibid., 223–224. As an example of Johnson's oversight, the 1928–1929 Army War College G-3 course dedicated one committee to current and future air forces, antiaircraft artillery, and joint employment, and another to the study of mechanized forces. See John L. DeWitt, "Course at the Army War College, 1928–1929, G-3, Outline of the Course, Committee Directives, September 4, 1928, to October 6, 1928," September 4, 1928, USAHEC, AWC Curricular Archives, 1928–1929.

19. Ball, *Of Responsible Command*, 185–186.

20. Matheny, *Carrying the War to the Enemy*, 57–58.

21. According to one senior officer's testimony, instructors at the Army War College encouraged original thought and respected opinions and ideas based on sound reasoning even if they conflicted with current doctrine or dealt with issues for which no doctrine existed. John L. DeWitt, "Orientation, the Army War College Course, 1928–1929," 2, September 4, 1928, USAHEC, AWC Curricular Archives, 1928–1929.

22. Pappas, *Prudens Futuri*, 115. Pappas argued that McGlachlin's influence on the college extended well beyond his tenure there, demonstrated by the later performance of prominent graduates who attended the school after he shaped the curriculum, which remained consistent with his philosophy through the 1920s.

23. Ibid.; Ball, *Of Responsible Command*, 191–194. The War Department G-1 had,

in previous classes, issued numerous waivers overriding the fifty-two-year-old student age limit.

24. Ball, *Of Responsible Command,* 194.

25. Matheny, *Carrying the War to the Enemy,* 73–74.

26. Ball, *Of Responsible Command,* 194–195.

27. Ibid., 195–197.

28. Ibid., 198–199.

29. Ibid., 205–206.

30. Ibid., 198.

31. Ibid., 210–211. Interestingly, the War Department assigned within the realm of instruction two fields not previously under the War College's explicit purview: "to instruct in those political, economic, and social matters which influence the conduct of war [and] . . . in the strategy, tactics, and logistics of large operations in past wars, with special reference to the World War." The latter modification to the War College's mission indicated a return to the history-based instruction favored by McGlachlin, which gradually disappeared from the War College curriculum during Ely's tenure as commandant. AG to Commandant, December 22, 1967, File 74-50, Army Regulation 350-5, Change 5, January 30, 1931, ¶3f(1), quoted in Ball, *Of Responsible Command,* 211.

32. Ball, *Of Responsible Command,* 211–212.

33. Ibid., 212; Ball quoted an earlier version, but for the relevant passage, Clausewitz, *On War,* 127; Bruscino, "Naturally Clausewitzian."

34. Ball, *Of Responsible Command,* 212–213.

35. Ibid., 209–219; Gole, *Road to Rainbow,* 18–19, 29–32.

36. DeWitt, "Orientation, the Army War College Course, 1928–1929."

37. Ibid., 1–2.

38. Ibid., 1; emphasis in original.

39. Ibid., 1–4. Later in the orientation, DeWitt emphasized that while some debate surrounded the division of the curriculum into command instruction and staff instruction, this did not imply a fundamental difference between the two. Rather, he pointed out that every function the General Staff performed comprised a command function, but the General Staff itself possessed no command authority; for this, they relied on the commander. Therefore, every General Staff officer must learn to think, act, plan, and lead like a commander, even when not in a command position. This teaching philosophy remains relevant in the US army's professional military education system. See ibid., 10.

40. Ibid., 5.

41. Ibid., 5–7. DeWitt emphasized that the faculty would disregard rank when making committee leadership decisions, noting, "The injection of it into consideration after assignments are made is productive of harm." He also emphasized the importance of creativity and initiative in committee work: "The officer who wants to

follow a model has not an aptitude for General Staff work." The same philosophy underpins the pedagogical methods at the military's leading professional military education institutions to this day.

42. John L. DeWitt, "Course at the Army War College, 1928–1929, G-3, Outline of the Course and Committee Directives," 1–2, September 4, 1928, USAHEC, AWC Curricular Archives, 1928–1929.

43. Ibid., 3–8. These records demonstrate that the officer education system did not neglect these topics in the 1920s and 1930s, a perception that exists in some histories of this period, probably as a result of overemphasis of the curriculum at the Leavenworth schools compared to that of the Army Industrial College and the Army War College.

44. E. H. Humphrey, "Course at the Army War College, 1928–1929, G-3, Orientation," 2–3, September 4, 1928, USAHEC, AWC Curricular Archives, 1928–1929.

45. T. W. Brown, "Course at the Army War College, 1928–1929, G-3: Report of Committee No. 3," October 4, 1928, USAHEC, AWC Curricular Archives, 1928–1929.

46. Ibid., 2.

47. Ibid., 3.

48. Ibid.

49. Ibid., 4.

50. Ibid.

51. John L. DeWitt, "Course at the Army War College, 1928–1929, G-1, Outline of the Course, Committee Directives, Orientation, October 8, 1928, to October 27, 1928," 1, October 8, 1928, USAHEC, AWC Curricular Archives, 1928–1929.

52. Ibid., 1–11.

53. Ibid., 4, 10.

54. Weigley, *History of the United States Army,* 400–401.

55. Lesley J. McNair, "Course at the Army War College, 1928–1929, G-1, Report of Committee No. 5. Subject: Reserve Systems for the Regular Army and National Guard," October 24, 1928, USAHEC, AWC Curricular Archives, 1928–1929.

56. Lesley J. McNair, "Course at the Army War College, 1928–1929, G-1, Synopsis of Report, Committee No. 5," October 24, 1928, USAHEC, AWC Curricular Archives, 1928–1929.

57. Harding Polk, "Course at the Army War College, 1928–1929, G-1, Supplement No, 1 to Report of Committee No. 5. Subject: The Reserve Systems of Foreign Countries," October 24, 1928, USAHEC, AWC Curricular Archives, 1928–1929.

58. W. N. Hill, "Course at the Army War College, 1928–1929, G-1, Supplement No, 2 to Report of Committee No, 5. Subject: The Reserve System of the Navy and the Marine Corps," October 24, 1928, USAHEC, AWC Curricular Archives, 1928–1929, 1–3.

59. Paul C. Paschal, "Course at the Army War College, 1928–1929, G-1, Supplement No, 3 to Report of Committee No. 5. Subject: The Enlisted Reserve System of the National Guard," October 24, 1928, USAHEC, AWC Curricular Archives, 1928–1929, 1–5.

60. Ibid., 3.

61. Ibid., 4. The subcommittee also emphasized the infeasibility of any system in which the War Department would align National Guard reserves with specific regular army units; the states held constitutional authority for unit alignment of their National Guard reservists.

62. Ibid., 5–6.

63. J. E. Ardrey, "Course at the Army War College, 1928–1929, G-1, Supplement No. 4 to Report of Committee No. 5. Subject: Reserve System for the Regular Army," October 24, 1928, USAHEC, AWC Curricular Archives, 1928–1929.

64. Ibid., 1–2.

65. Ibid., 2.

66. Ibid., 2–3.

67. McNair, "Course at the Army War College, 1928–1929, G-1, Report of Committee No. 5"; McNair, "Course at the Army War College, 1928–1929, G-1, Synopsis of Report, Committee No. 5." McNair was not a member of Committee No. 7, which searched for a feasible solution to the lack of a system of replacements—a problem that the army had never solved, and one that caused the AEF significant problems during the Great War. However, he did participate in the committee's conferences and attended its final briefing, benefiting from its detailed analysis of this similarly intractable problem.

68. DeWitt, "Orientation," October 8, 1928, to October 27, 1928, 4; John L. DeWitt, "Course at the Army War College, 1928–1929, G-2, Orientation and Outline of the Course," November 26, 1928, USAHEC, AWC Curricular Archives, 1928–1929, 1.

69. DeWitt, "Orientation and Outline," 2, November 26, 1928.

70. Ibid., 2–13.

71. John L. DeWitt, "Course at the Army War College, 1928–1929, War Plans: Orientation," 1, January 2, 1929, USAHEC, AWC Curricular Archives, 1928–1929. For a complete list of the war plans and their color designations, see Gole, *Road to Rainbow,* appendix E. War Plan Green dealt with US intervention in Mexico. Gole, *Road to Rainbow,* 166. The Conduct of War Course archives contain the guidance issued to each staff conducting map maneuvers based on the colored plans, but the actual war plans, returned to the War Department after the course, are at the National Archives in NARA 2.

72. DeWitt, "Orientation," January 2, 1929.

73. John L. DeWitt, "Course at the Army War College, 1928–1929, Conduct of War: Orientation Lecture," February 18, 1929, USAHEC, AWC Curricular Archives, 1928–1929.

74. Lesley J. McNair, "Course at the Army War College, 1928–1929: Conduct of War Course, First Period, Report of Command Group No. 3. Subject: French Operations on the Western Front in 1914, from the Concentration of Their Armies to Include the First Battle of the Marne," March 27, 1929, USAHEC, AWC Curricular Archives,

1928–1929; Lesley J. McNair, "Course at the Army War College, 1928–1929: Conduct of War Course, First Period, Supplement No. 5 to Report of Command Group No. 3," 1, March 27, 1929, USAHEC, AWC Curricular Archives, 1928–1929. McNair found Joffre a poor strategist but a strong leader who failed to see the shortcomings of his strategic plan and abandon it early enough, or establish an effective defense once he finally did abandon the offensive.

75. John L. DeWitt, "Course at the Army War College, 1928–1929, Conduct of War, Second Period, Outline of the Course, Oranization for Work and Assignments, General Instructions," 4, 6, April 1, 1929, USAHEC, AWC Curricular Archives, 1928–1929; Gole, *Road to Rainbow*, 166.

76. Colonel John L. DeWitt, "Memorandum from Colonel DeWitt to Student Command Group No. 3, War Plans Course. Subject: Report on Techniques of Green Map Maneuver," March 7, 1929, USAHEC, AWC Curricular Archives, 1928–1929.

77. "Notes on Reports on Techniques of Green Map Maneuver Submitted by Command Groups," March 1929, USAHEC, AWC Curricular Archives, 1928–1929.

78. "Memorandum from McNair to the Commandant, Subject: Technique of Green Map Maneuver," March 22, 1929, USAHEC, AWC Curricular Archives, 1928–1929.

79. John L. DeWitt, "Course at the Army War College, 1928–1929, Conduct of War, Third Period, Outline of the Course, Oranization for Work and Assignments, General Instructions," 2, May 13, 1929, USAHEC, AWC Curricular Archives, 1928–1929; John L. DeWitt, "Course at the Army War College, 1928–1929, Conduct of War, Fourth Period, Outline of the Course, Oranization for Work and Assignments, General Instructions," 3, May 27, 1929, USAHEC, AWC Curricular Archives, 1928–1929; John L. DeWitt, "Course at the Army War College, 1928–1929, Conduct of War, Fourth Period, Map Maneuver Red II, General Situation and First Special Situation," 1, May 27, 1929, USAHEC, AWC Curricular Archives, 1928–1929; Gole, *Road to Rainbow*, 166.

80. John L. DeWitt, "Course at the Army War College, 1928–1929, Conduct of War, Fifth Period, Command Post Exercise, Fort Du Pont, Delaware," 3–6, June 6, 1929, USAHEC, AWC Curricular Archives, 1928–1929, 3–6; emphasis in original.

81. Lesley J. McNair, "Course at the Army War College, 1928–1929, Memorandum for the Commmandent of the Army War College. Subject: The Apportionment of Appropriated Funds among the Components of the Army of the United States in Peace," May 6, 1929, USAHEC, AWC Curricular Archives, 1928–1929.

82. Ibid., 16–17.

83. William D. Connor, "Closing Address by Major General W. D. Connor, USA, Commandant," 1, June 27, 1929, USAHEC, AWC Curricular Archives, 1928–1929.

84. Ibid.

85. Jones, "Education of the Supreme Commander," 108.

86. William D. Connor, "Efficiency Report," July 5, 1929, McNair Papers, NARA, St.

Louis; William D. Connor, "Letter of Commendation for Efficiency Report," May 10, 1929, McNair Papers, NARA, St. Louis; AWC Adjutant General, "Index Sheet, the Adjutant General's Office," May 10, 1929, McNair Papers, NARA, St. Louis.

87. Connor, "Closing Address," 1.

CHAPTER 6. GETTING OVER THE HUMP

1. War Department, "Report of Change: Assigned to the Academic Division as Assistant Commandant, Headquarters, the Field Artillery School, Fort Sill, OK," July 23, 1929, McNair Papers, NARA, St. Louis.

2. As recalled by Thomas T. Handy, quoted in Coffman, *Regulars*, 265–266.

3. Comparato, *Age of Great Guns*, 258–259; Dastrup, *King of Battle*, 196–201; Coffman, *Regulars*, 265–267.

4. Russell A. Gugeler, "Fort Sill and the Golden Age of Field Artillery," 7, January 31, 1981, FA School Archives. Gugeler, author of the unpublished biography of Major General Orlando Ward, sent this unpublished article to Lester Miller, an archivist at the Morris Swett Library, Fort Sill, Oklahoma, in 1981.

5. Ibid. Massed fires in the Great War consisted of unobserved fire in the form of timed and rolling barrages, calculated using detailed maps and laborious surveying techniques. Observed fire would potentially increase the speed, accuracy, and effectiveness of fire, but many technological barriers hindered its feasibility in 1925.

6. A battery consisted of only six guns; by combining the fire of its three batteries, the battalion could achieve greater massed effects, and it could deliver fire more accurately by centralizing the preparation of fire data in one headquarters.

7. Gugeler, "Fort Sill and the Golden Age of Field Artillery," 8. Rapid-fire missions posed particular challenges because they would require replacing battalion siting and survey procedures that required at least six hours with a procedure the battalion could accomplish in minutes.

8. Ibid.

9. Brewer, "Flash-Sound Ranging."

10. Gugeler, "Fort Sill and the Golden Age of Field Artillery," 8–9.

11. Dastrup, *King of Battle*, 197; Gugeler, "Fort Sill and the Golden Age of Field Artillery," 9.

12. Lesley J. McNair, "Memorandum for the Commandant, Field Artillery School: Annual Report," 3, June 30, 1930, FA School Archives. McNair emphasized the increased proportion of time spent on reconaissance, fire direction, staff duties, and supply to prepare officers for field artillery command, arguing no other school could provide this vital instruction.

13. Lesley J. McNair, "Memorandum for the Commandant, Field Artillery School: Annual Report," June 28, 1931, FA School Archives.

14. Ibid., 2–3.

15. Ibid., 3–9.

16. Dastrup, *King of Battle,* 196–197; Gugeler, "Fort Sill and the Golden Age of Field Artillery," 10. Gugeler referred to the French officer merely as Tytler-Frazer.

17. Lesley J. McNair, "Memorandum for the Commandant, Field Artillery School: Annual Report," 3, June 15, 1932, FA School Archives.

18. "Field Artillery Notes: Gunnery Liaison Methods."

19. Carlos Brewer, "Recommendations for Changes in Gunnery Instruction and Battalion Organization," 1, June 2, 1932, FA School Archives.

20. McNair, "Extracts from 'Notes on Recent Operations,'" 229.

21. McNair, "Infantry Batteries and Accompanying Guns."

22. Brewer, "Recommendations for Changes in Gunnery Instruction and Battalion Organization," 3–4.

23. Ibid., 4–7.

24. Dastrup, *King of Battle,* 197; Gugeler, "Fort Sill and the Golden Age of Field Artillery," 8–9.

25. Gugeler, "Fort Sill and the Golden Age of Field Artillery," 11.

26. Ibid., 12–13.

27. Ibid.; Dastrup, *King of Battle,* 197–198.

28. Gugeler, "Fort Sill and the Golden Age of Field Artillery," 14.

29. Ibid., 15.

30. Ibid., 17.

31. Ibid., 17–18; Coffman, *Regulars,* 265–266; Dastrup, *King of Battle,* 198.

32. Lesley J. McNair, "Memorandum for the Commandant, Field Artillery School: Annual Report," June 7, 1933, FA School Archives.

33. William M. Cruikshank, "Efficiency Report," June 27, 1933, McNair Papers, NARA, St. Louis.

34. George P. Tyner, "Efficiency Report," February 8, 1930; William M. Cruikshank, "Efficiency Report," June 30, 1930; William M. Cruikshank, "Efficiency Report," June 30, 1931; William M. Cruikshank, "Efficiency Report," June 30, 1932; William M. Cruikshank, "Efficiency Report," June 27, 1933, all in McNair Papers, NARA, St. Louis. Cruikshank added and initialed this handwritten final comment to the typed efficiency report. He clearly held McNair in high regard.

35. Manus McCloskey, "Efficiency Report," June 30, 1934, McNair Papers, NARA, St. Louis.

36. McKenney, *Field Artillery,* 1:513–515.

37. Ibid., 2:965–967.

38. McCloskey, "Efficiency Report"; Manus McCloskey and George Van Horn Moseley, "Efficiency Report," September 1, 1934, McNair Papers, NARA, St. Louis. Most efficiency reports of this period include no special remarks in the 1st Indorsement section, with the adjutant simply signing for an unnamed indorsing officer, indicating his concurrence in the rating officer's evaluation.

39. Headquarters IV Corps Area, "Extract, Special Orders No. 118," n.d., McNair Papers, NARA, St. Louis. McNair remained assigned to the 83rd Field Artillery during this assignment, serving as detached personnel with the Civilian Conservation Corps.

40. L. D. Gasser, "Special Orders No. 118," July 16, 1934, McNair Papers, NARA, St. Louis.

41. Coffman, *Regulars*, 241–242. As Coffman pointed out, these officers often incurred unreimbursed travel costs due to offical travel requirements when serving in the CCC; Johnson, "Civilian Conservation Corps," ii.

42. Johnson, "Civilian Conservation Corps," ii. Even though members received no formal military training, they experienced military discipline, values, and leadership while gaining strength and physical endurance from regular meals and manual labor.

43. IV Corps Area Adjutant General, "Orders Directing McNair to Report to Fort McPherson, Georgia," August 18, 1934; Major General George Van Horn Moseley to Brigadier General Manus McCloskey, August 20, 1934, both in McNair Papers, NARA, St. Louis. He only had time to send his wife a brief telegram before departing: "For Mrs. L J McNair Slated to command Beauregard District Involves permanent change of station Date unknown at present Leave today for Beauregard . . . home Date later Love Lesley." Lesley J. McNair to Clare H. McNair, August 20, 1934, McNair Papers, NARA, St. Louis.

44. Major General George Van Horn Moseley to Brigadier General Manus Mc-Closkey, August 20, 1934; IV Corps Area Adjutant General, "T. H. Lowe to Commanding Officer, Barksdale Field, Louisiana," August 20, 1934, McNair Papers, NARA, St. Louis.

45. Various Special Orders, Headquarters, District E CCC, January 21–February 18, 1935, McNair Papers, NARA, St. Louis.

46. Manus McCloskey, "Brigadier General McCloskey to Major General Moseley," August 24, 1934, McNair Papers, NARA, St. Louis.

47. Lesley J. McNair, "Message from the Commanding Officer, District 'E' CCC," in "Progress in Education in District 'E' CCC," n.d., McNair Papers, NARA, St. Louis.

48. L. D. Gasser, "Special Orders No. 164," November 19, 1934, McNair Papers, NARA, St. Louis.

49. Ibid.

50. G. A. O'Connell, "Report of Physical Examination," January 12, 1934; James W. Duckworth, "Report of Physical Examination," November 27, 1934; H. P. Hobbs, "Report of Physical Examination," August 5, 1927; Ward Surgeon, "Walter Reed Diagnosis Card, 1927"; Charles W. Weeks et al., "Report of Examining Board for Promotion of Officers," November 27, 1934; P. T. Hayne, "War Department, the Adjutant General. Subject: Qualifications for Promotion," December 11, 1934; George Van Horn Moseley to Lesley J. McNair, February 1, 1935, all in McNair Papers, NARA, St. Louis.

51. George Van Horn Moseley, "George Van Horn Moseley to Lesley J. McNair, Subject: CCC Education," March 16, 1935, McNair Papers, NARA, St. Louis.

52. George Van Horn Moseley, "Efficiency Report," April 20, 1935, McNair Papers, NARA, St. Louis.

CHAPTER 7. RISE TO PROMINENCE, 1935–1940

1. War Department, "Special Orders No. 18," January 22, 1935; Lesley J. McNair, "Lesley McNair to the War Department Adjutant General, Subject: Travel Orders to Aberdeen Proving Grounds," May 13, 1935; War Department Adjutant General, "Promotion Orders and Oath of Office," May 17, 1935, all in McNair Papers, NARA, St. Louis.

2. Lesley J. McNair, "Lesley McNair to the War Department Adjutant General, Subject: Travel Orders to Aberdeen Proving Grounds," March 25, 1936, McNair Papers, NARA, St. Louis.

3. Parker, "Autogiro," 347–354.

4. "Field Artillery Notes."

5. Lesley J. McNair, "Auto-Giro," October 18, 1937, NARA 2, RG 337, Entry 58, Box 7. McNair began research for his article in June 1936. He traveled to the Kellett Autogiro Corporation to speak with project engineers in December 1936; McNair, "And Now the Autogiro."

6. McNair, "And Now the Autogiro," 5–6.

7. Ibid.

8. Ibid., 8–16.

9. Ibid., 17.

10. McNair, "Auto-Giro."

11. Raines, *Eyes of Artillery,* 21–22. Raines briefly described the army's experiments with the autogiro, but he made no mention of McNair's involvement or his article, "And Now the Autogiro."

12. Upton Birnie Jr., "Efficiency Report," June 30, 1935; Upton Birnie Jr., "Efficiency Report," June 30, 1936; Lesley J. McNair, "Acceptance of Appointment as Brigadier General," December 23, 1936; Upton Birnie Jr., "Efficiency Report (Promotion)," December 31, 1936; War Department Adjutant General, "Promotion Orders and Oath of Office," January 1, 1937; War Department, "Special Orders No. 1," January 1, 1937; War Department, "Special Orders No. 3," January 5, 1937, all in McNair Papers, NARA, St. Louis.

13. Kleber, "Lesley James McNair," 696; "Senior Field Artilleryman," 898; Wilson, *Maneuver and Firepower,* 126.

14. Ferrell, *America's Deadliest Battle,* 18–19. Despite the relatively greater efficiency and effectiveness of the prewar navy, it had devoted little effort to transport, leaving the AEF without a means to deploy overseas in 1917.

15. Schaffer, *America in the Great War,* 47–63.

16. Weigley, *History of the United States Army,* 415; Koistinen, *Planning War,* 38–39. Craig abruptly ended the ongoing update of the General War Plan of 1933, ordering

the initiation of a new planning effort that came to fruition near the end of his term as chief of staff in 1939.

17. Weigley, *History of the United States Army,* 416–417. As Weigley put it, "Roosevelt's tastes were nautical, and perhaps partly for that reason he was much slower to sympathize with Army requests for rebuilding" (417).

18. Watson, *War Department,* 42–43; Lesley J. McNair to Earl W. Bacon, June 20, 1940, NARA 2, RG 337, Entry 58, Box 8, "Anti-Tank Doctrines and Development" folder.

19. Wilson, *Maneuver and Firepower,* 125–126. The square division consisted of two infantry brigades with two infantry regiments each—four infantry regiments total—leading to the "square" designation. The division also possessed two field artillery regiments of two battalions each. The organizational problem existed at the battalion level: each infantry regiment had three battalions, not two, making task organization a challenge, and preventing habitual relationships and equivalent organization of sub-units. Total troops including all support elements amounted to a cumbersome 19,385. For a complete division organization, see Wilson's "Chart 5—Infantry Division, 7 October 1920" in *Maneuver and Firepower.* The infantry division retained this basic structure through 1936 while expanding to nearly 22,000 men.

20. Ibid., 129; Kretchik, *US Army Doctrine,* 140. As Kretchik pointed out, mechanization led every major nation to reorganize their military formations in the 1930s. Among other trends, all of the nations removed tanks from their infantry divisions, creating separate armored units. Similarly, every major power adopted the triangular division organization, with the US army last to make this change, finalizing and adopting the new design in 1939.

21. Proposed Infantry Division Test Files, NARA 2, RG 337, Entry 58C, Box 12. The War Department G-3 included a summary of the board's findings in the PID test guidance documents and orders sent to the 2nd Division; see also Wilson, *Maneuver and Firepower,* 125–126.

22. Proposed Infantry Division Test Files, NARA 2, RG 337, Entry 58C, Box 12. The War Department G-3 included a summary of the board's findings in the PID test guidance documents and orders sent to the 2nd Division.

23. Wilson, 126–130. For a complete division organization, see Wilson, "Chart 9—Proposed Infantry Division, 30 July 1936," in *Maneuver and Firepower.*

24. See "Tests of Proposed Infantry Division," memo from C. W. Christenberry to Commanding General, VIII Corps Area, December 15, 1936, Proposed Infantry Division Test Files, NARA 2, RG 337, Entry 58C, Box 12; and "Signal Corps Troops for Test of Proposed Infantry Division," memo from C. W. Christenberry to Commanding General, VIII Corps Area, December 17, 1936, Proposed Infantry Division Test Files, NARA 2, RG 337, Entry 58C, Box 12; Wilson, *Maneuver and Firepower,* 126–130.

25. "Tests of Proposed Infantry Division," December 15, 1936; Wilson, *Maneuver and Firepower,* 126–130.

26. Wilson, *Maneuver and Firepower*, 126–130.

27. H. J. Brees, "Field Service Test of Proposed Infantry Division," April 2, 1937, NARA 2, RG 337, Entry 58C, Boxes 12–13.

28. J. K. Parsons, "Efficiency Report on General Officer," June 30, 1937, McNair Papers, NARA, St. Louis.

29. Lesley J. McNair, "General Information—Field Service Test of the Proposed Infantry Division," June 4, 1937, NARA 2, RG 337, Entry 58C, Boxes 12–13; Lesley J. McNair, "Tentative Schedule of Field Service Test," July 13, 1937, NARA 2, RG 337, Entry 58C, Boxes 12–13; Lesley J. McNair, "Memorandum Number 23 (PID Umpires)," September 3, 1937, NARA 2, RG 337, Entry 58C, Boxes 12–13.

30. Lesley J. McNair, "Memorandum Number 29; Subject: Board of Review," September 20, 1937, NARA 2, RG 337, Entry 58C, Boxes 12–13. Although McNair did advocate equipping and employing cavalry for its primary role of reconnaissance, leading to an inability to engage in prolonged fighting, he did not base this view solely on his experience gained during the many tests and maneuvers that he had participated in or overseen. Rather, he followed guidance provided by the War Department for the conduct of the tests. Specifically, this guidance dictated emphasizing the cavalry's primary mission of reconnaissance while avoiding prolonged engagement in combat and handing off the fighting to infantry, armor, and artillery forces. This required optimizing the cavalry squadron organization for reconnaissance operations, which led to criticism from some cavalry personnel who believed the cavalry would never fully manage to avoid prolonged combat and therefore should be equipped like other combat units. McNair, responsible for implementing War Department guidance for the reorganization, might have seemed individually responsible for the shift in emphasis to reconnaissance over combat operations in cavalry unit organization and doctrine in the late 1930s. Archival records demonstrate that this is merely another example of oversimplifying processes as McNair's personal choices that actually originated in War Department guidance for implementation by McNair. In this case, McNair and the 2nd Division received this advice from the cavalry officers on the Leavenworth faculty months before the first PID test took place, and it was repeated as War Department guidance for design of the PID organization and test. Because McNair did not participate in the second round of tests of the triangular division, and because the War Department held veto power over all such matters, McNair could not have developed on his own the concept of the reconnaissance squadron as a light, "sneak and peek" focused unit that avoided combat whenever possible.

31. Various, "Observations, Questions, and Recommendations from Leavenworth and Branch Schools for PID Test of 1937," February–May 1937, NARA 2, RG 337, Entry 58C, Boxes 12–13. Lieutenant Colonel Ingles wrote to McNair on February 24, 1938, confirming receipt of the report and commending its quality despite the limited time available to prepare it as a result of Craig's insistence he receive it by February 20. The formatted and bound version of the report bears the date March 21, 1938, but

this report contains the same information provided by McNair on Craig's February 20 due date.

32. PID Test Review Board, "PID Test Report," October–November 1937, NARA 2, RG 337, Entry 58C, Boxes 12–13; H. C. Ingles to Lesley J. McNair, February 24, 1938, NARA 2, RG 337, Entry 58C, Boxes 12–13. The report's appendix A alone, "Supporting Data," is over 300 pages long.

33. J. K. Parsons, "Efficiency Report on General Officer," July 1, 1937–March 8, 1938; Malin Craig, "Letter of Commendation," April 5, 1938, both in McNair Papers, NARA, St. Louis.

34. PID and P2D Test Folders, NARA 2, RG 337, Entry 58C, Boxes 12–13.

35. S. M. Browne, "Report of Physical Examination," January 3, 1938, McNair Papers, NARA, St. Louis. The physical includes eleven endorsements, the first two recommending the special exam and the eleventh, on February 14, 1938, containing the surgeon general's recommendation McNair go before a medical board; S. U. Marietta, "Clinical Record: Request for Consultation—Special Examination," February 4, 1938, McNair Papers, NARA, St. Louis.

36. M. C. Stayer, "Report of Physical Examination," May 22, 1939, McNair Papers, NARA, St. Louis. McNair's 1939 physical includes an endorsement by the surgeon general recommending McNair go before a medical board. However, Chief of Staff Marshall responded to the surgeon general's recommendation to conduct a medical board with an order to issue a waiver for the condition, adding a handwritten note to the document explaining he saw no reason to pursue one. Although this could be construed as favoritism, at no point in three decades of medical history did any of McNair's exams indicate that he attempted to hide or downplay the severity of his hearing loss. Further, no evidence exists to indicate Marshall ordered the issuance of a waiver for any reason other than the one he described in his handwritten note attached to McNair's 1939 physical. Marshall (and Malin Craig, Marshall's predecessor and a huge admirer of McNair who helped propel his career forward despite his knowledge of McNair's hearing loss) knew through direct observation of McNair's duty performance in demanding general officer command and staff positions that the condition did not significantly hinder his duty performance or prevent his continued active service.

37. Wilson, *Maneuver and Firepower*, 130. As Wilson described, Lynch's concerns soon drew the attention of the media, leading to a *New York Times* report on Craig's plans to respond.

38. Ibid., 126–130.

39. J. K. Parsons, to General Malin Craig, June 13, 1938, NARA 2, RG 337, Entry 58C, Boxes 12–13.

40. Wilson, *Maneuver and Firepower*, 131–132; Holzimmer, *General Walter Krueger*, 65.

41. McNair voiced no opinions regarding the antitank issue or any other outcomes

of the tests; he merely designed, organized, and reported the results of a series of objective and thorough tests of the Modernization Board's updated division organization.

42. PID and P2D Test Division Files, NARA 2, RG 337, Entry 58C, Boxes 12–13; Wilson, *Maneuver and Firepower*, 131–133.

43. "Directive for Extended Field Service Test of New Division Organization," signed by order of the Secretary of War, January 24, 1939, NARA 2, RG 337, Entry 58C, Box 12; P2D Headquarters Staff, "File Number: 322.13 Provisional 2nd Division—General," March 9, 1939, NARA 2, RG 337, Entry 58C, Boxes 12–13. This consolidated folder contains correspondence between various personnel in the War Department, VIII Corps Area Headquarters, and the P2D Headquarters; however, the majority of P2D test planning documents bear McNair's signature.

44. "Directive for Extended Field Service Test of New Division Organization," January 24, 1939.

45. Ibid.

46. Marshall, *Soldierly Spirit*, 1:702–703.

47. F. W. Rowell, "Efficiency Report on General Officer," July 1, 1938–March 17, 1939, McNair Papers, NARA, St. Louis.

48. Wilson, *Maneuver and Firepower*, 132–133; Kevin C. Holzimmer, *General Walter Krueger*, 65–69. Wilson and Holzimmer differed in their account of Krueger's assessment of the P2D. Wilson wrote, "Krueger found the organization sound except for the quartermaster battalion and the need to make some minor adjustments in a few other elements." Holzimmer, perhaps because of his book's focus (and more detailed research) on Krueger, described Krueger's fundamental concerns over the division's organization in more detail, particularly its shortage of antimechanized capability and its limited fighting durability, which was the result of a lack of organic logistics assets. According to Holzimmer, Krueger also worried about a disconnect between the army's overarching doctrine, which stressed defeating the enemy through overwhelming combat power while relying on light divisions organized to emphasize mobility over firepower and limited logistics to support their intended mobility. In short, Krueger emerged as one of the first army officers to object to the concepts of pooling, streamlining, and task organization, believing the divisions should contain the same organic capabilities as army corps, only on a smaller scale.

CHAPTER 8. PROTECTIVE MOBILIZATION

1. Hopkins, *Pacific War*, 21–22.

2. Kennedy, *Freedom from Fear*, 400. The law included limits on the provision of war matériel to other nations, which some members of Congress believed led to the sinking of American ships by German submarines during World War I, resulting in the inevitability of American participation in the war. Therefore, legislators restricted such aid to the provision of raw materials only, on a cash-and-carry basis. However,

because American businessmen understood the profit potential of arms sales, this provision had a two-year limit.

3. Ibid., 401–402.

4. Ibid., 402–403; Stoler, *Allies and Adversaries*, 16. Stoler pointed out that in his first term Roosevelt focused on domestic matters, but in 1937 "he started to provide the direction and guidance his army and navy officers so desired." He began to show interest in war plans, as well as in the creation of new ones, and after the *Panay* sinking, he finally began talks with Britain regarding naval staff coordination, as his naval officers had recommended long before the incident.

5. Kennedy, *Freedom from Fear*, 403–405. When pressed by the British to take, as the positive measures he mentioned, specific actions to assist China in its defense against Japanese aggression, Roosevelt responded that American public opinion prevented him from merely acting as "a tail to the British kite." The *London Times* concluded from this that Roosevelt expressed more of an attitude than a program, an assessment Kennedy called "prophetic."

6. Ibid., 384–385.

7. Evans, *Third Reich*, 678–683.

8. For a detailed summary of the anti-Jewish pogroms of 1938, see ibid., 580–610.

9. Weinberg, *World at Arms*, 90–91. According to Weinberg, some evidence existed to suggest French foreign minister Georges Bonnet might have considered negotiating with Hitler to avoid war after the fall of Poland, but the prime minister, Edouard Daladier, removed Bonnet from office on September 13 and took personal responsibility for diplomatic relations with Nazi Germany; Kennedy, *Freedom from Fear*, 435–436.

10. Kennedy, *Freedom from Fear*, 466–468.

11. Stoler, *Allies and Adversaries*, 26; Kennedy, *Freedom from Fear*, 460–461.

12. Marshall, *Soldierly Spirit*, 1:702–703. No orders exist in McNair's personnel file assigning him to Fort Leavenworth.

13. Quoted in ibid., 705–706.

14. Quoted in ibid., 707. Marshall and McNair remembered the challenges that America's hastily mobilized divisions faced when attempting to master the complex fighting methods that Pershing's open warfare doctrine required, leading many to train primarily or even exclusively on trench-to-trench warfare before deploying to the front. Technology had apparently since emerged that many army leaders believed would change the nature of warfare to one more like the open warfare that Pershing and like-minded AEF officers envisioned (and that Germany's campaign in Poland would seem to verify). The challenge remained to train raw recruits for this complex, maneuver-focused form of warfare during a rapid mobilization—something the army failed to do to its satisfaction before World War I. Marshall believed McNair could establish the mind-set at CGSS that would enable its graduates to meet this challenge. As documents from years earlier demonstrate, when McNair spoke of the open nature of modern warfare, he expressed not his own personal vision but also a commonly

held view among army regulars. McNair merely sought to instill accepted army think-ing among many AEF veterans in the minds of young officers and new recruits, in ac-cordance with Marshall's guidance. Only time would tell whether this vision of future warfare would match reality.

15. Ibid., 707–708.

16. Ibid., 708. Such thinking dominated discourse among AEF veterans during the interwar period. In addition to using World War I terminology—still the common language among this core group of army leaders—stabilized warfare represented war at its worst, which the US army would avoid in the future through technology, instead fighting against dispersed units and exploiting gaps, rather than digging in and adopt-ing a seige warfare mentality.

17. Ibid., 710–714; Taaffe, *Marshall and His Generals*, 4–5.

18. Weigley, *History of the United States Army*, 415–421.

19. Lesley J. McNair, "Graduation Address to Command and General Staff School Graduating Class and Faculty, June 20, 1939," McNair Papers, CARL.

20. Schifferle, *America's School for War*, 167–168.

21. Ibid., 190.

22. Matheny, *Carrying the War to the Enemy*, 76. Analysis of McNair's AWC class curriculum supports this assertion. Although the CGSS curriculum might have neg-lected logistics and air power, these remained key topics at the AWC throughout the 1930s, preparing the officers bound for senior leadership far better than Leavenworth did for those aspects of the conduct of operational art by large formations.

23. McNair Papers, CARL.

24. Historian William O. Odom described the AEF's reliance on British and French doctrine and procedures both when preparing for the war and later evaluating its les-sons to write the 1923 manual. Odom, *After the Trenches*, 72–78. Postwar board re-ports are held at the NARA 2, RG 120, Entry 23.

25. Kretchik, *US Army Doctrine*, 138–139; for a detailed analysis of the vibrant and professional discourse that took place in several branch journals in the 1920s and 1930s, see Fullerton, "Bright Prospects, Bleak Realities."

26. Kretchik, *US Army Doctrine*, 138–139.

27. Ibid., 140.

28. Ibid., 143.

29. George C. Marshall to Lesley J. McNair, September 29, 1939, McNair Papers, CARL; Marshall, *We Cannot Delay*, 2:30.

30. Kretchik, *US Army Doctrine*, 143–144.

31. Ibid., 144.

32. Ibid., 143–147. Kretchik highlighted the many significant changes in the new manual; for a more critical assessment, see Odom, *After the Trenches*, 236. For more on the US army's modern definition of operational art, see US Army, *Unified Land Oper-ations*.

33. Kretchik, *US Army Doctrine*, 147.

34. Ibid., 143–147. Kretchik highlighted the many significant changes in the new manual; US Army, *Field Service Regulations (Tentative)*, 5; for a more critical assessment, see Odom, *After the Trenches*, 166. Despite his criticisms, Odom pointed out that "it is unfair to judge the army too harshly for its failure to prescribe more accurate doctrine on the eve of World War II. After all, at the time only the German Army had developed a correct formula for success on the modern battlefield, and it had done so through an expensive and extensive process of field testing and combat trials."

35. Kretchik, *US Army Doctrine*, 147; Odom, *After the Trenches*, 236–243.

36. Kretchik, *US Army Doctrine*, 147.

37. Schifferle, *America's School for War*, 149–150.

38. Marshall, *We Cannot Delay*, 236–237; emphasis in original. McNair responded in an undated memorandum, "As to the new courses, I see no clouds on the horizon," and he assured Marshall, "I am confident that the course will be thoroughly effective, although improvements doubtless will suggest themselves as we go along. You may be sure that we shall spare no effort to make the new setup all that you want it to be."

39. Schifferle, *America's School for War*, 149.

40. Ibid., 151.

41. George C. Marshall to Lesley J. McNair, April 12, 1940, McNair Papers, CARL. Marshall expressed his conviction that an abbreviated CGSS could still accomplish its mission, based on his five years' experience at the Infantry School, where Marshall observed much wasted time and a slow pace of instruction often caused by ill-prepared students or instruction gauged to the weakest students in each class. He believed sending future students well-designed preparatory materials, along with improved instructional methods and streamlining of the staff procedures taught could enable CGSS to produce equivalent results in less than half the time.

42. For example, contemporary doctrine anticipated that ground units, with their increased mobility, would often outpace their artillery support and specified that the AAC would provide fire support to ground units in such situations. However, some key leaders, including Marshall and McNair, doubted whether the AAC or the supported ground forces possessed the training and equipment necessary to accomplish this mission. See Lesley J. McNair to George C. Marshall, n.d., McNair Papers, CARL.

43. Marshall, *We Cannot Delay*, 2:144–145.

44. US Army, *Field Service Regulations*, 13–14. "Support by combat aviation is also required by mechanized and motmized units, particularly when operating beyond the range of friendly artillery. In all cases, the effectiveness of air support of ground troops is dependent upon careful coordination, close cooperation, and rapid signal communication."

45. Gabel, *US Army GHQ Maneuvers*, 39. As late as May 1941, US army doctrine still described an important role for the AAC in close air support of ground forces, long after an apparent shift in AAC focus to strategic bombing and aerial interdiction

missions seemed to limit its ability to provide such support. Although the strategic bombing and interdiction roles certainly provided important capabilities in the conduct of campaigns, the army's operations doctrine remained unchanged, leaving ground forces to expect timely close air support in combat even though it seemed that the AAC's interest in other missions overshadowed its dedication to the CAS role. Time would tell whether this remained merely a theoretical shortfall or a real limitation in practice.

46. Muller, "Close Air Support," 180.

47. For a detailed assessment of the Army Air Corps' (later USAAF's) views on air support to ground forces in the interwar years, see Rein, *North African Air Campaign*, 20–21. Rein argued that despite the AAC's shift in focus of equipment development to strategic bombers, it developed sound close air support procedures in the 1930s that formed an intellectual foundation for the development of doctrine for aviation support to ground forces by April 1942.

48. Cameron, *Mobility, Shock, and Firepower*.

49. Dunham, *Study No. 29*.

50. Lesley J. McNair, "Folder: Anti-Tank Doctrines and Development," 1940–41, NARA 2, RG 337, Entry 58, Box 8; Command and General Staff School, *Antimechanized Defense*.

51. For numerous examples of McNair's interactions with local community leaders, the media, and foreign military dignitaries while serving as Commandant, see McNair Papers, CARL.

52. Schifferle, *America's School for War*, 161.

53. Johnson, *Fast Tanks*, 224. To support this assertion, Johnson cited the letter Marshall wrote to McNair on February 23, 1939, informing him of his imminent appointment as commandant at Fort Leavenworth. One wonders how a letter written months before McNair's arrival at Leavenworth supports an assessment of his achievements at the end of his assignment there.

54. Adjutant General, "Creation of General Headquarters," July 26, 1940, McNair Papers, NARA, St. Louis.

55. Schaffer, *America in the Great War*, 63. See Kennedy, *Freedom from Fear*, 463.

56. Kennedy, *Freedom from Fear*, 463–464.

57. Ibid., 476. Kennedy credited this massive increase in military expenditures and the jobs it created with ending the Depression, not Roosevelt's New Deal programs. The impact of this increased spending on America's ability to prepare for war remained uncertain because, as Kennedy and many other historians have emphasized, by the end of 1940 the American military's most precious and scarce resourse was no longer money but time. America still had to prove that it could live up to Roosevelt's "arsenal of democracy" promise, and the demands on raw materials, manpower, and the military's ability to expand rapidly guaranteed that it would be no simple matter.

58. Kennedy, *Freedom from Fear*, 464–475; Murray and Millett, *War to Be Won*,

16–17. Roosevelt's interest in the war initially revolved around the potential of war production to salvage the US economy, but he also recognized that years of isolationism had led America to sit by as the Axis threat grew to great proportions, particularly with respect to America's crucial ally, Great Britain. This led him to support economic policies that required America to choose sides, face military engagement, and risk direct involvement in the war despite Roosevelt's public assurances that America would remain neutral.

59. Koistinen, *Arsenal of World War II*, 15.

60. Ibid., 15–16.

61. Higgs, *Depression, War, and Cold War*, 79–104.

62. Koistinen, *Arsenal of World War II*, 16–17.

63. Lacey, *Keep from All Thoughtful Men*, 19–22. In one major element of this book, Lacey convincingly dismantled the myth that General Albert C. Wedemeyer wrote the World War II victory plan—a myth that remains common to the modern understanding of World War II, as seen in works like Kirkpatrick, *Unknown Future*. Much of the accepted wisdom on American strategic planning from June 1940 to December 1941 stems from the official histories, such as Leighton and Coakley, *Global Logistics and Strategy*. For an alternative perspective, see Hopkins, *Pacific War*, 2.

64. Lacey, *Keep from All Thoughtful Men*, 20–22; Hopkins, *Pacific War*, 20. Roosevelt had just won an election after promising to keep America out of the war, so he could not officially approve any military strategy for direct American participation in it. However, had he disapproved of the plan, the secretaries knew he would not have been, in Lacey's words, "slow to demolish" it. The official history, however, implies Roosevelt officially endorsed this change in strategy, although Plan Dog only warranted a single mention, in a footnote. See Leighton and Coakley, *Global Logistics and Strategy*, 43n61.

65. Matheny, *Carrying the War to the Enemy*, 55–91; Lacey, *Keep from All Thoughtful Men*, 51.

66. Lacey, *Keep from All Thoughtful Men*, 17–18.

67. Ibid., 22. Paul A. C. Koistinen's three detailed studies of America's political economy from 1865 to 1945 remain essential references. Lacey supplemented and updated previous works like Koistinen's by providing a well-researched and accessible account that shatters several myths regarding the World War II industrial mobilization effort. See Koistinen, *Mobilizing for Modern War*; Koistinen, *Planning War*; and Koistinen, *Arsenal of World War II*.

68. Lacey, *Keep from All Thoughtful Men*, 30.

69. Koistinen, *Arsenal of World War II*, 187.

70. Lacey, *Keep from All Thoughtful Men*, 68–69.

71. Carew, *Becoming the Arsenal*, 163–167.

72. Lacey, *Keep from All Thoughtful Men*, 51. Lacey focused on the War Production Board, while acknowledging that it "was not the final or most powerful of the war

production agencies," because it was the lead industrial mobilization agency during the period he covered in his book. Koistinen highlighted the poor leadership qualities of the WPB chair, Donald M. Nelson, whose "guileless" desire for consent and consensus left him open to attack from more skillful bureaucratic infighters. Koistinen, *Arsenal of World War II*, 213.

73. Somervell and army undersecretary Robert Patterson worked together as the military representatives to the civilian industrialists they counted on to lead the transition to a war economy. David Kennedy described Patterson, a former soldier who still wore a belt he had stripped from the body of a German soldier he killed in 1918, as "not the sort of man who was likely to knuckle under to the pipe-smoking, pencil-pushing, former mail-order salesman at the WPB." Kennedy noted that Somervell "was cut from the same cloth" and described their approach to providing the WPB military requirement estimates as "brassing through the military's production program." Kennedy, *Freedom from Fear*, 621.

74. Lacey, *Keep from All Thoughtful Men*, 96–110. Only Somervell, of the three functional commanders, served on the WPB or participated in negotiations with civilian industrialists. Patterson theoretically represented the entire military, but he prioritized the needs of the Army Air Forces and the navy over that of the Army Ground Forces.

75. Lacey, *Keep from All Thoughtful Men*, 112.

76. Ibid., 112.

77. "World Battlefronts, SUPPLY: SOS," *Time*, June 15, 1942, 21.

78. Ibid., 21–22.

79. Lacey, *Keep from All Thoughtful Men*, 4.

80. Koistinen, *Arsenal of World War II*, 133.

81. Kennedy, *Freedom from Fear*, 646–647.

82. Ohl, *Supplying the Troops*, 85–86, at 85.

83. Ibid., 86–88, at 88. As David Kennedy described him, Somervell "was a man in whom organizational genius and Olympian arrogance were mixed in equal measure. In Sovervell's view, all the civilian war agencies amounted to nothing more or less than an effort by 'Henry Wallace and the leftists to take over the country.'" Kennedy, *Freedom from Fear*, 621.

84. "Army and Navy—Command, The Cost: God Help George Marshall," *Time*, October 19, 1942, 74

85. Lacey, *Keep from All Thoughtful Men*, 114–115; Kennedy, *Freedom from Fear*, 628.

86. Kennedy, *Freedom from Fear*, 629.

87. For one significant example of the works that created and supported the longevity of the interpretation that America's material production, rather than the effectiveness of its army, served as the nation's main contribution to the Allied war effort, see Weigley, *Eisenhower's Lieutenants*.

88. Kennedy, *Freedom from Fear*, 631–633, at 632.

89. National policy initially allowed volunteering during the mobilization for World War I, but this led to significant problems. Volunteers could avoid service in the combat arms, and often did so. During the mobilization for World War I, government officials quickly recognized the severity of this problem and suspended the practice. During the mobilization for World War II, the government initially used the same practice, although it created the same problems. Volunteering remained an option through December 1942, after which few options remained to reverse the damage done. See Kennedy, *Freedom from Fear*, 635–636.

90. Kennedy, *Freedom from Fear*, 635.

91. Palmer, Wiley, and Keast, *Procurement and Training*, 5.

92. Ibid., 3.

93. Ibid., 10.

94. Ibid., 9–10.

95. Palmer, "Study No. 5," 2.

96. Coffman, *Regulars*, 397.

97. Palmer, Wiley, and Keast, *Procurement and Training*, 91–95.

98. Wilson, *America and World War II*, 171. A sampling of test questions provided in Wilson's book makes it clear that recruits from less affluent backgrounds and possessing fewer years of quality education would fare poorly on the test simply because they had no exposure to various aspects of American culture referred to in the test. This meant the Army General Classification Test did a much better job of dividing recruits along lines of race and class than the intended measure of learning potential.

99. Ibid., 186.

100. Palmer, "Study No. 5," 9.

101. Kennedy, *Freedom from Fear*, 711; Palmer, Wiley, and Keast, *Procurement and Training*, 14–28.

102. Palmer, "Study No. 5," 2.

103. Kennedy, *Freedom from Fear*, 429. The Munich crisis took place in the fall of 1938, when Hitler met with European democratic leaders in Munich to convince them to endorse his recent annexation of the Sudetenland.

104. Kennedy, *Freedom from Fear*, 429–431. Marshall's response changed Roosevelt's interactions with Marshall, who from that day never addressed him by his first name. This episode might have led to a more formal relationship between the two men, but it apparently did not change Roosevelt's respect for Marshall's military capability. Roosevelt did not oppose Marshall's replacement of Craig as army chief of staff when Craig rose to secretary of the army. Marshall's morally courageous response also touched off a long and productive debate between Roosevelt and his service chiefs about the tension between providing military equipment to the Allies and producing equipment for mobilizing US military units. Total military production in America lagged far behind Roosevelt's goals well into 1941, largely because Congress saw the

European war as far away and not America's problem, causing the legislators to approve only small appropriations for military purchases.

105. Franklin D. Roosevelt to Secretary of the Navy Knox, January 2, 1942, NARA 2, RG 165, Entry 422, Office of the Director, Plans and Operations, Box 40, Folder 2. On the same day, the president forwarded a copy of this directive to Malin Craig to inform him of his orders for increased production; whether the nation's industrial capacity could enable industry to meet these demands remained uncertain.

106. Lesley J. McNair, "KRG Notes from Letter, Lesley J. McNair to George S. Patton," September 28, 1942, NARA 2, RG 319, Box 129, Folder 2.

107. Memorandum for Record, Papers of Dwight David Eisenhower, vol. 1, pt. 1, chap. 2, "Bolero," http://eisenhower.press.jhu.edu/.

108. Franklin D. Roosevelt to Secretary of the Army Craig, January 4, 1942, NARA 2, RG 165, Entry 422, Office of the Director, Plans and Operations, Box 40, Folder 2.

109. Operations Division Chief Gerow to Army Chief of Staff Marshall, January 8, 1942; Franklin D. Roosevelt to Secretary of the Navy Knox, January 2, 1942, both in NARA 2, RG 165, Entry 422, Office of the Director, Plans and Operations, Box 40, Folder 2.

110. Lacey, *Keep from All Thoughtful Men*, 22. President Roosevelt did not request munitions and equipment production estimates to support offensive operations until July 9, 1941, and did not receive a response until September 11.

111. Ibid., 25–27.

112. Ibid., 17. The United States produced and used almost ten million parachutes during the war.

113. P. P. Bishop, "Efficiency Report," April 6–July 1, 1939; Malin Craig, "Efficiency Report on General Officer," April 6–June 30, 1939, both in McNair Papers, NARA, St. Louis.

114. P. P. Bishop, "Efficiency Report," July 2, 1939–July 1, 1940, McNair Papers, NARA, St. Louis.

CHAPTER 9. TRAINING THE ARMY GROUND FORCES

1. Adjutant General, "Creation of General Headquarters"; Weigley, *History of the United States Army*, 429; Greenfield, Palmer, and Wiley, *Organization of Ground Combat Troops*, 1–6.

2. For example, Martin Blumenson wrote that when Marshall selected McNair to serve as GHQ chief of staff, he "gave him a free hand to fashion the combat units into a proficient fighting force." Blumenson, "Kasserine Pass," 236. This assertion overstates both the autonomy McNair enjoyed and the authority he possessed, given the many factors involved in achieving his mission that McNair did not control.

3. Marshall, *We Cannot Delay*, 2:236–237.

4. Marshall, *Aggressive and Determined Leadership;* see also other correspondence in Marshall, *We Cannot Delay.*

5. Greenfield, Palmer, and Wiley, *Organization of Ground Combat Troops,* 6–9. As Eli Kahn observed, McNair's role was a "purely domestic one of training troops for combat overseas, and thus he had no direct jurisdiction over any soldier outside the continental limits of the United States." Kahn, *McNair,* 2.

6. Greenfield, Palmer, and Wiley, *Organization of Ground Combat Troops,* 15.

7. Taaffe, *Marshall and His Generals,* 6; for another description of McNair's decreasing influence over time, see Pogue, *George C. Marshall: Organizer of Victory,* 71.

8. War Department Operations Division, "Operations Division Files: Office of the Director of Plans and Operations, War Department," January 1942–July 1944, NARA 2, RG 165, Entry 422, Boxes 40–48.

9. Many examples of Marshall's continued involvement in minor details are recorded in his personal papers. See, for example, his correspondence with McNair and Hugh Drum regarding a soldier's complaint at being passed over for promotion. Marshall, *We Cannot Delay,* 2:501. One can find much of McNair's correspondence with Marshall in the four-volume set of Marshall's papers. Other correspondence exists in various archival collections, including RG 165, 319, and 337 at NARA 2, and the McNair collections at NARA, St. Louis, and CARL. One rarely encounters critiques in American military history of General Marshall and his staff, but the redundancy and resulting inefficiency of this arrangement merits further study.

10. Gabel, *US Army GHQ Maneuvers,* 22–30.

11. Ibid., 13–14. As Gabel explained, "Few of the deficiencies exhibited in the August maneuvers were truly the fault of the National Guard. The War Department had neglected to form triangular divisions in the National Guard, and, in fact, would not do so until 1942" (13). The PID and P2D test results, as well as feedback from the field, indicated that the National Guard would not be able to reorganize to the triangular structure for quite some time, and in fact it took war to force the issue.

12. Greenfield, Palmer, and Wiley, *Organization of Ground Combat Troops,* 15–31. McNair showed greater interest in the GHQ training role than its operational responsibilities, despite his experience in the 1920s as Hawaiian Department G-3, but the headquarters excelled in both. The deputy chief of staff, Brigadier General Harry J. Maloney, led the operational side of GHQ as it assumed planning responsibility for an ever-growing list of task forces and locations, including Iceland, Greenland, Alaska, and three of the four US defense commands. By delegating the operational role to Maloney, McNair could concentrate on training. However, he retained overall control of each. Maloney ran an effective planning staff, and he later argued that the War Department could have improved its effectiveness by continuing to rely on GHQ to perform this role. Instead, by early 1942 further reorganization returned planning responsibility to the War Department General Staff. See Kent Roberts Greenfield, "Memorandum of Conversations with Maj. Gen. Harry J. Malony, Hq 94th Division," January 10, 1944, NARA 2, RG 319, Box 123.

13. Greenfield, Palmer, and Wiley, *Organization of Ground Combat Troops,* 131–141.

14. Quoted in ibid., 131.

15. Ibid., 153–155.

16. McNair disdained large staffs and the inertia their administrative requirements caused; see Greenfield, Palmer, and Wiley, *Organization of Ground Combat Troops,* 12; Kahn, *McNair,* 21.

17. Greenfield, Palmer, and Wiley, *Organization of Ground Combat Troops,* 26–30.

18. War Department Adjutant General, "Promotion Orders and Oath of Office for Promotion to Major General (Temporary)," December 1, 1940, McNair Papers, NARA, St. Louis.

19. Kahn, *McNair,* 41; Clark, *Calculated Risk,* 11–13. These various unit field maneuvers served as an important prelude to the large-scale GHQ maneuvers of 1941, and McNair's frequent presence enabled him to impart a common understanding of the latest doctrine to leaders of newly activated units.

20. Clark, *Calculated Risk,* 17; Marshall, *Aggressive and Determined Leadership,* 4:210.

21. Marshall, *We Cannot Delay,* 2:345.

22. Whitaker, "These Are the Generals—McNair," 12.

23. See, for example, McNair Papers, NARA, St. Louis; Kent Roberts Greenfield, "Notes of KRG on General McNair Correspondence," April 30, 1946, NARA 2, RG 319, Entry 488, CMH Manuscript File: AGF, Box 129; Maclyn P. Burg, "Interview with Leroy Lutes," General Services Administration, National Archives and Record Service, Dwight D. Eisenhower Library, http://www.eisenhower.archives.gov/; Robert M. Ward, "Interview with Thomas T. Handy," General Services Administration, National Archives and Record Service, Dwight D. Eisenhower Library, http://www.eisenhower .archives.gov/; and War Department Operations Division, "Operations Division Files: Office of the Director of Plans and Operations, War Department," January 1942–July 1944, NARA 2, RG 165, Entry 422, Boxes 40–48.

24. Faber, "Lesley James McNair," 164–165.

25. Greenfield, Palmer, and Wiley, *Organization of Ground Combat Troops,* 156–157.

26. Ibid., 33–34.

27. Gabel, *US Army GHQ Maneuvers,* 44–45.

28. Marshall, *We Cannot Delay,* 2:519.

29. War Department Adjutant General, "Promotion Orders and Oath of Office for Promotion to Lieutenant General (Temporary)," June 9, 1941, McNair Papers, NARA, St. Louis.

30. Even after Elihu Root's military reforms, motivated by the weaknesses revealed in America's military by the Spanish-American War, the relatively small-scale annual maneuvers served more as scripted training events than true competitive simulated battles. This contributed to the amateurism that some historians have described as evident in the American military in 1918, when after a year and a half of preparation the

AEF still barely possessed the skill necessary to conduct effective offensive operations at the Meuse-Argonne. See Gabel, *US Army GHQ Maneuvers*, 3–4; Ferrell, *America's Deadliest Battle*; Mark Grotelueschen's account of the 1st Division's reduction of St. Mihiel, in Grotelueschen, *AEF Way of War*, 106–125. This account describes both the ability of the AEF's 1st Division to conduct set-piece attacks when supported by massed fires, and the same unit's challenges transitioning to deep attacks and exploitation. Although many technological shortcomings contributed to the latter challenges, the division also had no opportunity to conduct large-scale maneuvers before engaging in combat.

31. Gabel, *US Army GHQ Maneuvers*, 4–5, 12.

32. Ibid.; Moenk, *History of Large-Scale Army Maneuvers*, 38–70.

33. Taaffe, *Marshall and His Generals*, 6. Although Marshall saw the promotion and assignment of general officers as one of his primary duties, he admitted his work pace forced him to rely on key subordinates for recommendations, "especially General Lesley McNair."

34. Marshall, *We Cannot Delay*, 2:6.

35. Coffman, *Regulars*, 397.

36. The press reported on McNair's tendency to recommend reclassification of officers who did not perform well in mobilization training. *Time* reported, "To many of these officers, the 1941 maneuvers mean the end of the road. Two weeks ago [McNair] told newsmen at Washington that the maneuvers would be more than a training school. For officers they will also be a test of fitness to lead troops in battle. The dull, the lazy, the careless, the generally incompetent, shown up in the field as well as by past records, will have to face the dreaded reclassification boards ("B-Boards"). Found substandard, they will get the gate." "National Defense: Test in the Field," *Time*, June 23, 1941, 23.

37. Taaffe, *Marshall and His Generals*, 7–8.

38. McNair frequently commented on the weeding-out process that would take place at the maneuvers, particularly for officers. See "Army: Discipline Wanted," *Time*, October 13, 1941, 36. In this article, McNair was quoted as saying, "There is no question that many of the weaknesses developed in these maneuvers are repeated again and again for lack of discipline. . . . A commander who cannot develop proper discipline must be replaced." McNair's insistence on tough, realistic training made national headlines as well, as in "Army: No More Phony Maneuvers," *Time*, June 16, 1941, 21. McNair did not spare subpar general officers from public criticism—although as a group, not by name: "Said Lieut General Lesley J. McNair, GHQ Chief of Staff, with characteristic frankness: 'A lot of these Generals who want to fire their Chiefs of Staff ought to fire themselves. We're going to start at the top and work down. We've got some bum Generals, and maybe I'm one of them, but we're going to weed them out. Have we the bright young Majors and Captains to replace them? Yes.'" "Army: Baffle of Louisiana," *Time*, September 29, 1941, 32.

39. Kretchik, *US Army Doctrine,* 148.

40. Odom, *After the Trenches,* 242.

41. Ibid., 242–243.

42. Kretchik, *US Army Doctrine,* 148–151.

43. Schifferle, *America's School for War,* 53–55.

44. Kretchik described the manual as "both a guide and a reference work, an operational and tactical education stuffed between two covers." Kretchik, *US Army Doctrine,* 150.

45. For just a few examples of the works that created and maintain this interpretation, see Weigley, *Eisenhower's Lieutenants;* van Creveld, *Fighting Power;* Hastings, *Overlord;* and Keegan, *Second World War.*

46. Gabel, *US Army GHQ Maneuvers,* 45.

47. Gabel pointed out that McNair fought hard to acquire actual equipment before the maneuvers, wanting to avoid situations like those in which "one man with a flag is a tank." Ibid., 49. New equipment received just before the GHQ manuevers included "the first M3 medium tanks, 105-mm howizters, halftracks, jeeps, and modern aircraft."

48. The antitank defense issue provides a particularly useful example of the misrepresentation of McNair's views and actions in many historical accounts, and shares much in common with other matters of controversy that have made him the target of criticism. Therefore, the following provides a detailed analysis of the issue of antitank defense while more briefly covering other issues due to space limitations.

49. Lesley J. McNair to Earl W. Bacon, June 20, 1940, NARA 2, RG 337, Entry 58, Box 8, "Anti-Tank Doctrines and Development" folder.

50. McNair's view of modern warfare, informed by years of involvement in recent division redesign tests, army maneuvers, and doctrine development, closely matched the views represented in current army doctrine and War Department views on ongoing modernization and reorganization efforts. See "Anti-Tank Doctrines and Development" folder, NARA 2, RG 337, Entry 58, Box 8; NARA 2, RG 337, Entry 58C, Test Division Files.

51. Lesley J. McNair, "Remarks by Lt. Gen. L. J. McNair, GSC," at Antitank Conference, Army War College, July 14, 1941, NARA 2, RG 319, Entry 488, CMH Manuscript File AGF, Box 136, Folder 2.

52. Ibid.

53. McNair, "AT Folder," McNair Papers, CARL; Lesley J. McNair, "Lesley J. McNair to Earl W. Bacon," June 20, 1940, NARA 2, RG 337, Entry 58, Box 8, "Anti-Tank Doctrines and Development" folder.

54. Gabel, *US Army GHQ Maneuvers,* 31–32; Winton, *Corps Commanders of the Bulge,* 88. Winton wrote a succinct critique that reflects the commonly encountered view: "McNair proved to be incorrect: combined arms of infantry, artillery, *and* tanks were the norm, not the exception." Unfortunately, Winton did not provide a reference

to support this assertion; this interpretation of McNair's views could stem from one interpretation of Command and General Staff School, *Antimechanized Defense,* or from reading War Department G-3 documentation on the topic that does describe tank masses as the norm—documents that McNair argued against in the early stages of the antitank debate.

55. US Army, *Tentative Field Service Regulations: Operations.* McNair oversaw the development of the Tentative FSR (1939), to which Marshall gave tentative approval in essentially unmodified form. It therefore serves as one of the best summaries of McNair's ideas about army operations in the late 1930s. One of the main ideas emphasized in the manual deals with the concept that the army now calls combined arms operations (referred to in the 1939 FSR as "combined action of all arms and services"). Chapter 2, paragraph 20, reads, "GENERAL—The units comprising the Army of the United States pertain to two functional subdivisions, the arms and the services. The arms engage directly in combat and are known collectively as the line of the Army. The arms are: the Infantry, the Cavalry, the Field Artillery, the Coast Artillery Corps, the Air Corps, the Corps of Engineers, and the Signal Corps. The services are charged with serving the line of the Army by performing the necessary functions of administration, supply, replacement, hospitalization, and evacuation." The manual provides further clarification in chapter 2, paragraph 21: "No one arm wins battles. The combined action of all arms and services is essential to success. The characteristics of each arm and service adapt it to the performance of its special function. The higher commander coordinates and directs the action of all, exploiting their powers to attain the ends sought."

56. Command and General Staff School, *Antimechanized Defense,* 7.

57. Ibid., table of contents.

58. Compared to the fantastical visions of future armored warfare propounded by theorists like J. F. C. Fuller and B. H. Liddell Hart, who both foresaw modern mechanized warfare defined by masses of tanks fighting independently and exploiting the "indirect approach," the concepts in *Antimechanized Defense* seem quite sensible. See ibid., 8–9.

59. Ibid., 10–11.

60. Ibid., 30.

61. Ibid., 31.

62. Ibid., 13–14, 18.

63. For example, see Matheny, *Carrying the War to the Enemy,* 70–74.

64. Lesley J. McNair correspondence with Earl W. Bacon, June 17–20, 1940, NARA 2, RG 337, Entry 58, Box 8.

65. Yeide, *Tank Killers,* 11; Gabel, *Seek, Strike, and Destroy,* 12–13. Gabel pointed out that Marshall "had reached the same impasse with regard to the mechanized forces," causing him to "withdraw all tanks from the existing arms and place them under the authority of a new 'quasi-arm,' the Armored Force."

66. Marshall, *We Cannot Delay*, 2:500–501; emphasis in original.

67. For a source that offers a less critical description of McNair's role in World War II antitank defense while leaving out key details and overemphasizing McNair's role, see House, *Combined Arms Warfare*, 144–145.

68. Johnson, *Fast Tanks*, 149–152.

69. Wedemeyer calculated, like McNair, that the 37mm gun could only penetrate armor up to 2½ inches thick, and therefore the army would require a more powerful gun to defeat new tanks with thicker armor. Wedemeyer, "Antitank Defense," 258–261; Gabel, *Seek, Strike, and Destroy*, 13.

70. Cameron, *Mobility, Shock, and Firepower*, 317–323. Cameron also notes that McNair's ideas about pooling accurately represented "the minimization tendency evident in the triangular division's organization." This guidance accompanied the order for 2nd Division to form and test the PID, issued before McNair was assigned to the division and given the responsibility of leading the PID test effort.

71. Gabel, *US Army GHQ Maneuvers*, 54. Gabel argued, "The Louisiana maneuvers revealed that virtually nobody but McNair believed in or practiced the aggressive antitank concept." Instead, most commanders, either unaware of or lacking faith in their intended method of use, deployed their antitank units in a passive defensive mode. This led Marshall and McNair to see the key problem as one of doctrine and education while staging demonstrations for dignitaries, including the vice president and secretary of war, to encourage continued support for rapid production of new weapons and fielding of units. See Gabel, *US Army GHQ Maneuvers*, 123–124.

72. Ibid., 175–176. Armor advocates also argued that the poor performance of armor during the Carolina maneuvers had more to do with flawed use than with the effectiveness of antitank guns, referring primarily to rushed, independent attacks by massed tanks. Although this did not halt the development of the antitank defense force, it did lead the Armored Force to recognize the vulnerability of independent tank formations and to work toward more effective combined arms operations and a division organization that improved the proportion of infantry to tanks. See Gabel, *Seek, Strike, and Destroy*, 17–18.

73. Greenfield, Palmer, and Wiley, *Organization of Ground Combat Troops*, 82–84; see 85–142 for an excellent summary of GHQ's role in the many other training matters and debates the headquarters dealt with throughout 1941, many of which remained unresolved at the end of the year. These included airborne and amphibious training, air support training and doctrine, organization of continental defense commands, questions of ground force control of antiaircraft and air units, and mostly unsuccessful efforts to increase GHQ's authority to achieve its many assigned missions.

74. To distill a long and bitter dispute, about which historians have produced volumes of material since the war, into a brief summation, McNair had little control over the outcome of this debate. He again sought to limit the burden on shipping and logistics requirements by arguing against a heavy tank, seeing the M-4 Sherman

medium tank as a reasonable balance between effectiveness and efficiency. Once again, the final decision rested with the War Department, and after troops had engaged in combat, field commanders held far more sway with the War Department than McNair. Even then, opinions remained mixed regarding the need for a heavy tank, which Eisenhower also argued against, largely because he too understood the huge demands that the fielding of a heavy tank would place on American shipping and the logistics network, which remained stretched to the breaking point until the end of the war.

75. Greenfield, Palmer, and Wiley, *Organization of Ground Combat Troops,* 143–155.

CHAPTER 10. THE ARMY GROUND FORCES AT WAR

1. Gaddis, *Landscape of History.*

2. Coffman, *Regulars,* 287.

3. Lesley J. McNair, "Assumption of Command, Army Ground Forces," March 9, 1942, McNair Papers, NARA, St. Louis; Greenfield, Palmer, and Wiley, *Organization of Ground Combat Troops,* 1–37; "Army: Streamlined Army," *Time,* March 9, 1942, 39; Kleber, "Lesley James McNair," 697. One finds many of the difficulties associated with Army Ground Forces' role in formation and training of new divisions at various training facilities described in H. Hildring, "Formation of a New Division—Memo from Major General H. Hildring to Lieutenant General McNair," October 14, 1942, NARA 2, RG 319, Box 122.

4. Greenfield, Palmer, and Wiley, *Organization of Ground Combat Troops,* 152.

5. Ibid., 170. KRG Notes, NARA 2, RG 319, Entry 488, Box 129.

6. Lesley J. McNair, "KRG Notes from Memo: Lesley J. McNair to Chief of Staff, US Army War Department," March 17, 1942, NARA 2, RG 319, Box 129, Folder 2. This memo mentions an attachment created by Mark Clark that compared staff officer numbers by position and rank in the Army Ground Forces, Army Air Forces, and Army Service Forces, but this table did not appear in Greenfield's notes.

7. "Army Aims to Lift Air Force Status: Stimson Says Reorganization Will Recognize That This Is Largely an 'Air War,'" *New York Times,* March 5, 1943. The article also reported that Somervell's authority would extend "much further than is indicated by his designation as Commander of the Service of Supply," including "the Judge Advocate General, the Provost Marshal General and the Adjutant General, as well as probably half a dozen other large branches of the Army."

8. Greenfield, Palmer, and Wiley, *Organization of Ground Combat Troops,* 153.

9. Greenfield, "Memorandum of Conversations with Maj. Gen. Harry J. Malony." Hopkins, a longtime adviser on economic issues to President Roosevelt, and his secretary of commerce from 1938 to 1940, served during the war as Roosevelt's unofficial emissary to Great Britain and overseer of lend-lease to the Soviet Union; Weinberg, *World at Arms,* 242–243.

10. Greenfield, "Memorandum of Conversations with Maj. Gen. Harry J. Malony."

11. For these two examples of Somervell's ever-expanding perceived scope of responsibility and quest for power, see War Department Operations Division, "Operations Division Files: Office of the Director of Plans and Operations, War Department," January 1942–July 1944, NARA 2, RG 165, Entry 422, Boxes 40–48. Both memos appear in Box 42, Book 8.

12. Greenfield, "Memorandum of Conversations with Maj. Gen. Harry J. Malony."

13. US Army Ground Forces. "AGF Staff Study No. 2." The inclusion of a large number of footnotes, referring to War Department orders and correspondence to support the findings of the study, indicate the controversial nature of this study. Additionally, the AGF classified the study "Restricted," further revealing the command's awareness of the sensitive nature of the analysis and the author's awareness of the debate it could generate if disseminated widely.

14. Quoted in ibid., 28.

15. Ibid., 18.

16. Ibid., 49.

17. Ibid.

18. Kennedy, *Freedom from Fear*, 516–526; Murray and Millett, *War to Be Won*, 177–178.

19. Lacey, *Keep from All Thoughtful Men*, 132; Stoler, *Allies and Adversaries*, 100–122. Stoler's account emphasizes the significance of Wedemeyer's role in preparation for attendance at the Casablanca Conference as a key planner. Lacey's account appears to provide the first evidence that Wedemeyer fabricated his role in these events.

20. Lacey, *Keep from All Thoughtful Men*, 129–132.

21. Matheny, *Carrying the War to the Enemy*, 42; Clausewitz, *On War*, 177.

22. "Army and Navy: War Babies," *Time*, March 30, 1942, 47; "Army, Small Yankees," *Time*, April 27, 1942, 56. Months would go by before the War Department developed a new mobilization schedule and acknowledged that the thirty-two divisions planned for mobilization in 1942 would never join the ranks.

23. As an example of the vague hints at the effect of production limitations leading to significant changes in strategy, see Matloff, *Strategic Planning*, 13–14.

24. Kennedy, *Freedom from Fear*, 631. As Kennedy pointed out, the awakening of 1942 identified the limits of personnel available for mobilization but "brought only partial resolution to the conundrum of manpower policy." For a detailed account of the 90-Division Gamble as described in the army's official history, see Matloff, "90-Division Gamble."

25. Kenney, *Freedom from Fear*, 585.

26. Ibid., 133. Lacey arrived at this conclusion on the basis of Somervell's exclusive role in the civil–military mobilization debate and his obstinacy and ignorance of economic realities throughout the process.

27. Koistinen, *Arsenal of World War II*, 235–236.

28. Lesley J. McNair to George S. Patton Jr., September 28, 1942, NARA 2, RG 319, Entry 488, Box 129, Folder 2.

29. Greenfield, Palmer, and Wiley, *Organization of Ground Combat Troops*, 227. The new troop basis as of July 1, 1943, supported an eighty-eight-division army. Two provisional light divisions later added soon gained permanent status, leading to the use of the phrase "ninety-division army."

30. Greenfield, Palmer, and Wiley, *Organization of Ground Combat Troops*, 290–299.

31. Gabel, *Seek, Strike, and Destroy*, 14.

32. War Department Operations Division, "Operations Division Files: Office of the Director of Plans and Operations, War Department," January 1942–July 1944, NARA 2, RG 165, Entry 422, Boxes 40–48.

33. Johnson, *Fast Tanks*, 145, 222.

34. Weigley, *History of the United States Army*, 471; note that Weigley, too, asserted that McNair possessed the authority to make such decisions on his own, overstating his autonomy and authority. McNair prepared the PID test report for Major General Parsons, his division commander, which, upon arrival at the War Department, generated so much debate that the chief of staff, Malin Craig, ordered an army-wide review and redesign, followed by another round of tests. McNair helped plan this next test phase—the P2D tests—but he did not participate in them.

35. Eisenhower, *Papers of Dwight David Eisenhower*, vol. 1, pt. 1, chap. 1, "All We Need Is Ships!," http://eisenhower.press.jhu.edu/.

36. In a July 1943 letter on unit organization revisions, McNair wrote, "Staffs are being revised downward. They are to be provided solely for combat needs. Operations cannot possibly be swift and effective if staffs are large and clumsy." Greenfield, Palmer, and Wiley, *Organization of Ground Combat Troops*, 377.

37. Kahn, *McNair*, 47.

38. Greenfield, Palmer, and Wiley, *Organization of Ground Combat Troops*, 293–294.

39. Ibid., 295–296.

40. Ibid., 296–297.

41. Ibid.

42. Comparato, *Age of Great Guns*, 258.

43. Weigley, *History of the United States Army*, 468–469.

44. Matheny, *Carrying the War to the Enemy*, 76–78.

45. Citino, *German Way of War*, 269–270.

46. For more on the concept of the discourse on war, see Lynn, *Battle*.

47. Atkinson, *Army at Dawn*, 159–160; Daubin, "Battle of Happy Valley," 1. For the official history of the campaign in Northwest Africa, which provides an excellent overview of the Kasserine Pass battles, see Howe, *Northwest Africa*.

48. Atkinson, *Army at Dawn*, 307–340; Howe, *Battle History of the 1st Armored Division*, 126–142.

49. Kelly, *Meeting the Fox,* 227–248. Eisenhower struggled with subordinate commanders' complaints regarding the inferiority of American armor ever since his first campaign in North Africa in 1942–1943, where he ordered Patton to conduct demonstrations of the M3 Stuart light tank penetrating the armor of captured German Panzer IVs to improve his troops' confidence in the 37mm gun. Eisenhower recognized his subordinates' frustration with their less capable weapons, but he also understood the limitations in American production and shipping capacity that made fielding new weapon systems particularly challenging. The appearance of upgraded and new models of tanks and tank destroyers later in the war demonstrates that the War Department continued to look for solutions; it simply could not design, produce, and deliver across the Atlantic and Pacific oceans new models of heavy equipment as quickly as field commanders desired.

50. Weinberg, *World at Arms* 446. Demonstrating the fact that American tanks could fight effectively if used with skill, Colonel Henry E. Gardiner's armor battalion participated in the final battle at Sidi Bou Zid and watched Rommel retreat after four hours of fighting without Gardiner's having lost a single tank. See Atkinson, *Army at Dawn,* 377–381.

51. Howe, *Battle History of the 1st Armored Division,* 136–142.

52. Weinberg, *World at Arms,* 443–444.

53. Atkinson, *Army At Dawn,* 335–336.

54. Kelly, *Meeting the Fox,* 247–248.

55. A twenty-six-week field artillery unit training program signed by McNair on February 15, 1942, reveals that the field artillery still emphasized massed fires, building on the efforts at the Field Artillery School during the interwar years while using improved equipment to add efficiency and effectiveness to those procedures. L. J. McNair, "Unit Training Program for Field Artillery," NARA 2, RG 337, AGF Files, Row 353, Box 672. The success of America's field artillery attracted attention in the press, as seen in an August 23, 1943, *Time* article. The article emphasized their effectiveness, noting that they originated well before the World War I but did not evolve into observed, easily adjusted mass fires until the experimentation at the Field Artillery School's gunnery department during the interwar years, combined with the development of adequate radios and mechanized guns before World War II. The article highlighted the fighting in North Africa to illustrate how the invention of the slide rule (created in two hours by a captain from the National Guard) added a critical capability that enhanced the efficacy of the Fire Direction Center (FDC). With the slide rule, "enlisted men, with grocery-store arithmetic and Harry Burns' GFT (Graphical Fire Table), could do computing that had demanded trained officers, complicated mathematics and 76 pages of firing tables in fine type." This enabled the FDC and its batteries "to deliver fire with wicked intensity and speed." "Artillery: Slide-Rule Boys," *Time,* August 23, 1943, 57.

56. Weigley, *Eisenhower's Lieutenants,* 730.

57. Kent Roberts Greenfield, "Memorandum for Record, Subject: McNair Correspondence," April 30, 1946, NARA 2, RG 319, Entry 488, Box 129, File 2.

58. Gabel, *Seek, Strike, and Destroy,* 24–27.

59. Yeide, *Tank Killers,* 6–7. As Yeide pointed out, the War Department originally designated Bruce's organization the Tank Destroyer Command, but later, on the basis of McNair's reminder that it possessed no command authority, redesignated it a center. Gabel, *Seek, Strike, and Destroy,* 24–26.

60. Gabel, *Seek, Strike, and Destroy,* 27–48. Gabel asserted tank destroyer doctrine proved more flawed during operations in North Africa than the weapon systems themselves, which commanders found useful through various field expedients, such as using the weapons as additional indirect fire assets or infantry support weapons to break through enemy strong points. He also pointed out that the towed antitank gun originally supported by McNair proved easier to conceal than self-propelled guns, but it was less versatile, particularly in fulfilling the field-expedient roles commanders found for self-propelled guns.

61. Lesley J. McNair to A. D. Bruce, April 12, 1943, NARA 2, RG 337, Entry 58, Box 9.

62. Ibid.

63. A. D. Bruce to Lesley J. McNair, June 5, 1943, NARA 2, RG 337, Entry 58, Box 8.

64. "Observer's Report on 37mm Gun," February 21, 1943, NARA 2, RG 160, Box 1.

65. Gabel, *Seek, Strike, and Destroy,* 49–65. In particular, see Gabel's description of antitank gun employment at Mortain on 60–61.

66. Yeide, *Tank Killers,* 9–10.

67. Equipment Review Board, "Equipment Review Board Report," June 20, 1945, NARA 2, RG 319, Entry 488, CMH Manuscript File: AGF, Box 128, Annex E, 2–3.

68. George S. Patton Jr. to Tom Handy, December 29, 1943, NARA 2, RG 165, Entry 422, Office of the Director, Plans and Operations, Box 45, Book 14.

69. G. S. Patton Jr. to Corps, Division, Tank Group and Tank Battalion Commanders, April 15, 1944, NARA 2, RG 165, Entry 422, Office of the Director, Plans and Operations, Box 46, Book 18.

70. Ibid. Patton urged commanders to use their tanks in combined arms maneuver, not to hold them in reserve waiting for the big opportunity to appear.

71. R. A. Meredith to Chief of Staff, US Army (Attention: New Development Division), April 29, 1944, NARA 2, RG 165, Entry 422, Office of the Director, Plans and Operations, Box 46, Book 18.

72. Eisenhower to Marshall, March 12, 1945, *Papers of Dwight David Eisenhower,* vol. 4, pt. 10, chap. 26, "Plans and Preparations," http://eisenhower.press.jhu.edu/.

73. Ibid., Eisenhower to Marshall, March 18, 1945.

74. Ibid., Eisenhower to Maurice Rose (notes), March 18, 1945.

75. Ibid., Eisenhower to Marshall, March 26, 1945.

76. Kent Roberts Greenfield, "Gen. Christiansen—Conversation with Col. Greenfield," February 7, 1945, NARA 2, RG 319, Entry 488, Box 136.

77. Equipment Review Board, "Equipment Review Board Report," June 20, 1945, NARA 2, RG 319, Entry 488, CMH Manuscript File: AGF, Box 128, 1–2.

78. Ibid., 3; emphasis in original. Although the Army Air Forces might have approached this level of unified effort, the Army Ground Forces complied with the War Department organization, leaving the technnical details of weapons design to the Army Service Forces.

79. Beaver, *Modernizing the American War Department,* 200.

80. Ibid., 203–204.

81. Thomas T. Handy, "Comments of General Patton Concerning Certain Aspects of the Sicilian Invasion," August 4, 1943, NARA 2, RG 165, Entry 422, Box 44.

82. Ibid.

83. Kent Roberts Greenfield, "Gen. Christiansen—Conversation with Col. Greenfield," February 7, 1945, NARA 2, RG 319, Entry 488, Box 136.

84. Ibid. General Marshall actually made the decisions Christiansen referred to when he described the Armored Force's being smothered. This centered on the Armored Force's relative independence, which Marshall did not allow to expand like that of the Army Air Corps', primarily because of the perceived difference in the need for close coordination of armor to other ground troops, as opposed to aviation. See Greenfield, Palmer, and Wiley, *Organization of Ground Combat Troops,* 56–72.

85. Comparato, *Age of Great Guns,* 258–259.

86. Palmer, Wiley, and Keast, *Procurement and Training,* 175.

87. Ibid., 175–176.

88. Palmer, Wiley, and Keast, *Procurement and Training,* 173–174.

89. McNair noted the poor performance of many replacement center commanders and sometimes brought the weakest performers to General Marshal's attention. For example, McNair recommended the relief, reduction to permanent grade of colonel, and retirement of Brigadier General Forrest E. Williford, commanding general of the Antiaircraft Replacement Training Center at Fort Eustis, Virginia, in a memo to the War Department G-1 on December 7, 1942. Lesley J. McNair, "Memorandum to Chief of Staff, US Army (Attention: G-1, War Department). Subject: Reduction of General Officer to Permanent Grade," December 7, 1942, NARA 2, RG 337, Entry 58A, Box 9, File A–C.

90. Palmer, Wiley, and Keast, *Procurement and Training,* 179–184. As the authors argue, "Faults in administration lay principally outside the jurisdiction of the Army Ground Forces, which in general had jurisdiction over training only." Processing problems still plagued the replacement system, from medical examination to equipment issue, and "the experience of replacements en route tended to destroy their morale and to undo the effects of their training" (182). Initial combat experience in North Africa in 1942–1943 exposed these various deficiencies to scrutiny by field commanders and War Department personnel alike, leading to further adjustments to the system in mid-1943.

91. George C. Marshall, "Memorandum for General McNair," November 28, 1942, NARA 2, RG 319, Box 5. Marshall noted his shock at learning some replacements who arrived in North Africa joined their regiments without ever having fired a rifle. He wrote, "I supposed this is a matter entirely beyond your control. Nevertheless I want to get your reactions to the administrative set-up that produces such a result." Marshall continued, "I have not had an opportunity to talk to Somervell, or to G-1 or G-3 about any of these matters, the assignment of replacements . . . etc., but I should like to have you present when I do talk to them."

92. Palmer, Wiley, and Keast, in *Procurement and Training,* related one of McNair's anecdotes: "One division commander . . . himself told me that when he needed replacements he went to the replacement depot and chose his men individually, regardless of arm or specialty, based primarily on their appearance and actions—somewhat as one would buy a horse" (182–183).

93. Ibid., 181–184.

94. Ibid., 184–185.

95. Ibid., 186–187.

96. Ibid., 186–188.

97. Ibid., 186.

98. The Army Ground Forces shipped eighty-seven divisions overseas and formed three more overseas; however, it inactivated one division upon arrival in theater and never committed two. Thus, eighty-seven divisions actually fought during the war. See ibid., 489–493.

99. Ibid., 226–231.

100. A survey conducted in September 1942 revealed that of 4,021 soldiers surveyed, 25 percent of infantrymen liked their branch the least, while only 3 percent of soldiers in other branches liked their branch the least of all branches. Special Services Division Research Branch, "What the Infantrymen Thinks about the Infantry," September 14, 1942, NARA 2, RG 160, Box 700. Additional question responses indicated infantrymen believed their training less effective than members of other branches in preparing them for war and postwar civilian employment.

101. Palmer, Wiley, and Keast, *Procurement and Training,* 7–8. The association of civilian skills to military specialties led to the assignment to each recruit a specification serial number (SSN), which, combined with the Army General Classification Test, justified assignment of skilled, intelligent recruits to noncombat roles.

102. Ibid., 6–10. Two War Department policies significantly added to the problem: preferential assignment of those who achieved high Army General Classification Test scores to the Army Air Forces and the diversion of recruits with skill in any civilian trade to the technical services (an obvious disadvantage to services like infantry and armor, for which no civilian equivalent existed—meaning that men who had developed no skill at any trade, and therefore probably did not represent the highest-quality recruits, filled most ground combat positions).

103. Wilson, "Who Fought and Why?," 300.

104. McNair, "The Struggle Is for Survival."

105. Ibid.

106. "Joy and Hate," *Time*, November 23, 1942, 23.

107. Miller, *Nothing Less Than Full Victory*, 16. Miller also incorrectly identified McNair as the "commander of GHQ."; Various, "Folder: 1942 Armistice Day Address"; Various, "Oversized Folder: Scrapbook of Clare McNair's Newspaper Clippings, 1940–1944," McNair Papers, US Library of Congress Archives. Clare collected every letter that she received about the speech, numbering them and organizing them according to whether they voiced support for or complaints about the speech. The former far outweighed the latter.

108. Palmer, Wiley, and Keast, *Procurement and Training*, 19–20. McNair made only one exception, allowing a higher proportion of quality troops in airborne units—but these made up only 2 percent of Army Ground Forces' total strength.

109. Ibid., 21–25. In short, of the personnel allocated to the Army Air Forces, at least 75 percent would come from the top 33 percent of inductees.

110. Ibid., 3. The seesaw nature of War Department policy on preferential quality assignment created significant disruption and stress during 1942–1943, but by the end of 1943, the policy of preferential assignment had done its work, resulting in a disproportionate number of the lowest-graded inductees' assignments to the ground combat arms. This greatly troubled McNair, who linked the quality problem directly to the disproportionately high casualty rates that ground force combat personnel sustained throughout the war.

111. Ibid., 24–28.

112. Ibid., 27.

113. Ibid., 30–31.

114. Eisenhower to Marshall, December 11, 1942, *Papers of Dwight David Eisenhower*, vol. 2, pt. 3, chap. 7, "The Race for Tunis," http://eisenhower.press.jhu.edu/.

115. Palmer, Wiley, and Keast, *Procurement and Training*, 29–30.

116. Ibid., 30–33.

117. Weigley, *Eisenhower's Lieutenants*, 13.

118. *Infantry Journal* quoted in "Army and Navy—Lessons of Combat," *Time*, March 15, 1943, 59.

119. Marshall, *Aggressive and Determined Leadership*, 4:266–267. In addition to McNair's recommendations, various field commanders highlighted the desperate need for more infantrymen of high quality and the need to "dignify the infantry" in the public eye.

120. Marshall, *Aggressive and Determined Leadership*, 4:266; Wilson, "Deposited on Fortune's Far Shore," 217.

121. "Army and Navy—Infantry: Credit for Doughboy," *Time*, April 10, 1944, 67.

122. Laurence Bergreen, "Irving Berlin: This Is the Army," *Prologue*, 28, no. 2 (Summer 1996), http://www.archives.gov/publications/prologue/1996/summer/irving-berlin-1.html.

123. "William I. Nichols to Lesley J. McNair," March 7, 1944, NARA 2, RG 337, Entry 58A–B, Box 9. Some members of the WPB and similar organizations who worked to provide combat material first to lend-lease, then to equip the US army, only accepted a government salary of $1 per year as a symbolic gesture to demonstrate their lack of profit motivation.

124. Lesley J. McNair, "Lesley J. McNair to Paul Gallico," March 18, 1944, NARA 2, RG 337, Entry 58A–B, Box 9. For many additional letters, memos, and photographs related to the Infantry Program, see RG 337, Entry 58A–B, Boxes 9–11.

125. Palmer, "Study No. 4," 38–39. See the Cook Board Report, "Inclosure No. 1, Overseas Strength and Casualties by Major Commands and Infantry, 1 June–31 December 1944," NARA 2, RG 319, Entry 488, CMH Manuscript File—AGF, Box 128.

126. MacDonald, *Time for Trumpets*, 28–32, 68–69, 418–421. Such comparisons still frequently appear and highlight the popularity of histories of World War II's great captains. See Showalter, *Patton and Rommel.*

127. For a succinct yet convincing argument for the wisdom of Eisenhower's broad front strategy as the realization of American operational art in World War II, see Lynch, "Supreme Allied Commander's Operational Approach."

EPILOGUE

1. Lesley J. McNair, "Diary," April 15–May 5, 1943, NARA 2, RG 337, CG AGF Files, Box 1. McNair appears to have kept no diaries during his long career, with the single exception of this short trip diary documenting his visit to the front in Tunisia.

2. Clay, *Blood and Sacrifice*, 167.

3. Various, "Clare McNair's Newspaper Clippings"; Lesley J. McNair, "Diary," April 15–May 5, 1943, NARA 2, RG 337, CG AGF Files, Box 1.

4. Levine, *Operation Fortitude*, 193–194; W. B. Smith to George Catlett Marshall, Cable S 55125, *Papers of Dwight David Eisenhower*, vol. 3, pt. 8, chap. 20, "Stalemate," http://eisenhower.press.jhu.edu/. As late as July 6, 1944, every senior German commander remained convinced that the Normandy invasion force was not the main Allied thrust. The 15th German Army remained north of the Seine River at nearly full strength, awaiting the expected Calais–Dunkirk area main assault.

5. MacIntyre, *Double Cross*, 332.

6. W. B. Smith to George Catlett Marshall, Cable S 55125, *Papers of Dwight David Eisenhower*, vol. 3, pt. 8, chap. 20, "Stalemate," http://eisenhower.press.jhu.edu/.

7. Levine, *Operation Fortitude*, 243; MacIntyre, *Double Cross*, 332.

8. Levine, *Operation Fortitude*, 194.

9. "Army and Navy: After Four Years," *Time*, July 24, 1944, 61.

10. Ambrose, *D-Day*, 82–83; European Theater of Operations Adjutant General, "Assignment of Command of First United States Army Group," July 21, 1944, McNair Papers, NARA, St. Louis.

11. Eisenhower to George Catlett Marshall, Cable FWD 12428.Secret, *Papers of Dwight David Eisenhower*, vol. 3, pt. 8, chap. 20, "Stalemate," http://eisenhower.press.jhu.edu/.

12. Ibid.

13. Ibid.

14. Kennedy, *Freedom from Fear*, 631.

15. Lesley McNair to Colonel Milton A. Elliot Jr., August 17, 1942, NARA 2, RG 319, Entry 488, CMH Manuscript File, AGF, Box 129, Folder 2.

16. Notes from McNair's farewell to his Army Ground Forces staff section chiefs, July 12, 1944, NARA 2, RG 319, Entry 488, Office of the Chief of Military History, Historical Manuscript File, Army Ground Forces, 1942–47, Box 136, File "McNair—General."

17. Levine, *Operation Fortitude*, 246.

18. Hodges, *Normandy to Victory*, 61–63.

19. Ibid., 65–71.

20. Atkinson, *Guns at Last Light*, 143.

21. Hodges, *Normandy to Victory*, 65–70.

22. "Army and Navy: From My Own Men," *Time*, August 14, 1944, 64.

23. Kahn, *McNair*, 1–2.

24. Various, "Letters of in Response to Lesley McNair's Death in Normandy," July–September 1944, McNair Papers, US Library of Congress Archives, 73. The McNair genealogy casts further doubt on speculation Clare might have burned her husband's papers in grief, remarking on her notable composure upon learning of his death; McNair, *McNair, McNair, and McNear, and McNeir Genealogies: Supplement, 1955.*

25. "Honor to Lesley J. McNair."

26. Second lieutenants in 1944 earned $2,595 a year; brigadier generals with dependents earned $8,000. The handful of generals with more than one star earned an average of only $10,000 a year. "Army and Navy: Soldiers' Rewards," *Time*, August 28, 1944, 66. The article concluded, "The military careerist, whose peacetime responsibilities should be large and whose wartime responsibilities may be awesome, can expect only to die poor."

27. Kahn, *McNair*, 1; Kleber, "Lesley James McNair," 697; McNair, *McNair, McNear, and McNeir Genealogies: Supplement, 1955*, 43–44; Herbert M. Jones to Mrs. Lesley J. McNair, September 10, 1954, McNair Papers, NARA, St. Louis. Many historians, unaware of McNair's posthumous promotion, refer to him as "Lieutenant General McNair" rather than "General McNair," his correct, permanent rank.

28. Panelist's statement noted by the author at the 2010 Conference of the Society for Military History.

Bibliography

ARCHIVAL SOURCES

US Library of Congress Archives, Washington, DC, Individual Papers and Photo Collections
McNair, Lesley J., Personal Papers and Memorabilia (donated by Clare H. McNair)

US National Archives I, Washington, DC (NARA 1)
McNair, Lesley J., Personnel File (through 1919)

US National Archives II, College Park, Maryland (NARA 2)
Record Group 94, Adjutant General's Office, Central Decimal Files, Bulky Files, 1917–1925
Record Group 120, Records of the American Expeditionary Forces (World War I)
Record Group 160, Records of US Army Service Forces (World War II)
Record Group 165, War Department General Staff, G1 Personnel, Numerical File, 1921–1942
Record Group 165, War Department Operations Division Files, 1942–1944
Record Group 319, Records of the Army Staff
Record Group 337, Records of Headquarters, Army Ground Forces
Record Group 395, Records of US Army Overseas Operations and Commands, 1898–1942
Record Group 407, Office of the Adjutant General, Central Files, 1917–1940

US National Archives, St. Louis, Missouri, Individual Personnel Files (NARA, St. Louis)
McNair, Lesley J., Personnel File (Post–1919)

US Army Heritage and Education Center, Carlisle Barracks, Pennsylvania, Army War College Curricular Files, Individual Papers, and Photographic Collections (USAHEC)
Curricular Files, Class of 1929
McNair, Lesley J.
Records Section, AWC Curricular Files
Ward, Orlando

US Army Command and General Staff College (CGSC) Records, Combined Arms Research Library (CARL) Archives, Lectures, Addresses, and School Texts, Fort Leavenworth, Kansas

Brees, Herbert J. *Combat Orders.* Fort Leavenworth, KS: General Service Schools Press, 1920.

Bundel, Charles M. *Selected Professional Papers of Chas. M. Bundel.* Fort Leavenworth, KS: Command and General Staff School Press, 1939.

Ely, Hanson E. *A Series of Addresses and Lectures Delivered by Major General Hanson E. Ely, United States Army.* Fort Leavenworth, KS: General Service Schools Press, 1927.

McNair, Lesley J. "Graduation Address to Command and General Staff School Graduating Class and Faculty, June 20, 1939." Typescript, Combined Arms Research Library Archives, McNair Files.

McNair, Leslie [*sic*] J., Maj. *Artillery Firing: Lectures to the Staff and Line Classes.* General Services Schools, Fort Leavenworth, October 1919. Fort Leavenworth, KS: General Service Schools Press, 1920.

US Army, Command and General Staff School. *Combat Orders (Tentative).* Fort Leavenworth, KS: Command and General Staff School Press, 1939.

US Army, Command and General Staff School. *Command and Staff Principles (Tentative).* Fort Leavenworth, KS: Command and General Staff School Press, 1937.

US Army, Command and General Staff School. *The Principles of Strategy for an Independent Corps or Army in a Theater of Operations.* Fort Leavenworth, KS: Command and General Staff School Press, 1936.

US Army, Command and General Staff School. *Tactical Employment of the Mechanized Division (Tentative).* Fort Leavenworth, KS: Command and General Staff School Press, 1937.

US Army, General Service School. *Combat Orders.* Fort Leavenworth, KS: General Service Schools Press, 1920.

US Army, General Service School. *General Principles of Employment of Cavalry.* Fort Leavenworth, KS: General Service Schools Press, 1920.

US Army, School of the Line. *General Tactical Functions of Large Units.* Fort Leavenworth, KS: General Service Schools Press, 1920.

US Army Field Artillery School Archives, Morris Swett Technical Library, Fort Sill, Oklahoma, Administrative Files and Personal Papers (FA School Archives)

Brewer, Carlos. "recommendations for Changes in Gunnery Instruction and Battalion Organization." Unpublished report.

Gugeler, Russell A. "Fort Sill and the Golden Age of Field Artillery." Unpublished article.

McNair, Lesley J. Annual Reports of the Assistant Commandant, Field Artillery School.

Purdue University Library and e-Archives (Purdue Archives)
"The Debris." Purdue University Yearbook.
"Minutes of the Purdue University Board of Trustees"
Bulletin of Purdue University

WORKS CITED

Ambrose, Stephen E. *D-Day, June 6, 1944: The Climactic Battle of World War II*. New York: Simon & Schuster, 1994.

Astore, William J. "Loving the German War Machine: America's Infatuation with Blitzkrieg, Warfighters, and Militarism." In *Arms and the Man: Military History Essays in Honor of Dennis Showalter*, edited by Michael S. Neiberg, 5–30. Boston: Brill, 2011.

Atkinson, Rick. *An Army at Dawn: The War in North Africa, 1942–1943*. New York: Henry Holt, 2002.

———. *The Day of Battle: The War in Sicily and Italy, 1943–1944*. New York: Henry Holt, 2007.

———. *The Guns at Last Light: The War in Western Europe, 1944–1945*. New York: Henry Holt, 2013.

Ball, Harry P. *Of Responsible Command: A History of the US Army War College*. Carlisle Barracks, PA: Alumni Association of the United States Army War College, 1983.

Beaver, Daniel R. *Modernizing the American War Department: Change and Continuity in a Turbulent Era, 1885–1920*. Kent, OH: Kent State University Press, 2006.

Blumenson, Martin. "America's World War II Leaders in Europe: Some Thoughts." *Parameters* 19, no. 4 (December 1989): 2–13.

———. "Kasserine Pass, 30 January–22 February 1943." In *America's First Battles, 1776–1965*, edited by Charles E. Heller and William A. Stofft, 226–265. Lawrence: University Press of Kansas, 1986.

———. *Kasserine Pass: Rommel's Bloody, Climactic Battle for Tunisia*. 1966. Reprint, New York: Cooper Square Press, 2000.

Bonn, Keith E. *When the Odds Were Even: The Vosges Mountains Campaign, October 1944–January 1945*. Novato, CA: Presidio Press, 1994.

Brewer, Carlos. "Flash-Sound Ranging." *Field Artillery Journal* 21, no. 4 (July–August 1931): 345–353.

Bruscino, Thomas. "Naturally Clausewitzian: US Army Theory and Education from Reconstruction to the Interwar Years." *Journal of Military History* 77, no. 4 (2013): 1251–1276.

Calhoun, Mark T. "Complexity and Innovation: Army Transformation and the Reality of War." Master's thesis, School of Advanced Military Studies, 2004.

———. "Defeat at Kasserine: American Armor Doctrine, Training, and Battle Command in Northwest Africa, World War II." Master's thesis, Command and General Staff College, 2003.

———. Review of David P. Colley, *Decision at Strasbourg: Ike's Strategic Mistake to Halt the Sixth Army Group at the Rhine in 1944*. *Army History* 78, no. 2 (2010): 51–52.

Cameron, Robert S. *Mobility, Shock, and Firepower: The Emergence of the US Army's Armor Branch, 1917–1945*. Washington, DC: United States Army Center of Military History, 2008.

Carew, Michael G. *Becoming the Arsenal: The American Industrial Mobilization for World War II, 1938–1942*. New York: University Press of America, 2010.

Citino, Robert M. *The German Way of War: From the Thirty Years' War to the Third Reich*. Lawrence: University Press of Kansas, 2005.

Clark, Mark. *Calculated Risk*. New York: Harper & Brothers, 1950.

Clausewitz, Carl von. *On War*. Translated by Michael Howard and Peter Paret. Princeton, NJ: Princeton University Press, 1984.

Clay, Steven E. *Blood and Sacrifice: The History of the 16th Infantry Regiment from the Civil War through the Gulf War*. Wheaton, IL: Cantigny First Division Foundation and the 16th Infantry Regiment Association, 2001.

Coffman, Edward M. *The Regulars: The American Army, 1898–1941*. Cambridge, MA: Belknap Press, 2004.

———. *The War to End All Wars: The American Military Experience in World War I*. Lexington: University Press of Kentucky, 1968.

Colley, David P. *Decision at Strasbourg: Ike's Strategic Mistake to Halt the Sixth Army Group at the Rhine in 1944*. Annapolis, MD: Naval Institute Press, 2008.

Collins, Leroy P. "Pack Saddles for Mountain Artillery." *Field Artillery Journal* 7, no. 3 (July–September 1917): 343–345.

Command and General Staff School. *Antimechanized Defense (Tentative)*. Fort Leavenworth, KS: Command and General Staff School Press, 1939.

Comparato, Frank E. *Age of Great Guns*. Harrisburg, PA: Stackpole, 1965.

Cooke, James J. *Pershing and His Generals: Command and Staff in the AEF*. Westport, CT: Praeger, 1997.

———. *The Rainbow Division in the Great War, 1917–1919*. Westport, CT: Praeger, 1994.

Creveld, Martin van. *Fighting Power: German and US Army Peformance, 1939–1945*. Westport, CT: Greenwood Press, 1982.

Dastrup, Boyd L. *Cedat Fortuna Peritis: A History of the Field Artillery School*. Fort Leavenworth, KS: Combat Studies Institute Press, 2011.

———. *King of Battle: A Branch History of the US Army's Field Artillery*. Fort Monroe, VA: Office of the Command Historian, United States Army Training and Doctrine Command, 1992.

Daubin, Freeland A., Jr. "The Battle of Happy Valley." Master's thesis, Armored School, Fort Knox, Kentucky, 1948.

Davis, Burke. *The Billy Mitchell Affair*. New York: Random House, 1967.

Doubler, Michael D. *Closing with the Enemy: How the GIs Fought the War in Europe, 1944–1945.* Lawrence: University Press of Kansas, 1994.

Dunham, Emory A. *Study No. 29: Tank Destroyer History.* Washington, DC: Historical Section, Army Ground Forces, 1946.

Eisenhower, Dwight D. *Crusade in Europe.* 1948. Reprint, New York: Da Capo Press, 1977.

Eisenhower, John S. D. *Intervention!* New York: Norton, 1993.

Evans, Richard J. *The Third Reich in Power: 1933–1939.* New York: Penguin Press, 2005.

Faber, Peter R. "Lesley James McNair." In *American National Biography,* edited by John A. Garraty and Mark C. Carnes, 164–165. New York: Oxford University Press, 1999.

Ferrell, Robert H. *America's Deadliest Battle: Meuse-Argonne, 1918.* Lawrence: University Press of Kansas, 2007.

"Field Artillery Notes." *Field Artillery Journal* 25, no. 3 (May–June 1935): 283–286.

"Field Artillery Notes: Gunnery Liaison Methods." *Field Artillery Journal* 22, no. 6 (November–December 1932): 631–635.

Fullerton, Dan C. "Bright Prospects, Bleak Realities: The US Army's Interwar Modernization Program for the Coming of the Second World War." PhD diss., University of Kansas, 2006.

Gabel, Christopher R. *Seek, Strike, and Destroy: US Army Tank Destroyer Doctrine in World War II.* Leavenworth Paper 12. Washington, DC: Combat Studies Institute, US Army Command and General Staff College, 1985.

———. *The US Army GHQ Maneuvers of 1941.* Washington, DC: Center of Military History, United States Army, 1992.

Gaddis, John Lewis. *The Landscape of History: How Historians Map the Past.* New York: Oxford University Press, 2002.

Gole, Henry G. *The Road to Rainbow: Army Planning for Global War, 1934–1940.* Annapolis, MD: Naval Institute Press, 2003.

Greenfield, Kent Roberts, Robert R. Palmer, and Bell I. Wiley. *The Organization of Ground Combat Troops.* 1947. Reprint, Washington, DC: US Army Center of Military History, 2004.

Grenville, J. A. S. "Diplomacy and War Plans in the United States, 1890–1917." In *The War Plans of the Great Powers, 1880–1914,* edited by Paul M. Kennedy, 23–38. Boston: Allen & Unwin, 1979.

Grotelueschen, Mark E. *The AEF Way of War: The American Army and Combat in World War I.* New York: Cambridge University Press, 2007.

Grow, H. B. "Bombing Tests on the 'Virginia' and 'New Jersey.'" *US Naval Institute Proceedings* 51/11/250 (December 1923): 1987–1996.

Grumelli, Michael L. "Trial of Faith: The Dissent and Court-Martial of Billy Mitchell." PhD diss., Rutgers University, 1991.

Hastings, Max. *Overlord: D-Day, June 6, 1944.* New York: Simon & Schuster, 1984.

Hauner, Milan. Book review of Martin van Creveld, *Fighting Power: German and US Army Peformance, 1939–1945. American Historical Review* 88, no. 5 (December 1983 1983): 1287–1288.

Higgs, Robert. *Depression, War, and Cold War: Challenging the Myths of Conflict and Prosperity.* Oakland, CA: Independent Institute, 2006.

Hinckley, W. G. "How Purdue Features Military Cermonies." *Field Artillery Journal* 16, no. 2 (March–April 1926): 184–189.

Hodges, Courtney H. *Normandy to Victory: The War Diary of General Courtney H. Hodges and the First US Army.* Edited by William C. Sylvan and Francis G. Smith Jr. Lexington: University Press of Kentucky, 2008.

Holzimmer, Kevin C. *General Walter Krueger: Unsung Hero of the Pacific War.* Lawrence: University Press of Kansas, 2007.

"Honor to Lesley J. McNair." *Field Artillery Journal* 35, no. 7 (July 1945): 386.

Hopkins, William B. *The Pacific War: The Strategy, Politics, and Players that Won the War.* Minneapolis, MN: Zenith Press, 2008.

House, Jonathan M. *Combined Arms Warfare in the Twentieth Century.* Lawrence: University Press of Kansas, 2001.

Howe, George F. *The Battle History of the 1st Armored Division.* Washington, DC: Combat Forces Press, 1954.

———. *Northwest Africa: Seizing the Initiative in the West.* 1957. Reprint, Washington, DC: US Army Center of Military History, 2002.

Johnson, Charles William. "The Civilian Conservation Corps: The Role of the Army." PhD diss., University of Michigan, 1968.

Johnson, David E. *Fast Tanks and Heavy Bombers: Innovation in the US Army, 1917–1945.* Ithaca, NY: Cornell University Press, 1998.

———. "From Frontier Constabulary to Modern Army: The US Army between the World Wars." In *The Challenge of Change: Military Institutions and New Realities, 1918–1941,* edited by Harold R. Winton and David R. Mets. Lincoln: University of Nebraska Press, 2000.

Jones, Grant W. "Education of the Supreme Commander: The Theoretical Underpinnings of Eisenhower's Strategy in Europe, 1944–45." *War and Society* 30, no. 2 (August 2011): 108–133.

Kahn, Ely J. *McNair, Educator of an Army.* Washington, DC: Infantry Journal, 1945.

Keegan, John. *The Second World War.* New York: Penguin Books, 1990.

Kelly, Orr. *Meeting the Fox: The Allied Invasion of Africa, from Operation Torch to Kasserine Pass to Victory in Tunisia.* New York: Wiley, 2002.

Kennedy, David M. *Freedom from Fear: The American People in Depression and War, 1929–1945.* New York: Oxford University Press, 1999.

Kingseed, Cole. "Marshall's Men." *Army,* December 2009, 50–59, http://marshallfound ation.org/.

Kirkpatrick, Charles Edward. *An Unknown Future and a Doubtful Present: Writing the Victory Plan of 1941.* Washington, DC: Center of Military History, United States Army, 1990.

Kleber, Brooks E. "Lesley James McNair." In *Dictionary of American Military Biography,* edited by Roger J. Spiller, 695–699. Westport, CT: Greenwood Press, 1984.

Koistinen, Paul A. C. *Arsenal of World War II: The Political Economy of American Warfare, 1940–1945.* Lawrence: University of Kansas Press, 2004.

———. *Mobilizing for Modern War: The Political Economy of American Warfare, 1865–1919.* Lawrence: University Press of Kansas, 1997.

———. *Planning War, Pursuing Peace: The Political Economy of American Warfare, 1920–1939.* Lawrence: University Press of Kansas, 1998.

Kretchik, Walter E. *US Army Doctrine: From the American Revolution to the War on Terror.* Lawrence: University Press of Kansas, 2011.

Lacey, James G. *Keep from All Thoughtful Men.* Annapolis, MD: Naval Institute Press, 2011.

Lehner, Larry, and Dorothy Lehner. "McNair: Verndale to St. Lô." Verndale, MN: Verndale Historical Society, 1976.

Leighton, Richard M., and Robert W. Coakley. *Global Logistics and Strategy: 1940–1943.* 1955. Reprint, Washington, DC: US Army Center of Military History, 2006.

Levine, Joshua. *Operation Fortitude: The Story of the Spies and the Spy Operation that Saved D-Day.* Guilford, CT: Lyons Press, 2012.

Linn, Brian McAllister, and Russell F. Weigley. "*The American Way of War* Revisited." *Journal of Military History* 66, no. 2 (April 2002): 501–533.

Lynch, Timothy B. "The Supreme Allied Commander's Operational Approach." Master's thesis, School of Advanced Military Studies, 2014.

Lynn, John A. *Battle: A History of Combat and Culture.* 2nd ed. Cambridge, MA: Westview Press, 2004.

MacDonald, Charles B. *A Time for Trumpets: The Untold Story of the Battle of the Bulge.* New York: Perennial, 2002.

MacIntyre, Ben. *Double Cross: The True Story of the D-Day Spies.* New York: Broadway, 2012.

Mansoor, Peter R. *The GI Offensive in Europe: The Triumph of American Infantry Divisions, 1941–1945.* Lawrence: University Press of Kansas, 1999.

Marshall, George Catlett. "*The Soldierly Spirit*": December 1880–June 1939. Vol. 1 of the Papers of George Catlett Marshall. Edited by Larry I. Bland and Sharon Ritenour Stevens. Baltimore, MD: Johns Hopkins University Press, 1981.

———. "*We Cannot Delay*": July 1, 1939–December 6, 1941. Vol. 2 of the Papers of George Catlett Marshall. Edited by Larry I. Bland, Sharon R. Ritenour, and Clarence E. Wunderlin Jr. Baltimore, MD: Johns Hopkins University Press, 1986.

———. "*The Right Man for the Job*": December 7, 1941–May 31, 1943. Vol. 3 of the Papers of George Catlett Marshall. Baltimore, MD: Johns Hopkins University Press, 1991.

———. *"Aggressive and Determined Leadership": June 1, 1943–December 31, 1944.* Vol. 4 of the Papers of George Catlett Marshall. Baltimore, MD: Johns Hopkins University Press, 1996.

Marshall, S. L. A. *World War I.* New York: American Heritage, 2001.

Masland, John W., and Laurence I. Radway. *Soldiers and Scholars: Military Education and National Policy.* Princeton, NJ: Princeton University Press, 1957.

Matheny, Michael R. *Carrying the War to the Enemy: American Operational Art to 1945.* Norman: University of Oklahoma Press, 2011.

Matloff, Maurice. "The 90-Division Gamble." In *Command Decisions,* edited by Kent Roberts Greenfield, 365–382. 1960. Reprint, Washington, DC: United States Army Center of Military History, 2002.

———. *Strategic Planning for Coalition Warfare, 1943–1944.* 1959. Reprint, Washington, DC: US Army Center of Military History, 2003.

McKenney, Janice E. *Field Artillery.* Washington, DC: United States Army Center of Military History, 2010.

———. *The Organizational History of Field Artillery, 1775–2003.* Washington, DC: United States Army Center for Military History, 2007.

McNair, James Birtley. *McNair, McNear, and McNeir Genealogies: Supplement, 1950.* Los Angeles: James Birtley McNair, 1950.

———. *McNair, McNear, and McNeir Genealogies: Supplement, 1955.* Los Angeles: James Birtley McNair, 1955.

McNair, Lesley J. "And Now the Autogiro." *Field Artillery Journal* 27, no. 1 (January–February 1937): 5–17.

———. "Extracts from 'Notes on Recent Operations,' by Brigadier General Leslie [*sic*] J. McNair, General Staff, GHQ, AEF." *Field Artillery Journal* 9, no. 2 (April–June 1919): 229–230.

———. "Infantry Batteries and Accompanying Guns." *Field Artillery Journal* 11, no. 2 (March–April 1921): 123–135.

———. "Military Training at Educational Insitutions." *Purdue Engineering Review* 20, no. 2 (1925): 6–7, 18.

———. "Military Training at Educational Institutions." *Purdue Engineering Review* 20, no. 2 (1925): 6.

———. "Pacifism at Purdue University." *Purdue Alumnus* 13, no. 7 (1926): 5–8.

———. "The ROTC." *Coast Artillery Journal* 68, no. 2 (February 1928): 172–176.

———. "The Struggle Is for Survival." *Vital Speeches of the Day* 9, no. 4 (1 December 1942): 4.

———. "Why Military Training in College." *Purdue Engineering Review* 23, no. 4 (May 1928): 5–6.

Miller, Edward G. *Nothing Less Than Full Victory: Americans at War in Europe, 1944–1945.* Annapolis, MD: Naval Institute Press, 2007.

———. *War Plan Orange: The US Strategy to Defeat Japan, 1897–1945.* Annapolis, MD: Naval Institute Press, 1991.

Millett, Allan R. "Cantigny, 28–31 May 1918." In *America's First Battles, 1776–1965,* edited by Charles E. Heller and William A. Stofft, 149–185. Lawrence: University Press of Kansas, 1986.

Millett, Allan R., and Williamson Murray, eds. *Military Effectiveness.* 3 vols. Boston: Allen & Unwin, 1988.

Moenk, Jean R. *A History of Large-Scale Army Maneuvers in the United States, 1935–1964.* Fort Monroe, VA: United States Continental Army Command, 1969.

Morgan, Patrick M. Book review of Martin van Creveld, *Fighting Power: German and US Army Peformance, 1939–1945. Annals of the American Academy of Political and Social Science* 471, no. 6 (January 1984): 175–176.

Muller, Richard R. "Close Air Support." In *Military Innovation in the Interwar Period,* edited by Williamson Murray and Allan R. Millett, 144–190. New York: Cambridge University Press, 1996.

Murray, Williamson, and Allan R. Millett, eds. *Military Innovation in the Interwar Period.* New York: Cambridge University Press, 1996.

———. *A War to Be Won: Fighting the Second World War.* Cambridge, MA: Belknap Press, 2000.

Odom, William O. *After the Trenches: The Transformation of US Army Doctrine, 1918–1939.* College Station: Texas A&M University Press, 1999.

Ohl, John Kennedy. *Supplying the Troops: General Somervell and American Logistics in WWII.* DeKalb: Northern Illinois University Press, 1994.

Page, Kirby. *War: Its Causes, Consequences and Cure.* New York: George H. Doran, 1923.

Page, Robert William, Jr. "Billy Mitchell: Cause Célèbre of American Air Power." Master's thesis, University of South Carolina, 1961.

Palmer, Robert R. "Study No. 4: Mobilization of the Ground Army." Washington, DC: Historical Section, Army Ground Forces, 1946.

———. "Study No. 5: Procurement of Enlisted Personnel for the AGF: The Problem of Quality." Washington, DC: Historical Section, Army Ground Forces, 1946.

Palmer, Robert R., Bell I. Wiley, and William R. Keast. *The Procurement and Training of Ground Combat Troops.* 1948. Reprint, Washington, DC: US Army Center of Military History, 1991.

Pappas, George S. *Prudens Futuri: The US Army War College, 1901–1967.* Carlisle Barracks, PA: Alumni Association of the US Army War College, 1980.

Parker, Edwin P., Jr. "The Autogiro and Its Value to the Field Artillery." *Field Artillery Journal* 24, no. 4 (July–August 1934): 347–354.

Pearlman, Michael D. *To Make Democracy Safe for America: Patricians and Prepared-ness in the Progressive Era.* Urbana: University of Illinois Press, 1984.

Pogue, Forrest C. *George C. Marshall: Education of a General, 1880–1939.* New York: Viking Press, 1963.

———. *George C. Marshall: Organizer of Victory, 1943–1945.* New York: Viking Press, 1973.

Raines Jr., Edgar F. *Eyes of Artillery: The Origins of Modern US Army Aviation in World War II.* Washington, DC: US Army Center of Military History, 2000.

Reardon, Mark J. *Victory at Mortain: Stopping Hitler's Panzer Counteroffensive.* Lawrence: University Press of Kansas, 2002.

Rein, Christopher. *The North African Air Campaign: US Army Air Forces from El Alamein to Salerno.* Lawrence: University Press of Kansas, 2012.

Rush, Robert S. *Hell in Hürtgen Forest: The Ordeal and Triumph of an American In-fantry Regiment.* Lawrence: University of Kansas Press, 2001.

Schaffer, Ronald. *America in the Great War: The Rise of the War Welfare State.* New York: Oxford University Press, 1991.

Schifferle, Peter J. *America's School for War: Fort Leavenworth, Officer Education, and Victory in World War II.* Lawrence: University Press of Kansas, 2010.

"Senior Field Artilleryman." *Field Artillery Journal* 32, no. 12 (December 1942): 898.

Showalter, Dennis. *Patton and Rommel: Men of War in the Twentieth Century.* New York: Berkley, 2005.

Smythe, Donald. *Pershing: General of the Armies.* Bloomington: Indiana University Press, 1986.

Stoler, Mark A. *Allies and Adversaries: The Joint Chiefs of Staff, the Grand Alliance, and US Strategy in World War II.* Chapel Hill: University of North Carolina Press, 2000.

Summerall, Charles Pelot. *The Way of Duty, Honor, Country: The Memoir of General Charles Pelot Summerall.* Edited by Timothy K. Nenninger. Lexington: University Press of Kentucky, 2010.

Taaffe, Stephen R. *Marshall and His Generals: US Army Commanders in World War II.* Lawrence: University of Kansas Press, 2011.

Tompkins, Frank. *Chasing Villa.* Harrisburg, PA: Military Service Publishing, 1934.

Trout, Steven. *On the Battlefield of Memory: The First World War and American Re-memberance, 1919–1941.* Tuscaloosa: University of Alabama Press, 2010.

US Army. *Field Service Regulations, Operations, May 22, 1941.* FM 100-5. Reprint, Fort Leavenworth, KS: US Army Command and General Staff College Press, 1992.

———. *Field Service Regulations, United States Army, 1923.* Washington, DC: Govern-ment Printing Office, 1924.

———. *Tentative Field Service Regulations: Operations.* FM 100-5. Washington, DC: Government Printing Office, 1939.

———. *Unified Land Operations.* Army Doctrine Reference Publication 3-0. Fort

Leavenworth, KS: Combined Arms Doctrine Directorate, United States Army Combined Arms Center, 2012.

US Army Ground Forces. "AGF Staff Study No. 2: A Short History of the AGF." Washington, DC: Historical Section, Army Ground Forces, 1944.

US Army War Department. *Drill Regulations for Mountain Artillery (Provisional), United States Army.* Washington, DC: Government Printing Office, 1908.

———. *Instructions for the Training of Platoons for Offensive Action, 1917.* Washington, DC: Government Printing Office, 1917.

US Ordnance Department. *Handbook of the 2.95-Inch Mountain Gun Matériel and Pack Outfit.* Washington, DC: Government Printing Office, 1912, Revised 1916.

Watson, Mark Skinner. *The War Department: Chief of Staff: Prewar Plans and Preparations.* 1949. Reprint, Washington, DC: US Army Center of Military History, 2003.

Wedemeyer, A. C. "Antitank Defense." *Field Artillery Journal* 31, no. 5 (May 1941): 258–272.

Weigley, Russell F. *Eisenhower's Lieutenants: The Campaign of France and Germany, 1944–1945.* Bloomington: Indiana University Press, 1981.

———. *History of the United States Army.* Enlarged ed. Bloomington: Indiana University Press, 1967.

Weinberg, Gerhard L. *A World at Arms: A Global History of World War II.* New York: Cambridge University Press, 1994.

West Point. "Official Register of the Officers and Cadets of the United States Military Academy." West Point, NY: USMA Press and Bindery, 1901–1904.

Wheeler, James Scott. "Marshall's Forgotten Men." *Army* 58, no. 11 (September 2010): 46–52.

Whitaker, John T. "Lieutenant General Lesley James McNair." In *These Are the Generals.* New York: Knopf, 1943.

Wilson, John. B. *Maneuver and Firepower: The Evolution of Divisions and Separate Brigades.* Washington, DC: United States Army Center for Military History, 1998.

Wilson, Theodore A. *America and World War II: Critical Issues.* Dubuque, IA: Kendall/Hunt, 2005.

———. "Deposited on Fortune's Far Shore: The 2d Battalion, 8th Infantry." In *D-Day 1944,* edited by Theodore A. Wilson, 213–237. Lawrence: University Press of Kansas, 1971.

———. "Who Fought and Why? The Assignment of American Soldiers to Combat." In *Time to Kill: The Soldier's Experience of War in the West, 1939–1945,* edited by Paul Addison and Angus Calder, 284–303. London: Random House UK, 1997.

Winton, Harold R. *Corps Commanders of the Bulge: Six American Generals and Victory in the Ardennes.* Lawrence: University of Kansas Press, 2007.

Yeide, Harry. *The Tank Killers: A History of America's World War II Tank Destroyer Force.* Havertown, PA: Casemate, 2004.

Index

Civilian Conservation Corps (CCC), 139,
142–147, 355n39, 355nn41–42
Clark, Mark, 220, 244, 252 (photo), 301, 346n12
Clausewitz, Carl von
and American operational art, 260
and US Army doctrine, 15, 185
and the US Army War College, 8, 108–109,
349n33
Clay, Steven E., 312
Coast Artillery, 373n55
cost effectiveness, 68
and defense from air and naval attack, 63–65,
67
separation from field artillery, 36
See also Field Artillery Branch
Coast Artillery Journal, 94–96. *See also* McNair,
Lesley J.: PMS&T at Purdue
Coe, Frank W., 71–72, 344n26. *See also* McNair,
Lesley J.: McNair Board of 1923–1924
Coffman, Edward M., 46, 84, 326, 333n4, 345n4,
355n41
Colley, David P., 11, 335n20
colored plans, 69, 118, 120, 351n71. *See also*
rainbow plans; World War II (WWII): and
American Strategy
combat command (CC), US army, 15, 225, 264,
269, 275. *See also* War Department: task
organization
combined arms warfare, 4–5, 185–187, 189, 228,
271, 330. *See also* Interwar Period
(1919–1939): and combined arms warfare;
McNair, Lesley J.: and combined arms
warfare; World War I (WWI): and
combined arms warfare; World War II
(WWII): and combined arms warfare
Command and General Staff School, US
(CGSS). *See* Fort Leavenworth schools
Congress, US, 36, 50, 53, 73, 86, 142, 174
approves lend-lease, 176 (*see also* lend-lease
program)
and executive branch power, 174
and funds for military bases in Pacific, 63
and funds for ROTC, 96
and interwar foreign affairs, 173
isolationism and, 23, 154
and military preparedness, 23, 47–48, 82
and military spending, 193
and National Defense Act of 1916, 82
and National Defense Act of 1920, 82, 84, 114,
117

and Neutrality Act of 1937, 174
and Protective Mobilization, 194
See also Protective Mobilization of 1940;
Selective Service Act of 1917; Selective
Training and Service Act of 1940
Coolidge, Calvin, President, 72, 91
Craig, Malin, 164, 180, 213, 247, 326–328,
356n16, 359nn36–37, 367n104
and the 1939 Field Service Regulations (FSR)
(Tentative), 185
cuts weapons research programs in 1936,
154–155
and equipment development programs,
154–155
and FDR on WWI as air war, 209
forms the Modernization Board, 156
as "a Pershing protégé," 153
and redesign of infantry division, 153, 156,
158, 161–162, 164–166, 169, 358n31,
377n34
selects McNair as CGSS commandant, 2, 168,
170, 177–178
and war plans versus capabilities, 154
and WWII anti-tank defense, 233–234, 241
and WWII War Economy, 193, 209, 211,
368n105
Crosby, H. B., 103
Crozier, William, 47
Cruikshank, William M., 139, 354n34

Dastrup, Boyd, 52
Davis, Dwight D., Acting Secretary of War, 72
Department of Defense, US, 3
Depression, 9, 123, 142, 154, 173, 193–194, 207,
248, 345n4, 346n12, 364n57
Devers, Jacob L., 40
on advantages of observed fire, 127–128
on antitank guns, 244
and Field Artillery School, Gunnery
Department, 127–128, 135
on McNair's leadership, 35
on pooling, 268
on tank gun caliber, 290
See also Field Artillery School, Gunnery
Department
Doctrine, US army, 44
and McNair at CGSS, 182–187
modernization of, 3–5
and moral versus technical factors, 44
and primacy of infantry, 44

Snow, William J., 92–94. *See also* McNair, Lesley
J.: as PMS&T at Purdue
"Soldier for a Day" initiative, 307
Somervell, Brehon B.
appointed ASF commander, 250
and civilian industrialists, 199–202
and competition with AAF and AGF, 256
and dysfunction in WPB, 260, 366nn73–74,
366n83, 376n11, 376n26
and inefficiency of staff, 253
and manpower crisis of 1942, 262–263
as Marshall's "attack dog," 263
and military war requirements, 204, 212
and redundancy with War Department G-4,
254
and replacements, 381n91
and War Department efficiency measures,
267
and War Department logistics functions,
255
and WWII as air war, 319, 375n7
See also mobilization for WWII, industrial
Soviet Union, 201, 271, 375n9. *See also* Russian
Army
square division, US army, 49, 156, 158, 319,
357n19. *See also* triangular division, US
army
Stark, Harold R., 196, 258. *See also* colored plans;
rainbow plans; War Plan Dog
Stevens, Robert, 212
Stimson, Henry L.
appoints Marshall GHQ commander, 214
and McNair's posthumous awards, 323, 325
(photo)
and McNair promotion to Lieutenant
General, 224
and military war requirements, 198
and National Guard officers, 225–226
on War Department reorganization, 253
on WWII as an air war, 375n7
and WPB dysfunction, 202
Stoler, Mark A., 177, 361n4, 376n19
Strategic bombers (B-24s) as close air support,
321–322
Summerall, Charles P.
as Army chief of staff and AWC, 108
on artillery pre-WWI, 340n24
at Billy Mitchell court martial, 76–77
as firepower advocate post-WWI, 58
as Hawaiian Department commander, 63
and McNair Board, 65, 68, 342n10

and McNair during WWI, 342n3
and McNair's reputation, 342n4
on Oahu plan of defense, 68, 70, 343n22
retained square division organization, 156
on weapon development process, 288
Supreme Court, US and FDR's New Deal, 173

Taaffe, Stephen R., 23, 180, 217, 226, 371n33
tank destroyers
Andrew D. Bruce and, 243–244
and Bruce on "tank hunting," 281
and Cook Board, 283
on decision to develop, 240–243
and expedients' combat performance, 280
and Marshall's views on, 244
and McNair on "tank hunting," 281–282
and McNair's views on, 279
as member of combined arms team, 283
and Palmer Board, 280
and Patton's views on, 280
and Tank Destroyer Tactical and Firing
Center, 244
War Department on AT unit organization,
243
War Department control of, 243–244
War Department tank destroyer board, 244
Wedemeyer envisions "tank chaser," 343
See also anti-tank (AT) guns
triangular division, US army
and division tests of 1929, 156
and Modernization Board, 156
and open warfare, 156
and War Department test guidance, 157
See also proposed infantry division (PID)
tests; Provisional 2nd Division (P2D)
test design
Trout, Steven, 81
Tyner, George P., 139

Very pistol, 65
Vichy France, 275
Victory Plan, US
"90-division gamble" and functional
commands, 318–319
and British-preferred "underbelly" strategy,
260, 274
and changes upon manpower crisis of 1942,
260
Wedemeyer's role in Victory plan, 365n63,
376n19
von Clausewitz, Carl. *See* Clausewitz, Carl von

World War II (WWII)

and American isolationism, 9, 23, 174, 179, 329, 365n58

and American strategy, 196–197, 258–262

and artillery effectiveness, 16–17, 270, 276, 278, 282–284, 286, 290–291, 310, 341n39, 358n30, 378n55

Battle of the Bulge, 110

and battle hardening, 274, 303 (*see also* learning versus adaptation, US Army)

Battle of Okinawa, 49

and combined arms warfare, 16, 22, 24, 189, 222, 228, 243, 247, 250, 264, 266, 268, 270–271, 274, 276–277, 279–280, 282–283, 285, 291, 310, 372n54, 374n72, 379n70 (*see also* learning versus adaptation, US Army)

Cook Board (postwar army effectiveness study) and, 283, 288, 308

D-Day, Operation Overlord, June 6, 1944, 5, 21–22, 259, 305, 314

and doctrine, 227–228

efficiency and effectiveness, 264–265, 271–272

European Theater of Operations, Eastern Front, 5, 286

European Theater of Operations, Western Front, 5

and "Germany First" strategy, 258

and individual replacements, 296

and industrial mobilization, 203 (*see also* mobilization for WWII, industrial)

Kasserine Pass battles, 13, 270, 275–278

lack of reserve forces, US and, 115–117

McNair on the "infantry problem," 303–308

McNair prepares AGF for war, 247

Mediterranean Theater of Operations, 5

mobilization training for, 1, 3–7

official histories of, 1

and operational art, 260

"overhead" in unit staffs and, 251

Pacific Theater of Operations, 5, 258

personnel procurement, US and, 206

and tank destroyers (*see* tank destroyers)

and unconditional surrender, 15, 20

and US Army casualty rates, 208–209, 263, 303–304

as a "war of machines," 246 (*see also* Army Air Forces: and WWII as an air war; Roosevelt, Franklin Delano (FDR): on WWII as a "War of Machines")

war plan (US) adjustments to fit strategic situation, 196, 258

"workmanlike" US Army generals and, 4, 8, 12, 19, 309, 328, 331

See also Army General Classification Test (AGCT); mobilization for WWII, industrial; mobilization for WWII, military; shipping capacity, US)

Writers' War Board, 307